OXFORD COMPARATIVE CONSTITUTIONALISM

A Theory of African Constitutionalism

OXFORD COMPARATIVE CONSTITUTIONALISM

Comparative constitutional law has a long and distinguished history in intellectual thought and in the construction of public law. As political actors and the people who create or modify their constitutional orders, they often wish to learn from the experience and learning of others. This cross-fertilization and mutual interaction has only accelerated with the onset of globalization, which has transformed the world into an interconnected web that facilitates dialogue and linkages across international and regional structures. Oxford Comparative Constitutionalism seeks to publish scholarship of the highest quality in constitutional law that deepens our knowledge of local, national, regional, and global phenomena through the lens of comparative public law.

ALSO PUBLISHED IN THIS SERIES

Abusive Constitutional Borrowing
Legal Globalization and the Subversion of Liberal Democracy
Rosalind Dixon and David Landau

Deliberative Peace Referendums
Ron Levy, Ian O'Flynn, Hoi L Kong

Eternity Clauses In Democratic Constitutionalism
Silvia Suteu

Scales of Memory
Constitutional Justice and Historical Evil
Justin Collings

The Global South and Comparative Constitutional Law
Edited by Philipp Dann, Michael Riegner, and Maxim Bönnemann

City, State
Constitutionalism and the Megacity
Ran Hirschl

Constitutional Change in the Contemporary Socialist World
Ngoc Son Bui

Poland's Constitutional Breakdown
Wojciech Sadurski

A Theory of African Constitutionalism

BERIHUN ADUGNA GEBEYE

OXFORD
UNIVERSITY PRESS

OXFORD
UNIVERSITY PRESS

Great Clarendon Street, Oxford, OX2 6DP,
United Kingdom

Oxford University Press is a department of the University of Oxford.
It furthers the University's objective of excellence in research, scholarship,
and education by publishing worldwide. Oxford is a registered trade mark of
Oxford University Press in the UK and in certain other countries

First Edition published in 2021

Impression: 1

Published in the United States of America by Oxford University Press
198 Madison Avenue, New York, NY 10016, United States of America

British Library Cataloguing in Publication Data
Data available

Library of Congress Control Number: 2020952643

ISBN 978–0–19–289392–5

DOI: 10.1093/oso/9780192893925.001.0001

Printed and bound by
CPI Group (UK) Ltd, Croydon, CR0 4YY

Contents

Acknowledgements

This book could not have been written without the generous support of many individuals and institutions. From the inception of this project to its conclusion, I have been extremely lucky to work with and blessed by the support, guidance, and encouragement of many kind people.

The book began as my doctoral dissertation at the Central European University (CEU). So, first and foremost, I wish to thank my doctoral supervisor Mathias Möschel for his exceptional guidance throughout the project. His critical engagements with the various drafts of this book and his constructive criticisms and comments along the way have pushed me to think with more clarity. I am indebted to his unwavering support and full confidence throughout this project. I must thank my doctoral examiners, H. Kwasi Prempeh and Markus Böckenförde, for their insightful comments and constructive suggestions that helped me sharpen and clarify my ideas. I also owe huge thanks to my teachers, doctoral colleagues, and staff at CEU who supported and advised me in numerous ways over the years.

After my doctoral studies, I joined Ran Hirschl's Alexander von Humboldt Chair of Comparative Constitutionalism at the University of Göttingen as a postdoctoral research fellow. This provided me a terrific intellectual, personal, and institutional environment to revise, sharpen, and further develop my ideas. This book would not have been brought to the world in this form without the intellectual guidance, mentorship, and personal devotion of Ran Hirschl to me and my work. He took a special interest in my ideas early on and generously helped and guided me in numerous ways to bring them in a much advanced and improved form in this book. At the Alexander von Humboldt Chair of Comparative Constitutionalism, Mariana Velasco Rivera, Alexander Hudson, Lisa Harms, and Esther Lauer, among many others, have been a constant source of support and inspiration. I also would like to thank the Department of Ethics, Law and Politics at the Max Planck Institute for the Study of Religious and Ethnic Diversity for being an additional intellectual hub and support when I was a Visiting Scholar at the Max Planck Fellow Group in Comparative Constitutionalism. I am especially grateful to Ayelet Shachar for her invaluable support and guidance, from which this book and I have benefited immensely.

Much of the book was written in a pre-Covid-19 world. I had the good fortune of traveling and discussing my ideas in person in many places. I spent some research time at the Centre for Socio-Legal Studies at the University of Oxford, the Columbia Law School and its Human Rights Institute, and most recently at the Max Planck Institute for Comparative Public Law and International Law. I also presented parts of the book at several conferences organized by different institutions including the Queen Mary University of London, Addis Ababa University, the Institute for Global Law and Policy at Harvard Law School, University of Oxford, Columbia Law School, McGill Law School, WZB Berlin Social Science Center, University of Milan, and the Melbourne Law School. This book benefited from the excellent and vibrant intellectual environments and the scholarly conversations I had with so many people in these institutions. I also owe huge gratitude to the Open Society Foundation London, which generously funded my research at Oxford as a Civil Society Scholar and to CEU for generously funding my doctoral studies and awarding me the Doctoral Research Support Grant, which enabled me to conduct an important part of my research at Columbia University in the City of New York.

While writing this book, I have received different kinds of support, advice, and guidance from so many people, and I want to especially thank Csilla Kollonay-Lehoczky, Gedion Timothewos Hessebon, Getahun Walelgn, Hiwot Aboye, Hodan Mohamed, Marina Kurkchiyan, Michael Imran Kanu, Nancy Elsamanoudi, Renáta Uitz, Seid Yimam, Shimles Sisay, Sejal Parmar, and Shimon Shemtov. I am especially grateful to Richard Albert—a global leader of comparative constitutionalism and a selfless advisor, mentor, and opportunity creator for the comparative constitutional law community worldwide - for his guidance, invaluable comments, and suggestions and for giving me the opportunity to deliver a plenary lecture based on parts of the book at the first of its kind Global Summit on the Future of Constitutionalism alongside the leading scholars of public law and comparative constitutionalism.

I am profoundly grateful to the editors of the *Oxford Comparative Constitutionalism* series Richard Albert and Robert Schütze as well as OUP commissioning editor Jamie Berezin, for their confidence and guidance in this project from its inception. I wish to thank the anonymous reviewers of Oxford University Press, whose critical reviews and constructive comments helped me write a much better book. I am very grateful to Brianne Bellio at OUP and Mark Ajin at Newgen, who made everything easy for me in the production of the book.

Last, but not least, I am hugely indebted to my parents, Fikrie Kassie and Adugna Gebeye, for making it possible for me to be the person that I am today. Their unwavering and continuing support, prayer, and encouragement are my great source of strength and inspiration. I dedicate this book to them as a small gesture of love and gratitude knowing that I could never repay them for all they have done. I wish to acknowledge my large extended family and friends for their continued support and encouragement over the years. Finally, I am grateful to Giulia Priora for her able support and joyful companion throughout the writing of this book. I couldn't thank her enough for listening and discussing many of the ideas in this book firsthand over the years.

***

Some earlier short versions and parts of this work have been included in "Global Constitutionalism and Cultural Diversity: The Emergence of Jurisgenerative Constitutionalism in Africa" (2021) 10 *Global Constitutionalism* 1, 40–71; "Federal Theory and Federalism in Africa" (2020) 52 *Verfassung und Recht in Übersee/World Comparative Law* 2, 95–115; and "The Janus Face of Legal Pluralism for the Rule of Law Promotion in Sub-Saharan Africa" (2019) 53 *Canadian Journal of African Studies/Revue canadienne des études africaines* 2, 337–353.

Berihun Adugna Gebeye
Heidelberg, Germany
January 2021

Table of Cases

ETHIOPIA

KENYA

NIGERIA

SOUTH AFRICA

Table of Legislation

NATIONAL CONSTITUTIONS AND LEGISLATION

INTERNATIONAL LAWS AND CONVENTIONS

Introduction

The major scholarly and policy discussions on African constitutionalism revolve around two main theoretical frameworks: legal centralism and legal pluralism. Legal centralists explain the idea and practice of African constitutionalism through the prism of liberal constitutionalism, focusing primarily on written constitutions. Their temporal starting point is the 1950s and 1960s, when many African states got independence from colonial rule. From the perspective of the legal centralists—ie, based on the practice of limited government, the protection of individual rights, and the rule of law—the performance of African constitutionalism has been a tragic failure, at worst, and very disappointing, at best.[1]

In contrast, legal pluralists understand and explain African constitutionalism from two distinct vantage points: the first is through the lens of the state and the second is through the lens of society. Inherent in this view is the bifurcation of the public sphere into the civic public, which operates—or claims to operate—under the civil structures of the state created during colonialism, and the primordial public, which functions in accordance with indigenous custom since precolonial times.[2] Legal pluralists hold that these two publics operate under different senses of morality, rationality, and justice. As a result, they posit that there are dual and parallel constitutional systems in African states. For legal pluralists, this state of affairs not only distinguishes African constitutionalism from the liberal constitutional systems of Western states, but it also renders the liberal constitutional project in Africa simply a chimera. While legal centralists turn to the universe of liberal constitutionalism to find a cure for the perennial ills of African constitutionalism, legal pluralists believe the solution lies within the historical and cultural milieu of Africans.

There is an impasse between the legal centralist and legal pluralist account of African constitutionalism. As these theoretical frameworks stand on different epistemological, historical, and legal accounts, it is difficult to fully understand African constitutionalism in its normative and empirical manifestations without choosing one over the other. As such, the legal centralist and legal pluralist impasse limits the range of theoretically cogent and practically sound constitutional solutions to the problems of constitutional government in Africa. The solution to such impasse is not to be found in the emphatic support of one against the other, but rather in subjecting them both

[1] HWO Okoth-Ogendo, 'Constitutions without Constitutionalism: Reflections on an African Political Paradox' in Douglass Greenberg and others (eds), *Constitutionalism and Democracy: Transitions in the Contemporary World* (Oxford University Press 1993) 65–80. Okoth-Ogendo's 'Constitutions without Constitutionalism' is the classic legal centralist account of constitutions and constitutionalism in Africa.

[2] Peter P Ekeh, 'Colonialism and the Two Publics in Africa: A Theoretical Statement' (1975) 17 Comparative Studies in Society and History 91, 92–93. Ekeh's 'Two Publics' epitomize the legal pluralist approach of constitutions and constitutionalism in Africa.

A Theory of African Constitutionalism. Berihun Adugna Gebeye, Oxford University Press.
DOI: 10.1093/oso/9780192893925.003.0001

to proper critical exposition and analysis. As both legal centralists and legal pluralists grapple with similar constitutional problems in similar constitutional spaces, problematizing them in order to attend to the constitutional realities may help transcend such impasse in constitutional thinking in Africa.

This book develops a theory of African constitutionalism that transcends the legal centralist and legal pluralist impasse through a comprehensive study of African constitutionalism from precolonial times to the present, along with the attendant constitutional designs and practices ranging from the nature and operation of the state, to its vertical and horizontal government structures, to its Bill of Rights. Two main questions guide the inquiry of the book: Why we need a new theoretical framework for African constitutionalism, and how this could offer us better theoretical and practical tools with which to understand, improve, and assess African constitutionalism on its own terms. In the book, the term 'African constitutionalism' refers to a set of concepts, principles, and practices that arise from the experiences, interactions, and contestations of power and governance from precolonial times to the present, and are, in turn, used to organize, limit, and enable political power and authority in African states.[3] The use of the term 'African constitutionalism' here does not imply or suggest the existence of a uniform and singular experience of constitutionalism in all African states. Quite the opposite. African states have a rich and diverse experience with constitutionalism. However, as this book demonstrates, there are some unique constitutional features that all African states have in common. By locating the phenomenology of African constitutionalism from precolonial times to the present, and by building on, and simultaneously departing from, the theoretical and practical insights of both legal centralism and legal pluralism, the book aims to rectify their pitfalls in a way that is attentive to both the normative configurations and empirical manifestations of constitutionalism on the continent.

The central argument presented herein is that legal syncretism is a better theoretical framework for understanding African constitutionalism than legal centralism and legal pluralism. Legal syncretism has two facets: *a process* and *a result* facet. *Legal syncretism as a process* more clearly accounts for the development and transformation of African constitutionalism from precolonial times to the present, while *legal syncretism as a result* better captures and explains the designs and practices of African constitutionalism across time and space. I attempt to advance the hypothesis that legal syncretism not only offers a better theoretical framework for understanding the nature, travails, pathologies, and incremental successes of African constitutionalism, but also provides very useful theoretical and practical insights for its diagnosis, consolidation, and assessment. For the purposes of this book, legal syncretism refers to *the process and the result of adoption, rejection, invention, and transformation of diverse and seemingly opposite legal rules, principles, and practices into a constitutional state with imperial or colonial legacies.* As I consider legal syncretism as a general or meta theory that captures and explains African constitutionalism and as a theoretical framework like that of legal centralism and legal pluralism, I use 'theoretical framework' or 'theory' interchangeably throughout the book. The constitutional matrix that sets legal

[3] See also Mark Tushnet, 'Varieties of Constitutionalism' (2016) 14 International Journal of Constitutional Law 1, 1–5. African constitutionalism is one variety in the universe of constitutionalism.

syncretism in motion is composed of international law, colonial laws, African indigenous laws, and liberal constitutional norms and practices.

By taking the Berlin West Africa Conference of 1884–1885 as a frame of reference, due to its radical effect on the socio-economic and political lives of Africans and its enduring legacy for constitutionalism throughout the continent, this book first decodes how a particular synergy of international law and European colonial laws ended the precolonial constitutional systems of African societies—societies that hosted numerous indigenous constitutional systems that considered custom as their normative order and traditional government as their institutional setup. Second, it shows how colonial constitutionalism took root on the continent via the accommodation, rejection, and invention of some variants of custom and traditional authority, such as customary law and native authority, and how this constitutional engineering, on the one hand, created unity at the constitutional level by affirming the supremacy of the colonial government, but on the other hand, it recognized diversity at the sub-constitutional level by incorporating precolonial indigenous laws and institutions as part of the colonial legal order. Third, it examines how postcolonial constitutionalism accepts the colonially-constituted states, but grapples with devising a theory of government that legitimates these states and addresses their pressing challenges and needs within an international legal order that takes democracy, the rule of law, and human rights as 'the global constitutionalist trinity'.[4] Through this genealogical exploration of African constitutionalism, I present how the syncretic processes of rejection, acceptance, accommodation, and transformation of the constitutive elements of the constitutional matrix—ie, international law, colonial laws, African indigenous laws, and liberal constitutional norms and practices—have informed constitutional change and transformation across time and space.

These syncretic constitutional processes within the constitutional matrix have also brought about syncretic constitutional designs and practices related to the nature of the state, government, and the notion of rights in Africa. The state in Africa, in a departure from classic theories of state, first came into being and took root in society through the technology of law. The *constitution* of the African state is the product of the syncretic configuration of international law *from above* and African indigenous laws *from below*. International law *from above* incorporated Africa into world society as a colony in the late nineteenth century, and then recognized it as an equal sovereign in the community of nations in the mid-twentieth century in the form of a European-style territorial state. Along with these recognitions, it bestowed on the territorial state (both colonial and postcolonial) formal internal autonomy and external protection through the doctrine of sovereignty. Within the contours of these territorial states, African indigenous laws were reconfigured *from below* to provide the state with the necessary infrastructure and resources for its internal operation. Within the context of international law *from above* and African indigenous laws *from below*, the written constitutions primarily have provided legitimacy and, to the extent possible, the institutional and normative context for the practice of constitutionalism. Due to its origin, the African state has syncretic forms of morality, justice, and rationality that establish

[4] Mattias Kumm and others, 'How Large Is the World of Global Constitutionalism?' (2014) 3 Global Constitutionalism 1, 3–4.

it, to begin with, and then maintain it even if it may not have the monopoly of violence (in the Weberian sense) throughout its territory.

Like with the *constitution* of the state, legal syncretism permeates the entire spectrum of African constitutional designs and practices ranging from the vertical organization of the state, to its horizontal government structures, to its Bill of Rights. For a detailed exploration and examination of how legal syncretism captures and explains these constitutional designs and practices, I use federalism, the executive branch, and women's constitutional rights as themes of analysis. The choice of these themes is based on two considerations. The first is that these themes represent the three major aspects of constitutional design and practice: federalism is one form of vertical organization of government, the executive is the representative of government in the horizontal division of powers, women's constitutional rights are one element in the Bills of Rights. Thus, a study of these themes provides a comprehensive idea of the structures, values, and rights in African constitutionalism. The second reason for choosing these themes is their relevance and capacity to highlight the nature, identity, and challenges of African constitutionalism. Although African countries are either less interested in, or have a general distaste for, federalism, there is an increasing trend of, or demand for, decentralization which a focus on federalism can illuminate.[5] The executive is the most powerful government branch that has influenced the trajectory of African constitutionalism and making it part of this study offers some useful insights regarding the design and practice of limited government.[6] Women's constitutional rights are good intersection points in the designs and practices of liberal constitutionalism and multiculturalism.[7] Furthermore, a focus on women's constitutional rights not only extends the discussion to human rights as more broadly conceived, but it also helps with an exploration of the organization and philosophy of the judiciary.

To show how legal syncretism captures and explains federalism, the executive, and women's constitutional rights in Africa, I focus on Nigeria, Ethiopia, and South Africa as comparative case studies. I have chosen these case studies since not only do they represent strikingly different African historical experiences, but they also share some key similarities. For example, while Nigeria had a colonial experience, Ethiopia did not, and South Africa had the unique experience of apartheid. Nonetheless, the Western imperial and colonial encounters played a critical role in the emergence of all three of these countries in their present forms and textures; Western colonialism brought about the formation of Nigeria and South Africa, and it contributed to the development of Ethiopia in its current territorial form.[8] Furthermore, these states are representative of the ethnic, racial, religious, and regional diversities that are prevalent in Africa, which influence the designs and practices of constitutionalism on

[5] See Charles M Fombad, 'Constitutional Entrenchment of Decentralization in Africa: An Overview of Trends and Tendencies' (2018) 62 Journal of African law 2, 175–99; Yonatan Fessha and Coel Kirkby, 'A Critical Survey of Subnational Autonomy in African States' (2008) 38 Publius: The Journal of Federalism 248, 248–71.

[6] See Oda van Cranenburgh, '"Big Men" Rule: Presidential Power, Regime Type and Democracy in 30 African Countries' (2008) 15 Democratization 952, 952–73.

[7] See for instance, Fareda Banda, *Women, Law and Human Rights: An African Perspective* (Hart Publishing 2005) 41–57.

[8] Bahru Zewde, *A History of Modern Ethiopia, 1855–1991* (2nd ed, James Currey 2001) 111–47.

the continent. Additionally, while South Africa is a good example of the practice of 'liberal constitutionalism' in Africa, Nigeria and Ethiopia—like most other African countries—continue to grapple with it.

Moreover, these states are suitable case studies with which to explore and examine the specific themes of this book. With respect to federalism, Nigeria, Ethiopia, and South Africa are the only established African federal countries. Regarding the executive, Nigeria adopted the type of presidential system that is predominant in Africa, while Ethiopia follows the less-preferred parliamentary system, and South Africa has a hybrid system. Related to women's constitutional rights, these case studies are representative of the various constitutional treatments and practices of women's constitutional rights found in many African countries. Hence, not only do the striking differences and similarities in the constitutional histories, challenges, designs, and practices of Nigeria, Ethiopia, and South Africa—in addition to them being representative of the various African experiments of constitutionalism—render them good comparative case studies, but they also demonstrate the theoretical fitness of legal syncretism to clearly account for and explain African constitutionalism with all its diversities and subtleties.[9]

I approach African constitutionalism from a multidisciplinary perspective. The objective of deploying multidisciplinary perspectives and materials is to retrieve and construct an account of African constitutionalism in different times and places. This is particularly useful for my thesis as it situates the phenomenology of African constitutionalism within the dynamics of power and governance from precolonial times to the present. Although this book is mainly a legal study and, consequently, uses methods and materials from the fields of constitutional law, international law, constitutional theory, and legal theory, it also draws heavily from the fields of political science, anthropology, sociology, religious studies, international relations, and history in order to better understand both the normative configurations and empirical manifestations of African constitutionalism. In particular, this book develops legal syncretism—as a theoretical framework—from the notion of syncretism in religious studies and anthropology.

Furthermore, this book is comparative as it is theoretical. It is comparative not only in the sense of using Nigeria, Ethiopia, and South Africa as case studies for testing and demonstrating the theoretical framework of this book, but also in its quest to include and interrogate the constitutional experiences of many African countries and Western liberal democracies in the process of developing the theoretical framework itself. In this respect, it makes extensive use of the constitutional experiences of numerous African societies and countries and features the experiences of liberal constitutional democracies along the way. It is the aim of developing a theoretical framework for African constitutionalism that is behind this broader comparative approach within and beyond Africa.[10]

[9] See Ran Hirschl, *Comparative Matters: The Renaissance of Comparative Constitutional Law* (Oxford University Press 2014) 244–66.

[10] See also Masamichi Sasaki, 'Comparative Research' in Michael S Lewis-Beck, Alan Bryman, and Tim Futing Liao (eds), *The SAGE Encyclopedia of Social Science Research Methods* (Sage Publications 2004) 152–53.

In sum, this book has three main objectives. The first is to develop a theoretical framework for African constitutionalism that breaks the impasse between legal centralism and legal pluralism. The second is to offer some useful theoretical and practical insights and perspectives for the constitution-building processes—constitution-making, revisions, and amendments—in Africa. The third and final objective is to present African constitutionalism to the universe of comparative constitutionalism and, hopefully, set a new research agenda in comparative constitutionalism, particularly in the global south. The general drivers of constitutional histories, politics, laws, and practices; the local, national, and international dynamics that shape constitutional experience; and the legacies of colonialism and imperialism I discuss in this book are also relevant to much of Asia, Latin America, and the Middle East. As a result, the theory advanced in this book may be relevant beyond Africa. And if so, the book will bring a new global conversation with a richly African experience as a comparative resource. Following from these objectives, I believe that the significance of this book lies in its contribution to the scholarship on constitutional theory, comparative constitutionalism, constitutional sociology, constitutional identity, and constitution-building.

In pursuing these objectives, this book is organized into seven chapters. The first three chapters are theoretical; and their main purpose is to develop a theoretical framework for understanding African constitutionalism. In this regard, Chapter 1 sets the basis for the development of the theoretical framework of this book by showing why we should look through the prism of *legal syncretism* to understand and appreciate the complexities of African constitutionalism. Chapter 2 assesses how *legal syncretism as a process* explains the development and transformation of African constitutionalism from precolonial times to the present. And Chapter 3 goes on to examine how *legal syncretism as a result* captures and explains the designs and practices of African constitutionalism with respect to the nature of the African state, its vertical and horizontal organization of government, and the Bills of Rights.

The following three chapters are comparative case studies, which aim to demonstrate the theoretical fitness of legal syncretism to capture and explain the selected themes in greater detail. Chapters 4, 5, and 6 take—respectively—federalism, the executive, and women's constitutional rights as themes of analysis and Nigeria, Ethiopia, and South Africa as comparative case studies. Before delving into the specific experiences of the case studies, these chapters first develop a conceptual framework for these themes against which the case studies can be evaluated. The conceptual frameworks regarding federalism, the executive, and women's constitutional rights are important not only to show how legal syncretism animates their design and practice, but also to make a normative case for how they may figure in constitutional design in Africa.

Chapter 7 brings the elements of legal syncretism to the attention of future constitutional designs and practices by outlining some of the major gaps, limits, and potential of previous African constitutional experiences. The book concludes with demonstrating how legal syncretism as a theoretical framework more than legal centralism and legal pluralism clearly accounts for and explains the complexities of African constitutionalism, and how it offers novel theoretical and practical tools for understanding, improving, and assessing African constitutionalism on its own terms.

PART I
THEORY

1

Legal Syncretism as a Theoretical Framework for African Constitutionalism

Constitutions assume a dual role of both constraining and enabling political power for socio-economic and political transformation in Africa.[1] In this regard, a high premium is given to constitutions and constitutionalism in order to ensure, among other things, the practice of multi-party democracy, the rule of law, human rights, and overall development.[2] Although many agree on the importance and transformative potential of constitutions and constitutionalism for Africa's multi-faceted challenges, there is still no uniform account of constitutions and constitutionalism in Africa. This mainly has to do with the 'African triple heritage'—that is informed by African indigeneity, the spread of Islam, and European colonialism[3]—and the hegemony and universalization of liberal constitutionalism.[4] The attendant historical, epistemological, methodological, and ideological accounts give rise to plural, and sometimes competing, understandings of constitutions and constitutionalism in Africa.[5]

For many, constitutions and constitutionalism in Africa are postcolonial phenomena, and the independence constitutions of the 1950s and 1960s are the starting point for Africa's constitutional analysis.[6] The essential features of these constitutions are the incorporation of liberal constitutional ideals, such as limited government and the Bill of Rights, into a written constitution. Despite passing through numerous waves of constitution-making since independence, the proclaimed aims of constitutions in Africa are to entrench and practice liberal constitutionalism.[7] Even though there are several challenges for the practical enforcement of said constitutions, ranging from their alleged unfitness to the African context to the commitment of African

[1] NW Barber, *The Principles of Constitutionalism* (Oxford University Press 2018) 9–10; Upendra Baxi, 'Preliminary Notes on Transformative Constitutionalism' in Oscar Vilhena Vieira, Upendra Baxi, and Frans Viljoen (eds), *Transformative Constitutionalism: Comparing the Apex Courts of Brazil, India and South Africa* (Pretoria University Law Press 2013) 19–47.

[2] H Kwasi Prempeh, 'Africa's "Constitutionalism Revival": False Start or New Dawn?' (2007) 5 International Journal of Constitutional Law 469, 485.

[3] See Ali A Mazrui, *The Africans: A Triple Heritage* (Little, Brown and Company 1986).

[4] Francis M Deng, *Identity, Diversity, and Constitutionalism in Africa* (United States Institute of Peace Press 2008) 12–13.

[5] See also Abdullahi Ahmed An-Na'im, *African Constitutionalism and the Role of Islam* (University of Pennsylvania Press 2006) 20; Mahmood Mamdani, 'The Social Basis of Constitutionalism in Africa' (1990) 28 The Journal of Modern African Studies 359, 363–66.

[6] Charles M Fombad, 'The Evolution of Modern African Constitutions: A Retrospective Perspective' in Charles M Fombad (eds), *Separation of Powers in African Constitutionalism* (Oxford University Press 2016) 14.

[7] See Charles Manga Fombad, 'Constitution-Building in Africa: The Never-Ending Story of the Making, Unmaking and Remaking of Constitutions' (2014) 13 African and Asian Studies 429, 429–51.

A Theory of African Constitutionalism. Berihun Adugna Gebeye, Oxford University Press. © Berihun Adugna Gebeye 2021.
DOI: 10.1093/oso/9780192893925.003.0002

governments to live by their rules, they are nevertheless presented as the supreme source of political power and authority in African states.[8]

For others, however, as constitutions and constitutionalism can be traced back to precolonial times, there are two constitutional systems in postcolonial Africa. While the first is a constitutional system based on written constitutions, the second is a constitutional system based on indigenous custom. This is because, the argument goes, there are 'two publics' in Africa.[9] The first is a 'civic public' created by Europeans through their colonization of Africa and which operates—or claims to operate—under a Western-style constitutional system. The second is a 'primordial public' that survived colonialism and operates under the logic and morality of indigenous custom. Hence, it is posited that—unlike in the West—there are two parallel constitutional systems in Africa, each with a different morality, rationality, and sense of justice.

Appreciating the nature, identity, and contours of African constitutionalism is necessary when trying to foster constitutional government and consolidate its dividends on the continent. To this end, one should address the singularity or duality of the constitutional order, the relationship between the written constitutional system and the indigenous customary order, and their overall interaction and impact on the system of constitutional government. These require a theoretical framework that adequately captures and explains the idea of constitution and constitutionalism in Africa across time and space. This book proposes legal syncretism as a theoretical framework capable of capturing and explaining the full transformation of African constitutionalism and the attendant constitutional designs and practices across time and space. Legal syncretism in this book refers to *the process and the result of adoption, rejection, invention, and transformation of diverse and seemingly opposite legal rules, principles, and practices into a constitutional state with imperial or colonial legacies.*

The objective of this chapter is, therefore, to justify the necessity of having a theoretical framework for African constitutionalism and to present legal syncretism as a better theoretical framework for the African constitutional universe than legal centralism and legal pluralism. After providing the reasons for needing a new theoretical framework for African constitutionalism, the chapter proceeds to explore the existing theoretical frameworks of law—legal centralism and legal pluralism—and examines their relevance to African constitutionalism. After showing both the potential and limits of these frameworks, the chapter proposes legal syncretism as a new and better theoretical framework that captures and explains the transformation of African constitutionalism from precolonial times to the present, as well as the attendant constitutional designs and practices, in theoretically defensible and practically sound ways.

[8] See HWO Okoth-Ogendo, 'Constitutions without Constitutionalism: Reflections on an African Political Paradox' in Douglass Greenberg and others (eds), *Constitutionalism and Democracy: Transitions in the Contemporary World* (Oxford University Press 1993) 65–80; Charles Manga Fombad, 'Constitutional Reforms and Constitutionalism in Africa: Reflections on Some Current Challenges and Future Prospects' (2011) 59 Buff L Rev 1007, 1020–35.

[9] See Peter P Ekeh, 'Colonialism and the Two Publics in Africa: A Theoretical Statement' (1975) 17 Comparative Studies in Society and History 91, 92–93; Mahmood Mamdani, *Citizen and Subject: Contemporary Africa and the Legacy of Late Colonialism* (Princeton University Press 1996) 16–18; Wale Adebanwi, 'Africa's "Two Publics": Colonialism and Governmentality' (2017) 34 Theory, Culture & Society 65, 74–77.

I. Why We Need a Theoretical Framework for African Constitutionalism

With few exceptions, the Westphalian state system was imported to the African continent at the end of the nineteenth century through European colonialism. While the colonial state in Africa brought with it Western law as a technology of governance, it neither found a lawless society nor did it totally erase the laws of the pre-existing societies.[10] Before the importation of Western laws, customary or indigenous laws had been performing constitutionalist functions, ranging from the exercise of political authority to the protection of individual rights, in precolonial societies in Africa.[11] With the advent of colonialism, customary or indigenous laws were officially subordinated to the imported Western laws. Similarly, after independence customary laws have been applicable within the limits of the constitutional framework. Nonetheless, the interaction between laws that emanate from the state—both colonial and postcolonial—and from society is not as clear as its official proclamation.[12]

Even though the postcolonial written constitutions were declared as supreme legal codes within the states, they have been unable—in practical terms—to broadcast their institutions and laws throughout the entire territory.[13] In much of Africa, constitutional rules and institutions are mainly applicable—when they are applicable—at the center, or in cities and towns. At the same time, although the application of customary laws is limited in constitutions, they do regulate—in actual terms—the socio-economic and political life of much of the population in rural and pastoral areas.[14] Due to this non-uniform application of constitutions and customary laws, some argue that these postcolonial states are bifurcated states operating under the realm of both modern constitutional systems and customary or indigenous constitutional systems.[15] Consequently, as noted in the Introduction, it is contended that two parallel constitutional systems co-exist in regulating these 'two publics' in postcolonial Africa.[16]

The relationship between the 'written-based constitutional systems' and the 'custom-based constitutional systems' is often characterized in binaries, such as official vs unofficial, formal vs informal, state vs society, and modern vs traditional,

[10] See T Olawale Elias, *The Nature of African Customary Law* (Manchester University Press 1956).

[11] M Fortes and EE Evans-Pritchard, 'Introduction' in M Fortes and EE Evans-Pritchard (eds), *African Political Systems* (Oxford University Press 1940) 12–14.

[12] Olaf Zenker and Markus Virgil Hoehne, 'Processing the Paradox: When the State has to Deal with Customary Law' in Olaf Zenker and Markus Virgil Hoehne (eds), *The State and the Paradox of Customary Law in Africa* (Routledge 2018) 1–30.

[13] See also Jeffrey Herbst, *States and Power in Africa: Comparative Lessons in Authority and Control* (Princeton University Press 2000) 11–13.

[14] Jeanmarie Fenrich, Paolo Galizzi, and Tracy E Higgins, 'Introduction' in Jeanmarie Fenrich, Paolo Galizzi, and Tracy E Higgins (eds), *The Future of African Customary Law* (Cambridge University Press 2011) 1–2.

[15] See Mamdani, *Citizen and Subject* (n 9) 16–18; Lungisile Ntsebeza, *Democracy Compromised: Chiefs and the Politics of the Land in South Africa* (Brill 2005) 295–99.

[16] See also Bruce Baker, 'Justice and Security Architecture in Africa: The Plans, The Bricks, The Purse and The Builder' (2011) 43 The Journal of Legal Pluralism and Unofficial Law 25, 27. Baker further states that the customary justice systems are the most efficient and more widely used than the constitutional based justice systems.

respectively.[17] In fact, the relationship between these two systems in postcolonial Africa is far more complex and transcends the aforementioned binaries.[18] The discrepancy between the proclamation of constitutional monopoly and actual practice on the one hand,[19] and the vitality of customary or indigenous systems as sources of political power and rights protection on the other,[20] necessitate a clearer account of constitutions and constitutionalism in postcolonial Africa.

The constitutional experience of postcolonial Africa begs more questions and casts more doubts as to what constitutions and constitutionalism actually mean than what it actually tells. For instance, how do we understand and conceive constitutions and constitutionalism in Africa across time and space? Are there single or plural constitutional systems in postcolonial Africa? How are customary or indigenous systems related to constitutional government? And what role do they play in postcolonial Africa? For this purpose, a theoretical framework that addresses these questions and contributes to the consolidation of constitutional government in Africa becomes necessary. It goes without saying that a clearer account of constitutions and constitutionalism can also be helpful in identifying the pathologies of constitutional government and offer some useful diagnostic prescriptions for its health and improvement going forward.

Furthermore, this book builds on previous justifications for a theoretical study of constitutions and constitutionalism. In this respect, Richard Fallon notes that both descriptive and prescriptive constitutional theory should—or at least claim to—advance the rule of law, democracy, and substantive justice that protects individual rights.[21] Despite the variations in the meanings they attach, or in the ways they claim to advance them, the rule of law, democracy, and respect for individual rights are the main justifications for all constitutional studies. Thus, the quest for a theoretical framework of constitutionalism in Africa is ultimately related to advancing the rule of law, promoting democracy, and protecting basic individual rights, for these all depend on a clearer account of constitutions and their attendant operating systems.

II. Theoretical Frameworks of Law and their Relevance to Constitutional Law

Law has been understood in diverse ways by many great thinkers.[22] One fundamental element in the description of law is its relationship to the state. Legal theorists in the legal positivism school hold that law is fundamentally tied to the state. For instance, John Austin defines law as 'a general command of a sovereign addressed to his

[17] Carolyn Logan, 'Traditional Leaders in Modern Africa: Can Democracy and the Chief Co-Exist?' Afrobarometer Working Papers 35 Working Paper No 93 <http://afrobarometerorg/sites/default/files/publications/Working%20paper/AfropaperNo93pdf> accessed 23 August 2018.

[18] See Kate Baldwin, *The Paradox of Traditional Chiefs in Democratic Africa* (Cambridge University Press 2015) 6–13; Christian Lund, 'Twilight Institutions: Public Authority and Local Politics in Africa' (2006) 37 Development & Change 685.

[19] Herbst, *States and Power in Africa* (n 13) 21–23.

[20] Pierre Englebert, 'Patterns and Theories of Traditional Resurgence in Tropical Africa' (2002) 118 Mondes en développement 51.

[21] Richard H Fallon, 'How to Choose a Constitutional Theory' (1999) 87 California Law Review 535, 539.

[22] HLA Hart, *The Concept of Law* (2nd ed, Oxford University Press 1994) 1–2.

subjects'.[23] HLA Hart, in contrast with Austin, considers law as 'a union of primary and secondary rules'.[24] Scott Shapiro, by considering laws as plans, asserts that law is 'a self-certifying compulsory planning organization whose aim is to solve those moral problems that cannot be solved, or solved as well, through alternative forms of social ordering'.[25] Even if these legal theorists approach law differently, they all consider the existence, normativity, and force of law from the perspective of the state. This understanding of law is dubbed 'legal centralism' as it situates law within the centralized, singular, and supreme legal order of the state.[26]

Others, however, including legal pluralists, legal anthropologists, and law and society scholars, conceive law independently of, or unlimited by, the state; they consider the state as one among many sources of law.[27] For example, John Griffiths, in his influential article 'What is Legal Pluralism?', defines law as 'the self-regulation of the semi-autonomous social field'.[28] Boaventura de Sousa Santos, seeing law from a post-modern perspective, defines law as 'a body of regularized procedures and normative standards, considered justiciable in any group, which contributes to the creation and prevention of disputes, and to their settlement through an argumentative discourse, coupled with the threat of force'.[29] Viewing law from a global perspective, William Twining conceives law '[. . .] as a species of institutionalised social practice that is oriented to ordering relations between subjects at one or more levels of relations and of ordering'.[30] Unhappy with these essentialist definitions or conceptions of law,[31] Brian Z Tamanaha contends that law is '[. . .] whatever social groups conventionally attach the label "law" to'.[32] Despite the differences in their definitions or conceptualizations of law, these jurists unite on the plural sources of law. They posit that law is neither the exclusive domain of the state nor is non-state law inferior to state law. This description of law is usually called 'legal pluralism' as it ascribes plural sources for law.

Even though legal centralism and legal pluralism are broad descriptive frameworks directed at understanding and explicating the identity, nature, source, and application of law generally, they have constitutional relevance as well. This is due to the fact that they deal with how a legal order is constituted and structured, and how it functions. For legal centralists, there is either a supreme written constitution or a master rule in any legal system that ultimately determines the legality and validity of the laws within that legal system. Consider, for instance, Hans Kelsen and Hart. Kelsen, in his *General Theory of Law and State*, puts the constitution at the top of the legal order.[33] As the highest

[23] Wilfrid E Rumble (eds), *John Austin: The Province of Jurisprudence Determined* (Cambridge University Press 1995) XV and 18; Joseph Raz, *The Concept of a Legal System: An Introduction to the Theory of Legal System* (2nd ed, Oxford University Press 1980) 4.

[24] Hart, *The Concept of Law* (n 22) 79.

[25] Scott J Shapiro, *Legality* (Harvard University Press 2013) 225.

[26] John Griffiths, 'What Is Legal Pluralism?' (1986) 24 Journal of Legal Pluralism and Unofficial Law 1, 3.

[27] For instance, see DJ Galligan, *Law in Modern Society* (Oxford University Press 2007) 162.

[28] Griffiths, 'What Is Legal Pluralism?' (n 26) 38.

[29] Boaventura de Sousa Santos, *Toward a New Legal Common Sense: Law, Globalization, and Emancipation* (Cambridge University Press 2002) 428–29.

[30] William Twining, *General Jurisprudence: Understanding Law from a Global Perspective* (Cambridge University Press 2009) 117.

[31] See Brian Z Tamanha, 'A Non-Essentialist Version of Legal Pluralism' (2000) 27 Journal of Law and Society 296.

[32] Brian Z Tamanaha, *A Realistic Theory of Law* (Cambridge University Press 2017) 194.

[33] Hans Kelsen, *General Theory of Law and State* (Anders Wedberg tr, Harvard University Press 1945) 124.

law, Kelsen posits, every other law should conform to the constitution or else it will be deemed null and void.[34] To this end, Kelsen introduces the idea of a special constitutional court that is in charge of constitutional review in a centralized manner.[35] Hart, in his *The Concept of Law*, introduces the idea of the rule of recognition as an ultimate and master metarule in any legal system.[36] Hart's rule of recognition has constitutional relevance as it is this rule that provides the supreme and ultimate criterion for the validity and legality of rules in a legal system.[37] For example, acts of parliament in the United Kingdom and the amendment clause in the United States Constitution[38] are both considered rules of recognition.[39] In contrast, legal pluralists contend that multiple legal orders can co-exist in a society or territory independently.[40] Consequently, they advance the claim that there is no superior law that settles conflicts between, or among, legal orders in society as each legal order has a different source of legality and validity.[41]

As the idea of constitutions and constitutionalism in Africa is discussed within the prism of both written and custom-based constitutional systems, as noted in the previous section, applying legal centralism and legal pluralism can be helpful in problematizing and clarifying the constitutional phenomenon of Africa. The following sections present a concise account of legal centralism and legal pluralism in order to show both their potential and limits as theoretical frameworks for African constitutionalism.

III. Legal Centralism

Legal centralism is related to, and associated with, the development of the modern state. The state as an historically contingent entity claims primacy over any other entity within it. Regardless of any differences in the development of the state across the world, once they came into being, states project a legal order that is supreme and universal within their jurisdiction. Consequently, state institutions and their officials advance the supreme and universal power of the state, and scholars and philosophers theorize about this phenomenon in a systematic manner. Legal centralism is the result of two phenomena: the projection of *state law* as a singular legal order by the state as a manifestation and practice of sovereignty on the one hand, and the consideration of *law*—by legal scholars and philosophers in their scientific study of law—as the sole business and domain of the state on the other. In order to understand the fundamentals of legal centralism, this section explores the notion of the state, how it projects its legal order as supreme and universal within its domain, and how scholars and

[34] ibid 125–28.

[35] See Georg Schmitz, 'The Constitutional Court of the Republic of Austria 1918–1920' (2003) 16 Ratio Juris 240.

[36] Hart, *The Concept of Law* (n 22) 100–03.

[37] ibid 103.

[38] United States Constitution 1789, Article V.

[39] Hart, *The Concept of Law* (n 22) 106; Kent Greenawalt, 'The Rule of Recognition and the Constitution' in Matthew Adler and Kenneth Einar Himma (eds), *The Rule of Recognition and the US Constitution* (Oxford University Press 2009) 11–16.

[40] Griffiths, 'What Is Legal Pluralism?' (n 26) 5–7; Galligan, *Law in Modern Society* (n 27) 162–63.

[41] NW Barber, *The Constitutional State* (Oxford University Press 2012) 147–48.

philosophers, particularly legal scientists, posit and advance the idea that the state is the only source of law and legality.

The state as externally immune (from interference) and internally autonomous (in its course of action) emerges after the 1648 Treaty of Westphalia. Even if the Westphalian state system is particular to Europe, it has become the universal template for states everywhere.[42] From a legal perspective, the idea of the state can be seen through the prisms of international law and constitutional law. For the purposes of international law,[43] the state should possess a permanent population, a defined territory, a government, and a capacity to enter into relations with other states in order to assume rights and duties as such.[44] The rich body of scholarship on international law takes these criteria of statehood into account when identifying entities as states for the purpose of their discipline. For instance, Antonio Cassese,[45] Malcolm Shaw,[46] and Ian Brownlie[47] write their treatises on international law by taking these essential requirements of statehood into consideration. For Cassese, states need to have (a) 'a central structure capable of exercising effective control over a human community living in a given territory'; (b) 'a territory which does not belong, or no longer belongs, to any other sovereign state'; and (c) 'effective possession of, and control over, a territory'.[48] By the same token, Shaw discusses the notion of the state within these legal criteria and interrogates it with the international law practice.[49] Similarly, Brownlie considers the existence of 'population, defined territory, government and independence' as the legal criteria for statehood.[50] Despite new developments in international law that challenge the Westphalian idea of the state, international law still accords states external protection through the recognition of sovereignty and internal autonomy through the recognition of the right to self-determination.[51]

Constitutional law also gives substance to the international law conception of statehood: it defines the state's population, territorial limit, and form of government, and proclaims the sovereign power of the state.[52] By providing the institutional architecture as well as the systems of operation and interaction, the constitution gives the state not only its own form and texture, but also confers the unity of authority and power onto the state.[53] Fundamentally, in its classic European context, the constitution constitutes, or establishes, the state.[54] Through this *constitution* of the state, the

[42] Martin van Creveld, *The Rise and Decline of the State* (Cambridge University Press 1999) 263–335; explaining how the idea of the state spread from few Western European states to Eastern Europe, Latin America, Asia, and Africa.

[43] James R Crawford, *The Creation of States in International Law* (2nd ed, Oxford University Press 2007) 45.

[44] Montevideo Convention on the Rights and Duties of States 1933, article 1.

[45] Antonio Cassese, *International Law* (2nd ed, Oxford University Press 2005) 71–80.

[46] Malcolm N Shaw, *International Law* (8th ed, Cambridge University Press 2017) 155–63.

[47] Ian Brownlie, *Principles of Public International Law* (7th ed, Oxford University Press 2008) 69–83.

[48] Cassese, *International Law* (n 45) 73.

[49] Shaw, *International Law* (n 46) 155–63.

[50] Brownlie, *Principles of Public International Law* (n 47) 70–71.

[51] See for instance, Jean L Cohen, *Globalization and Sovereignty: Rethinking Legality, Legitimacy, and Constitutionalism* (Cambridge University Press 2012) 1–8, 76–79.

[52] Barber, *The Constitutional State* (n 41) 17–25.

[53] Gianfranco Poggi, *The Development of the Modern State: A Sociological Introduction* (Stanford University Press 1978) 92–93; Andrew Vincent, *Theories of the State* (Wiley-Blackwell 1991) 118–19.

[54] Olivier Beaud, 'Conceptions of the State' in Michel Rosenfeld and András Sajó (eds), *The Oxford Handbook of Comparative Constitutional Law* (Oxford University Press 2012) 273–74.

constitution—both written and unwritten—enables the state to exercise its sovereign power while also disabling it from exercising the same by introducing some limitations.[55] Indeed, this constitutional state is a later development, or progression, of the Westphalian state associated with the French and American revolutions in the late eighteenth and nineteenth centuries.[56] In the current century, despite variations in form, substance, and practice, states either operate, or claim to operate, under their own supreme constitutional systems. Under these systems, constitutional law proclaims and claims the supreme authority and power of the state in both its internal actions and external relations.

In addition to these self-projections and claims of the state, scholars and philosophers of social,[57] political,[58] and legal theory[59] also advance the grander claims of the state, with Max Weber offering the most influential account of the state in this respect. He posited that '[a] compulsory political association with continuous organization […] will be called a "state" if and in so far as its administrative staff successfully upholds a claim to the monopoly of the legitimate use of physical force in the enforcement of its order'.[60] While the international law and constitutional law accounts of the state are normative, the Weberian state is empirical and descriptive. As such, according to Weber, states have the monopoly and legitimate use of violence over their populations and within their territories. Building on Weber, other social and political theorists assert that the state is not only a supreme entity, but also the source of law and legality.[61] Peter Steinberger goes even further, claiming that the state is more a 'structure of judgment about what is true and what is not' than merely a geographically-defined piece of earth, a collection of people, or a pattern of social interactions.[62] In a similar vein, Alexander d'Entrèves observes that the state is an 'omnipresent entity' that uses law in the exercise of its indefinite and irresistible power.[63] Common to the various notions of state in social and political theory is the supremacy of the state as an entity and the use of law as a legitimate use of force.

The supremacy of the state and state law are given unmatched expression in legal theory. Among the legal philosophers of the twentieth century, Kelsen gave the most legalistic account of the state and positioned state law as the supreme arbiter in the operation and functioning of the state and those within it. He considers the state as 'the personification of the legal order', or a 'juristic expression of law'.[64] While he agrees with using the conventional elements of the state—such as territory, population, and sovereignty—when assessing whether to consider a certain entity a state, he also offers a legalistic account of these elements. For Kelsen, the territory of the state is 'the

[55] See for instance András Sajó and Renáta Uitz, *The Constitution of Freedom: An Introduction to Legal Constitutionalism* (Oxford University Press 2017) 22–23.

[56] Vincent, *Theories of the State* (n 53) 96–98; Ernst-Wolfgang Böckenförde, *Constitutional and Political Theory: Selected Writings* (Mirjam Künkler and Tine Stein (eds), Oxford University Press 2017) 141–42.

[57] Poggi, *The Development of the Modern State* (n 53) 1.

[58] See Alessandro Passerin d'Entrèves, *The Notion of the State: An Introduction to Political Theory* (Oxford University Press 1967) 1; Christopher Pierson, *The Modern State* (3rd ed, Routledge 2011) 8–34.

[59] Kelsen, *General Theory of Law and State* (n 33) 207–43.

[60] Max Weber, *Theory of Social and Economic Organization* (Talcott Parsons and AM Henderson tr, Oxford University Press 1947) 154.

[61] Vincent, *Theories of the State* (n 53) 19–21.

[62] Peter J Steinberger, *The Idea of the State* (Cambridge University Press 2005) 13.

[63] d'Entrèves, *The Notion of the State* (n 58) 1.

[64] Kelsen, *General Theory of Law and State* (n 33) 181.

territorial sphere of validity of the national legal order'.[65] This means that the reach of the legal order determines the territory of the state. Similarly, he considers people of the state as nothing but 'the personal sphere of validity of the national legal order'[66] and sovereignty of the state as 'the validity and efficacy of the national legal order'.[67] Thus, for Kelsen, the legal order both identifies the people of a state and imposes its sovereign power over them. By doing so, the legal order constitutes, or establishes, a state with 'one people, one territory, and one power'.[68] As the Kelsenian legal order is a hierarchical structure of laws which places the Constitution at the top, he unifies the theory of law with the theory of state.[69]

Unlike Kelsen, Hart takes the state for granted and offers a general concept of state law.[70] In order to understand the concept of law in general, Hart introduces the notion of 'primary and secondary rules' which he considers to be the 'key to the science of jurisprudence'.[71] He posits that law is 'the union of primary and secondary rules', and, thereby, the legality of a rule rests on its fitness within these systems of rules.[72] Even though Hart states from the outset that his theory of law is a theory of municipal law, he tries to apply his system of rules to primitive or pre-state societies as well.[73] He contends that while there are primary rules (duty-imposing rules) in primitive societies, secondary rules (power-conferring rules) are absent, and, consequently, the concept of law is non-existent in these societies.[74] According to Hart's conception, law is the sole domain of the state, and non-state or pre-state societies lack law as so understood.

Likewise, even though Joseph Raz admits to the parochial nature of legal theory and insists that it should also take into consideration the experiences of non-Western societies if it is to be universal,[75] his conception of law and legality is in line with the traditions of analytical legal theory, like that of Kelsen and Hart. While Raz approaches law differently than his predecessors, and his theory of legal systems has much more currency with regard to non-Western contexts,[76] law and legality in his conception still emanate from the hierarchical structure of legal systems of states and their institutions.[77] Raz holds that '[a] theory of law must be based, at least partly, on a theory of state, and ... [a] theory of state is partly based on a theory of law—the two are intimately interrelated'.[78] According to Raz, without a theory of state, a theory of law is

[65] ibid 207.
[66] ibid 233.
[67] ibid 255.
[68] ibid.
[69] See also Hans Kelsen, *Introduction to the Problems of Legal Theory: A Translation of the First Edition of the Reine Rechtslehre Or Pure Theory of Law* (Bonnie Litschewski Paulson and Stanley L Paulson tr, Clarendon Press 1996) 63–64.
[70] Hart, *The Concept of Law* (n 22) 3, 239–40.
[71] ibid 81.
[72] ibid 79.
[73] ibid 91–99.
[74] ibid 99.
[75] Joseph Raz, *Between Authority and Interpretation: On the Theory of Law and Practical Reason* (Oxford University Press 2010) 31–32, 41–46.
[76] Raz, *The Concept of a Legal System* (n 23) 1–4.
[77] See also Keith Culver and Michael Giudice, *Legality's Borders: An Essay in General Jurisprudence* (Oxford University Press 2010) 62–64.
[78] Joseph Raz, *The Authority of Law: Essays on Law and Morality* (Oxford University Press 1979) 99.

inconceivable. Hence, like Kelsen and Hart, the Razian account of law and legality is that of the state.[79]

Legal centralism, therefore, is a term used to describe the projection of state law as a supreme and singular legal order of the state, as well as the consideration of law by legal philosophers as the sole business and sphere of the state. Indeed, as is evident from this discussion, legal centralism contains no consensus as to what law is nor does it put forth a uniform method for studying it. The essential feature of legal centralism, as discussed above and eloquently put by John Griffiths, is the following:

> Law is and should be the law of the state, uniform for all persons, exclusive of all other law, and administered by a single set of state institutions. To the extent that the other lesser normative orderings, such as the church, the family, the voluntary association and the economic organizations exist, they ought to be and in fact are hierarchically subordinate to the law and institutions of the state.[80]

And it is in this sense that legal centralism is used in this book.

IV. Legal Pluralism

Originally related to the phenomenon of law in colonial societies,[81] legal pluralism has since been used to describe the nature of law and legality globally.[82] Posited in sharp contrast with legal centralism, legal pluralism claims that law is neither the exclusive domain of the state nor is state law superior to non-state law. It holds, rather, that law is essentially plural in its source, and, consequently, multiple legal orders coexist in any social field, with the state being only one among many sources of law. Legal pluralism has primarily been presented and advanced by sociologists, anthropologists, and lawyers working at the intersection of law, society, and state, at both the local and international levels. It should be clear from the outset that there is neither agreement about what law is nor a consensus on the definition of legal pluralism itself within the legal pluralism scholarship. The aim of this section is not to settle the controversy of the 'legal' in legal pluralism, or the debate over legal pluralism itself, but rather, as with the previous section, to briefly present the idea of legal pluralism with the aim of testing its descriptive potential for the purposes of this book.

Legal pluralism is usually defined as 'a situation in which two or more legal systems coexist in the same social field',[83] or 'that state of affairs, for any social field, in which behavior pursuant to more than one legal order occurs'.[84] This conception of legal

[79] See also Roger Cotterrell, 'Transnational Communities and the Concept of Law' (2008) 21 Ratio Juris 1, 6–7.

[80] Griffiths, 'What Is Legal Pluralism?' (n 26) 3.

[81] See MB Hooker, *Legal Pluralism: An Introduction to Colonial and Neo-Colonial Laws* (Clarendon Press 1975). Explaining how British, French, and Dutch laws interact with customary and religious laws in colonial and post-colonial Africa, Asia, and the Middle East.

[82] See Sally Engle Merry, 'Legal Pluralism' (1988) 22 Law & Society Review 869, 869; Brian Z Tamanaha, 'Understanding Legal Pluralism: Past to Present, Local to Global' (2008) 30 Sydney L Rev 375.

[83] Merry, 'Legal Pluralism' (n 82) 870.

[84] Griffiths, 'What Is Legal Pluralism?' (n 26) 2.

pluralism rests in the intellectual works of the early sociology of law and legal anthropology scholarship. In the 1930s and 1940s, Georges Gurvitch argued that the positivist sources of law—statutes and judicial decisions—are not only secondary sources, but also depend on other primary or material sources for their authority and effectiveness.[85] He contended that the monist claim of the state being the only source of law is not only dogmatic, but also socially unscientific.[86] As long as there are multiple sources of law, Gurvitch observed, the state cannot claim the monopoly of legality.[87] Like Gurvitch, Eugen Ehrlich gave further impetus to the view of plural ethos and qualities of law through his idea of 'living law', which he describes as 'the law which dominates life itself though it has not been posited in legal propositions'.[88]

In the 1970s, legal anthropologists produced a more advanced scholarship related to legal pluralism which has informed its development. Among the most influential works in this respect are Leopold Pospisil's theory of legal levels,[89] Michael Garfield Smith's theory of corporations,[90] and Sally Falk Moore's theory of the semi-autonomous social field.[91] Building on the works of Adamson Hoebel which describe primitive societies as having laws that are distinct from, but arise out of, culture, rituals, magic, and customary ordering,[92] Pospisil argues that 'no society has a single consistent legal system'.[93] He posits that every society has multiple legal levels which arise out of the existence of subgroups—such as family, lineage, community, and political confederacy—which each have their own laws.[94] Society as a mosaic of specifically patterned subgroups, notes Pospisil, has a multiplicity of legal systems ordered hierarchically based on their inclusiveness.[95]

By identifying how power is organized in society and how individuals are subject to different social organizations, Smith proposes the theory of corporations as a framework with which to understand law in society. Unlike Pospisil, Smith advances the universality of corporations and corporate life, and states that 'law provides the medium of expression and adjustment of the corporate relations'.[96] He further argues that as there are many corporations that are established based on religion, occupation, sex, ethnicity, age, or similar attributes—beyond a mere collection of people that run 'the

[85] Georges Gurvitch, *L'Expérience juridique et la philosophie pluraliste du droit* (Éditions A Pedone, Librairie de la Cour d'Appel et de l'Ordre des Avocats 1935) 145 as cited by Gordon R Woodman, 'Ideological Combat and Social Observation: Recent Debate about Legal Pluralism' (1998) 30 The Journal of Legal Pluralism and Unofficial Law 21, 28–29.

[86] ibid.

[87] See for instance Georges Gurvitch, *Sociology of Law* (Kegan Paul, Trench, Trubner & Co Ltd 1947) 166–80.

[88] Eugen Ehrlich, *Fundamental Principles of the Sociology of Law [1936]* (Transaction Publishers 2009) 493.

[89] See Leopold J Pospisil, *Anthropology of Law: A Comparative Theory* (Harper & Row 1971).

[90] See MG Smith, *Corporations and Society: The Social Anthropology of Collective Action* (Transaction Publishers 1974).

[91] See Sally Falk Moore, 'Law and Social Change: The Semi-Autonomous Social Field as an Appropriate Subject of Study' (1973) 7 Law & Society Review 719, 719–46.

[92] See E Adamson Hoebel, *The Law of Primitive Man: A Study in Comparative Legal Dynamics* (Harvard University Press 1954) 28.

[93] Pospisil, *Anthropology of Law* (n 89) 98.

[94] ibid 107 and 125.

[95] ibid 107.

[96] Smith, *Corporations and Society* (n 90) 128.

politics of public affairs'—there are and will be multiple laws in society.[97] Moore, on the other hand, develops her theory of the semi-autonomous social field not by taking social organizations as corporations, nor by recognizing them as hierarchical fields, but rather by considering the capacity of social fields 'to generate rules and coerce compliance'.[98] As long as there are multiple social fields with the capacity to generate and execute rules, there will be plural laws in society. Hence, the gist of all their theories is that legal pluralism is the feature of law in society, and that not only is legal centralism not reflective of socio-legal phenomena, but it is also deceptive with regard to real societal structure and interaction.[99]

By building on and reacting to such scholarship, John Griffiths offers a descriptive conception of legal pluralism by classifying it as both strong and weak. While strong legal pluralism refers to a situation where multiple legal orders coexist in parallel—independently of each other—within the same social field, weak legal pluralism refers to situations where non-state law and state law are applicable in the same social field, with the former being recognized by the latter as a 'technique of governance on pragmatic reasons'.[100] He notes that as the application of customary and religious laws in colonial societies was conditioned upon their recognition by the respective Western laws, legal pluralism in colonial societies was an archetype of weak legal pluralism.[101] And, for him, weak legal pluralism is not legal pluralism in the full sense of the term as it is permeated by legal centralism by virtue of the fact that it is the state that authorizes the application of the non-state laws. He holds that as law is 'neither systematic nor uniform' but rather 'the self-regulation of the semi-autonomous social field', the true version of legal pluralism is strong legal pluralism.[102] Hence, legal pluralism for him is an empirical situation in every society in which multiple legal orders are applicable in the same social field without the authorization of the state. By doing so, Griffiths liberates law from being solely associated with the state.[103]

Other significant perspectives include those of Boaventura de Sousa Santos and Gunther Teubner who place the notion of legal pluralism in a post-modern context, and, consequently, add some new layers and dimensions to the legal pluralism scholarship. After defining law in normative and institutional terms, Sousa Santos identifies six types, or clusters, of laws that are applicable in the same social field. These include domestic law (the law of the household), production law (the laws of the factory and corporation), exchange law (the laws of the market), community law (the laws of groups, whether hegemonic or oppressed), territorial or state law (the law of the citizen place), and systemic law (the law of the world place).[104] Teubner theorizes about the complexities of these clusters of laws through his idea of 'constitutional fragments'. He

[97] ibid 84–85; Griffiths, 'What Is Legal Pluralism?' (n 26) 18.

[98] Moore, 'Law and Social Change' (n 91) 722.

[99] See also Marc Galanter, 'Justice in Many Rooms: Courts, Private Ordering, and Indigenous Law' (1981) 13 The Journal of Legal Pluralism and Unofficial Law 1, 17–27.

[100] Griffiths, 'What Is Legal Pluralism?' (n 26) 5.

[101] ibid; see also Jacques Vanderlinden, 'Return to Legal Pluralism: Twenty Years Later' (1989) 21 The Journal of Legal Pluralism and Unofficial Law 149, 153–56.

[102] Griffiths, 'What Is Legal Pluralism?' (n 26) 5 and 38.

[103] See also Franz von Benda-Beckmann, 'Who's Afraid of Legal Pluralism?' (2002) 34 The Journal of Legal Pluralism and Unofficial Law 37, 74.

[104] ibid 429–38; see also Sousa Santos, *Toward a New Legal Common Sense* (n 29).

argues that constitutionalism is neither the sole arena of the nation-state, nor the only domain of global constitutionalism; constitutional problems can arise in transnational political processes, and 'at the same time outside the institutionalized political sector, in the "private sectors" of global society'.[105] He holds that transnational political processes and private sectors of global society can have transnational and sectorial constitutionalism, respectively, that both constitute their power and limit it under their own rule of law.[106] He suggests that conflicts among these constitutional systems should not be solved by appeal to a state or global constitutionalism,[107] but rather to a 'multilevel constitutionalism'.[108] Strong legal pluralism animates Teubner's conception of constitutional fragments.[109]

Without engaging in a definitional exercise on the precise meanings of law and legal pluralism,[110] Tamanaha considers legal pluralism as a 'common historical condition' evident in every society across time and space.[111] Multiple legal orders with competing claims of authority, conflicting—and sometimes complementing—normative demands, as well as diverse styles and orientation have existed in society from the medieval period to the present.[112] While the emergence of the nation-state in Europe reduced the medieval type of legal pluralism, it brought legal pluralism to colonial societies and into the wider international legal system.[113] Colonialism, globalization, and privatization have all made the uniform and monopolistic claim of state law obsolete.[114] Tamanaha identifies six types of normative orderings that give rise to legal pluralism.[115] The first is the *official/positive legal system* that includes those of the state, regional systems (such as the European Union or the African Union), and international systems (such as the United Nations or the World Trade Organization).[116] The second is *customary normative systems,* including indigenous/traditional laws and other forms of dispute-resolution mechanisms. The third is *religious normative systems*, such as Islamic law. The fourth is *economic/capitalist normative systems* that regulate capitalist production and market transactions. The fifth is *functionalist normative systems* that are organized and established to pursue particular purposes or functions, such as Universities, hospitals, and sports leagues. And the final one is

[105] Gunther Teubner, *Constitutional Fragments: Societal Constitutionalism and Globalization* (Gareth Norbury tr, Oxford University Press 2014) 1–2.

[106] ibid 17, for sectorial constitutionalism see Chapter 2 and for transnational constitutionalism see Chapter 3.

[107] Global constitutionalism refers to 'the gradual emergence and deliberate creation of constitutionalist elements in the international legal order'. See Anne Peters, 'The Merits of Global Constitutionalism' (2009) 16 Indiana Journal of Global Legal Studies 397, 397–411.

[108] ibid 35–36, 155–73.

[109] See also Gunther Teubner, 'The Two Faces of Janus: Rethinking Legal Pluralism' (1991) 13 Cardozo Law Review 1443, 1444–52.

[110] See Brian Z Tamanaha, 'A Non-Essentialist Version of Legal Pluralism' (2000) 27 Journal of Law and Society 2, 296–321.

[111] Tamanaha, 'Understanding Legal Pluralism' (n 82) 376.

[112] ibid 377–86.

[113] See William W Burke-White, 'International Legal Pluralism' (2004) 25 Michigan Journal of International Law 963.

[114] Tamanaha, 'Understanding Legal Pluralism' (n 82) 409.

[115] ibid 397–99.

[116] See also Paul Schiff Berman, *Global Legal Pluralism: A Jurisprudence of Law Beyond Borders* (Cambridge University Press 2012) 23–57, mapping out the details of legal pluralism at the global level.

community normative systems that are organized mainly around identity. Despite their differences in power, influence, and organizational structure, these normative systems all apply to the same social arena.

In a nutshell then, legal pluralism refers to the existence and application of multiple legal orders in the same social field—with or without the recognition of the state. As discussed above, there is no consensus in the legal pluralism scholarship with regard to *what law is* or the precise definition of *legal pluralism*. Nonetheless, there is some unanimity in this scholarship according to which law is neither the sole domain of the state nor is state law superior to non-state law. However, building on this general idea of legal pluralism, for the purposes of this book legal pluralism will refer to the existence and application of customary, religious, and state laws within a state—with or without its recognition. This narrower conception of legal pluralism was chosen simply because this book deals with the legal and constitutional systems of postcolonial states in Africa where this type of legal pluralism finds its classic expression and is still predominant today.

V. The Potential and Limits of Legal Centralism and Legal Pluralism as Theoretical Frameworks for African Constitutionalism

In order to test the potential and limits of legal centralism and legal pluralism as theoretical frameworks for African constitutionalism, it is important to discuss the concept of constitutionalism in general, and its application to the African context in particular. After a working concept of constitutionalism in Africa is established, this section applies legal centralism and legal pluralism to this phenomenon. The objective is to show how legal centralism and legal pluralism can be helpful, yet inadequate, in trying to understand and explain constitutionalism in Africa. By demonstrating the inadequacies of these two concepts for this purpose, this section not only paves the way for unearthing a new theoretical framework that captures the essence and nature of constitutionalism in Africa, but also provides new methods and approaches of doing so.

Constitutionalism is a generic term that does not have a single shape or form, neither in the past nor the present.[117] In its conventional understanding, however, constitutionalism is often described as the idea of limited government and the protection of fundamental rights under the rule of law.[118] This idea of constitutionalism is set in motion (albeit not always) through the instrumentality of a written document, called a constitution, that provides the institutional and functional features of government and its operation, along with some fundamental rights.[119] The constitution, in turn, is usually referred to as a social contract, a collective promise, an expression of values, a manifestation of power, a pre-commitment, and a co-ordination device of a state.[120]

[117] See Charles Howard McIlwain, *Constitutionalism: Ancient and Modern* (Revised edition, Cornell University Press 1947) 23–24; Mark Tushnet, 'Varieties of Constitutionalism' (2016) 14 International Journal of Constitutional Law 1, 1–5.

[118] Dieter Grimm, *Constitutionalism: Past, Present, and Future* (Oxford University Press 2016) 363–64.

[119] The famous exception to this is the United Kingdom with its unwritten constitution.

[120] Keith E Whittington, 'Constitutionalism' in Gregory A Caldeira, R Daniel Kelemen, and Keith E Whittington (eds), *The Oxford Handbook of Law and Politics* (Oxford University Press 2008) 289–91;

As such, the constitution is authored by a people using their liberty through their constituent power.[121]

In order to effectuate an 'order of liberty', the constitution allocates separate powers and responsibilities to the legislative, executive, and judicial branches of government, and at the same time, instills systems of checks and balances between them.[122] By doing so, the constitution not only establishes limited government, but also self-sustains itself by limiting the powers of constitutional amendment.[123] Furthermore, as the supreme law of the land, all other laws and normative orderings are required to conform to the constitution and derive their authority from it, or else they will be null and void.[124] Hence, in its classic form, constitutionalism 'stands for a set of interrelated concepts, principles, and practices of organizing, and thereby limiting, government power in order to prevent despotism'.[125]

This idea of constitutionalism, or *liberal* constitutionalism to be precise, is a late eighteenth-century phenomenon associated with the development of the modern state in North America and France.[126] Despite numerous innovations and novelties, the American and French systems of constitutional government are informed by, and built on, Enlightenment thinking.[127] The ideas of a written constitution, judicial review, the separation of powers, and the Bill of Rights, among other constitutional principles and concepts, have since traveled from their original homelands and have been adopted by many other nations worldwide.[128] Indeed, the migration of constitutional ideas is not limited to the spread of liberal constitutionalism to other parts of the world, but also includes the mutual learning and cross-fertilization among the liberal constitutional systems on both sides of the Atlantic.[129] In the case of Africa, liberal constitutionalism arrived quite late, in the 1950s and 1960s, when the colonies gained independence from colonial rule and were recognized as equal members in the community of nations.[130] And when it came to Africa, it did so in the image of

Denis J Galligan and Mila Versteeg, 'Theoretical Perspectives on the Social and Political Foundations of Constitutions' in Denis J Galligan and Mila Versteeg (eds), *Social and Political Foundations of Constitutions* (Cambridge University Press 2013) 8–39.

[121] Alexander Somek, *The Cosmopolitan Constitution* (Oxford University Press 2014) 1–2.

[122] Sajó and Uitz, *The Constitution of Freedom* (n 55) 14.

[123] Yaniv Roznai, *Unconstitutional Constitutional Amendments: The Limits of Amendment Powers* (Oxford University Press 2017) 228–33.

[124] See also Jutta Limbach, 'The Concept of the Supremacy of the Constitution' (2001) 64 The Modern Law Review 1, 1–10.

[125] Sajó and Uitz, *The Constitution of Freedom* (n 55) 13.

[126] Grimm, *Constitutionalism* (n 118) 6.

[127] Stephen Holmes, 'Constitution and Constitutionalism' in Michel Rosenfeld and András Sajó (eds), *The Oxford Handbook of Comparative Constitutional Law* (Oxford University Press 2012) 195–98.

[128] See Ran Hirschl, *Towards Juristocracy: The Origins and Consequences of the New Constitutionalism* (Harvard University Press 2007); Vlad Perju, 'Constitutional Transplants, Borrowing, and Migrations' in Michel Rosenfeld and András Sajó (eds), *The Oxford Handbook of Comparative Constitutional Law* (Oxford University Press 2012) 1305.

[129] Sujit Choudhry, 'Migration as a New Metaphor in Comparative Constitutional Law' in Sujit Choudhry (ed), *The Migration of Constitutional Ideas* (Cambridge University Press 2006) 1–16.

[130] See Robert B Seidman, 'Constitutions in Independent, Anglophonic, Sub-Saharan Africa: Form and Legitimacy' (1969) 1969 Wisconsin Law Review 83, 94; Victor T Le Vine, 'The Fall and Rise of Constitutionalism in West Africa' (1997) 35 The Journal of Modern African Studies 181, 183–86; YP Ghai, 'Constitutions and the Political Order in East Africa' (1972) 21 The International and Comparative Law Quarterly 403, 410–12.

the constitutional systems of the former colonizers, predominantly the British and the French.

Nonetheless, liberal constitutionalism was not transplanted to Africa—on the eve of independence—onto a tabula rasa, but was rather situated in, and configured within, the complex historical trajectories of state formation, resistance and conquest, colonial rule, and the struggle for decolonization.[131] These, in turn, are located within the background of the socio-economic and political organizations of African societies that existed before and during the birth of the colonial state, as well as throughout its operation and end, and continued after the inauguration of the liberal world order with the end of the Second World War.[132] Consequently, the phenomenology of constitutional studies in Africa is not—or should not be—limited to the arrival of liberal constitutionalism at the time of independence, but also lies in the experiences, interactions, and contestations of power and governance in precolonial, colonial, and postcolonial times.

The liberal constitutional system of the postcolonial period is a superstructure built on top of precolonial and colonial structures, laws, rules, discursive practices, and behaviors.[133] This is due to the fact that—as history has it—the independence constitutions which ushered in liberal constitutionalism were transition devices from colony to sovereign statehood and mechanisms of transfer of government power from the hands of colonial powers to the indigenous Africans.[134] Thus, the body politic of the postcolonial state is formed during the colonial period.[135]

As a result, in order to fully understand and appreciate the nature and practice of constitutionalism in postcolonial Africa, it becomes necessary to investigate the precolonial and colonial systems of governance as well as the international system within which Africa is situated. After all, the state in Africa is constituted out of the interactions of precolonial and colonial dynamics within, and in light of the broader international system without.

The plethora of scholarship attests to the fact that precolonial societies in Africa had their own way of organizing, constituting, and limiting political power.[136] According to the original definition of a 'constitution', namely, to set up and organize a people for common defense, prosperity, and territorial aggrandizement,[137] precolonial societies

[131] An-Na'im, *African Constitutionalism and the Role of Islam* (n 5) 27.

[132] See Tukumbi Lumumba-Kasongo, 'The Origin of African Constitutions, Elusive Constitutionalism, and the Crisis of Liberal Democracy' in Said Adejumobi (ed), *Democratic Renewal in Africa: Trends and Discourses* (Palgrave Macmillan 2015) 66–67; André Mbata B Mangu, 'Africa's Long and Hard Road to Constitutionalism and Democracy: Two Decades On' in Said Adejumobi (ed), *Democratic Renewal in Africa: Trends and Discourses* (Palgrave Macmillan 2015) 104–09.

[133] See also Issa G Shivji, *Where Is Uhuru?: Reflections on the Struggle for Democracy in Africa* (Fahamu/Pambazuka 2009) 51.

[134] Crawford Young, *The Postcolonial State in Africa: Fifty Years of Independence, 1960–2010* (University of Wisconsin Press 2012) 11–12.

[135] See for instance Crawford Young, *The African Colonial State in Comparative Perspective* (Yale University Press 1994) 180–81.

[136] See for instance An-Na'im, *African Constitutionalism and the Role of Islam* (n 5) 35–42; John Hatchard, Muna Ndulo, and Peter Slinn, *Comparative Constitutionalism and Good Governance in the Commonwealth: An Eastern and Southern African Perspective* (Cambridge University Press 2004) 13; Mangu (n 141) 104–10.

[137] See Holmes, 'Constitution and Constitutionalism' (n 127) 195; McIlwain, *Constitutionalism* (n 117) 23–24.

in Africa had various forms of constitutions.[138] To the extent that they relied on these constitutions to organize and operate their overall socio-economic and political life, they also practiced some sort of constitutionalism. Furthermore, these practices of constitutionalism included the respect for, and protection of, some basic rights and freedoms.[139] Nonetheless, many of these precolonial societies had neither the attributes of modern statehood, nor a similar type of political organization, although they did have various forms of non-state constitutional practices and organizations.

The advent of colonialism superimposed a 'new constitutional system' over the precolonial constitutions. Indeed, there is nothing truly constitutional about the colonial constitutional systems if we relate constitutionalism with sovereignty, limited government, and the protection of fundamental rights.[140] It is merely constitutional in the empirical sense of *constituting or establishing the state* in Africa.[141] In this regard, the Berlin Africa Conference of 1884–1885 provided the basic rules of the colonial constitutional dispensation. On the one hand, it (a) provided the rules of engagement among Europeans in the partitioning of Africa; (b) legitimized prior colonial possessions; and (c) exported the doctrine of European sovereignty to the African universe in order to avoid conflict between the colonial powers. Consequently, the territories of precolonial societies were redrawn according to the possessions and wishes of the colonial powers. On the other hand, it also gave the colonial powers absolute power in their African territories and denied Africans' claims to—and exercise of—power based on their own terms within this colonial enterprise.[142]

In light of these fundamental pillars of the colonial dispensation, the colonial state in Africa was formed. This colonial state possessed a people, a territory, a government, and sovereignty. Yet even though the colonial state in Africa had these attributes, it was strikingly different from the kind of state that we see in Europe, as noted in the previous sections. This is due to the fact that the various peoples that inhabited these colonial states neither consented to live under the new territorial states, nor did they share a common history, culture, language or tradition; they were simply lumped together for reasons of colonial and imperial expediency. Furthermore, the government and sovereign power in these colonial states resided in the imperial capitals outside its territorial reach, and even within the colonial state itself, the colonial government had neither the monopoly of violence throughout the territory nor the interest to establish a rational-legal authority in the Weberian sense.[143]

The postcolonial state maintained this *founding constitutive identity* of the colonial state through the aid of international law externally, and constitutional law internally. The Charter of the Organization of African Unity (OAU), now the African Union, affirmed the colonial borders and made the defense of 'sovereignty, territorial integrity,

[138] See RS Rattray, *Ashanti Law and Constitution* (Clarendon Press 1929).

[139] See Makau Mutua, *Human Rights: A Political and Cultural Critique* (University of Pennsylvania Press 2009) 74–81.

[140] Hatchard, Ndulo and Slinn, *Comparative Constitutionalism and Good Governance in the Commonwealth* (n 136) 14–15.

[141] An-Na'im, *African Constitutionalism and the Role of Islam* (n 5) 42–43.

[142] See Jörg Fisch, 'Africa as Terra Nullius: the Berlin Conference and International Law' in Stig Förster, Wolfgang Justin Mommsen, and Ronald Edward Robinson (eds), *Bismarck, Europe and Africa: The Berlin Africa Conference 1884-1885 and the Onset of Partition* (Oxford University Press 1988) 347–75.

[143] Herbst, *States and Power in Africa* (n 13) 67–70 and 78–79.

and independence' its purpose.[144] Furthermore, the Charter recognized the principle of '[r]espect for the sovereignty and territorial integrity of each State and for its inalienable right to independent existence'.[145] Such recognition by the OAU legitimized the artificial borders of postcolonial states in Africa and, consequently, provided them with the necessary shield from any external aggression and interference, including from each other.[146] Internally, the independence constitutions introduced a new theory of government without much alteration of the colonial laws, structures, rules, and practices.[147] Unlike the colonial constitutional arrangements which made the colonial governments unlimited, the independence constitutions introduced limited government under the system of constitutional democracy. Moreover, these constitutions proclaimed supremacy over any other form of law and positioned the state as the ultimate and supreme power within their bounds.

While post-independence constitution-making in Africa has involved the negation and affirmation of the liberal theory of government[148]—as seen with the constitution of one-party systems, 'Big man rule',[149] and multi-party democracy[150]—the paradoxical nature of postcolonial African states continues unabated. On the one hand, the postcolonial African states are weak internationally, for they either depend on handouts from Western governments and donor agencies, and international organizations or civil society groups have to perform some of their essential functions.[151] Additionally, they are either unable and/or unwilling to perform basic state functions—such as the provision of welfare, law and order, and security—throughout their territories.[152] As such, internally they lack empirical sovereignty in the Weberian sense, even though they enjoy juridical sovereignty internationally.[153] On the other hand, the postcolonial African states are strong internally as they are equipped with financial, human, bureaucratic, security, and armed infrastructures that are more powerful than other groups and are more able to deploy coercion and violence anywhere in their territory.[154] Due to the lack of empirical sovereignty, postcolonial governments in Africa do not usually rely on the democratic will of the population at large to stay in office, but primarily on extra-constitutional mechanisms, such as the control of the government apparatus and patronage systems or the incorporation and support of key

[144] The Charter of the Organization of African Unity 1963, art II.

[145] Ibid, art III.

[146] See also Saadia Touval, 'The Organization of African Unity and African Borders' (1967) 21 International Organization 102, 127.

[147] Prempeh, 'Africa's 'Constitutionalism Revival' (n 2) 502; Sabelo J Ndlovu-Gatsheni, *Coloniality of Power in Postcolonial Africa* (Council for the Development of Social Science Research in Africa 2013) 6–7.

[148] Michel Rosenfeld, 'Constitutional Identity' in Michel Rosenfeld and András Sajó (eds), *The Oxford Handbook of Comparative Constitutional Law* (Oxford University Press 2012) 766.

[149] For details of 'Big men rule' see Robert H Jackson and Carl G Rosberg, *Personal Rule in Black Africa: Prince, Autocrat, Prophet, Tyrant* (University of California Press 1982).

[150] Young, *The Postcolonial State in Africa* (n 134) 8–31.

[151] Yash Ghai, 'Chimera of Constitutionalism: State, Economy, and Society in Africa' in Swati Deva (eds), *Law and (In) Equalities: Contemporary Perspectives* (Eastern Book Company 2010) 319–23.

[152] Jonathan Hill, 'Beyond the Other? A Postcolonial Critique of the Failed State Thesis' (2005) 3 African Identities 139, 145–46; Herbst, *States and Power in Africa* (n 13) 254–57.

[153] See Robert H Jackson and Carl G Rosberg, 'Why Africa's Weak States Persist: The Empirical and the Juridical in Statehood' (1982) 35 World Politics 1.

[154] Ghai, 'Chimera of Constitutionalism' (n 151) 321–22.

ethnic actors or leaders.[155] Thus, like with empirical sovereignty, popular sovereignty is lacking in many postcolonial African states.

In light of these constitutional trajectories, legal centralism and legal pluralism possess conceptual appeal and practical relevance in understanding the multiple and complex constitutional systems, experiences, practices, and aspirations in Africa. Legal centralism is relevant, since the state and its projection of state law as a universal and supreme legal order do exist in Africa. As discussed above, precolonial systems of political organization were transformed into territorial colonial states, and these, in turn, were further transformed into 'constitutional states' upon their independence.[156] Along with these transitions and transformations, state law was positioned to be the ultimate and universal legal order. Consider, for example, Nigeria: Section 1(1) of their 1999 Constitution proclaims that '[t]his Constitution is Supreme and its provisions shall have binding force on the authorities and persons throughout the Federal Republic of Nigeria'. Based on this constitutional proclamation, the legal centralist theory can be utilized to understand and explain the idea and practice of constitutionalism in Nigeria. By the same token, however, legal pluralism is also relevant as multiple types of laws coexist in Nigeria; in addition to Islamic law, there are more than 250 ethnic groups in Nigeria, each with their own customary laws.[157] This means that both Islamic and numerous customary laws all coexist in Nigeria along with state law. Moreover, these laws apply with or without recognition by their Constitution.[158] Accordingly, legal pluralism can also be deployed to capture the essence and practice of constitutionalism in Nigeria.

However, in spite of their potential to serve as theoretical frameworks for understanding African constitutionalism, legal centralism and legal pluralism also have inherent limitations. Both misunderstand, or misconstrue, the full nature of the state, government organization, and the notion of rights in Africa. As discussed above, the state does not possess the necessary empirical sovereignty to enforce its laws throughout its territory—save through specific actions of coercion and violence—nor is the existence and application of customary and/or Islamic laws contingent upon state recognition and conformation by liberal constitutional standards. At the same time, customary and/or religious laws neither claim supremacy and universality like the constitutions, nor do their enforcers challenge the authority of the state and its institutions. Thus, the legal centralist approach fails to account for the specific empirical realities of the state, while also missing the role, position, and function of customary and/or religious laws in the operation of the state. Similarly, the legal pluralist approach misinterprets the nature of the state, its organization, as well as its configuration with society.

155 An-Na'im, *African Constitutionalism and the Role of Islam* (n 5) 51–53.

156 Okoth-Ogendo, 'Constitutions without Constitutionalism' (n 8) 70–71.

157 Abdulmumini A Oba, 'Religious and Customary Laws in Nigeria' (2011) 25 Emory Int'l L Rev 881, 881–84.

158 See Rotimi Suberu, 'The Sharia Challenge: Revisiting the Travails of the Secular State' in Wale Adebanwi and Ebenezer Obadare (eds), *Encountering the Nigerian State* (Palgrave Macmillan 2010) 217–38; Vincent O Nmehielle, 'Sharia Law in the Northern States of Nigeria: To Implement or Not to Implement, the Constitutionality Is the Question' (2004) 26 Human Rights Quarterly 730, 741–57.

Thus, a proper theoretical framework for African constitutionalism should rectify the limitations of both legal centralism and legal pluralism. The search for this theoretical framework should seriously consider the constitutional developments in Africa from precolonial times to the present without falling into the trap of either legal centralism or legal pluralism. This includes the investigation and critical assessment of constitutional design and practice in light of the socio-economic and political factors that influence constitutional government in Africa, as well as the general idea of constitutionalism and the migration of constitutional ideas. In the search for a proper theoretical framework for African constitutionalism, the nature and organization of the state, its government structure, and the notion of constitutional rights should all be the units of analysis across time and space. Such an endeavor obviously requires the use of multi-disciplinary approaches and materials in order to transcend the impasse between legal centralism and legal pluralism. Building on religious studies and anthropology, the following section introduces legal syncretism as a theoretical framework for African constitutionalism in order to clearly account for the constitutional transformations and developments—from precolonial times to the present—and to explain the attendant constitutional designs and practices.

VI. Legal Syncretism as a Theoretical Framework for African Constitutionalism

Legal syncretism, unlike legal centralism and legal pluralism, is not a widely discussed subject in the fields of law, socio-legal studies, or legal anthropology. Even if some scholars use the term legal syncretism, they neither define the term nor give it content.[159] For instance, MA Jaspan employed legal syncretism as an appealing normative legal theory for Indonesia in the 1960s. Nevertheless, he argues that the existence of a complex legal system composed of Dutch law, Adat or customary law, and Islamic law make it difficult to adopt 'a syncretic philosophy of law based on diverse Indonesian tradition and a modified socialist ideology'.[160] The main challenge to the development of a syncretic philosophy of law, according to Jaspan, is the impasse between unification and plurality. However, he neither explains what legal syncretism means nor does he elaborate on what he calls a syncretic philosophy of law. Similarly, Neil J Diamant uses legal syncretism—without offering a definition or explanation—in lieu of legal transplants to assess the changes in the family law of China.[161] In the African context, Xavier Blanc-Jouvan proposed the idea of *mixitè* as a trend and normative argument for the establishment of law and legal reform.[162] He contends that the only way to have

[159] See Paschalis M Kitromilides, 'The Making of a Lawyer: Humanism and Legal Syncretism in Venetian Crete' (1993) 17 Byzantine and Modern Greek Studies 57, 57–81. In this article, the term legal syncretism is mentioned only in the title.

[160] MA Jaspan, 'In Quest of New Law: The Perplexity of Legal Syncretism in Indonesia' (1965) 7 Comparative Studies in Society and History 252, 252 and 265.

[161] Neil J Diamant, 'Legal Syncretism and Family Change in Urban and Rural China' in Dennis Galvan and Rudra Sil (eds), *Reconfiguring Institutions Across Time and Space: Syncretic Responses to Challenges of Political and Economic Transformation* (Palgrave Macmillan 2007) 164–88.

[162] Xavier Blanc-Jouvan, 'Du Pluralisme a la mixite dans les nouveaux droits africains' in Dalloz-Sirey (ed), *Liber amicorum: Mélanges en l'honneur de Camille Jauffret-Spinosi* (Dalloz 2013) 123–50.

uniform and coherent legal regulation in Africa is through the mixture of traditional African law with modern law. In this process, Blanc-Jouvan notes, traditional African law should not be relegated to an inferior position in its relationship with modern law. While *mixitè* may be an aspect of legal syncretism, the latter has a much broader notion and can give more nuance to the legal universe in Africa.[163] Hence, to develop the concept of legal syncretism, I turn to religious studies and anthropology where syncretism has been studied extensively.

Syncretism has multiple meanings: the Oxford English Dictionary defines it as '(1) an attempted union or reconciliation of diverse or opposite tenets or practices, (2) the merging of two or more inflectional categories, and (3) the process of fusing diverse ideas or sensations into a general (inexact) impression'.[164] The word syncretism comes from the Greek 'prefix *syn*, "with," and *krasis*, "mixture" … *synkrasis*, which means "a mixing together." '[165] It was first used by Plutarch (AD 45–125) in the *Moralia*, in the chapter entitled *On Brotherly Love*, to describe the coming together of the quarreling inhabitants of Crete against a common enemy.[166] While Cretans warred and quarreled amongst each other, they had a culture of setting aside their differences and standing united against an outside enemy or aggressor, and this was called syncretism.[167] The original use of the word was associated—with its sense of belonging and self-defense in a community—with a political field of human affairs.[168]

Syncretism in religious studies is usually defined as 'a blending of religious ideas and practices, by means of which either one set adopts more or less thoroughly the principles of another or both are amalgamated in a more cosmopolitan and less polytheistic shape'.[169] This state of religious mixture is of a momentary nature that can either lead to a further accretive mixture or to an unravelling of past syntheses.[170] Erasmus of Rotterdam (1469–1536) first introduced the term to the domain of religion in the Renaissance era. Following the ethos of Plutarch's syncretism, Erasmus used syncretism to reconcile various theological differences in Christianity and to show how Christianity also absorbed Classical ideas, such as those of Plato and Aristotle, and how this, in turn, enriched and strengthened Christianity.[171] Erasmus' syncretism, in addition to uniting different followers of Christian doctrine against

163 See also Charles Stewart, 'Syncretism and Its Synonyms: Reflections on Cultural Mixture' (1999) 29 Diacritics 40, 41–48.

164 The Oxford English Dictionary, 'Syncretism, N' <http://wwwoedcom/view/Entry/196428> accessed 28 November 2018.

165 Rosalind Shaw and Charles Stewart, 'Introduction: Problematizing Syncretism' in Rosalind Shaw and Charles Stewart (eds), *Syncretism/Anti-Syncretism: The Politics of Religious Synthesis* (Routledge 2003) 3.

166 Anita Maria Leopold and Jeppe Sinding Jensen, 'Introduction to Part II' in Anita Maria Leopold and Jeppe Sinding Jensen (eds), *Syncretism in Religion: A Reader* (Routledge 2016) 14; Andre Droogers and Sidney M Greenfield, 'Recovering and Reconstructing Syncretism' in Andre Droogers and Sidney M Greenfield (eds), *Reinventing Religions: Syncretism and Transformation in Africa and the Americas* (Rowman & Littlefield Publishers 2001) 27.

167 Leopold and Jensen, 'Introduction to Part II' (n 166) 14.

168 ibid 14–15.

169 James Moffatt, 'Syncretism' in James Hastings (eds), *Encyclopedia of Religion and Ethics* (Charles Scribner's Sons 1922) 157.

170 Charles Stewart, 'Relocating Syncretism in Social Science Discourse' in Anita Maria Leopold and Jeppe Sinding Jensen (eds), *Syncretism in Religion: A Reader* (Routledge 2014) 278.

171 ibid 15; Shaw and Stewart, 'Introduction' (n 165) 3–4; Irina A Levinskaya, 'Syncretism—The Term and Phenomenon' (1993) 44 Tyndale Bulletin 117, 119.

the Barbarians—just as with the Cretans—infused a human idea (non-Christian) onto godly Christian thought. In the sixteenth and seventeenth centuries, however, syncretism acquired a pejorative connotation as the quest to reconcile the various Protestant denominations, as well as the mutual access to each other's rituals of communion and baptism, were considered to be an unprincipled jumbling and mixing of religions.[172] In the nineteenth century, the negative connotation of syncretism resurfaced once again as scholars of comparative religion presented the state of Christianity and religious life in the New World, Africa, and Asia, as one of disorder, confusion, and merely a pathway to full Christianity.[173] In these respects, syncretism was used as an assimilation tool to bring historically and geographically distant societies into the Christian empire, and at the same time, as an 'othering' tool for those same societies as their syncretic religion was considered as inferior and impure.[174]

Unlike some of the negative connotations in religious studies, syncretism has been associated with neutrality and even conferred a positive significance in anthropology.[175] It was introduced as a reinterpretation of acculturation—a phenomenon which results in the blending of cultures via cultural contact in the context of imperialism and colonialism.[176] As acculturation studies emerged as an alternative method to evolutionism in anthropology, a further refinement and reinterpretation of acculturation was necessary in order to overcome 'the problems and methods of the discipline' and to account for the specific manners and ways in which the blending of cultures happen.[177] To this end, syncretism was deployed at the center of anthropological studies to refer to both the incorporation, reformulation, invention, and transformation of cultural traits, forms, meanings, and practices as the result of cultural contacts and encounters, and to describe the processes of such syncretic cultural makeups.[178] Through such processes, syncretism reconnects the past with the present.[179] The increasingly globalized and interconnected world order has made syncretism a basic predicament of both culture and religion.[180] Consequently, cultural purity and authenticity are relegated to the periphery and are substituted by multiculturalism and cultural pluralism—in practical terms—and are heavily criticized as unappealing normative claims in the social sciences. Hence, it is held that as anthropology is a 'discourse about syncretism', syncretism is considered a form of anthropology.[181]

Whether in its original Plutarchic version or in its later religious and cultural usages, syncretism happens in a dynamic cultural matrix. It requires the existence of multiple and diverse cultural, political, or religious ideas and practices within a

[172] Shaw and Stewart, 'Introduction' (n 165) 4.
[173] ibid 4–5.
[174] ibid.
[175] ibid 1.
[176] Droogers and Greenfield, 'Recovering and Reconstructing Syncretism' (n 166) 26.
[177] ibid 24–27; Melville J Herskovits, 'The Significance of the Study of Acculturation for Anthropology' (1937) 39 American Anthropologist 259, 261–62.
[178] Droogers and Greenfield, 'Recovering and Reconstructing Syncretism' (n 166) 26.
[179] Shaw and Stewart, 'Introduction' (n 165) 5.
[180] ibid 1 and 12–20.
[181] ibid 20–21.

specific social field at a specific time.[182] The encounter and contact of these diverse and multiple ideas and practices set syncretism in motion; this encounter leads to both conflict and tension, to exchange and interaction.[183] Given the balance of power between these diverse cultural, political, and religious ideas, these encounters can lead to their (1) symbiotic relationship, (2) fusion, adaptation, and assimilation, (3) metamorphosis or transformation, and/or (4) isolation and dissolution.[184] Acceptance and resistance, integration and accommodation, unity and diversity are all inherent elements in these syncretic processes.[185] In the Plutarchic sense of syncretism, conflict and disagreement within a community are transformed into unity and brotherhood. In the religious sense of syncretism, it can either lead to different religions opt for a symbiotic relationship as we see with Confucianism, Taoism, and Buddhism in China, or to incorporation and adaptation like with Classical ideas into Christian doctrine in Europe, or to a fusion and transformation like that of Christianity and Islam[186] in Africa, or to the development of an entirely new popular religion or superstition.[187] In the cultural context, syncretism creates a dynamic which is mutually intelligible and practically acceptable to all subjects and participants in the cultural matrix.[188] In all of these cases syncretism can be the result of a conscious and reflective action and undertaking, and/or an unconscious, naïve, and spontaneous engagement within the cultural matrix.[189] Similarly, it can either be driven from *above* or *below*, consequently setting into motion complex processes of syncretism in the spectrum of hierarchies of power within the social field.[190]

As *a process* and *a result* of this dynamic cultural matrix, syncretism offers a practical tool to solving some of its existential problems.[191] This is because syncretism has a reconciliatory power in contexts where diverse and opposing ideas and practices exist in the same social field. Although it involves varied forms of acceptance and rejection, or synthesis and erasure, depending upon the balance of power between or among the different cultural, religious, or political ideas and practices at a given time and place, syncretism brings together different norms, ideas, symbols, and discursive practices in order to solve and transcend challenges or problems posed by the encounters in the cultural matrix. By appealing to phenomenological similarities, complementarities, or comparable similar experiences and practices, syncretism transforms the dynamic in the cultural matrix from one of wild animosity and perpetual opposition or

182 Hans G Kippenberg, 'In Praise of Syncretism: The Beginning of Christianity Conceived in the Light of a Diagnosis of Modern Culture' in Anita Maria Leopold and Jeppe Sinding Jensen (eds), *Syncretism in Religion: A Reader* (Routledge 2016) 34.

183 ibid.

184 Kurt Rudolph, 'Syncretism: From Theological Invective to a Concept in the Study of Religion' in Anita Maria Leopold and Jeppe Sinding Jensen (eds), *Syncretism in Religion: A Reader* (Routledge 2016) 81–82.

185 Michael Pye, 'Syncretism and Ambiguity' (1971) 18 Numen 83, 89–93.

186 An-Na'im, *African Constitutionalism and the Role of Islam* (n 5) 107–13.

187 Rudolph, 'Syncretism' (n 184) 81–82.

188 Shaw and Stewart, 'Introduction' (n 165) 18–19.

189 Leopold and Jensen, 'Introduction to Part II' (n 166) 52–53.

190 Shaw and Stewart, 'Introduction' (n 165) 19–20; Birgit Meyer, '"If You Are a Devil, You Are a Witch and, If You Are a Witch, You Are a Devil" the Integration of "Pagan" Ideas Into the Conceptual Universe of Ewe Christians in Southeastern Ghana1' (1992) 22 Journal of Religion in Africa 98, 119–23.

191 Andre Droogers, 'Syncretism and Fundamentalism: A Comparison' (2005) 52 Social Compass 463, 465.

conflict into one of integration, accommodation, respect, tolerance, and new modes of resistance and change.[192] Yet although syncretism is helpful in solving these problems, it cannot satisfy everyone in the social field. For instance, for the advocates of religious and cultural purity and authenticity, syncretism is a process to be arrested and a problem to be solved.[193] For others, however, it is a process to be supported and a result to be celebrated as it offers a space and opportunity for the negotiation between opposing identities and hegemonies in situations such as imperial and colonial conquest, migration, and religious dissemination.[194] The syncretic process of absorption, rejection, affirmation, transformation, and reconstruction opens new avenues for participation and negotiation in the cultural matrix.[195]

Due to its normative appeal and descriptive potential, syncretism has also been used in the field of political science. Dennis Galvan and Rudra Sil, in their edited book *Reconfiguring Institutions across Time and Space: Syncretic Responses to Challenges of Political and Economic Transformation*, demonstrate the analytical potential and theoretical fitness of syncretism to explain institutional transformations and changes in the political and economic fields.[196] Drawing from diverse regional experiences and multiple perspectives in institutions, they give special emphasis to what they call 'institutional syncretism', which they define as 'a set of interpretive processes through which actors in local settings selectively transform newly imposed or transplanted institutional features (norms, rules—formal and informal—organizational principles, and operational procedures) while adapting portable elements of preexisting social institutions to produce innovative institutional configurations'.[197] Within the theoretical framework of institutional syncretism, the contributors analyze and discuss how the syncretism of numerous practices, norms, and institutions explain the institutional frameworks or normative practices, in different societies across time and space.

To give a particular example, Thomas Bickford chooses the military as a space for syncretic inquiry, and China as a case study.[198] Bickford considers the military as an institution the 'most universally prone to convergence in terms of their organizational structures, routines, and practices'.[199] However, what he finds in his study of the People's Liberation Army (PLA) is 'a radical departure from the ideal-typical model of Modern military organization' like we find in the West.[200] The reason for this

[192] ibid.

[193] See Siv Ellen Kraft, '"To Mix or Not to Mix": Syncretism/Anti-Syncretism in the History of Theosophy' (2002) 49 Numen 142, 142–70.

[194] Shaw and Stewart, 'Introduction' (n 165) 18.

[195] ibid 18–19; Peter van der Veer, 'Syncretism, multiculturalism and the Discourse of tolerance' in Rosalind Shaw and Charles Stewart (eds), *Syncretism/Anti-Syncretism: The Politics of Religious Synthesis* (Routledge 2003) 185–86.

[196] See Dennis Galvan and Rudra Sil (eds), *Reconfiguring Institutions Across Time and Space: Syncretic Responses to Challenges of Political and Economic Transformation* (Palgrave Macmillan 2007).

[197] Dennis Galvan and Rudra Sil, 'The Dilemma of Institutional Adaptation and the Role of Syncretism' in Dennis Galvan and Rudra Sil (eds), *Reconfiguring Institutions Across Time and Space: Syncretic Responses to Challenges of Political and Economic Transformation* (Palgrave Macmillan 2007) 7.

[198] Thomas J Bickford, 'Institutional Syncretism and the Chinese Armed Forces' in Dennis Galvan and Rudra Sil (eds), *Reconfiguring Institutions Across Time and Space: Syncretic Responses to Challenges of Political and Economic Transformation* (Palgrave Macmillan 2007) 61–80.

[199] ibid 63.

[200] ibid 62.

departure is the syncretism of Chinese, European, and Soviet modes of military and economic organization.[201] Bickford argues that this is 'a result of a deliberate attempt by Communist Party elites to selectively combine and reinterpret traditional organizational frameworks with the formally modern organizational characteristics of the military that justifies the political authority of the elites and serves as an ideological and organizational vehicle for social transformation'.[202] The consequence, according to him, is the establishment of a military with extensive military and economic roles.

Thus, just as syncretism has been applied as an analytical tool or theoretical framework in religious studies, anthropology, and political science, the application of syncretism in the legal field, what I call legal syncretism—*the process and the result of adoption, rejection, invention, and transformation of diverse and seemingly opposite legal rules, principles, and practices into a constitutional state with imperial or colonial legacies*—offers a better theoretical framework for African constitutionalism than legal centralism and legal pluralism. As the discussion in the next chapters illustrate the dynamic cultural matrix which sets it in motion exists in the African constitutional experiences. As *a process*—as discussed in Chapter 2—legal syncretism captures and explains the transformation and development of African constitutionalism from precolonial times to the present. And as *a result*—as discussed in Chapter 3—legal syncretism explains and decrypts the designs and practices of African constitutionalism.

Legal syncretism is capable of accommodating different theories within itself. The subsequent chapters illustrate the range of theoretical possibilities regarding different aspects of African constitutionalism, such as the theory of state, federal and unitary theory, the separation of powers, and constitutional rights. Legal syncretism, then, is a meta and foundational theory of African constitutionalism that can serve as a basis for wider constitutional studies and practice in Africa.

VII. Conclusion

This chapter introduced legal syncretism as a theoretical framework for African constitutionalism in order to clearly account for the constitutional transformations and developments from precolonial times to the present, and to explain the attendant constitutional designs and practices. The chapter also demonstrates that understanding the nature, practice, and manifestations of African constitutionalism is necessary when trying to foster constitutionalism and consolidate its dividends on the continent. While existing theoretical frameworks such as legal centralism and legal pluralism offer useful theoretical and practical insights for the understanding of the phenomenon of African constitutionalism, they are inadequate to fully capture the complex, multifaceted, and interwoven constitutional ideas, practices, and aspirations on the continent. This is because legal centralism ignores the empirical realities of the state and fails to account for the role and function of customary and/or religious laws in the operation of the state, and legal pluralism misinterprets the true nature of the African state and its configuration with the society. In contrast, however, *legal*

[201] ibid.
[202] ibid 62.

syncretism as a process accounts for—in theoretically defensible and practically sound ways—the transformation of African constitutionalism from precolonial times to the present, and *legal syncretism as a result* captures and explains the designs and practices of African constitutionalism. Legal syncretism, therefore, is a general theory of African constitutionalism that can serve as a basis for wider constitutional studies and practice in Africa.

2
The Transformation of African Constitutionalism

Chapter 1 introduced legal syncretism as a general theory or theoretical framework for African constitutionalism, since neither legal centralism nor legal pluralism could fully capture and explain the blend of constitutional ideas, principles, and practices that undergird constitutionalism throughout the continent. Legal syncretism explains, and clearly takes into account, all African constitutional transformations and developments, as well as the attendant constitutional designs and practices, both in their normative and empirical manifestations. This chapter investigates how *legal syncretism as a process* explains the constitutional transformations and developments from precolonial times to the present, while Chapter 3 discusses how *legal syncretism as a result* captures and explains the attendant constitutional designs and practices.

Through the lens of legal syncretism, the objectives of this chapter are to (a) explore and examine the idea and practice of constitutionalism in precolonial Africa, (b) trace the transformation of precolonial constitutionalism with the introduction of colonial constitutionalism, and (c) show how postcolonial constitutionalism builds on and departs from the previous constitutional systems. The investigation in this chapter shows how the encounters and interactions between international law, colonial laws, African indigenous laws, and liberal constitutional norms and practices since the late nineteenth century have all established the territorial, political, and theoretical contours of African constitutionalism.

I. Constitutionalism in Precolonial Africa

As the dynamic constitutional matrix that sets legal syncretism into motion arises as a result of imperial or colonial encounters, it is important to explore and ascertain the African constitutional contexts and identities before these encounters in order to trace the subsequent syncretic constitutional transformations and developments. Therefore, the purpose of the inquiry into constitutionalism in precolonial Africa in this section is not to demonstrate the existence of a constitutional system best suited for Africa, and, consequently, feed into the romanticism of constitutional autochthony, nor is it to discover new insights and materials that boost African historical memory. This inquiry is primarily important to, on the one hand, help understand the present state of African constitutionalism and its persistent challenges, and on the other hand, to help identify the pathologies of constitutional practices and discourses and then take remedial actions for their diagnosis, as there are some continuities, as

A Theory of African Constitutionalism. Berihun Adugna Gebeye, Oxford University Press. © Berihun Adugna Gebeye 2021.
DOI: 10.1093/oso/9780192893925.003.0003

well as discontinuities, in the practice of constitutionalism from precolonial times to the present.[1]

In the study of constitutionalism in precolonial Africa, there are a number of caveats that should be mentioned from the outset. The first is the availability, nature, and sources of data related to this study; it is widely known that there are few written sources on precolonial Africa, and that even these sources are those of travelers and missionaries who wrote based on their observations about the state of affairs as they saw them.[2] The second is the issue of time within both the range and end of the precolonial period. On the one hand, due to the vastness of time, it is difficult—to say the least—to fully comprehend constitutionalism in this period. On the other hand, due to variations in the beginnings of imperial and colonial relations in Africa, it is difficult to clearly and generally delineate one precolonial period for the whole of Africa within which constitutionalism should be discussed. The third is the notion of change which is universal to all human societies and further complicates the investigation of constitutionalism in this period. The fourth and final caveat is the difficulty of attempting to employ a modern concept when trying to understand a different time period.

In light of all these caveats, this section considers the Berlin Africa Conference as the end of the long precolonial period due to the radical changes it brought about with regard to the socio-economic and political life of Africans as well as its enduring legacy in connection with constitutional government in Africa. In order to understand the idea and practice of constitutionalism in precolonial Africa, this section first explores and examines—at a higher level of abstraction and generality—their political organizations through the prisms of traditional government and traditional conceptions of power, and their legal orders through the lens of custom in the political universe of precolonial African societies.

A. Traditional Government and Traditional Conceptions of Power

Precolonial Africa hosted a mosaic of societies with different types of political organization across its vast geography. Based on the nature of their political organization, three types of political systems existed in precolonial Africa.[3] The first type operated based on a centralized administrative system, such as empires, states, kingdoms, and chiefdoms (usually referred to as *states*).[4] The second type functioned based on a lineage structure, such as clans or tribes (usually referred to as *stateless societies*). And the third type was based on kinship and consisted of small communities tied to each other by that kinship. For the purpose of this section, I will focus on the first two types

[1] Sabelo J Ndlovu-Gatsheni, 'Genealogies of Coloniality and Implications for Africa's Development' (2015) 40 Africa Development/Afrique et Développement 13, 14–15; Alex Thomson, *An Introduction to African Politics* (3rd ed, Routledge 2010) 9.

[2] AN Allott, AL Epstein, and M Gluckman, 'Introduction' in Max Gluckman (ed), *Ideas and Procedures in African Customary Law* (Oxford University Press 1969) 19–21.

[3] M Fortes and EE Evans-Pritchard, 'Introduction' in M Fortes and EE Evans-Pritchard (eds), *African Political Systems* (Oxford University Press 1940) 12–14. Needless to say, there were diverse and complex ways of interactions that transcends these classifications within and among these political systems.

[4] See also Mueni wa Muiu and Guy Martin, *A New Paradigm of the African State: Fundi Wa Afrika* (Palgrave Macmillan 2009) 23–46.

of political systems due to their relevance to current discourses and practices of constitutionalism. I will use the terminology of 'traditional government' and 'traditional conceptions of power' to refer to these different types of political organization and political conceptions in precolonial Africa following common usage of these terms in African constitutional scholarship, and also in order to distinguish them from the modern government and the modern conceptions of power in Africa. The objective of this section is to briefly present the origin, nature, and power of traditional government in these political organizations and traditional political conceptions, and to highlight the identities, projections, and manifestations of traditional political power and authority in precolonial Africa. This section also aims to draw some common and salient features in the conception, organization, and exercise of traditional political power and authority in precolonial Africa.

The origins and sources of political power in centralized political systems in Africa—despite some exceptions and variations in form and degree—were hereditary and related to lineage, kinship, real or imagined common ancestry, and/or the consent of the people. This was backed by a myth that confers political power with a special type of royalty and divinity.[5] Hereditary succession to the throne was the rule in many of the centralized political systems. For instance, succession to the throne was hereditary along the maternal line in the empires of Ghana and Mali,[6] along the paternal line in the empires of Songhai, Asante, and Benin,[7] and along both lines in the Ethiopian Empire.[8] Nonetheless, it was not always the case that the rule of hereditary succession to the throne was guaranteed, nor was it always practically possible that this rule yielded the right person for the throne. For example, in the Mossi Empire, succession to the throne was hereditary, but it was subject to confirmation by four dignitaries who themselves were governors of provinces along other specialized functions in the empire.[9] Additionally, the kingdom of Cayor imported kings from the outside—but maintained other political positions for hereditary succession—due to its seven dynasties' equal rights to the throne and their perpetual disagreement in choosing their king from among themselves.[10] Moreover, the Oromo have an egalitarian political system where political office is open to all members of the group who are categorized into five generations, or sets, which rotate every eight years.[11]

The king, the chief, or the ruler in these centralized political systems was both the reservoir and custodian of political power bestowed with the supreme powers of legislation, execution, and adjudication. In addition, in empires, kingdoms, or chiefdoms that practiced traditional African religions, the king was endowed with temporal and spiritual powers.[12] The king was a symbol that linked the living with the dead, as well

[5] George BN Ayittey, *Indigenous African Institutions* (2nd ed, Transnational Publishers 2006) 181; Naomi Chazan, 'Myths and Politics in Precolonial Africa' in Shmuel Noah Eisenstadt, Michael Abitbol, and Naomi Chazan (eds), *The Early State in African Perspective: Culture, Power, and Division of Labor* (Brill 1988) 28–29.

[6] Cheikh Anta Diop, *Precolonial Black Africa* (Harold Salemson tr, Seventh Printing edition, Chicago Review Press 1988) 48–53.

[7] Ayittey, *Indigenous African Institutions* (n 5) 233–53.

[8] See Hanna Rubinkowska, *Ethiopia on the Verge of Modernity: The Transfer of Power During Zewditu's Reign 1916-1930* (Agade Publishing 2010).

[9] Diop, *Precolonial Black Africa* (n 6) 43–44.

[10] ibid 56.

[11] See Asmarom Legesse, *Oromo Democracy: An Indigenous African Political System* (Red Sea Press 2001).

[12] Diop, *Precolonial Black Africa* (n 6) 65–66.

as supernatural power that protected and comforted the living and ensured the continuity of their posterity.[13] For instance, the Zulu king was a supreme legislator, administrator, chief justice, spiritual head, and healer of his kingdom.[14] Nonetheless, with the introduction of Islam and Christianity into certain African empires and kingdoms, including Songhai and Ethiopia respectively, the power of the king was limited to the temporal element of the empire, while the Muslim clergy and Christian priests were in charge of the eternal.[15] The power of the king, chief, or ruler, whether temporal and/or eternal, was expressed in singular, unified, personal, and absolute terms in the domain of their empire or kingdom.[16] Hence, in theory, the traditional conception of political power was centralized, indivisible, and resided in the person of the king, chief, or ruler,[17] who were actually considered as 'the manifestation of the gods' and were thus painted as 'physically dangerous to touch and politically absolute'.[18]

In practice, however, this seemingly centralized and personalized political power was dispersed both horizontally and vertically. Horizontally, the king, chief, or ruler had to share political power with—among others—the King's or Chief's Council, the Council of Elders, their Cabinet, the Queen-mother, the women of the royal house, the village heads, and ritual functionaries.[19] Accordingly, the king or chief was not an absolute monarch who simply commanded and executed their policies and laws as they wished.[20] Even though the king or chief was not generally obliged to follow the advice or decisions of these councils and officials, ignoring such advice and contradicting council or cabinet decisions was done at their own peril as it could invite chaos at the palace and rebellion in the empire or kingdom.[21] Furthermore, the king or chief was neither beyond the reach of law, nor—at least in some empires and kingdoms such as the Mossi Empire—could they remove their ministers at will.[22]

Vertically, as the empire or kingdom was divided into provinces and villages, political power was devolved from the king or chiefs to the provincial governors or chiefs, as well as to other subordinate chiefs and village heads.[23] Hence, both as representatives of their own people in the empire or kingdom as well as representatives of the king or chief amongst their people, these provincial and village administrators had

[13] Ayittey, *Indigenous African Institutions* (n 5) 39–40, 131–32.

[14] Max Gluckman, 'The Kingdom of the Zulu' in M Fortes and E E Evans-Pritchard (eds), *African Political Systems* (Oxford University Press 1940) 29–30.

[15] Diop, *Precolonial Black Africa* (n 6) 66–69.

[16] Chancellor Williams, *Destruction of Black Civilization: Great Issues of a Race from 4500 BC to 2000 AD* (Third World Press 1974) 179–81.

[17] Basil Davidson, *The African Genius: An Introduction to African Social and Cultural History* (Little, Brown and Company/ An Atlantic Monthly Press Book 1969) 190–96.

[18] SE Finer, *The History of Government from the Earliest Times: Ancient Monarchies and Empires; The Intermediate Ages; Empires, Monarchies and the Modern State* (Oxford University Press 1999) 144.

[19] Muiu and Martin, *A New Paradigm of the African State* (n 4) 47; Ayittey, *Indigenous African Institutions* (n 5) 111; Fortes and Evans-Pritchard, 'Introduction' (n 3) 11–12; Robert William July, *Precolonial Africa: An Economic and Social History* (Scribner 1975) 112–13; Davidson, *The African Genius* (n 17) 198–99; Robert S Smith, *Kingdoms of the Yoruba* (2nd ed, University of Wisconsin Press 1988) 92–93; KA Busia, *Africa in Search of Democracy* (Routledge & Kegan Paul PLC 1967) 23–24.

[20] Peter G Lloyd, 'The Political Structure of African Kingdoms: An Exploratory Model' in Michael Banton (ed), *Political Systems and the Distribution of Power* (Routledge 2011) 73–82.

[21] Williams, *Destruction of Black Civilization* (n 16) 174.

[22] Diop, *Precolonial Black Africa* (n 6) 44–45.

[23] Ayittey, *Indigenous African Institutions* (n 5) 280–83; Diop, *Precolonial Black Africa* (n 6) 111–12.

some autonomy of action within their jurisdictions.[24] Thus, as the actual practice and exercise of political power was configured with webs of checks and balances, there were multiple sites of power and, consequently, decision by consensus was the norm rather than the exception.[25]

In uncentralized political systems, however, in addition to the lack of centralized political authority and power, there existed a general distaste for organized power.[26] In these political systems, there was no single person or institution vested with the ultimate and supreme political power and authority. Unlike the centralized political systems, where social status and class defined and determined one's access to, and participation in, the political system, in uncentralized political systems, social status, wealth, and rank were less important, albeit still significant.[27] Furthermore, in sharp contrast to centralized political systems, in uncentralized political systems such as the Tiv, Igbo, and Dagaaba, '[k]ings or chiefs are often portrayed [in their mystic conception of power] as unimaginative, unintelligent, lacking common sense, and likely to use brute force' in order to discourage the centralization of power, either by an individual or institution.[28]

The basic unit of the political system in stateless societies was a joint or extended family based on some number of generational lineage.[29] Every such unit had a single head who acted both as a domestic authority concerning its internal affairs and as a representative of the unit in its relationship with other units.[30] In these systems, political power was exercised through an equilibrium between a number of segments that were 'spatially juxtaposed and structurally equivalent'.[31] For instance, a '[c]onflict between local segments necessarily [meant] conflicts between lineage segments ... and the stabilizing factor [was] not a superordinate judicial or military organization, but [was] simply the sum total of inter-segment relations'.[32] As a result, the political systems were organized in unilineal descent groups and political power was balanced through the dialectic of co-operation and competition among, or between, the various lineages.[33]

The lack of a centralized authority and administrative system in uncentralized political systems did not mean that they lacked a systematically organized political organization that maintained internal peace and order, and guaranteed and ensured

[24] T Olawale Elias, *The Nature of African Customary Law* (Manchester University Press 1956) 19–20; Fortes and Evans-Pritchard, 'Introduction' (n 3) 12.

[25] Ayittey, *Indigenous African Institutions* (n 5) 137–40, 266–67; Fortes and Evans-Pritchard, 'Introduction' (n 3) 11–12; Finer, *The History of Government from the Earliest Times* (n 18) 145–61; Basil Davidson, *The Black Man's Burden: Africa and the Curse of the Nation-State* (James Currey 1992) 74–98.

[26] Kenneth Carlston, *Social Theory and African Tribal Organization: The Development of Socio-Legal Theory* (University of Illinois Press 1968) 211; Paul Bohannan, *Africa and Africans* (The Natural History Press 1964) 195.

[27] Fortes and Evans-Pritchard, 'Introduction' (n 3) 6.

[28] Kojo Yelpaala, 'Circular Arguments and Self-Fulfilling Definitions: "Statelessness" and the Dagaaba' (1983) 10 History in Africa 349, 357.

[29] John Middleton and David Tait, 'Introduction' in John Middleton and David Tait (eds), *Tribes Without Rulers: Studies in African Segmentary Systems* (Routledge & Kegan Paul PLC 1970) 8.

[30] ibid 8–9.

[31] Fortes and Evans-Pritchard, 'Introduction' (n 3) 13.

[32] ibid 13–14.

[33] Middleton and Tait, 'Introduction' (n 29) 6–7; Elias, *The Nature of African Customary Law* (n 24) 20.

external defense and protection. Indeed, many of them did have systematic organizations informed by a number of factors, including their size, geography, livelihood, and way of life.[34] They had rulers named as chiefs, elders, sultans, or headmen; village or elder assemblies as deliberative bodies; age grades as functional organizations; as well as adjudicatory bodies.[35] Through such forms of political organization, and with the aid of commonly accepted customary and religious traditions, uncentralized political systems were able to maintain internal cohesion and order.[36] Whenever there was an external attack or other form of aggression, they organized and channeled their violence through self-help, feud, and warfare into the dialectic of co-operation and competition, along with the balance of powers between and among the lineage systems.[37]

Hence, all that was missing in these societies was a personalized, indivisible, permanent, and supreme political power vested in either a single individual or institution. For instance, in Somali society, families and extended families form corporate groups such as *qabiil, qolo, jilib,* and *reer,* often under the leadership of a *sultan* or *ugaz,* for common defense and the protection of property.[38] Nonetheless, they are entitled to leave these groups and join other groups—or even form new ones—in order to protect their best interests at any time, and no one can stop them.[39] Furthermore, even in times of external defense or war, the centralized systematic organization of violence was not of a permanent nature, but was demand-driven and contingent upon need in any particular time and place.[40] Thus, in uncentralized political systems there was a fundamental fear of centralized political power and the entire framework of political organizations was aimed at avoiding the emergence and development of such power, and to significantly limit any ambitions of centralization.[41]

Both centralized and uncentralized political systems, despite their striking differences, had some common conceptions and articulations about political power and political authority. In both systems, genealogical ties and connections played a crucial role in both the foundation and development of political power and authority. Moreover, these genealogical ties and connections broadcasted political power and authority from the center to the peripheries, in the case of centralized political systems, and to distant lineages, in the case of uncentralized political systems. Obviously, however, in both political systems, political power and authority were projected in geographically-limited territories.[42] Nonetheless, for reasons of political geography, such as low population densities, inhospitable environments, and the availability of large areas of open land, territory did not hold a central place in the imagination and

[34] See Carlston, *Social Theory and African Tribal Organization* (n 26).

[35] Middleton and Tait, 'Introduction' (n 29).

[36] Ayittey, *Indigenous African Institutions* (n 5) 113–27.

[37] Middleton and Tait, 'Introduction' (n 29) 19–22.

[38] IM Lewis, *A Pastoral Democracy: A Study of Pastoralism and Politics Among the Northern Somali of the Horn of Africa* (James Currey 1999) 132–34.

[39] Ibid 133; Ayittey, *Indigenous African Institutions* (n 5) 121; see also Michael van Notten, *The Law of the Somalis: A Stable Foundation for Economic Development in the Horn of Africa* (Spencer Heath MacCallum ed, The Red Sea Press 2005).

[40] Ayittey, *Indigenous African Institutions* (n 5) 113.

[41] Yelpaala, 'Circular Arguments and Self-Fulfilling Definitions' (n 28).

[42] AI Asiwaju, 'The Concept of Frontier in the Setting of States in Pre-Colonial Africa' (1983) 127–128 Présence Africaine 43.

conception of power in precolonial Africa—unlike in Europe where the opposite was true.[43]

As a result, a territorial-based explanation of the political power of the state—like that offered by Weber—not only misses the political conception and imagination of precolonial Africa, but it also misconfigures it. More than territory, it was genealogical ties, connections, and alliances, along with their dynamics across societies that accounted for the conception and practice of political power and authority in precolonial Africa.[44] Additionally, in both political systems—as multiple sites of political power existed—sovereignty was divided, shared, and diffused among different actors. This was very clear in uncentralized political systems where the balance of powers and the dialectic of co-operation and competition of the lineage groups guided political behavior and political action. In centralized political systems, too, the paradox of political theory—ie, the projection of a centralized, indivisible, supreme, and absolute power vested in the person of the king in principle, contrasted with the existence of a horizontal and vertical division of powers in practice—ultimately channeled a shared and diffused sovereignty. The traditional governments in both systems did not operate in a willy-nilly or random fashion, but were rather constituted, and acted upon, pursuant to established custom.

B. Custom as an Indigenous Constitution

Custom was the constitution of precolonial societies in Africa. First, it provided the fundamental rules for governing society in general, including the relationships between the governor and the governed in the case of centralized political systems, and between individuals and lineages in uncentralized political systems.[45] Second, custom outlined the powers and responsibilities of government along with its organization, operation, and change.[46] And third, it recognized the protections available to individuals and groups within their respective political communities.[47] Building on the

[43] Jeffrey Herbst, *States and Power in Africa: Comparative Lessons in Authority and Control* (Princeton University Press 2000) 35–57; Ali A Mazrui, *The Africans: A Triple Heritage* (Little, Brown and Company 1986) 41–61.

[44] See Jan M Vansina, *Paths in the Rainforests: Toward a History of Political Tradition in Equatorial Africa* (University of Wisconsin Press 1990) 142–65; Igor Kopytoff, 'The Internal African Frontier: The Making of African Political Culture' in Igor Kopytoff (ed), *The African Frontier: The Reproduction of Traditional African Societies* (Indiana University Press 1987) 29; Max Gluckman, *Politics, Law and Ritual in Tribal Society* (Transaction Publishers 1965) 163–64.

[45] These are some of the fundamental elements for a constitution. See for instance, David Dyzenhaus, 'The Idea of a Constitution: A Plea for Staatsrechtslehre' in David Dyzenhaus and Malcolm Thorburn (eds), *Philosophical Foundations of Constitutional Law* (Oxford University Press 2016) 9–12; Hanna Fenichel Pitkin, 'The Idea of a Constitution' (1987) 37 Journal of Legal Education 167; Charles Howard McIlwain, *Constitutionalism: Ancient and Modern* (Revised edition, Cornell University Press 1947) 146.

[46] See Ayittey, *Indigenous African Institutions* (n 5); Fortes and Evans-Pritchard, 'Introduction' (n 3); Middleton and Tait, 'Introduction' (n 29).

[47] See Makau Mutua, *Human Rights: A Political and Cultural Critique* (University of Pennsylvania Press 2009) 74–83; Vincent Obisienunwo Orlu Nmehielle, *The African Human Rights System: Its Laws, Practice, and Institutions* (Martinus Nijhoff Publishers 2001) 11–17; Josiah AM Cobbah, 'African Values and the Human Rights Debate: An African Perspective' (1987) 9 Human Rights Quarterly 309, 320–25. See also the Charter of Manden (*Charte de Manden*) of the Empire of Mali, that dates back 1236 AC, which recognized fundamental rights.

previous discussion, this section demonstrates how custom was the constitutional basis for the existence and operation of traditional government in precolonial Africa. The discussion begins by clarifying the concept of 'custom' and its multiple functions and manifestations, and then proceeds to explore its constitutional function and relevance.

Custom had multiple meanings and functions in precolonial Africa. As the Oxford English Dictionary defines it, custom is 'a mode of behavior or procedure which is widely practiced and accepted in a particular community' and 'an established usage which by long continuance has acquired the force of a law or right'; this was the case in precolonial Africa as well.[48] Furthermore, custom was a normative order that managed and regulated the way of life of societies.[49] As a normative order, custom was formed though regular social behavior accompanied by general public observance and a sense of obligation.[50] The Nigerian Supreme Court in *Oyewumi v Ogunesan* defined custom as 'the organic and living law of the indigenous people of Nigeria regulating their lives and transactions'.[51] Similarly, the South African Constitutional Court in *Alexkor Limited v the Richtersveld Community* defines custom as:

> a system of law that was known to the community, practiced and passed on from generation to generation. It is a system of law that has its own values and norms. Throughout its history, it has evolved and developed to meet the changing needs of the community.[52]

From these conceptions and definitions, at least three different functions and manifestations of custom emerge: custom as a way of life, as law, and as constitution.

Although custom was unwritten, it is possible to distinguish its different functions and manifestations as well as their subsequent socio-legal and political consequences. Indeed, the multifarious nature of custom in the socio-political imagination of precolonial Africa on the one hand, and the lack of theoretical and conceptual tools with which to understand these African realities on the other, have led some to conclude that precolonial Africa was 'pre-law'.[53] It is argued that the absence of clear distinctions in the African imagination as to whether rules of social conduct are law or custom,

[48] Oxford English Dictionary, 'Custom,' <http://wwwoedcom/view/Entry/46306> accessed 29 October 2018.

[49] Henry Louis Gates and Kwame Anthony Appiah, *Encyclopedia of Africa* (Oxford University Press 2010) 35.

[50] Gordan Woodman, 'A Survey of Customary Law in Africa: In Search of Lessons for the Future', in Jeanmarie Fenrich, Paolo Galizzi, and Tracy E Higgins (eds), *The Future of African Customary Law* (Cambridge University Press 2011) 10; TW Bennett, *Customary Law in South Africa* (Juta 2004) 1; Ian Hamnett, *Chieftainship and Legitimacy: An Anthropological Study of Executive Law in Lesotho* (Routledge & Kegan Paul Limited 1975) 14.

[51] *Oyewumi v Ogunesan* [1990] 3 NWLR PT 137 P182, 207.

[52] *Alexkor Ltd and Another v Richtersveld Community and Others* (CCT19/03) [2003] ZACC 18; 2004 (5) SA 460 (CC); 2003 (12) BCLR 1301 (CC) (14 October 2003) 53.

[53] Makau W Mutua, 'Africa and the Rule of Law' (2016) 13 Sur-International Journal on Human Rights 159, 163. Indeed, the recognition of the so called 'customary law' by colonial powers was a later development due to what Mahmood Mamdani called 'a crisis of mission and a crisis of justification' that changed colonial policy from 'civilization to conservation and from progress to order'. See Mahmood Mamdani, *Define and Rule: Native as Political Identity* (Harvard University Press 2012) 8–25.

coupled with the difficulty of identifying social practices and usages as either ordinary social conduct or law, made custom a non-legal subject matter.[54] Nevertheless, the different functions of custom were clearly known to the respective communities in precolonial Africa. For instance, traditional dances and drumming at marriage ceremonies in many African societies are customary. It is also customary to pay a dowry for the conclusion of marriage. However, marriage can be concluded even without dances and drumming, but it cannot be valid without the payment of a dowry—despite a weeklong performance of dances and drumming.[55]

The overriding values of *cieng* of the Dinka, personhood of the Akan, and Ubuntu of the Southern Africa are all customary values which guide human behavior and relations towards humanness, compassion, community, and unity.[56] However, the inability and/or unwillingness of one to live up to these values does not bring legal consequences, but social ones, such as the lack of respect, honor, and dignity in the community. In contrast, if one fails to pay their debt, takes someone's property, or kills another human being, that person faces legal sanctions of civil or criminal nature, according to the respective custom.[57] Furthermore, if the king, chief, or headman acts without the consultation and participation of their counsels, other subordinate administrators, elders, or the community at large, or if one attempts to be a king, chief, or headman by force, the politico-legal core of custom would be triggered.[58]

Custom as a constitution in precolonial Africa provided the fundamental rules of organization of society, the government structures, and the rights and duties of individuals and groups.[59] In centralized political systems, custom divided society both horizontally and vertically.[60] Horizontally, some—due to their birth—were entitled to rule,[61]while others were entitled to elect the rulers, and others still were only entitled to say how the king or chief should rule.[62] Additionally, some—due to their special functions, training, and skills, such as priests, craftsmen, fishermen, or singers—had special privileges or (dis)advantages in the social strata.[63] In some centralized political systems, there were also some categories of people who did not have any say at all, but had to simply obey the rules.[64] Vertically, as centralized political

[54] Elias, *The Nature of African Customary Law* (n 24) 29.

[55] ibid.

[56] Francis M Deng, *Identity, Diversity, and Constitutionalism in Africa* (United States Institute of Peace Press 2008) 85–100; Y Makgoro, 'Ubuntu and the Law in South Africa' (1998) 1 Potchefstroom Electronic Law Journal/Potchefstroomse Elektroniese Regsblad 1; Kwame Gyekye, *Tradition and Modernity: Philosophical Reflections on the African Experience* (Oxford University Press 1997) 48–52.

[57] See Elias, *The Nature of African Customary Law* (n 24) chapters VII, VIII, and IX.

[58] Ayittey, *Indigenous African Institutions* (n 5) 216–31; Elias, *The Nature of African Customary Law* (n 24) 18–19.

[59] See also Jeanmarie Fenrich, Paolo Galizzi, and Tracy E Higgins, 'Introduction' in Jeanmarie Fenrich, Paolo Galizzi, and Tracy E Higgins (eds), *The Future of African Customary Law* (Cambridge University Press 2011) 2.

[60] Basil Davidson, *A History of West Africa, 1000–1800* (Revised edition, Addison-Wesley Longman Ltd 1978) 178.

[61] See also EG Parrinder, 'Divine Kingship in West Africa' (1956) 3 Numen 111, 111–21.

[62] Davidson, *A History of West Africa* (n 60) 178; Cheikh Anta Diop, *Civilization or Barbarism: An Authentic Anthropology* (Yaa-Lengi Meema Ngemi tr, 3rd ed, Lawrence Hill Books 1991) 117–18.

[63] Davidson, *A History of West Africa* (n 60) 179; Diop, *Civilization or Barbarism* (n 62) 117–18.

[64] Davidson, *A History of West Africa* (n 60) 180–82; Robert William July, *Precolonial Africa: An Economic and Social History* (Scribner 1975) 225.

systems were heterogeneous and they each had their own customs, there were divisions which separated one clan from another, one village from another, and the descendants of one ancestor from the descendants of another.[65] Status, wealth, age, sex, ability, disability, and beauty—among others—were also intersecting themes that affected the individual's place and position within the respective customs of many of the centralized political systems.[66] As the customs of uncentralized political systems were more egalitarian, and as lineages were their corporate political units, these societies were more homogenous vertically and less-stratified horizontally. Surely, there were still customary, functional, and other divisions—such as sex, secret-society affiliation, age grades, or age sets—that defined the individual's place and position within these societies.[67]

In addition to constituting the social makeup of precolonial societies, by taking into consideration the size of their population, the customs of the centralized political systems also established and organized government power, both horizontally and vertically. Horizontally, as noted in the previous discussion, the government of the empire or kingdom was organized around the king or chief who held legislative, executive, and judicial powers, but shared these powers with their Counsel, the Cabinet, the Queen-mother, the women of the royal house, the ritual functionaries, etc. And vertically, the government power of the empire or kingdom was devolved to the provinces and villages under the custodianship of the provincial chiefs or princes, as well as the village leaders. In the case of uncentralized political systems, custom authorized and conferred the headman with governmental authority in collaboration with his lineage. In both political systems, custom provided sanctions and punishments for the abuse or misuse of powers, and recognized a set of rights and freedoms for individuals and groups within the political community.

Chancellor Williams developed an archetype of the 'African Constitution' in precolonial Africa by examining the customs of 105 language groups in twenty-six African countries over the course of sixteen years of research and two years of field study.[68] Building on the discussions here and in the previous section, along with Williams' version of the 'African Constitution' and George Ayittey's 'Indigenous African Constitution',[69] I would like to briefly restate and summarize the theory of government and the idea of rights as produced by the customs of precolonial societies in Africa:

Indigenous theory of government and ideas of rights in precolonial Africa[70]

[65] Davidson, *A History of West Africa* (n 60) 178–79; Szymon Chodak, 'Social Stratification in Sub-Saharan Africa' (1973) 7 Canadian Journal of African Studies/Revue Canadienne des Études Africaines 401, 402–408.

[66] Elias, *The Nature of African Customary Law* (n 24) 98–108; July (n 276) 111–14.

[67] Ayittey, *Indigenous African Institutions* (n 5) 112–131; Middleton and Tait, 'Introduction' (n 29); Susan Keech McIntosh, 'Pathways to complexity: An African Perspective' in Susan Keech McIntosh (eds), *Beyond Chiefdoms: Pathways to Complexity in Africa* (Cambridge University Press 2005) 9–19.

[68] Williams, *Destruction of Black Civilization* (n 16) 20–21, 171–86.

[69] Ayittey, *Indigenous African Institutions* (n 5) 295–97.

[70] Adopted with modifications from Williams, *Destruction of Black Civilization* (n 16) 181–86 and Ayittey, *Indigenous African Institutions* (n 5) 295–97.

I General Principles

1. He who founded the empire, kingdom, or chiefdom by uniting many as one is the leader.
2. The people will elect rulers from the founder's family in honor of him if the heirs demonstrate the founder's character, bravery, and intelligence.
3. The will of the people is the supreme law.
4. The king or chief is the custodian of the will of the people and its supreme and ultimate executor.

II Fundamental Rights

Every member of the community has

1. The right to work and economic livelihood.
2. The right to the use of land.
3. The right to defend the family against intruders, and even against harassment by the king or chief.
4. The right to aid in time of trouble including the right to family or community care in case of sickness and accidents.
5. The right to a fair trial.
6. The right to participate in government and the decision-making process.
7. Freedom of expression and worship.
8. Freedom of movement and association.

III Government

1. The king or chief in line with his powers and functions is obligated to:
   a. Provide a vital link between the living and the ancestors.
   b. Maintain order, balance, and harmony among the cosmological elements: the sky, the earth, and the world.
   c. Promote peace, justice, social harmony, and prosperity among the people.
   d. Respect the laws of the ancestors and abide by the will of the people.
   e. Collect money, taxes, gifts, and other donations and dispose them for the welfare of society.
   f. Present the prayers of the people to his and their ancestors in Heaven.
2. The king or chief shall govern with a Council.
   a. The king or chief must remain silent as the Council deliberates on an issue.
   b. Important decisions must be debated until unanimity is reached. If not, the issue shall be placed before a Village Assembly of commoners and debated until a consensus is reached.
   c. The king or chief, together with the Council, shall ensure that the will of the people, arrived at by consensus, is carried out. The king or chief shall not unilaterally abrogate the expressed will of the community.
   d. The king or chief shall not entertain or enter into any contract with a foreigner or stranger without the full approval of the Council.
   e. All decisions initiated by the king should be approved by the Council.
3. The Council should be composed of the elders of the extended family or clan based on hereditary or meritocratic considerations. The king or chief may nominate other persons of high regard to the Council upon concurrence of the Council.
4. The family is the primary social, economic, judicial, and political unit in society that entertains all internal matters firsthand.

5. The primary duties of the government are to defend the community against external aggression, maintain law and order, and ensure the survival of the ethnic group by promoting peace, justice, harmony, and economic prosperity. It is not the function of the tribal government to operate commercial enterprises to the total exclusion of the subjects. The king or chief may operate a farm or business if they so wish. But he cannot prohibit others from engaging in the same economic activity.
6. Grounds for removal and/or regicide of a king or chief.
   a. Failure to perform the duties listed in III (1);
   b. Drunkenness;
   c. Cowardice in war;
   d. Failure to listen to advice;
   e. Physical disfigurement;
   f. Oppression of the people; and
   g. Looting the tribal treasury.

Thus, as is evident, custom animated the normative universe of both traditional government and traditional conceptions of power, and was the ultimate compass in the practical exercise of political power. Accordingly, custom was the indigenous constitution that regulated the politico-legal life of precolonial societies in Africa.

C. Indigenous Constitutionalism

The indigenous constitutions, as described in the previous section, were enforceable in practice. Granted, there should not be any illusion that the constitutional theory envisioned in the constitutional arrangements was exactly what was implemented in practice. Nonetheless, there was a general compliance with, and commitment to, the practical enforcement of the indigenous constitution. If rule by consent, the rule of law, limited government, and the protection of rights constitute the fundamental elements of constitutionalism, then precolonial societies in Africa did have indigenous constitutionalism.[71] This section explores the practical enforcement of the indigenous constitutions in light of these fundamental elements of constitutionalism. The objective of this discussion is to demonstrate that custom as indigenous constitution did matter in the operation and functioning of traditional government in precolonial Africa.

The general will of the people had paramount importance in bestowing the king or chief with the type of authority and legitimacy necessary for voluntary compliance to his political power. As discussed in the previous sections, the indigenous constitutions provided different rules of access to political office and allocated different powers and functions to these offices. As a result, illegal seizure of a political office, abuse and/or misuse of political powers, and non-performance of political functions were all sanctioned, either through the institutional political process, or through popular rebellion—including secession—or a combination of both. For instance, the kings

[71] See Bruce P Frohnen, 'Is Constitutionalism Liberal?' (2011) 33 Campbell Law Review 31, 529–58.

of Buganda, Lubu, Zulu, Ankole, Mende, Fanti, Yoruba, and Asante were all held in check through these processes.[72] To give a specific example, the Asante destooled, or impeached, three kings: Osei Kwame in 1799 for absenting and failing to perform his religious duties during the *Adae* festivals, Karikari in 1874 for extravagance, and Mensa Bonsu in 1883 for excessive taxation.[73] While indigenous constitutions could not always prevent rulers from behaving like tyrants or dictators, the recourse to rebellion, secession, and regicide tamed the temptations of dictatorship. In this regard, the demise and death of Shaka of the Zulu Kingdom were instructive as it shows how the lack of popular consent ended the king's rule and, ultimately, cost him his life.[74] Hence, rule by consent was one of the cornerstones of political legitimacy and authority in precolonial Africa.[75]

Indigenous constitutions applied to rulers and subjects alike. In addition, both the rulers and their subjects were fully aware of their rights and duties to each other and agreed to live accordingly.[76] One of the fundamental rules of indigenous constitutions echoes the familiar French maxim of *noblesse oblige*.[77] As the kings, chiefs, or rulers held power and influence unmatched by any member of their societies, they also assumed corresponding obligations and responsibilities towards those societies.[78] In as much as kings, chiefs, or rulers collected taxes, tributes, and labor services—among others—from their subjects, they also had to disperse welfare and justice to them, protect their lives and properties, and perform ritual acts and observances.[79] Failure to perform these duties would result in impeachment, removal, or even regicide, as noted above. Hence, the idea of constitutionalism as manifested in precolonial Africa was not only concerned with limiting government for the benefit of individual or communal liberty, but was also tasked with enabling government for the same purposes.[80] As NW Barber argued in *The Principles of Constitutionalism,* indigenous constitutionalism both *limited* and *enabled* government to effectuate political power for the betterment and common prosperity of society in accordance with the principles and rules of the indigenous constitutions.[81]

In a similar vein, the rights and freedoms recognized in the indigenous constitutions were enforceable. The right to use land, the right to a fair trial, the right to participation in decision-making, freedom of expression and movement—among others—were all enforceable rights in precolonial Africa. There is an abundance of scholarship that shows how Africans used their rights to land, settled their disputes,

[72] Ayittey, *Indigenous African Institutions* (n 5) 185–200; Elias, *The Nature of African Customary Law* (n 24) 18 and 99; Gluckman, 'The Kingdom of the Zulu of South Africa' (n 14) 30–36; K Oberg, 'The Kingdom of Ankole in Uganda' in M Fortes and EE Evans-Pritchard (eds), *African Political Systems* (Oxford University Press 1940) 157–61.

[73] ibid 174.

[74] Gluckman, 'The Kingdom of the Zulu of South Africa' (n 14) 26.

[75] Williams, *Destruction of Black Civilization* (n 16) 179–85; Elias, *The Nature of African Customary Law* (n 24) 19–20; Fortes and Evans-Pritchard, 'Introduction' (n 3) 12–13; Middleton and Tait, 'Introduction' (n 29).

[76] Fortes and Evans-Pritchard, 'Introduction' (n 3) 12.

[77] Elias, *The Nature of African Customary Law* (n 24) 20.

[78] Fortes and Evans-Pritchard, 'Introduction' (n 3) 12.

[79] ibid 12.

[80] See also Graham Walker, 'The Idea of Nonliberal Constitutionalism' (1997) 39 Nomos 154, 154–84.

[81] NW Barber, *The Principles of Constitutionalism* (Oxford University Press 2018) 9–10.

participated in the government of their societies, expressed their ideas and views, and freely moved from one place to another within and beyond their political communities.[82] These rights and freedoms were inherent in the indigenous constitutional dispensation and remained so in the constitutional practices as well. Nonetheless, I am not claiming that precolonial Africa practiced human rights as we know them today, nor am I suggesting that there was full equality in the practice and enforcement of these rights and freedoms. Indeed, not everyone in the political community was equal, and discrimination based on sex, status, and ethnicity, for example, was quite prevalent. However, precolonial societies in Africa did maintain and practice the rights that were recognized in their respective constitutions. Therefore, seen in the light of the general ideas and principles of constitutionalism, we can affirm that precolonial societies in Africa practiced an indigenous constitutionalism which can be considered as one legitimate variety of constitutionalism.[83]

II. Constitutionalism in Colonial Africa

As with constitutionalism in precolonial Africa, the nature and identity of the colonial constitutionalism that encountered indigenous constitutionalism in colonial Africa should first be investigated and ascertained on its own in order to properly locate it within the dynamic constitutional matrix that sets legal syncretism in play. Even if it is, indeed, a contradiction in terms to talk about colonial constitutionalism in Africa, it is difficult to fully understand and explain the dynamic constitutional matrix that changed and transformed indigenous constitutionalism and, consequently, established a syncretic postcolonial constitutional design and practice, without properly accounting for the colonial constitutional setup. As highlighted in the previous chapter, colonialism superimposed a new constitutional system over precolonial Africa under a new theory of government and new conceptions of power. This section examines and explores the nature of colonial constitutional theory and practice, as well as their interactions with the indigenous constitutional systems. First we will deal with the nature of colonial constitutions and their theory of government and conception of power. This will then be followed by a discussion about how colonial constitutions dissolved the indigenous constitutional systems by transforming and reconfiguring the traditional governments and customs into the colonial constitutional systems through acts of rejection, accommodation, and invention. Needless to say, there were different types of colonial constitutions in Africa, inasmuch as there were different colonial powers as well as different circumstances and exigencies within the respective

[82] See Mutua, *Human Rights* (n 47) 74–81; Elias, *The Nature of African Customary Law* (n 24) chapter IX (for land rights), XI (for participation in decision making), and XII (for the judicial processes); Lewis, *A Pastoral Democracy* (n 38) (for the democratic decision making among the Somalis); Kwasi Wiredu, 'An Akan Perspective on Human Rights' in Abdullahi Ahmed An-naim and Francis M Deng (eds), *Human Rights in Africa: Cross-Cultural Perspectives* (Brookings Institution Press 1990) 243–60; Francis M Deng, 'A Cultural Approach to Human Rights Among the Dinka' in Abdullahi Ahmed An-naim and Francis M Deng (eds), *Human Rights in Africa: Cross-Cultural Perspectives* (Brookings Institution Press 1990) 261–89.

[83] See Mark Tushnet, 'Varieties of Constitutionalism' (2016) 14 International Journal of Constitutional Law 1, 1–5; Frohnen, 'Is Constitutionalism Liberal?' (n 71); Walker, 'The Idea of Nonliberal Constitutionalism' (n 80).

colonial states. Hence, the reference to colonial constitutions here is to their fundamental common elements.

A. Colonial Constitutions

The colonial constitutions in Africa were framed and structured through the aid of international law as well as domestic imperial and colonial laws. Indeed, imperial and colonial laws were the main tools, structural prerequisites, and cutting edge of the colonial project elsewhere.[84] Nonetheless, the emergence of new states with colonial ambitions in Africa put international law at the forefront of late colonialism.[85] In this regard, the Berlin Conference, building on nineteenth-century international law, provided the frame of reference for the colonization of Africa and acted as the fundamental basic law for colonial Africa.[86] Within the framework of the Berlin Conference, the respective imperial and colonial laws crafted, administered, and managed the African colonial states. Through the help of international law as well as imperial and colonial laws, new territories, peoples, governments, and sovereignties were established and superimposed over the indigenous constitutional arrangements of precolonial Africa. In the paragraphs that follow, the constitutional design and theory built into the colonial constitutions in Africa will be discussed.

The Berlin Conference provided the basic law, or constitution, *ex nihilo*[87] for colonial Africa without the participation of Africans. At the Berlin Conference, indigenous constitutions were considered non-existent. So were the numerous precolonial societies along with their centralized and uncentralized political systems. International law neither recognized the personality of precolonial African states and societies, nor did it provide a theory of international relations that included them,[88] and as a result, Africa was a place without rights and duties under international law. The exclusion of Africa from the Berlin Conference on African affairs, and the invitation and participation of other states—such as the United States, Austria-Hungary, Denmark, and Sweden-Norway, all of which did not have any colonial interests in Africa—is

[84] Lauren Benton, *Law and Colonial Cultures: Legal Regimes in World History, 1400–1900* (Cambridge University Press 2002) 18–19; Sally Engle Merry, 'Law and Colonialism' (1991) 25 Law & Society Review 889, 890; Res Schuerch, *The International Criminal Court at the Mercy of Powerful States: An Assessment of the Neo-Colonialism Claim Made by African Stakeholders* (Springer 2017) 44–47; Martin Chanock, *Law, Custom, and Social Order: The Colonial Experience in Malawi and Zambia* (Cambridge University Press 1985) 4.

[85] Wolfgang Justin Mommsen, 'Bismarck, the Concept of Europe, and the Future of West Africa, 1883–1885' in Stig Förster, Wolfgang Justin Mommsen, and Ronald Edward Robinson (eds), *Bismarck, Europe and Africa: The Berlin Africa Conference 1884–1885 and the Onset of Partition* (Oxford University Press [for] German Historical Institute 1988) 151–70.

[86] Matthew Craven, 'Between Law and History: The Berlin Conference of 1884–1885 and the Logic of Free Trade' (2015) 3 London Review of International Law 31, 49–54; Antony Anghie, *Imperialism, Sovereignty and the Making of International Law* (Cambridge University Press 2007) 90–91.

[87] Thomas C Grey, 'The Constitution as Scripture' (1984) 37 Stanford Law Review 1, 16.

[88] Ibrahim J Gassama, 'International Law, Colonialism, and the African' in Martin S Shanguhyia and Toyin Falola (eds), *The Palgrave Handbook of African Colonial and Postcolonial History* (Palgrave Macmillan 2018) 554–59; Makau wa Mutua, 'Why Redraw the Map of Africa: A Moral and Legal Inquiry' (1995) 16 Michigan Journal of International Law 1113, 1120–22.

evidence of international law treating Africa as a legal object.[89] Consequently, Africa was considered as a *terra nullius* and, hence, a legitimate object of occupation and conquest by European states. As the power of Europeans to occupy and colonize Africa was accepted as a truism, the Berlin Conference simply concerned itself with how this can be achieved. Consider, for example, the opening paragraphs of the General Act of the Berlin Conference:

> WISHING, in a spirit of good and mutual accord, to regulate the conditions most favourable to the development of trade and civilization in certain regions of Africa, and to assure to all nations the advantages of free navigation on the two chief rivers of Africa flowing into the Atlantic Ocean;
>
> BEING DESIROUS, on the other hand, to obviate the misunderstanding and disputes which might in future arise from new acts of occupation (prises de possession) on the coast of Africa; and concerned, at the same time, as to the means of furthering the moral and material well-being of the native populations;

The Berlin Conference incorporated what Achille Mbembe called 'the founding violence' into the colonial constitutions.[90] On the one hand, this created the right to colonization and the space within which it was to be exercised. On the other hand, it negated all indigenous constitutions and made the colonial constitutions supreme. Chapter 6 of the General Act of the Berlin Conference speaks about this founding violence:

> Any Power which henceforth takes possession of a tract of land on the coasts of the African continent outside of its present possessions, or which, being hitherto without such possessions, shall acquire them, as well as the Power which assumes a Protectorate there, shall accompany the respective act with a notification thereof, addressed to the other Signatory Powers of the present Act, in order to enable them, if need be, to make good any claims of their own.[91]
>
> The Signatory Powers of the present Act recognize the obligation to insure the establishment of authority in the regions occupied by them on the coasts of the African continent sufficient to protect existing rights, and, as the case may be, freedom of trade and of transit under the conditions agreed upon.[92]

The chief aim of these provisions was the legitimization of the partitions of Africa among the European colonial powers and the management of conflicts that might have arisen in this respect. Through this act of legitimization, colonial sovereignty was born in the graveyards of the sovereignty of Africans.

[89] Jörg Fisch, 'Africa as Terra Nullius: the Berlin Conference and International Law' in Stig Förster, Wolfgang Justin Mommsen, and Ronald Edward Robinson (eds), *Bismarck, Europe and Africa: The Berlin Africa Conference 1884–1885 and the Onset of Partition* (Oxford University Press 1988) 347.

[90] Achille Mbembe, *On the Postcolony* (University of California Press 2001) 25.

[91] General Act of the Berlin Conference on West Africa 1885, art 34.

[92] ibid art 35.

Building on the founding violence and frame of reference engineered at the Berlin Conference, the imperial and colonial powers added a further 'legitimation and maintenance violence' to the colonial constitutional architecture.[93] The legitimation violence was brought to Africa with the importation of imperial and colonial laws in order to justify, order, and structure colonial government. To ensure the maintenance, spread, and permanence of the colonial government, the colonial powers enacted new laws and rules—maintenance violence—as necessitated by the exigencies of the respective situations in every colony. As a result, precolonial states and societies were forced to come together or be separated from each other in order to form new territorial colonial states, and new colonial governments animated by violence and a colonial sovereignty alien to the Africans were implanted in these states.

Even though the structures and rules of colonial constitutions varied between the Anglophone, Francophone, and Lusophone colonies—and within these colonies themselves—their effect on terminating the indigenous constitutional systems were the same.[94] For instance, in Anglophone Africa, the colonial constitutional structures were composed of an Order in Council which established the general framework of colonial governance by applying the laws of England; Acts of the Westminster parliament; and local legislation of the colonies by their Governors and/or Legislative Councils.[95] In Sierra Leone and Gambia, there was a Governor and a Legislative Council—comprised of a Chief Justice, a colonial secretary, and some merchants—with both legislative and judicial powers.[96] In the colony of the Gold Coast, however, there was only a Lieutenant Governor, while the Governor and Legislative Council of Sierra Leone held legislative and judicial powers over it.[97] In addition, the Order in Council provided the application of the codified laws of India in Eastern Anglophone Africa.[98] In a similar vein, in Francophone Africa, the colonial constitutional structures and rules were provided in the *senatus-consult* of 3 May 1854 which authorized the administration of the colonies by the decree of the Emperor—which the President inherited in the Third Republic, legislation of the Ministers of the Navy and the Colony, and local legislation by the governors, administers, or councils.[99] Despite their variations, however, all of these colonial constitutions changed the rules, institutions, procedures, and meanings of the indigenous constitutional systems in the new territorial states.[100]

[93] ibid; Mamdani, *Define and Rule* (n 53) 43–44.

[94] See MB Hooker, *Legal Pluralism: An Introduction to Colonial and Neo-Colonial Laws* (Clarendon Press 1975) chapters II–IV.

[95] See the constitutional structure of Tanganika as a sample; The Tanganyika Order in Council 1920.

[96] Arthur Mills, *Colonial Constitutions: An Outline of the Constitutional History and Existing Government of the British Dependencies: With Schedules of the Orders in Council, Statutes, and Parliamentary Documents Relating to Each Dependency* (J Murray 1856) 163–64, 168.

[97] ibid 170.

[98] JND Anderson, 'Colonial Law in Tropical Africa: The Conflict between English, Islamic and Customary Law' (1960) 35 Ind LJ 433, 434–35.

[99] Ruth Ginio, *French Colonialism Unmasked: The Vichy Years in French West Africa* (University of Nebraska Press 2008) 3–4; Jean Suret-Canale, *French Colonialism in Tropical Africa: 1900–1945* (Pica Press 1971) 71–72; Hooker, *Legal Pluralism* (n 94) 196–203.

[100] Richard Roberts and Kristin Mann, *'Law in Colonial Africa' in* Kristin Mann and Richard Roberts (eds), *Law in Colonial Africa* (Heinemann Educational Books & James Currey 1991) 3–5.

B. The Transformation of Traditional Government

With the superimposition of colonial constitutions in Africa, the traditional governments ceased to be the ultimate decision-making bodies as they had been. Their power and final decision-making authority over the people within their precolonial territorial or genealogical ties were stripped and rejected by the new colonial governments. Their fundamental sources and conceptions of power were subordinated, transformed, and incorporated into the systems of the colonial governments. In this section, I demonstrate how the colonial constitutions rejected, incorporated, invented, and accommodated traditional governments into the colonial states and governments through complex legal syncretic processes.

As the importation of European laws and institutions were part of the alleged civilizing mission of the colonial project in Africa, the powers of traditional government were not formally recognized from the beginning.[101] Indeed, the purpose of the importation of these new laws and institutions was not simply to use them as dispute-settlement mechanisms, or as an apparatus of control,[102] but rather—as the core part of the legitimation violence—to present Western civilization as possessing universal normative appeal and institutional sophistication which could and should be applied to the colonies.[103] In fact, as noted elsewhere, colonial states had neither the interest nor the capacity to apply European laws to all Africans within their territory. However, the maintenance of the colonial state and colonial rule of law did require some formal recognition of the traditional governments.[104] The exigencies of colonial administration, including, but not limited to, the need to contain threats to the continuity of colonial rule, protecting the authority and dignity of local colonial governors and European citizens, as well as collecting taxes from the African masses, all made the recognition of certain limited powers of traditional government necessary.[105]

The recognition of traditional government by the colonial states introduced new changes to the precolonial structures and normative bases of traditional government and traditional conception of power. These changes brought new terminologies, or political vocabularies, to colonial Africa, such as 'native authority' or 'native administration'. In this native authority or native administration, the native chief was appointed or confirmed by the colonial authorities.[106] The basis of these appointments and confirmations of the chief was not custom, but rather the chief's agreement with

[101] See also Alice L Conklin, *A Mission to Civilize: The Republican Idea of Empire in France and West Africa, 1895–1930* (Stanford University Press 1997).

[102] Mahmood Mamdani, *Citizen and Subject: Contemporary Africa and the Legacy of Late Colonialism* (Princeton University Press 1996) 109.

[103] ibid; Nasser Hussain, *The Jurisprudence of Emergency: Colonialism and the Rule of Law* (University of Michigan Press 2003) 35–68 .

[104] Mamdani, *Define and Rule* (n 53) 8; Karen E Fields, *Revival and Rebellion in Colonial Central Africa* (Princeton University Press 1985) chapters 1 and 2.

[105] Henri Labouret, 'France's Colonial Policy in Africa' (1940) 39 African Affairs 22, 25–29; David Killingray, 'The Maintenance of Law and Order in British Colonial Africa' (1986) 85 African Affairs 411, 412–19; Emmanuelle Saada, 'The Empire of Law: Dignity, Prestige, and Domination in the "Colonial Situation"' (2002) 20 French Politics, Culture & Society 98, 103–106.

[106] Lord Hailey, *Native Administration and Political Development in British Tropical Africa: Report, 1940–42* (London: HMSO 1944) 85–87.

the colonial authorities and their commitment to the colonial missions.[107] Precisely because of this, colonial authorities recognized chiefs who submitted to their policies and dismissed those who stood against them, and, thus, appointed persons who otherwise could not have been chiefs or traditional leaders according to custom.[108] Furthermore, they created the institution of native authority in communities that did not have prior centralized political systems.[109] By doing so, colonial states incorporated new sources of power and authority into the institution of native authority by displacing customary rules and practices.

Along with these new sources of power, the colonial states also changed the functions and powers of the traditional governments. Depending upon the circumstances and contexts of the specific colonial administrations, colonial states either added powers and functions to traditional authorities, or they severely limited their powers and functions.[110] Generally speaking, in British colonial Africa, the powers of traditional authorities increased, more often than not, while still being subject to the oversight of colonial authorities,[111] whereas in French colonial Africa, the powers of traditional authorities were severely limited.[112] For instance, in British colonial Africa, as sole native authority was vested in the chiefs under the authority of colonial administrators, they became stronger as holders of political power.[113] In French colonial Africa, however, the main tasks of native authorities included the collection of taxes, the recruitment of men for labor, and the execution and management of the infamous *indigènes*.[114] As part of the corpus of colonial administrations, salaries and bonuses were paid to the chiefs in colonial Africa.[115]

Furthermore, the institution of native authority was not a purely native institution run by natives applying native laws, but rather one that heavily incorporated Europeans and European laws into its structure and operation. In this respect, the British form of native rule consisted of a native authority who was an indigenous chief appointed and backed by the British, a native treasury which included British tax assessors and

[107] Colin Newbury, *Patrons, Clients, and Empire: Chieftaincy and over-Rule in Asia, Africa, and the Pacific* (Oxford University Press 2003) 121–22.

[108] Suret-Canale, *French Colonialism in Tropical Africa* (n 99) 82–83.

[109] ibid 79–80; Adiele Eberechukwu Afigbo, *The Warrant Chiefs: Indirect Rule in Southeastern Nigeria, 1891–1929* (Longman 1972) 37–45; Robert L Tignor, 'Colonial Chiefs in Chiefless Societies' (1971) 9 The Journal of Modern African Studies 339, 339–59.

[110] Martin Chanok, 'Making Customary Law: Men, Women, and Courts in Colonial Northern Rhodesia' in Margaret Jean Hay and Marcia Wright (eds), *African Women & the Law: Historical Perspectives* (Boston University, African Studies Center 1982) 59–60; Suret-Canale, *French Colonialism in Tropical Africa* (n 99) 79–82.

[111] Peter K Tibenderana, 'The Irony of Indirect Rule in Sokoto Emirate, Nigeria, 1903–1944' (1988) 31 African Studies Review 67, 67–92.

[112] Michael Crowder, 'Indirect Rule: French and British Style' (1964) 34 Africa: Journal of the International African Institute 197, 197–205.

[113] For details see Michael Crowder and Obaro Ikime (eds), *West African Chiefs: Their Changing Status under Colonial Rule and Independence* (Africana Publishing Corporation and the University of Ife Press 1970).

[114] Crowder, 'Indirect Rule' (n 112) 200; Gregory Mann, 'What Was the "Indigénat"? The "Empire of Law" in French West Africa' (2009) 50 The Journal of African History 331, 333–337; Suret-Canale, *French Colonialism in Tropical Africa* (n 99) 80–83.

[115] Newbury, *Patrons, Clients, and Empire* (n 107) 114; Elise Huillery, 'The Black Man's Burden: The Cost of Colonization of French West Africa' (2014) 74 The Journal of Economic History 1, 14; Tignor, 'Colonial Chiefs in Chiefless Societies' (n 109).

African tax collectors, and a native court run by Africans and supervised by British colonial officials.[116] When we further explore the native court systems in many parts of British colonial Africa, we find that the judges were actually British and that the natives were simply advisors, translators, or aids in the disposition of colonial justice.[117] Similarly, chiefs and headmen acted mainly as assessors and interpreters of customary laws in native courts.[118] Even when natives did run the native courts, their decisions were subject to review and appeal in higher courts staffed by the British.[119] Hence, the native authority and administration was an arrangement of mixed persons, laws, and institutions where syncretism took place as a matter of colonial governmentality.

These changes significantly transformed the relationship between traditional governments and their respective African societies. On the one hand, traditional authorities represented the colonial states as part of the colonial administration or bureaucracy in their societies, while on the other hand, they were divorced from the indigenous constitutional systems of checks and balances; the precolonial supreme custodians of sovereignty were reduced to subordinate administrators. In lieu of their new source of power and legitimacy, they were neither accountable to their precolonial councils and peers, nor to their people.[120] As long as they had the backing and support of the colonial states, they exercised their power without—or with little limitations from—their people.[121] Despite the differences in the degree of despotism within the native authorities of the British and French colonies—or even within individual colonies—the colonial states all channeled and configured violence to the body of native authorities as a means of exploitation, domination, and tribalization that fundamentally altered the nature of traditional government and the traditional conception of power in Africa.

C. The Transformation of Custom

Like traditional authorities, customs were also transformed by the intrusion of colonial constitutions through a complex process of legal syncretism. In fact, in pursuing the alleged civilizing mission, as noted above, colonial powers attempted to apply

[116] T Walter Wallbank, 'The Principles and Organization of British Native Rule in Tropical Africa' (1934) 3 Pacific Historical Review 142, 147–49.

[117] Julius Lewin, 'Native Courts and British Justice in Africa' (1944) 14 Africa: Journal of the International African Institute 448, 448.

[118] Bonny Ibhawoh, 'Historical Globalization and Colonial Legal Culture: African Assessors, Customary Law, and Criminal Justice in British Africa' (2009) 4 Journal of Global History 429, 434–35; AN Allott, 'The Judicial Ascertainment of Customary Law in British Africa' (1957) 20 The Modern Law Review 244, 249–51; see also Sally Falk Moore, 'Treating Law as Knowledge: Telling Colonial Officers What to Say to Africans about Running "Their Own" Native Courts' (1992) 26 Law & Society Review 11.

[119] Roger Gocking, 'British Justice and the Native Tribunals of the Southern Gold Coast Colony' (1993) 34 The Journal of African History 93, 95; David N Smith, 'Native Courts of Northern Nigeria: Techniques for Institutional Development' (1968) 48 Boston University Law Review 49, 56; AN Allott, 'Native Tribunals in the Gold Coast 1844–1927 Prolegomena to a Study of Native Courts in Ghana' (1957) 1 Journal of African Law 163, 168–69; Julius Lewin, 'The Recognition of Native Law and Custom in British Africa' (1938) 20 Journal of Comparative Legislation and International Law 16, 20–21.

[120] Mamdani, *Define and Rule* (n 53) 43–45.

[121] ibid 52–61.

their own imported laws to their colonies.[122] Nonetheless, due to changes in colonial policy—from direct rule to indirect rule in the case of the British, and from assimilation to association in the case of French—the colonial mission transformed from one of 'civilization to conservation' and 'from progress to order.'[123] While for Mamdani this change in colonial policy was a new technology of governmentality, one of *define and rule*, it was one of accommodation and adaption for Lord Lugard, the then-governor of Nigeria and the engineer of indirect rule in Anglophone Africa. Lugard rationalized his policy as follows:

> The task of the administrative officer is to cloth his principles in the grab of evolution, not of revolution; to make it apparent alike to the educated native, the conservative Moslem, and the primitive pagan [*sic*], each in his own degree, that the policy of the government is not antagonistic but progressive–sympathetic to his aspirations and the safeguard of his natural rights.[124]

Regardless of the complexities of the deriving logic or reasons for these changes in colonial policy, these changes—in practical terms—transformed the domain of custom.

As a matter of colonial laws, the application of custom in the colonial states and its recognition as *native law*, *indigenous law*, or *customary law*, was conditional upon the fulfillment of some *uncustomary* requirements. The first such requirement was that custom should not contravene any written law or legislation; these included the imperial and colonial laws of the metropoles as well as all local laws enacted by colonial administrators, councils, or officials.[125] In French colonial Africa, in particular, the application of custom was further limited to private law, while public law was under French civil law. Moreover, in matters of private law, the application of customary and religious laws—in the case of Muslims—was limited to civil status, marriage, succession, gifts, and wills.[126] Within such confinement, custom, either by its very terms or by implication, should not have contradicted imperial and colonial laws.[127] As a result, the domain of the customary was fractured and fragmented by the imposition of 'legislative non-contradiction' as an essential element of its application and recognition.

The second requirement was that custom should not be repugnant to the European sense of natural justice, equity, morality, public order, good conscience, and civilization.[128] This is the so-called *repugnancy test* employed to further transform and align the application of custom so as to conform to the European and Christian normative systems. In this regard, woman-to-woman marriages or liability for the faults of family

[122] Hooker, *Legal Pluralism* (n 94) 220; Robert B Seidman, 'The Reception of English Law' in Yash P Ghai, Robin Luckham, and Francis G Snyder (eds), *The Political Economy of Law: A Third World Reader* (Oxford University Press 1987) 107–16.

[123] Mamdani, *Define and Rule* (n 53) 8.

[124] Frederick John Dealtry Lugard, *The Dual Mandate in British Tropical Africa* (William Blackwood and Sons 1922) 194.

[125] Muna Ndulo, 'African Customary Law, Customs, and Women's Rights' (2011) 18 Indiana Journal of Global Legal Studies 87, 95.

[126] Hooker, *Legal Pluralism* (n 94) 221–22.

[127] Ndulo, 'African Customary Law, Customs, and Women's Rights' (n 125) 95.

[128] Mamdani, *Citizen and Subject* (n 102) 115–19; Moore, 'Treating Law as Knowledge' (n 118) 18–19; Antony N Allott, *New Essays in African Law* (Butterworths 1970) 158–81.

members—among others—were considered repugnant.[129] Even if there were no written laws to contravene, the practical application of custom was contingent upon its conformity with the general moral and legal considerations of the colonial states. Consequently, as it was difficult to determine *ex ante* the conformity of the numerous customs with the repugnancy test, it was neither evident whether a custom which did not contravene written laws was applicable or not, nor whether the outcomes of actions and behaviors pursuant to custom were predictable, as they were in precolonial times. These twin requirements of legislative conformity and passing the repugnancy test not only subordinated the constitutional status of custom as compared to precolonial times, but they also introduced changes to the substantive and procedural aspects of custom from the outside, ie, the colonial states.

Additionally, as with the invention of chiefs in chief-less societies, new customary laws were also invented in colonial Africa,[130] and these inventions took two forms. The first was the creation of customary law by the colonial states. For example, the French colonial administration created the central feature of *Banjal* customary land law, which radically separated land use 'between the master of the land and the users'.[131] In solving a dispute between the natives, the colonial court decided that the 'rain priest', who had been created by the colonial administration, owned the land, which went against an established *Banjal* custom.[132] Despite being a colonial invention, such land law was treated as customary law.[133] The second form of invention of custom came from the struggles, contestations, and resistance between Africans and the colonial authorities, as well as among the Africans themselves.[134] In this respect, both the colonial authorities and the African elites created many of the customary laws in Malawi and Zambia.[135] While the British were protective of women at first, they created and ossified many patriarchal rules in co-operation with the male African elders for the sake of order and stability.[136] The *Chagga* of Tanzania also constructed new customary

[129] Ndulo, 'African Customary Law, Customs, and Women's Rights' (n 125) 95–96; see also Jackton B Ojwang and Emily Nyiva Kinama, 'Woman-to-Woman Marriage: A Cultural Paradox in Contemporary Africa's Constitutional Profile' (2014) 47 Verfassung und Recht in Übersee/Law and Politics in Africa, Asia and Latin America 412; CO Akpamgbo, 'A "Woman to Woman" Marriage and the Repugnancy Clause: A Case of Putting New Wine into Old Bottles' (1977) 9 The Journal of Legal Pluralism and Unofficial Law 87, 87–92.

[130] Simon Roberts, 'Introduction: Some Notes on "African Customary Law"' (1984) 28 Journal of African Law 1, 1–5; Franz von Benda-Beckmann, 'Law out of Context: A Comment on the Creation of Traditional Law Discussion' (1984) 28 Journal of African Law 28, 28–33.

[131] Francis G Snyder, 'Colonialism and Legal Form: The Creation of "Customary Law" in Senegal' (1981) 13 The Journal of Legal Pluralism and Unofficial Law 49, 51.

[132] ibid 64–69.

[133] ibid 74; see also Francis Snyder, 'Customary Law and the Economy' (1984) 28 Journal of African Law 34, 34–43.

[134] Thomas Spear, 'Neo-Traditionalism and The Limits of Invention in British Colonial Africa' (2003) 44 The Journal of African History 3, 3–27; Peter Fitzpatrick, 'Traditionalism and Traditional Law' (1984) 28 Journal of African Law 20, 20–27; Terence Ranger, 'The Invention of Tradition in Colonial Africa' in Eric Hobsbawm and Terence Ranger (eds), *The Invention of Tradition* (Cambridge University Press 1983) 247–62.

[135] Chanock, *Law, Custom, and Social Order* (n 84) 4–10.

[136] ibid 145–50; Chanok, 'Making Customary Law' (n 110) 53–67.

laws out of their precolonial customary practices and colonial rules in order to adjust to new realities.[137]

Furthermore, in some instances and places in colonial Africa, Islamic law was considered as a variant of customary law, while in others it was treated as a distinct category of law, like customary law or imported law. For instance, Islamic law was treated as a form of native law and custom in Northern Nigeria, Ghana, Sierra Leone, Uganda, and Nyasaland.[138] In French West Africa, too, Islamic law was lumped together with custom under the disposition of native courts.[139] Citing Article 75 of the 1903 Code, which recognized the application of customary and Islamic laws in the native courts, the then-Governor-General of French West Africa noted to his local administrators that '[n]ative courts will judge [by] applying either Malikite rites, which are accepted in a large portion of our territories and are more or less modifications of Quranic law by local practice, or by applying local traditions in regions where Muslim influence is not yet strong'.[140] As a result, in the operation of native courts, Islamic law was fused and forged with custom in these colonies.[141] Unlike in Kenya, Sudan, Somaliland, and Zanzibar, among others, where Islamic law was recognized as a distinct category of law,[142] Islamic law and custom were mixed or (con)fused with one another in the colonial vocabulary of native law and custom, as well as in the adjudication of the customary in the native courts.[143]

Thus, the combined influences of the requirement of legislative conformity with imported laws, the repugnancy test, the creation of new customary laws, and the mix of Islamic laws with custom all ended the constitutional status of custom, as discussed earlier in this chapter; custom was simply subordinated and made part of colonial laws. And unlike in precolonial times, changes in the domain of the customary happened both through the agency of Africans—in their interaction with the colonial states, as well as with each other in light of new circumstances—and through the agency of colonial powers in the process of legitimating and maintaining their colonies.[144] Accordingly, what (de)legitimated custom was the colonial states and the new realities, and not solely their conformity with their respective precolonial constitutional systems. This heralded the disruption and end of indigenous constitutional systems.[145]

137 See Sally Falk Moore, *Social Facts and Fabrications 'Customary' Law on Kilimanjaro, 1880–1980* (Cambridge University Press 1986).

138 Anderson, 'Colonial Law in Tropical Africa' (n 98) 437.

139 Richard Roberts, 'Custom and Muslim Family Law in the Native Courts of the French Soudan, 1905–1912' in Shamil Jeppie, Ebrahim Moosa, and Richard L Roberts (eds), *Muslim Family Law in Sub-Saharan Africa: Colonial Legacies and Post-Colonial Challenges* (Amsterdam University Press 2010) 89–90.

140 ibid 90.

141 Barbara M Cooper, 'Injudicious Intrusions: Chiefly Authority and Islamic Judicial Practice in Maradi, Niger' in Jeppie, Moosa, and Roberts, *Muslim Family Law in Sub-Saharan Africa* (n 139) 187–88.

142 Anderson, 'Colonial Law in Tropical Africa' (n 98) 437–38; Shamil Jeppie, 'The Making and Unmaking of Colonial Sharia in the Sudan' in Jeppie, Moosa, and Roberts, *Muslim Family Law in Sub-Saharan Africa* (n 139) 165.

143 JND Anderson, *Islamic Law in Africa Vol II* (Reprinted edition, Routledge 2008) 1–10.

144 See also Benton, *Law and Colonial Cultures* (n 84) 3–5; Peter Fitzpatrick, 'Terminal Legality: Imperialism and the (De)Composition of Law' in Diane Elizabeth Kirkby and Catharine Coleborne, *Law, History, Colonialism: The Reach of Empire* (Manchester University Press 2001) 9–21.

145 See also Yash Ghai and Jill Cottrell, 'The State and Constitutionalism in Postcolonial Societies in Africa' in Upendra Baxi, Christopher McCrudden, and Abdul Paliwala (eds), *Law's Ethical, Global and Theoretical Contexts: Essays in Honour of William Twining* (Cambridge University Press 2015) 172–73.

III. Constitutionalism in Postcolonial Africa

Constitutionalism in postcolonial Africa has aimed to redeem the legitimacy deficit of the alien origin of the state—through the legal syncretic processes of rejection or negation of the colonial state and its theory of government on the one hand, and the affirmation or acceptance of the colonial state structures on the other—in order to broadcast and channel the fruits of independence and self-determination. While anti-colonial resistance, decolonization, and the materialization of independence all signify the rejection or negation of the colonial state and its *modus operandi,* the continuity of the colonial state makeup—its territorial borders, peoples, and sovereignties—demonstrate the affirmation or acceptance of the colonial legacy. Constitutionally speaking, the independence of African states marked the transfer of government power from the hands of Europeans to the Africans. It is no wonder, then, that the chief purpose and function of constitutions and constitutionalism since independence have been to devise a theory of government that legitimizes government power and authority, and, consequently, enables it to deliver the promises of liberation and self-determination in the postcolonial states. In the following sections, I explore and examine the continuous legal syncretic processes of negation and affirmation of the theory of limited government as presented by the liberal constitutional tradition and the attendant constitutional treatments, as well as the broader constitutional discourse on customary law and traditional authority taking place in postcolonial constitutionalism in Africa. The objective of this discussion is to demonstrate the fact that constitutionalism in postcolonial Africa is neither singular, as legal centralists posit, nor plural, as legal pluralists comfortably claim, but rather legally syncretic. Past constitutional experiences along with present constitutional realities make constitutionalism in postcolonial Africa a blend of constitutional ideas, textures, and meanings that transcend both legal centralists and legal pluralist accounts.

A. The Continuous Negation and Affirmation of Liberal Constitutionalism

Just like the Berlin Conference provided the constitutional basis for the establishment of colonial states in Africa, the independence constitutions heralded the end of colonial states and the birth of new independent and sovereign African states within the community of nations. Unlike the Berlin Conference, however, many of the colonies—with few exceptions[146]—achieved their independence in a bargain, albeit an unequal one, between the former colonizers and the African political elites, and the independence constitutions were the results of these bargains. In sharp contrast to the colonial theory of unlimited government, these independence constitutions incorporated and/or imposed a system of limited government for the newly independent states. Largely

[146] For instance, in some colonies such as Algeria and in Portuguese colonies, independence was achieved through wars of national liberation; see JNC Hill, *Identity in Algerian Politics: The Legacy of Colonial Rule* (Lynne Rienner Publishers 2009) 55–67; Patrick Chabal, 'The Post-Colonial State in Portuguese-Speaking Africa' (1992) 8 Portuguese Studies 189, 192–95.

modeled after the constitutional systems of the former colonizers, the independence constitutions established either a Westminster-style parliamentary system or a presidential system with horizontal—and in some cases vertical—separation of powers with checks and balances and recognized fundamental human rights.[147] Furthermore, they made electoral democracy the only basis for accessing government power and they provided the rules of election as well. Hence, Africa was set to begin its self-government under a system of liberal constitutional democracy.

Aside from the legitimacy deficit of the independence constitutions in general,[148] and the continuity of the Queen of England as the titular head of state for the former British colonies in particular, the theory of government engineered by these constitutions has been defensible in retrospect.[149] This is due to the fact that the quest to have limited government under a system of multi-party democracy as well as the protection of human rights both continue to permeate the constitutional and political struggles of postcolonial Africa to date.[150] As a result, the idea of limited government in the independence constitutions had moral legitimacy, if not sociological legitimacy, at the time.[151] Nonetheless, the desire to manufacture the legitimacy of the new states and governments, and the urge and need to change from a monarchy to a republic in the case of the former British colonies, were understandable.[152] By virtue of their condition, the newly independent states were compelled to overcome the inherent contradictions of being born from colonies while, at the same time, being expected to reimagine independence and operate with a decisive break from their colonial past.[153] In these attempts, the independence constitutions were changed or altered and the idea of limited government and multi-party democracy were rejected as alien and colonial impositions.[154]

Soon after independence, one-party systems replaced multi-party democracy, and personal rule displaced the separation of powers and checks and balances by leaders claiming to fulfill the fruits of independence—nation-building, development, and overall social transformation—and to found and institute a new government based on African autochthonous conceptions and new realities.[155] The new African leaders

[147] Victor T Le Vine, 'The Fall and Rise of Constitutionalism in West Africa' (1997) 35 The Journal of Modern African Studies 181, 184–87; YP Ghai, 'Constitutions and the Political Order in East Africa' (1972) 21 The International and Comparative Law Quarterly 403, 410–13; Robert B Seidman, 'Constitutions in Independent, Anglophonic, Sub-Saharan Africa: Form and Legitimacy' (1969) 1969 Wisconsin Law Review 83.

[148] BO Nwabueze, *Constitutionalism in the Emergent States* (Fairleigh Dickinson University Press 1973) 24–28.

[149] See Robert Mattes and Michael Bratton, 'Do Africans Still Want Democracy?' (Afrobarometer 2016) Afrobarometer Policy Paper No 36, 1–27.

[150] See Eunice N Sahle, 'Introduction' in Eunice N Sahle (ed), *Democracy, Constitutionalism, and Politics in Africa: Historical Contexts, Developments, and Dilemmas* (Springer 2017) 1–4; Peter Anayang Nyong'o, *Popular Struggles for Democracy in Africa* (Zed Books 1987).

[151] A constitution can be morally justifiable if it has an inherent trustworthiness in its substantive standards of justice although it may be imposed. For details see Richard H Fallon, 'Legitimacy and the Constitution' (2005) 118 Harvard Law Review 1787, 1794–96.

[152] Nwabueze, *Constitutionalism in the Emergent States* (n 148) 23.

[153] Leela Gandhi, *Postcolonial Theory: A Critical Introduction* (Allen & Unwin 1998) 6.

[154] Nwabueze, *Constitutionalism in the Emergent States* (n 148) 28–30.

[155] Young, *The Postcolonial State in Africa* (n 143) 16–19; Pal Ahluwalia, *Politics and Post-Colonial Theory: African Inflections* (Routledge 2002) 56–59.

argued that the limited government instituted by the independence constitutions was a hurdle for development, social transformation, and nation—building, in addition to its origin and nature being alien to the African experience. It was contended that an African theory of government would accelerate development, enable government, and bestow upon the state the power and resources it needed to defeat 'Africa's real enemies—ignorance, poverty, and diseases'.[156] In light of these ideas it was claimed that multi-party democracy is a brake and a recipe for tribalism.

Accordingly, one-party systems were constitutionalized and the powers of presidents were enlarged in the new republican constitutions. Such constitutional undertakings were rationalized based on the alleged existence of an African system of government that favors consensus and co-operation over competition, the unity of power over its division, and the centrality of a unifying personality like the kings or chiefs in precolonial times.[157] As discussed elsewhere, this claim is not true not only because there were numerous governance systems in precolonial Africa, but also because they, too, all had inbuilt systems of separation of powers and checks and balances and, consequently, also had a limited theory of government. Nevertheless, the new leaders centralized and personalized both the powers of the government and their political parties, and made themselves the main sources of power and wealth in the newly independent states.[158]

However, the practice of one-party systems and personal rule did not bring economic development and build unified nations, nor did it confer the much-needed legitimacy upon the states and governments.[159] The primacy that personal patronage, loyalty, and dependence around the presidency enjoyed over the constitutional rules and laws with regard to opportunities in politics and business drained the new independent states of any hope for development and progress.[160] The tendency and propensity towards corruption among those in government (the public sector) and their affiliates in business (the private sector), and the similar drive to exit among those marginal to these systems, further weakened the legitimacy of the states and governments.[161] The newly independent states became captive to their new presidents and their cronies, and were ready for capture by their opponents when circumstances permitted. The alleged claims of nation-building and development turned out to be mere justifications for the personal rule of presidents and, at the same time, organizing principles for state capture by their opponents.[162] Furthermore, the ethnic, religious, and

[156] H Kwasi Prempeh, 'Africa's "Constitutionalism Revival": False Start or New Dawn?' (2007) 5 International Journal of Constitutional Law 469, 475.

[157] H Kwasi Prempeh, 'Presidential Power in Comparative Perspective: The Puzzling Persistence of Imperial Presidency in Post-Authoritarian Africa' (2007) 35 Hastings Const LQ 761, 764–65.

[158] See also Robert H Jackson and Carl G Rosberg, *Personal Rule in Black Africa: Prince, Autocrat, Prophet, Tyrant* (University of California Press 1982).

[159] See also Peter Anyang' Nyong'o, 'Africa: The Failure of One-Party Rule' (1992) 3 Journal of Democracy 90, 90–96.

[160] Michael Bratton and Nicholas van de Walle, 'Neopatrimonial Rule Regimes and Political Transitions in Africa' (1994) 46 World Politics 453, 458.

[161] Mamdani, *Citizen and Subject* (n 102) 11.

[162] See Davidson, *The Black Man's Burden* (n 25) 290–94; Liisa Laakso and Adebayo O Olukoshi, 'The Crises of the Post-Colonial Nation-State Project in Africa' in Adebayo O Olukoshi and Liisa Laakso (eds), *Challenges to the Nation-State in Africa* (Nordic Africa Institute 1996) 11–16; Claude Ake, 'The Unique Case of African Democracy' (1993) 69 International Affairs 239, 239.

regional diversities in these newly independent states made one-party systems and personal rule unpalatable and unappealing to many, especially minorities.[163]

As their political elites held these states hostage, the military was invited by the prevailing circumstances—or simply invited itself—into the realm of politics by transforming its role from protecting the territorial integrity of the states to cleansing them of 'incorrigible politicians.'[164] With the exception of few states where one-party autocracies survived, from the late 1960s up to the end of the 1980s, the military took over power from the civilian regimes in the African states.[165] While the military justified its intervention with claims of failure on the part of the constitutional governments, as well as the prevalence of corruption and bad governance on the part of civilian leaders, it subscribed to the theory of government, and used the playbooks, of the very civilian leaders they deposed.[166]

The military leaders aimed to civilize or demilitarize their powers by either adopting a new constitution entirely, or by altering only few parts of the existing one-party state constitutions. They neither had a commitment to practice constitutionalism, nor an interest in transferring power to a civilian regime,[167] nor the will to deliver good government and prevent corruption while in office.[168] It is no wonder, then, that there were eighty successful coups, 108 failed attempts, and 139 reported plots in forty-eight African states between 1956–2001.[169] The ultimate objective of the military leaders was to institutionalize their personal power under a theory of unlimited government, just like their civilian predecessors.[170]

Nonetheless, the general distaste, protest, and struggle against unlimited government at home, and the triumph of liberal democracy abroad with the end of the Cold War,[171] coerced African states to reaffirm and accept liberal constitutionalism with multi-party democracy in the 1990s. Starting in Algeria, with the opening up of multi-party elections in 1988 and followed by the organization of a national conference for democratic transition in Benin in 1990, the 'tsunami of democratization swept over

163 See also Philip Roessler, *Ethnic Politics and State Power in Africa: The Logic of the Coup-Civil War Trap* (Cambridge University Press 2016) 60–81.

164 See Paul Nugent, *Africa Since Independence: A Comparative History* (2nd ed, Palgrave Macmillan 2012) chapter 6; George Klay Kieh, Jr, 'Military Engagement in Politics in Africa' in George Klay Kieh, Jr and Pita Ogaba Agbese (eds), *The Military and Politics in Africa: From Engagement to Democratic and Constitutional Control* (Ashgate 2004) 37–54; Samuel Decalo, 'Military Coups and Military Regimes in Africa' (1973) 11 The Journal of Modern African Studies 105, 105–27.

165 Young, *The Postcolonial State in Africa* (n 143) 16–19.

166 See also Samuel Decalo, *Coups and Army Rule in Africa: Studies in Military Style* (Yale University Press 1976).

167 Even if the military handed over power to the civilian regimes after the military coup in Ghana and Nigeria, they recaptured power from the civilian regimes again; Nugent, *Africa Since Independence* (n 164) chapter 6.

168 HWO Okoth-Ogendo, 'Constitutions without Constitutionalism: Reflections on an African Political Paradox' in Douglass Greenberg and others (eds), *Constitutionalism and Democracy: Transitions in the Contemporary World* (Oxford University Press 1993) 78.

169 Patrick J McGowan, 'African Military Coups d'état, 1956–2001: Frequency, Trends and Distribution' (2003) 41 The Journal of Modern African Studies 339, 339; See also GS Mmaduabuchi Okeke, 'Theories of Military in African Politics,' in Samuel Ojo Oloruntoba and Toyin Falola, *The Palgrave Handbook of African Politics, Governance and Development* (Palgrave Macmillan 2018) 219–36.

170 Okoth-Ogendo, 'Constitutions without Constitutionalism' (n 168) 78.

171 See Francis Fukuyama, *The End of History and the Last Man* (The Free Press 1992).

Africa' throughout the 1990s.[172] For better or worse, multi-party democracy, with its protection of some fundamental human rights under a constitutionally limited government, has been put forward to address the troubles of post-independence, including political instability, dictatorship, bad governance, grave violation of human rights, corruption, and pervasive poverty. With few exceptions,[173] the majority of African states revised or adopted brand new constitutions that incorporated and affirmed the principles of democratic politics, established independent constitutional review systems along with independent constitutional institutions, and recognized fundamental human rights and freedoms.

Even though the post-Cold War African constitutions have had more vitality and a stronger influence in shaping and taming the actions and behaviors of African governments than the previous constitutions, they, too, have carried over the authoritarian textures of their predecessors and managed to negate many of the liberal constitutional promises and commitments. On the one hand, in addition to affirming the idea of limited government in a constitutional democracy as a matter of constitutional law and politics, these constitutions also helped bring about the peaceful transfer of power through elections, end the tenure of presidents for life, enable courts to annul unconstitutional legislative and executive actions and decisions,[174] contributed to the emergence of the nascent free media and civil society, and created the space for the practice of human rights.[175] On the other hand, however, despite these positive developments, multiple decades of these constitutional experiments have led to the development of dominant and single-party systems,[176] maintained authoritarian rules and practices,[177] and faced the resurgence of personal rule,[178] and sometimes even military coups.[179] Thus, as Michel Rosenfeld noted, the postcolonial constitutional experiment

[172] Young, *The Postcolonial State in Africa* (n 143) 26–27; see also Samuel P Huntington, *The Third Wave: Democratization in the Late Twentieth Century* (University of Oklahoma Press 1993).

[173] For instance, Botswana only revised its 1966 Constitution in 2005.

[174] Recently, the Supreme Court of Kenya annuls the presidential election result for election irregularities ordering reelection. See *Raila Amolo Odinga and another v Independent Electoral and Boundaries Commission and others* [2017] Supreme Court of Kenya, Presidential Petition No 1 of 2017. See also Rachel Ellett, *Pathways to Judicial Power in Transitional States: Perspectives from African Courts* (Routledge 2013) 6–7.

[175] Prempeh, 'Africa's "Constitutionalism Revival"' (n 156) 471–72.

[176] Gero Erdmann and Matthias Basedau, 'An Overview of African Party Systems' in Renske Doorenspleet and Lia Nijzink (eds), *One-Party Dominance in African Democracies* (Lynne Rienner Publishers 2010) 25–46; Matthijs Bogaards, 'Counting Parties and Identifying Dominant Party Systems in Africa' (2004) 43 European Journal of Political Research 173, 173–97.

[177] See Gabrielle Lynch and Gordon Crawford, 'Democratization in Africa 1990–2010: An Assessment' (2011) 18 Democratization 275, 275–310.

[178] See Oda van Cranenburgh, '"Big Men" Rule: Presidential Power, Regime Type and Democracy in 30 African Countries' (2008) 15 Democratization 952, 952–73; Larry Diamond, 'The Rule of Law versus the Big Man' (2008) 19 Journal of Democracy 138, 138–49.

[179] For instance Niger (2010), Mali (2012), Guinea Bissau (2012), Lesotho (2014), and Burkina Faso (2017) had military coups; see Virginie Baudais and Grégory Chauzal, 'The 2010 Coup d'état in Niger: A Praetorian Regulation of Politics?' (2011) 110 African Affairs 295, 295–304; Adam Nossiter, 'Soldiers Overthrow Mali Government' *The New York Times* (22 March 2012) <https://wwwnytimescom/2012/03/23/world/africa/mali-coup-france-calls-for-electionshtml> accessed 16 November 2018; Adam Nossiter, 'Guinea-Bissau Coup Removes Presidential Front-Runner' *The New York Times* (13 April 2012) <https://wwwnytimescom/2012/04/14/world/africa/guinea-bissau-coup-removes-presidential-front-runnerhtml> accessed 16 November 2018; Everisto Benyera, 'Towards an Explanation of the Recurrence of Military Coups in Lesotho' (2017) 3 ASPJ Africa & Francophonie 56, 56–73; Hervé Taoko, 'African Leaders Call for Reinstatement of

in Africa is a dialectic process—one that involves a continuous affirmation and absorption of liberal constitutionalism as implanted on the eve of independence, and a negation and rejection of the same—while these states operate in a system of constitutional government.[180] In this dialectic process of negation and affirmation, as discussed in the next chapter, the theory of government focuses more on changing the office holder than reforming the office itself.

B. Customary Law and Traditional Authority in Postcolonial Constitutions

In the dialectic continuum of the negation and affirmation of liberal constitutionalism in postcolonial Africa, the constitutional treatment of customary laws and traditional authorities present a paradox to the theory of government as advanced by African civilian and military leaders. The paradox arises, firstly, in the claims by African leaders to be instituting a government based on the African autochthonous political traditions while simultaneously rejecting and/or undermining customary laws and traditional authorities. While post-independence leaders retrieved an alleged African theory of government that bestows unified political power upon the chief executive of the state,[181] they rejected, at worst, and undermined, at best, the usefulness of customary laws and traditional authorities to the postcolonial states with claims of their incompatibility with modernity and the theory of the nation-state.[182] Secondly, the affirmation of liberal constitutionalism and multi-party democracy in the post-1990 constitutions have brought customary laws and traditional authorities into the constitutional space as the alleged African theory of government was negated and the idea of the nation-state withered away. In this section I discuss and present the constitutional treatment of customary laws and traditional authorities in postcolonial constitutions, and in the following section I examine and explore the general constitutional debates about customary laws and traditional authorities in the postcolonial states.

The independence constitutions adopted three major approaches with respect to customary laws and traditional authorities.[183] The first approach, which was applied mainly in Anglophone Africa,[184] was to maintain the colonial legal systems which recognized the application of customary laws and the powers of traditional authorities. The second approach, which was mainly followed in Francophone and Lusophone Africa, was to abolish the colonial customary or native courts and to establish a general court

President of Burkina Faso' *The New York Times* (21 December 2017) <https://wwwnytimescom/2015/09/23/world/africa/military-coup-burkina-fasohtml> accessed 16 November 2018.

180 Michel Rosenfeld, 'Constitutional Identity' in Michel Rosenfeld and András Sajó (eds), *The Oxford Handbook of Comparative Constitutional Law* (Oxford University Press 2012) 766; Michel Rosenfeld, *The Identity of the Constitutional Subject: Selfhood, Citizenship, Culture, and Community* (Routledge 2010) 179–80.

181 BO Nwabueze, *Presidentialism in Commonwealth Africa* (St Martin's Press 1974) 106.

182 Davidson, *The Black Man's Burden* (n 25) 99–107.

183 Fareda Banda, *Women, Law and Human Rights: An African Perspective* (Hart Publishing 2005) 20.

184 See also Lloyd Fallers, 'Customary Law in the New African States' (1962) 27 Law and Contemporary Problems 605, 606–16.

system which also applied customary laws. And the third approach was to adopt an integrated court system where customary courts handled the first instance customary law claims, while higher courts reviewed their decisions through appeal. Given that traditional authorities were considered as the custodian of customary laws, the recognition of these customary laws implied the concomitant recognition of the powers of traditional authorities—at least in the states that followed the first and third approaches. In many of these states, in addition to the judicial powers possessed by the traditional authorities as it related to the adjudication of customary laws, the traditional authorities were also incorporated into the state administration through regionalism (Ghana and Kenya), federalism (Nigeria and Uganda), constitutional monarchy (Swaziland and Lesotho), and chieftaincy (Zambia and Zimbabwe).[185] The independence constitutions recognized customary laws and traditional authorities subject to their constitutional conformity. Needless to say, the constitutional role and influence of traditional authorities varied not only across states, but also within states at the central and regional levels.[186] Traditional authorities had much more power and influence at regional levels, particularly on matters of land, family, and personal issues. In short, the independence constitutions were open to accommodating customary laws and traditional authorities in the constitutional governments of the newly independent states.

The constitutions of the one-party systems and military regimes, however, either rejected or seriously undermined the role and status of customary laws and traditional authorities. As their objective was building a nation-state, the ethnic diversity of these states and their respective customary laws and traditional authorities were suppressed, or repressed by the leaders. The constitution, and for that matter all laws, policies, and development interventions, were tools for creating a homogeneous political entity rather than serving as accommodation mechanisms for the actual diversity of these states.[187] Moreover, colonial languages were adopted as national languages and their usage was aggressively promoted, while the teaching of local languages was abolished.[188] Social, political, and legal pluralism were all abandoned in the unitary projects of nation-building. New unifying ideologies under new leaders, such as *Ujamma* (Julius Nyerere), *Authenticité* (Mobutu Sese Seko), variants of *African socialism* (Sékou Touré and Kwame Nkrumah), *African humanism* (Kenneth Kaunda), and *Harambee* (Jomo Kenyatta), substituted the role and function of customary laws and traditional authorities.[189] As a result, the application of customary laws and traditional authorities was abolished in some states, such as Burkina Faso, Tanzania, and Mozambique, while seriously limited in others, such as Ghana, Nigeria, and Zimbabwe.[190]

[185] Okoth-Ogendo, 'Constitutions without Constitutionalism' (n 168) 71; Seidman, 'Constitutions in Independent, Anglophonic, Sub-Saharan Africa' (n 147) 95–96.

[186] Seidman, 'Constitutions in Independent, Anglophonic, Sub-Saharan Africa' (n 147) 95.

[187] See also Benyamin Neurberger, 'State and Nation in African Thought' in John Hutchinson and Anthony D Smith (eds), *Nationalism* (Oxford University Press 1994) 231–35.

[188] Solomon A Dersso, *Taking Ethno-Cultural Diversity Seriously in Constitutional Design: A Theory of Minority Rights for Addressing Africa's Multi-Ethnic Challenge* (Martinus Nijhoff Publishers 2012) 68.

[189] Laakso and Olukoshi, 'The Crises of the Post-Colonial Nation-State Project in Africa' (n 162) 14–15.

[190] See Lars Buur and Helene Maria Kyed, 'Contested Sources of Authority: Re-Claiming State Sovereignty by Formalizing Traditional Authority in Mozambique' (2006) 37 Development & Change 847, 850–51; Banda, *Women, Law and Human Rights* (n 183) 21; Englebert (n 28) 51; Richard Rathbone, *Nkrumah & the Chiefs: The Politics of Chieftaincy in Ghana, 1951–60* (Ohio State University Press 2000); EI

Customary laws and traditional authorities showed some resurgence after the end of the one-party systems and military regimes, and figure prominently in the post-1990 constitutions.[191] In many of these constitutions—such as in Ethiopia, Ghana, Malawi, Mozambique, Namibia, Niger, Nigeria, South Africa, and Uganda, just to mention a few—specific constitutional provisions are allotted to customary laws and traditional authorities.[192] Additionally, the recognition of the right to culture in many of the African constitutions opens the opportunity for the application of customary laws and the exercise of traditional powers by traditional authorities.[193] Moreover, along with customary laws, Islamic law was also recognized in many African states with significant Muslim populations.[194] The trend of recognition and accommodation of customary laws, Islamic law, and traditional authorities continues in the recent waves of constitution-making in Africa.[195] The new constitutions of Angola, Kenya, Zambia, Zimbabwe, and South Sudan all recognize customary and/or Islamic laws and traditional authorities.[196] While the specific subject matter and procedures of application differ in every state, customary and Islamic laws are generally applicable in personal and family matters.[197] Similarly, despite differences in their roles and influence, the powers of traditional authorities are usually confined to the domain of the customary, and their power waxes in the rural areas and wanes in the urban.

Thus, in terms of approach, postcolonial constitutional treatment of customary laws and traditional authorities shares many commonalities with their colonial constitutional treatment. This is due to the fact that the colonial state originally wanted to replace customary laws with imported laws during direct rule—at least by denying them official recognition—which is also what the post-independence leaders attempted to do in their nation-state projects. In addition, the recognition of customary laws and traditional authorities in the colonial state (during the system of indirect rule and association) was conditional upon their conformity with the written colonial laws and their ability to pass the repugnancy test; in a similar vein, in the postcolonial state (in the system of constitutional democracy) they have to conform to constitutional standards. The recognition of traditional authorities—both in the colonial and postcolonial state—is in itself an act

Nwogugu, 'Abolition of Customary Courts—The Nigerian Experiment' (1976) 20 Journal of African Law 1, 1–19.

191 Katrina Cuskelly, 'Customs and Constitutions: State Recognition of Customary Law around the World' (International Union for Conservation of Nature and Natural Resources 2011) 6–11 <https://portalsiucnorg/library/efiles/documents/2011-101pdf> accessed 8 March 2017.

192 Ndulo, 'African Customary Law, Customs, and Women's Rights' (n 125) 98–101; Akua Kuenyehia, 'Women, Marriage, and Intestate Succession in the Context of Legal Pluralism in Africa' (2006) 40 UC Davis L Rev 385, 399–401.

193 Barbara Oomen, *Chiefs in South Africa: Law, Power & Culture in the Post-Apartheid Era* (James Currey 2005) 50–58; Harri Englund, 'Introduction: Recognizing Identities, Imagining Alternatives' in Harri Englund and Francis B Nyamnjoh, *Rights and the Politics of Recognition in Africa* (Zed Books 2004) 1–29; Bennett, *Customary Law in South Africa* (n 50) 1–24.

194 Abdullahi Ahmed An-Na'im, *African Constitutionalism and the Role of Islam* (University of Pennsylvania Press 2006) 8–16.

195 See also Gedion T Hessebon, 'The Fourth Constitution-Making Wave of Africa: Constitutions 40?' (2014) 28 Temple International & Comparative Law Journal 185, 189–90.

196 M Christian Green, 'Religious and Legal Pluralism in Recent African Constitutional Reform' (2013) 28 Journal of Law and Religion 401, 432–39.

197 Banda, *Women, Law and Human Rights* (n 183) 34–36.

of subordination to their precolonial position. Even though constitutional design fails to attend to constitutional practice, the subordination of customary laws and traditional authorities is undoubtedly a constitutional reality in Africa today. In the next section I explain why this is so by engaging with the general constitutional discourse in Africa, with a particular emphasis on customary laws and traditional authorities.

C. Customary Law and Traditional Authority in the Postcolonial Constitutional Discourse

The postcolonial discourse on customary laws and traditional authorities has two strands involving the legal syncretic processes of rejection, acceptance, incorporation, and accommodation. The first strand of the debate is related to a larger postcolonial discourse that deals with what course the postcolonial state and its people should take in order to achieve liberation and self-determination in the full sense of these terms. This, in turn, has four major themes. The first calls for the complete redrawing of the maps in Africa—either going back to precolonial times or forming a new political geography based on African terms and African values. The second proposes a new African theory of government within the existing borders that would redeem the illegitimate origin and logic of the state and enable it to serve the needs, rights, and interests of its people. The third posits liberal constitutionalism as the future of the postcolonial state and its people. And the fourth calls for the contextualization of liberal constitutionalism within African values, realities, and needs.

The second strand of the debate on customary laws and traditional authorities is related to their constitutional (non)recognition and their empirical applications and manifestations—with or without official state recognition. In the paragraphs that follow, I explore how customary laws and traditional authorities figure in these debates and themes, and examine their role, status, and function in the postcolonial state.

A strong case for customary laws and traditional authorities exists in the aforementioned theme that calls for the rejection of the postcolonial state and the complete redrawing of its borders.[198] It is argued that the postcolonial state is incapable of salvation or redemption in its current form as it was established and maintained as an apparatus of violence in order to serve the colonial and imperial powers during and after colonialism.[199] It is contended that the very logic and mode of operation of the postcolonial state is alien to Africans, did not serve them well in the past, and will not serve them in the future.[200] The importation of democracy, human rights, and constitutionalism at independence have not rectified the violence inherent in the makeup of the

[198] Laurence Caromba, 'Redrawing the Map of Southern Africa? A Critical Analysis of the Arguments for the Unification of South Africa and Lesotho' (2017) 44 Politikon: South African Journal of Political Studies 93, 93–109; Muiu and Martin, *A New Paradigm of the African State* (n 4) 193–205; Pita Ogaba Agbese and George Klay Kieh Jr, 'State Renewal in Africa: The Lessons' in Pita Ogaba Agbese and George Klay Kieh Jr (eds), *Reconstituting the State in Africa* (Palgrave Macmillan 2007) 279–93; Kelechi A Kalu, 'The Political Economy of State Reconstitution in Africa' in Obioma M Iheduru, *Contending Issues in African Development: Advances, Challenges, and the Future* (Greenwood Press 2001) 34–39; Mutua, 'Why Redraw the Map of Africa' (n 88) 1113–76.

[199] Mutua, 'Why Redraw the Map of Africa' (n 88) 1160–62.

[200] Muiu and Martin, *A New Paradigm of the African State* (n 4) 193–94.

postcolonial state, nor have they tamed the raw violence of its government. Moreover, these liberal ideas as developed in a particular socio-economic, cultural, and political condition have inherent limitations, both in legitimating the fundamentally illegitimate postcolonial state as well as in responding to its pressing challenges and the problems facing the peoples of Africa.[201] The postcolonial state—undemocratic, illegitimate, and alien at its core by its very nature, form, and substance—is impossible to democratize without completely unscrambling, disassembling, or dismantling it.[202]

The democratization of Africa, therefore, starts with the dismantling of the physical barriers and confinements of the colonial borders that delineate the postcolonial states, and then continues with the subsequent reconfiguration of precolonial African ideas and principles of government onto these new geographical spaces. Going back to African roots and thinking through African epistemology, it is claimed, will herald the African renaissance and true liberation. In this process of renewal and reformation of the postcolonial state and its theory of government, a high premium is given to the idea of custom and traditional authority as practiced in precolonial times.

Customary laws and traditional authorities also figure prominently, albeit less radically, in the second theme which aims to institute an African theory of government within the postcolonial state as currently formed. The main argument that runs through this theme is that a theory of government based on African ideas, values, principles, and practices is necessary in order to legitimize the postcolonial state, hold its government accountable, deliver development, and arrest the pressing socio-economic, political, and cultural challenges of Africans.[203] It is held that a theory of government based on African values would have a cultural appeal, practical utility, and a diagnostic capacity for the ills and misfortunes of liberal democracy.[204]

To this end, a consensual democracy in a 'non-party polity' is proposed, while liberal democracy with its multi-party system is rejected.[205] The case for a consensual democracy is made building on the African tradition of consensus in decision-making, the culture of inclusive participation, the general responsiveness of participants to striking a balance between individual and communal interests, and the resultant compromise and harmony in the outcomes of the decisions.[206] It is surmised that multi-party democracy with its spirit of competition in the process, and the production of winners and losers in the outcome, is fundamentally unfit for the postcolonial state with its diverse religious, linguistic, and ethnic composition.[207]

201 Makau Mutua, *Human Rights Standards: Hegemony, Law, and Politics* (State University of New York Press 2016) 165–183; Mutua, 'Africa and the Rule of Law' (n 265); Mutua, *Human Rights* (n 47) 126–53.

202 Mutua, 'Why Redraw the Map of Africa' (n 88) 1162; Makau wa Mutua, 'Putting Humpty Dumpty Back Together Again: The Dilemmas of the Post-Colonial African State' (1995) 21 Brooklyn Journal of International Law 505, 534–36.

203 Ake, 'The Unique Case of African Democracy' (n 162) 239–44; Claude Ake, 'Rethinking African Democracy' (1991) 2 Journal of Democracy 32, 32–44.

204 See Claude Ake, *Democracy and Development in Africa* (Brookings Institution Press 2001) 132–39.

205 Kwasi Wiredu, 'Democracy and Consensus in African Traditional Politics: A Plea for a Non-Party Polity' (1995) 39 The Centennial Review 53, 53–64.

206 Kwasi Wiredu, 'Democracy by Consensus: Some Conceptual Considerations' (2001) 30 Philosophical Papers 227, 227–44; Gyekye, *Tradition and Modernity* (n 56) 259–60.

207 See Tukumbi Lumumba-Kasongo, 'The Problematics of Liberal Democracy and Democratic Process: Lessons for Deconstructing and Building African Democracies' in Tukumbi Lumumba-Kasongo

Furthermore, it is claimed that multi-party democracy, with its majoritarian primacy, configures—both by design and effect—a deep sense of exclusion, alienation, and hostility among the diverse ethno-linguistic groups, especially given the numerical composition of the groups that inhabit the postcolonial state.[208] The African theory of government, in contrast to liberal democracy, channels a form of economic and social democracy that brings socio-economic improvement to the African people on the one hand, and focuses on people-centered participation and engagement with the state on the other.[209] The idea of customary laws and traditional authorities is at the heart of this quest for an African theory of government as it endeavors to offer an appropriate governance system for the postcolonial state and aspires to (re)connect it with the African cultural universe.[210]

In contrast to the first and second themes, customary laws and traditional authorities have a limited role and function in the third theme which posits liberal constitutionalism and democracy as a panacea for the challenges and problems of the postcolonial state. It is argued that even though the African state has a foreign and colonial origin, we need a system of limited government that can ensure accountability and responsibility, while also protecting fundamental human rights and civil liberties as long as the state exists.[211] Without the system of liberal constitutionalism and multiparty democracy, an ordered life and liberty, along with good governance, the rule of law, and development—among other aspirations of Africans—would be difficult to achieve in the postcolonial state.[212] Just as driving a car requires the use of seatbelts and an understanding of traffic rules in order to avoid accidents, the operation of a modern state needs a liberal constitutional system and the observance of the will of the people as manifested in regular elections—the lack of which have bedeviled postcolonial states ever since independence.[213]

While the state has a commitment to having a written constitution as a basis for its sovereign existence, if not for its operation, what is mainly required is the actual practice of the written constitution.[214] Moreover, in light of its tortuous constitutional past,

(ed), *Liberal Democracy and Its Critics in Africa: Political Dysfunction and the Struggle for Progress* (Zed Books 2005) 1–22.

[208] Kwasi Wiredu, *Cultural Universals and Particulars: An African Perspective* (Indiana University Press 1996) 177, 182–90; See also Claude Ake, *The Feasibility of Democracy in Africa* (Council for the Development of Social Science Research in Africa 2000).

[209] Issa G Shivji, *Where Is Uhuru?: Reflections on the Struggle for Democracy in Africa* (Fahamu/Pambazuka 2009) 60–63.

[210] Gyekye, *Tradition and Modernity* (n 56) 234–37.

[211] Yash Ghai, 'Chimera of Constitutionalism: State, Economy, and Society in Africa' in Swati Deva (eds), *Law and (In) Equalities: Contemporary Perspectives* (Eastern Book Company 2010) 313–331; Yash Pal Ghai, 'Creating a New Constitutional Order: Kenya's Predicament' in W Gachenga, G Franceschi, and Migai Akech (eds), *Governance, Institutions and the Human Condition* (LawAfrica Publishing 2009) 18–30.

[212] HWO Okoth-Ogendo, 'The Quest for Constitutional Government' in Göran Hydén, Dele Olowu, and HWO Okoth-Ogendo (eds), *African Perspectives on Governance* (Africa World Press 2000) 43–58; Okoth-Ogendo, 'Constitutions without Constitutionalism' (n 168) 65–84.

[213] See also Wiktor Osiatyński, *Human Rights and Their Limits* (Cambridge University Press 2009) 161.

[214] Prempeh, 'Africa's "Constitutionalism Revival"' (n 156) 486–94; H Kwasi Prempeh, 'Marbury in Africa: Judicial Review and the Challenge of Constitutionalism in Contemporary Africa' (2007) 80 Tulane Law Review 42–84; Okoth-Ogendo, 'Constitutions without Constitutionalism' (n 168) 65–84; HWO Okoth-Ogendo, 'The Politics of Constitutional Change in Kenya Since Independence, 1963-69' (1972) 71 African Affairs 9, 33–34; Nwabueze, *Constitutionalism in the Emergent States* (n 148) 300–07.

a constitutional system should be engineered that (a) effectively limits the power of the executive branch through the reduction of presidential powers, term limits, judicial review, and decentralization; (b) empowers the legislature through the control of the legislative agendas and various oversight mechanisms; (c) ensures the independence of the judiciary; (d) fosters the practice of human rights, free media, and civil society; and (e) advances democracy, accountability, and transparency through the establishment of independent constitutional institutions.[215]

The common thread that runs through this theme is the prescription of liberal constitutionalism and multi-party democracy for the constitutional challenges and problems of the postcolonial state.[216] In this theme, customary laws and traditional authorities have a role and function only if they are compatible with these liberal constitutional ideals, or else they are rejected or put aside.

In the fourth theme, however, which calls for the contextualization of constitutionalism in Africa, customary laws and traditional authorities in their many facets are reconfigured and retrieved. The central claim of this theme is that constitutionalism will not take root in Africa unless it takes into account African values and realities in both its normative articulation and institutional design. It holds that the lack of cultural content and context, along with other factors, have contributed to the tragic failure of constitutionalism and democracy in the two decades following independence, and to their continuous fragility since the 1990s with the return of multi-party democracy.[217] The postcolonial state, being a foreign creation itself and still struggling to gain legitimacy, cannot simply wish away the African systems of government, or its laws and practices, and substitute them with some liberal constitutional templates developed in Western historicity.[218] At the same time, the postcolonial state cannot reject liberal constitutional ideas simply because they emerged in a foreign land, provided that these ideas are open to contestation and reconceptualization in light of the given socio-cultural, economic, and political contexts.[219]

The theoretically defensible and practically sensible way to advance and foster constitutional government is to incorporate the historical, social, and political experiences of every postcolonial state—not only in the normative and institutional conception of constitutionalism, but also in its practical assessment.[220] As a result, the African worldview and culture should inform and permeate the entire spectrum of constitutional government—including the notion and practice of human rights, democracy, development, environment, and gender relations—otherwise a sustainable constitutional government will simply be wishful thinking.[221] Hence, customary laws

[215] Fombad (n 16) 1035–89; Prempeh, 'Africa's "Constitutionalism Revival"' (n 156) 494–505; H Kwasi Prempeh, 'African Judges, in Their Own Cause: Reconstituting Independent Courts in Contemporary Africa' (2006) 4 International Journal of Constitutional Law 592, 598–604.

[216] Prempeh, 'Africa's "Constitutionalism Revival"' (n 156) 485.

[217] See Deng, *Identity, Diversity, and Constitutionalism in Africa* (n 56) 195.

[218] See also Gedion Timothewos Hessebon, *Contextualizing Constitutionalism: Multiparty Democracy in the African Political Matrix* (Eleven International Publishing 2017) 185–91.

[219] An-Na'im, *African Constitutionalism and the Role of Islam* (n 194) 16–20.

[220] ibid 27–30.

[221] Deng, *Identity, Diversity, and Constitutionalism in Africa* (n 56) chapters 8 and 9; Ali Mazrui, 'Constitutional Change and Cultural Engineering: Africa's Search for New Directions' in Joseph Oloka-Onyango (ed), *Constitutionalism in Africa: Creating Opportunities, Facing Challenges* (Fountain Publishers 2001) 18–36.

and traditional authorities, along with their numerous manifestations, are given due consideration in this quest for the contextualization of constitutionalism in Africa.

With the exception of the first theme, variants of these general normative arguments on the role and function of customary laws and traditional authorities in postcolonial Africa have been used as justifications for the (non)recognition of said customary laws and traditional authorities in the constitutions. As noted in the previous section, the quest for an African theory of government by the post-independence leaders led to the rejection of customary laws and traditional authorities as they existed in colonial Africa, and to the incorporation of some customary and traditional principles of government into the normative conceptions and institutional architectures of the constitutions. Similarly, the implantation of liberal constitutionalism at independence and its return in the 1990s have led to the resurgence of customary laws and traditional authorities in the constitutions of many African states. Liberal constitutional arguments, such as the recognition of cultural pluralism and democratization on the one hand, and the quest for the contextualization of constitutionalism, ie, the Africanization of constitutionalism on the other, have contributed to the recognition of customary laws and traditional authorities in the post-1990 constitutions.[222]

Beyond these general normative arguments on the role and function of customary laws and traditional authorities and their constitutional (non)recognition in postcolonial Africa, there is an empirical state of affairs in which customary laws and traditional authorities exist and operate. Despite differences in breadth and width, they have always had a stronghold in the so-called collapsed or failed states, the weak states, as well as the relatively stable and democratic states, ever since independence.[223] The empirical applications and manifestations of customary laws and traditional authorities transcend the normative arguments advanced in their support or opposition, as well as the constitutional texts that either define their scope and extent or deny their very application. In the postcolonial condition that customary laws and traditional authorities find themselves, their actors and machinery are neither equal partners to the state, nor do they have the ambition to be so, nor do they consider themselves as distinctively different and separate from the state or its constitutional order. Herein lies one of the puzzles of the postcolonial state which the next chapter attempts to decrypt.

IV. Conclusion

Through the lens of legal syncretism, this chapter unearthed the constitutional matrix that sets in motion the transformation and development of African constitutionalism

[222] David Pimentel, 'Legal Pluralism in Post-Colonial Africa: Linking Statutory and Customary Adjudication in Mozambique' (2011) 14 Yale Hum Rts & Dev LJ 59, 61–69; Helene Maria Kyed and Lars Buur, 'Introduction: Traditional Authority and Democratization in Africa' in Lars Buur and Helene Maria Kyed (eds), *State Recognition and Democratization in Sub-Saharan Africa: A New Dawn for Traditional Authorities* (Palgrave Macmillan 2007) 1–24; Englebert (n 28) 51–52; Peter Skalník, 'Authority Versus Power: Democracy in Africa Must Include Original African Institutions' (1996) 28 The Journal of Legal Pluralism and Unofficial Law 109, 109–19.

[223] Godsglory O Ifezue, 'Understanding Chieftainship in Botswana: The Status and Powers of Chiefs in Present Day Botswana' (2015) 59 Journal of African Law 271, 271–93; J Michael Williams, *Chieftaincy, the State, and Democracy: Political Legitimacy in Post-Apartheid South Africa* (Indiana University Press 2010) 217–18; Kyed and Buur (n 222) 4–5.

from precolonial times to the present. The genealogical orientation of legal syncretism provides the necessary analytical tools and resources with which to retrieve and register the African experience of constitutionalism in precolonial times as the first element in the constitutional matrix. This, in turn, rectifies one of the epistemological problems associated with legal centralism, namely, that Africa was pre-constitution before European colonialism. Similarly, by presenting international law into the African constitutional matrix, legal syncretism captures theoretical and practical insights that escaped the attention of legal pluralism, for the latter focuses exclusively on the dynamics of customary, religious, and imported European laws within the colonial and postcolonial states.

Using legal syncretism, this chapter also demonstrates that precolonial Africa experienced and hosted numerous indigenous constitutional systems that considered custom as their normative order and traditional government as their institutional setup. With the aid of international law, however, these indigenous constitutional systems were aborted, rejected, and formally subordinated with the conclusion of the Berlin Conference. By considering the General Act of the Berlin Conference as a basic law, European colonial powers introduced their own colonial constitutional systems to Africa. In addition to dissolving the operation of indigenous constitutional systems, the colonial constitutional systems significantly transformed the nature of custom and traditional authority through acts of rejection, accommodation, and invention.

Accepting the colonially constituted states, the postcolonial constitutional systems have been grappling with devising a theory of government that legitimates the newly independent states and addresses their pressing challenges and needs. In these attempts, the postcolonial constitutional systems have been engaging with the continuous legal syncretic processes of negation and affirmation of liberal constitutionalism on the one hand, and the rejection, accommodation, and tolerance of customary laws and traditional authorities on the other. These constitutional transformations and developments have been informed by the interactions, changes, and reconfigurations of constitutional ideas, principles, and practices from the indigenous, colonial, international, and liberal constitutional systems and experiences. These legal syncretic processes, in turn, bring a blend of constitutional ideas, principles, and practices into the constitutional designs and practices, which the following chapter examines.

3
The Design and Practice of African Constitutionalism

Chapter 2 has demonstrated how legal syncretism animates African constitutional transformations and developments across time and place. This chapter continues to explore and examine how *legal syncretism as a result* permeates the design and practice of African constitutionalism. By taking the constitutional structures and rights seriously, as well as their practical applications, this chapter attempts to decrypt the identity, nature, and texture of African constitutionalism through legal syncretism. The first section explicates the nature of the African state and its various modalities of organization, the second section examines the African government architecture, and the final section investigates the constitutional rights regime. Through a closer look at the texts and contexts of constitutions and constitutionalism in Africa, and building on social, legal, constitutional, political, and international relations theories, this chapter aims to reveal the distinctive features of African constitutionalism. The overarching objective of this chapter is to underscore why appreciating the syncretic features of African constitutionalism is necessary in order to understand, improve, and foster constitutionalism on the continent.

I. The African State and its Vertical Organization

Based on the dominant theories of state, as discussed in Chapter 1, the African state is often described as weak, fragile, a quasi-state, immature, or a state by simple courtesy of international law. This book challenges this conventional view and presents an alternative theory. I argue that the African state is neither weak and bifurcated, nor is it a quasi-state, or a state by simple courtesy of international law, but rather a syncretic state that has a syncretic sense of morality, justice, and rationality which emanates from its unique use of international law along with some tenets of the indigenous constitutional systems in order to establish and maintain itself.

In order to develop this theory of state, in this section I explore and evaluate the nature, identity, and texture of the African state and its various modalities of organization. I show how African constitutionalism uses international law and some tenets of indigenous constitutional systems to constitute or establish the African state, and how these elements, in turn, bring about a state with a different power configuration and expression than the Weberian state. Additionally, I demonstrate how the syncretic nature of the African state blends and fuses—in its constitutional design and practice—federal and unitary systems of organization into its vertical division of powers.

A Theory of African Constitutionalism. Berihun Adugna Gebeye, Oxford University Press. © Berihun Adugna Gebeye 2021.
DOI: 10.1093/oso/9780192893925.003.0004

A. The *Constitution* of the African State

Without understanding the anatomy of the African state, it is difficult to comprehend and explain its constitutional system. Thus, in order to understand the nature and/or anatomy of the African state, as well its *constitution* and mode of operation, I will first examine how the African state is explained and described in social, political, and international relations theory.[1] By doing so, my objective is to show the limitations of these theories in explaining the nature of the African state and, subsequently, to construct a constitutional framework based on legal syncretism that accounts for its complexities of *constitution* and mode of operation. For this purpose, I would like to identify three major themes within which the nature of the African state has been discussed: the 'two publics' thesis, the 'weak state' thesis, and the 'state survival' thesis. As the focus of the discussion here is on the structural anatomy of the state, the particular ways in which the state acts are excluded and will be considered in the later sections related to its system of government.

The 'two publics' thesis, proposed by Peter P Ekeh, has been an influential account of the nature of the African state.[2] Ekeh posits that the African state hosts two publics with different relationships with the private realm. The first public is based on 'primordial groupings, ties, and sentiments [that] influence and determine the individual's public behavior'.[3] This primordial public—which is mainly based on ethnic affiliation—'is moral and operates on the same moral imperatives as the private realm'.[4] The individual in the primordial public considers their duties as a moral obligation in order to benefit and sustain their own primordial public.[5] The second public is the civic public implanted by the colonial state and is based on the civic structures of the colonial state, such as the military, the civil service, and the police.[6] Unlike the primordial public, the civic public is amoral to the private realm. Accordingly, the individual emphasizes their rights in their engagement with the civic public by de-emphasizing their attendant duties.[7] As there is no moral urge on the part of the individual to give back to the civic public, the civic public is up for grabs or capture for the enrichment of the primordial public. Ekeh contends that while the two publics share similar actors, they are essentially rivals as they each operate with a fundamentally different and opposite sense of morality, justice, and rationality.[8]

Building on Ekeh's two publics thesis, and drawing from Michel Foucault's theory of governmentality, Wale Adebanwi argues that the African state is 'neither real nor illusory', but rather a 'transactional reality'.[9] As such, the public is always up for capture,

[1] To the best of my knowledge, there is no legal or constitutional theory of the state in Africa. The legal and constitutional law scholarship takes the state for granted.

[2] Peter P Ekeh, 'Colonialism and the Two Publics in Africa: A Theoretical Statement' (1975) 17 Comparative Studies in Society and History 91, 92–93.

[3] ibid 92.

[4] ibid.

[5] ibid 106.

[6] ibid 92.

[7] ibid 107.

[8] ibid 93.

[9] Wale Adebanwi, 'Africa's "Two Publics": Colonialism and Governmentality' (2017) 34 Theory, Culture & Society 65, 76.

adjustment, and adaptation. In these processes, 'while the civic public *notionally* addresses itself to the question of how to save and improve *the state*, the primordial public practically focuses on the question of how to save and improve the *community*, or "*our*" *people*'.[10] Consequently, this has led to the 'bifurcation of public reason, apparatus of rule, mentalities of rule, and rationality'.[11] Furthermore, the dualization of the public makes the actors of these publics both 'ethical and unethical at the same time' and 'provides them with the material and ideological tools to live with, live well within, as well as defend the existence of this dual public'.[12] Similarly, Mamdani uses the concept of a bifurcated state to describe and explain the African state as it relates to the rural and urban divide, the domain of state law and state authority, as well as the domain of customary and traditional authority.[13]

Indeed, the two publics thesis offers a unique analytical tool with which to explain and decrypt the *constitution* of the African state, but it does not explain it fully. True, there are seemingly two separate publics, or bifurcation, within the African state, and it is also true that there is a parasitic relationship between these two publics. Nevertheless, these two publics are neither purely divided in their sense of morality, justice, and rationality, nor are they always parasitic in their relationship. As discussed in Chapter 2, the civic public builds on some tenets of the primordial public and the primordial public accepts and depends on some tenets of the civic public. Acceptance and co-operation, as much as rejection and competition, symbolize the relationship between these two publics. Precisely because of this, what we get is not a 'bifurcation of public reason, apparatus of rule, mentalities of rule, and rationality', but rather syncretic public reason, apparatus of rule, mentalities of rule, and rationality that develop in a particular way according to the balance between the two publics in a given time and place. Moreover, it is not the dualization of the public that makes the actors of these publics 'ethical and unethical at the same time' and 'provides them with the material and ideological tools to live with, live well within, as well as defend the existence of this dual public', but it was rather the syncretic configuration of the civic public with the primordial public during the colonial encounter as well as its affirmation at independence. As a result, there is a syncretic public rather than two publics in the African state, the makeup of which is explained later in this section.

The weak state thesis focuses primarily on Ekeh's civic public by ignoring the primordial public, in order to explain the nature of the African state. It holds that the African state is not a state in the Weberian sense,[14] as it has neither the capacity and authority to broadcast its power over its territory and population, nor the adequate resources to finance its operation.[15] The African state, according to this thesis, is

[10] ibid.

[11] ibid 72.

[12] ibid 76.

[13] Mahmood Mamdani, *Citizen and Subject: Contemporary Africa and the Legacy of Late Colonialism* (Princeton University Press 1996) 16–22.

[14] See Max Weber, *Theory of Social and Economic Organization* (Talcott Parsons and AM Henderson tr, Oxford University Press 1947) 154.

[15] Jeffrey Herbst, *States and Power in Africa: Comparative Lessons in Authority and Control* (Princeton University Press 2000) 15–17; Robert H Jackson and Carl G Rosberg, 'Sovereignty and Underdevelopment: Juridical Statehood in the African Crisis' (1986) 24 The Journal of Modern African Studies 1, 1–3.

an empirical illusion without empirical sovereignty.[16] Moreover, due to its colonial origin, the African state is considered as alien to the people and, consequently, lacks moral and cultural legitimacy; the people who live within the African state do not have a common history and past cultural experience, nor do they currently have a common national identity or cohesion.[17] Thus, this view contends, the African state is only a state due to the courtesy of international law.[18] Unlike nineteenth-century international law which denied the sovereignty of Africans, post-World War II international law, under the auspices of the United Nations, extended juridical sovereignty to the former colonies in Africa without the need for them to have empirical sovereignty.[19] The replacement of empirical statehood with juridical statehood by international law has enabled African states to join the community of nations without acquiring the necessary capacity and infrastructure for their empirical existence. As such, being that sovereignty is the foundation and basis of the African state, unlike the Weberian state where sovereignty is an empirical reality and manifestation of the state, the African state is fundamentally too weak to perform standard state functions and responsibilities.

Indeed, the weak state thesis, like the two publics thesis, does explain some aspects of the African state. It is true, for example, that the African state is not like the Weberian state which asserts sovereignty as an empirical fact and deploys it through its monopoly of violence. Equally true is the constitutive role of international law in the sovereignty of the African state: it played a significant role in the *constitution* of both the colonial and postcolonial states, since, as discussed in Chapter 2, it provided their basic rules of organization and operation. The General Act of the Berlin Conference—with its guiding principles of international law—conferred juridical sovereignty on the colonial state without it having acquired the necessary capacity and infrastructure to assert empirical sovereignty. And, in a similar vein, the principles of territorial integrity and sovereignty of the United Nations and the Organization of African Unity (OAU) affirmed the sovereignty of the colonial state, which the postcolonial state then inherited.

However, there are a number of outstanding questions that the weak state thesis fails to answer. For example, how an alien political entity can operate—or even exist—in a population which neither shares a common history and culture, nor has a common sense of national identity or cohesion. Or why its inhabitants still commit to living under this entity while they can easily break away from it and form a new state of their own.[20] The truth of the matter is, that despite all of the prevalent ethno-linguistic and religious tensions and conflicts that exist, secessionist movements remain rare.[21] In the more than the fifty states that Africa consists of, secessionist movements have only

[16] Robert H Jackson, 'Juridical Statehood in Sub-Saharan Africa' (1992) 46 Journal of International Affairs 1, 1.

[17] Crawford Young, *The Postcolonial State in Africa: Fifty Years of Independence, 1960–2010* (University of Wisconsin Press 2012) 299; Francis M Deng, *Identity, Diversity, and Constitutionalism in Africa* (United States Institute of Peace Press 2008) 31.

[18] Robert H Jackson, 'Juridical Statehood in Sub-Saharan Africa' (n 16) 1–16.

[19] ibid 2.

[20] Young, *The Postcolonial State in Africa* (n 17) 299.

[21] ibid.

been raised in small numbers by specific groups in specific states. For instance, the Katanga in Congo, the Biafra in Nigeria, the Cabinda in Angola, the Casamance in Senegal, the South Sudan in Sudan, and the Eritrea in Ethiopia are the most notable secessionist movements, and it was only the South Sudanese and Eritrean secession that actually materialized.[22] Moreover, behind these secessionist movements are the real or imagined lack of cultural recognition, as well as a desire for more political participation and representation in the national state.[23] Hence, despite the acute lack of empirical sovereignty of the African state, its inhabitants willfully remain attached to it.

The state survival thesis comes to the rescue of the weak state thesis in explaining why the African state still exists despite all the odds. Robert Jackson and Carl Rosenberg offer four reasons why African states persist despite their apparent weakness and legitimacy deficit.[24] The first is the ideology of Pan-Africanism, or African nationalism, that cemented the consensus that the freedom of Africans would best be achieved within the contours of the colonial states, and this has led to the legal and political commitment to respect the sovereignty and territorial integrity of each newly independent state.[25] This legal and political commitment to respect the colonial borders avoids the possibility of external threats. The second reason is the rational choice theory, namely, that it is in the interest of each African state to respect the territorial integrity and sovereignty of the other states amidst the lack of empirical sovereignty internally.[26] The internal insecurity of both the states and their leaders demand the respect of the sovereignty of other states. The third reason is associated with the conservativeness of the United Nations-led international order for state fragmentation. And the fourth reason is the absence of interference in African affairs by non-Africans.[27] Like Jackson and Rosenberg, Christopher Clapham holds that 'negative sovereignty,' that is, the principle of respect for existing colonial borders and the principle of non-interference in international affairs, helps African states to secure their viability.[28]

While Pierre Englebert and Crawford Young agree with some of the above explanations, they offer more specific reasons that are internal to the African state. Although they agree that Pan-Africanism and its concomitant impact on the norms of the OAU are significant in maintaining the African state intact in legal and political terms, they do not believe it is a sufficient reason given 'the norm violating behavior of African states'. For instance, by violating the principles of sovereignty and territorial integrity, Tanzania, Cote d'Ivoire, Gabon, and Zambia gave recognition to Biafra in the 1960s; Libya supported separatist groups in Chad; Chad, Ethiopia, and Uganda supported the South Sudanese; Sudan supported separatists in Ethiopia; and Tanzania even invaded Uganda at the end of the 1970s.[29] And recently, the African Union readmitted

[22] Solomon A Dersso, *Taking Ethno-Cultural Diversity Seriously in Constitutional Design: A Theory of Minority Rights for Addressing Africa's Multi-Ethnic Challenge* (Martinus Nijhoff Publishers 2012) 51–52.

[23] ibid 60.

[24] Robert H Jackson and Carl G Rosberg, 'Why Africa's Weak States Persist: The Empirical and the Juridical in Statehood' (1982) 35 World Politics 1, 17.

[25] ibid 18.

[26] ibid 19.

[27] ibid 20–21.

[28] Christopher Clapham, *Africa and the International System: The Politics of State Survival* (Cambridge University Press 1996) 34–38, 44–50.

[29] Pierre Englebert, *Africa: Unity Sovereignty and Sorrow* (Lynne Rienner Publishers 2009) 33; Young, *The Postcolonial State in Africa* (n 17) 301–02.

Morocco as a member state while its annexation of Western Sahara was still ongoing, which reinforces Englebert and Young's argument.[30] They also agree with the rational choice theory as well as with the conservativeness of the international system for state fragmentation. In particular, the secessionist movements were mostly discouraged, and the Eritrean and South Sudanese secessions were only accepted after many decades of civil war and prior recognition by Ethiopia and Sudan, respectively.[31]

However, the most compelling reason for the survival of many of the African states, for Englebert at least, is the diffusion of sovereignty in the form of 'legal command' to many state institutions, agents, and officials.[32] He claims that the legal power that enables different state institutions, agents, and officials—such as customs officials, courts, municipal workers, civil servants, soldiers, police, and the like—emanates from the juridical and diffused sovereignty of the state.[33] As a result, what makes the state endure is the contextualization of sovereignty in the form of legal command by different state actors. But Engleberg's argument also only explains part of the story, since his conception of contextualized sovereignty and its manifestation in the form of legal command is valid in urban areas, or in areas where formal state institutions or officials exist, but in many rural areas, where the majority of inhabitants live, there is an acute lack of state agents and officials. Hence, in the absence of state institutions, agents, or officials that use the legal command, how the majority of the population leads a socio-economic and political life under the umbrella of the state remains a mystery.

Young, on the other hand, contends that the weak African states survive simply because their citizens or populations want them to endure.[34] He observes that the catastrophic failure of states to provide basic security, freedoms, and opportunities erases neither the attachment of the citizens to their states, nor the hope that their states can be reformed.[35] Young gives the examples of Congo-Kinshasa, South Sudan, and Somalia to demonstrate the attachment of citizens to their states. Despite the ongoing civil war and its horrendous impact in their lives, many Congolese and opposition rebel groups have a high attachment to their state.[36] In a similar vein, many South Sudanese had an ambition to live in a single Sudan.[37] And, similarly, without a central government for more than two decades, Somalia still exists in the social imagination of Somalis.[38] Hence, for Young, 'territorial nationalism' is the reason behind the survival of the African state. Even once 'failed' or 'collapsed' states, like Ghana, Uganda, Mozambique, Sierra Leone, and Liberia, just to mention a few, have recovered from their failure or collapse.[39] Moreover, Ghana is now one of the states in Africa where

30 Ben Quinn and agencies, 'Morocco Rejoins African Union after More than 30 Years' *The Guardian* (31 January 2017) <https://wwwtheguardiancom/global-development/2017/jan/31/morocco-rejoins-african-union-after-more-than-30-years> accessed 16 February 2017.

31 Young, *The Postcolonial State in Africa* (n 17) 301.

32 Englebert, *Africa* (n 29) 62.

33 ibid 62–64.

34 Young, *The Postcolonial State in Africa* (n 17) 314.

35 ibid.

36 ibid 305–06.

37 ibid.

38 ibid 299.

39 See I William Zartman (ed), *Collapsed States: The Disintegration and Restoration of Legitimate Authority* (Lynne Rienner Publishers 1995).

electoral democracy brings peaceful political transition. Somalia is also recovering from its tragic failure and is marching towards rebuilding institutions under a constitutional system.[40] For the continuous viability of the African state and its propensity for recovery, Young's thesis of territorial nationalism is a convincing explanation. However, territorial nationalism alone neither explains how the socio-economic and political biosphere of the populace operates, nor does it indicate how these are (dis) connected to the state.

The *constitution* of the African state, therefore, lies in the syncretic configuration of international law and customary laws and traditional authorities which all three aforementioned theses fail to take into account. While the two publics thesis emphasizes the incompatibility and perpetual rivalry between the customary and traditional conceptions of power (primordial public) and the modern rational-legal authority (civic public) without sufficiently considering international law, the weak state and state survival theses focus too heavily on international law by ignoring the roles and functions of customary and traditional conceptions of power and authority in the African state. As noted elsewhere, international law created and maintained the sovereignty of the African state, as we know it today, both in colonial and postcolonial times; it reimagined and reconfigured precolonial Africa into its current territorial form. Accordingly, it implanted the territorial state with its attendant attributes, such as defined population, territory, government, and sovereignty. Along with these, it bestowed on the territorial state internal autonomy and external protection. By doing so, international law incorporated Africa into the community of nations on its own terms and played a *constitutive* role in the formation of the African states *from above*.

Additionally, the OAU Charter provided the general principles and the territorial space within which such principles apply in postcolonial Africa. Furthermore, with the transformation of the OAU to the African Union (AU), constitutional democracy and governance are not matters entirely left to states. In response to the recurring coup d'état and the never-ending processes of constitutional change, the AU adopted a Charter on Democracy, Elections, and Governance (the Charter) in 2007 to collectively protect constitutionalism and democratic governance. The objectives of this Charter as outlined in article 2 include the adherence to the universal values of democracy, human rights, the rule of law, and constitutionalism. Article 10, in particular, obliges states parties to entrench the principle of constitutional supremacy, to amend or revise their constitutions only based on national consensus including a referendum, and to protect the right to equality as a fundamental precondition for a just and democratic society. Such regulation of constitutional change or amendment means that member states are not entirely free, at least in principle, to make and unmake their own constitutions. In the AU's vision of constitutional democracy, there is a *mutual dependence* between member states and the AU in the making or unmaking of national constitutions.

These are not simply mere aspirations without a practical impact on the constitutional behavior of state parties. The African Court on Human and Peoples' Rights

[40] The Constitution of Somalia 2012.

takes some practical steps in enforcing these constitutional standards.[41] For instance, in *Actions Pour la Protection des Droits de L'Homme (APDH) v The Republic of Cote d'Ivoire*, the African Court on Human and Peoples' Rights found the composition of the Electoral Commission to be in violation of the Charter and incompatible with the right to equality before the law and equal protection by the law as recognized under article 10(3).[42] Moreover, there are also sub-regional mechanisms that contribute to the collective protection of constitutionalism and democratic governance in various regions of Africa.[43] Hence, beyond reaffirming the territorial states, these regional and sub-regional laws aim to regulate the internal operation of these states in a certain way *from above*.[44]

At the same time, within the contours of the territorial state, customary laws and traditional authorities, in all their various manifestations, have been reconfigured in the government of the African state. The encounter between the rational-legal authority of the state—which is created *from above* through the aid of international law—and the customary and traditional conception of power and authority have transformed both conceptions of power and authority in Africa. As discussed in Chapter 2, the rational-legal authority has incorporated some elements of the customary and traditional conceptions of power, and in so doing, has changed its nature or identity. Similarly, the customary and traditional conceptions of power and authority have accepted the existence of the rational-legal authority and, accordingly, have transformed, reconfigured, and channeled their principles and practices into the operation of the territorial state. Thus, as international law gives the state internal autonomy and external protection *from above*, customary and traditional conceptions of power and authority provide the state with the necessary infrastructure and resources for internal operation *from below*.

If we consider the powers and resources available in the domain of the customary and traditional authority as only one aspect of the state configuration—as I believe we should—the African state is, indeed, strong in its bureaucratic arrangement and disposition, as well as its maintenance of internal law and order, as these exist everywhere throughout the territory. Obviously, these customary and traditional conceptions of power go beyond the simple constitutional recognitions and include their empirical applications and manifestations as well. As noted in Chapter 2, customary laws and traditional authorities perform state functions both in the so-called weak or collapsed states, as well as in the more stable and democratic ones. For instance, customary laws and traditional authorities play a significant state function in Mozambique,[45]

[41] See Adem Kassie Abebe, 'Taming Regressive Constitutional Amendments: The African Court as a Continental (Super) Constitutional Court' (2019) 17 International Journal of Constitutional Law 89, 89–117.

[42] *Actions Pour la Protection des Droits de L'Homme (APDH) v The Republic of Cote d'Ivoire*, App No 001/2014, Judgment of 18 November 2016; Ben Kioko, 'The African Charter on Democracy, Elections and Governance as a Justiciable Instrument' (2019) 63 Journal of African Law 39, 49–55.

[43] See Sègnonna Horace Adjolohoun, 'The Making and Remaking of National Constitutions in African Regional Courts' (2018) 2018 African Journal of Comparative Constitutional Law 1, 35–70.

[44] See also Nico Steytler, 'Domesticating the Leviathan: Constitutionalism and Federalism in Africa' (2016) 24 African Journal of International and Comparative Law 272.

[45] Lars Buur and Helene Maria Kyed, 'Contested Sources of Authority: Re-Claiming State Sovereignty by Formalizing Traditional Authority in Mozambique' (2006) 37 Development & Change 847, 850–51.

Angola,[46] Sierra Leone,[47] Somalia,[48] Tanzania,[49] Ethiopia,[50] South Africa,[51] Namibia,[52] and Botswana[53]—all of which have different levels of state existence, capacity, and legitimacy according to the Weberian conception of state.

Thus, the colonial encounter set into motion the development of a syncretic African state that repudiates the indigenous constitutional configurations, as discussed in Chapter 2, yet incorporates, reforms, and reconfigures some of their underlying rules, principles, and practices into its current constitutional system in order to extend its institutional reach in its territory and ensure internal law and order. By doing so, the state, in turn, also transformed its rational-legal authority as it fused it with a traditional political authority that operates with a different sense of morality, justice, and rationality. As a result, the African state is neither bifurcated nor does it host two publics, nor is it solely dependent on international law for its survival. Rather, the African state is *constituted* through a syncretic configuration of international law *from above,* and customary laws and traditional authorities *from below*. Within such syncretic configuration, the written constitution primarily has provided legitimacy and, to the extent possible, the institutional and normative context for the practice of constitutionalism in the African state. Due to its origin, therefore, the African state has syncretic forms of morality, justice, and rationality that establish it, to begin with, and then maintain it even if it may not have the monopoly of violence (in the Weberian sense) throughout its territory. Thus, the African state and its constitutional system is both a product and a space of legal syncretism.

B. The Vertical Organization of the African State: Between Federalism and Unitarism

Configured between the twin pillars of international law *from above* and customary laws and traditional authorities *from below*, African constitutionalism grapples with a theory of government in order to organize the state which is somewhere between federalism and unitarism. The ethno-linguistic and regional diversity, along with the lack of a prior shared history and culture beyond the colonial experience, have made

46 Aslak Orre, 'Integration of Traditional Authorities in Local Governance in Mozambique and Angola: The Context of Decentralization and Democratisation' in Armando Marques Guedes and Maria José Lopes (eds), *State and Traditional Law in Angola and Mozambique* (Almedina 2007) 139–99.

47 Richard Fanthorpe, 'On the Limits of Liberal Peace: Chiefs and Democratic Decentralization in Post-War Sierra Leone' (2006) 105 African Affairs 27.

48 Michael van Notten, *The Law of the Somalis: A Stable Foundation for Economic Development in the Horn of Africa* (Spencer Heath MacCallum ed, The Red Sea Press 2005).

49 Mahmood Mamdani, *Define and Rule: Native as Political Identity* (Harvard University Press 2012) 107.

50 See Bahru Zewde and Siegfried Pausewang (eds), *Ethiopia: The Challenge of Democracy from Below* (Nordic Africa Institute 2002).

51 See Barbara Oomen, *Chiefs in South Africa: Law, Power & Culture in the Post-Apartheid Era* (James Currey 2005).

52 Oliver C Ruppel and Katharina Ruppel-Schlichting, 'Legal and Judicial Pluralism in Namibia and Beyond: A Modern Approach to African Legal Architecture?' (2011) 43 The Journal of Legal Pluralism and Unofficial Law 33, 33–57.

53 Godsglory O Ifezue, 'Understanding Chieftainship in Botswana: The Status and Powers of Chiefs in Present Day Botswana' (2015) 59 Journal of African Law 271, 271–93.

the nation-state project difficult, yet have made the unitary system of government the preferred system of state organization in Africa. Nonetheless, this has been achieved through the reinterpretation of both the logic and principles of said unitary systems of government. In transposing the unitary system of government, the syncretic African state redeployed it as both a device for holding the diverse ethno-linguistic groups together as well as a means of expanding the power of the central government. In doing so, it also incorporated some federalist ideas and principles of state organization into its unitary system. By the same token, those states which adopted a federal form of government not only transformed the nature and function of federalism, but also fused it with some unitary principles and ideas. As a result, the theory of state organization in Africa—both federal and unitary at the same time—possesses an underlying purpose or function and aims to address a common problem posed by the syncretic nature of the African state.

The African federal and unitary theories, therefore, diverge from the classic federal and unitary theories, even though they share some common structural norms, principles, and discursive practices with them. This section explores both the federalist ambition in unitary states and the unitary impulse in federal states on the one hand, and the divergences and convergences of African federalism and unitarism with classic theories on the other, in order to demonstrate how the theory of vertical state organization in Africa builds on legal syncretism. The discussion begins with a restatement of classic unitary and federal theory in order to trace their transformation and reconceptualization in the African state.

Unitary systems of government trace their origin to the Westphalian state system which conceived the state 'ideally as a unitary, centralized, homogeneous, self-sufficient, and politically sovereign polity encompassing a single nation, a territory, and a unitary government'.[54] Accordingly, in a classic unitary system of government, the state expresses, and is expressed by, the homogeneous national identity of its citizens who share common socio-cultural and linguistic identities, among others.[55] As diversity is a fact of the human or social experience, the unitary theory of government employs a political theory in order to achieve unity or homogeneity. In this respect, John Stuart Mill, for example, suggested having a common language if free institutions are to work in a nation-state;[56] Jean-Jacques Rousseau emphasized the necessity of having a common religion as the ultimate moral reservoir of a nation;[57] and Ernest Barker proposed social cohesion as a necessary condition for the exercise and operation of sovereignty.[58] All of these require, and indeed required, the imposition of a dominant culture—and its animating attributes for all within a given state—as a unification tool, by the use of force, or at least the threat of force (as in France), and in some exceptional circumstances, with 'center-periphery political dynamics' (as in the United Kingdom).[59] Hence, the unitary system of government has a strong cultural

[54] Daniel J Elazar, 'Contrasting Unitary and Federal Systems' (1997) 18 International Political Science Review / Revue internationale de science politique 237, 237.

[55] Sergio Bartole, 'Internal Ordering in a Unitary State' in Michel Rosenfeld and András Sajó (eds), *The Oxford Handbook of Comparative Constitutional Law* (Oxford University Press 2012) 610–11.

[56] John Stuart Mill, *Utilitarianism, Liberty & Representative Government* (JM Dent & Sons 1910) 365.

[57] Jean-Jacques Rousseau, *The Social Contract* (Maurice Cranston tr, Penguin Classics 1968) 181.

[58] Ernest Barker, *Principles of Social & Political Theory* (Clarendon Press 1951) 42.

[59] Elazar, 'Contrasting Unitary and Federal Systems' (n 54) 244–46.

current of homogeneity and cohesion, along with the consequent indivisibility of the state and its inseparability with the identity of its people.

As a product and manifestation of the homogeneous and unified cultural current of a state, and as a mechanism for extending, consolidating, and ensuring the application of uniform laws, policies, and practices throughout its territory, the unitary state creates one locus of power. Government in a unitary state is either organized hierarchically, as in France, where those at the top of the power pyramid control and dispense the ultimate power to the regions or departments, or it is organized centrally, as in the United Kingdom, where the center holds the supreme and final power in its relationship with the peripheries.[60] The key consideration in the unitary system of government is the efficient organization of state power. State efficiency, in this respect, is associated with the maximization of control over the lower levels by the top of the power pyramid, or the control of the peripheries by the center.[61] Depending on the particular needs, as well as how democratic or republican the government is, those at the top or at the center decide when and how to decentralize power—whether in the form of deconcentration, delegation, and devolution—to the lower administrative bodies.[62] At the same time, the national or central government can either recentralize the powers of the lower administrative bodies, or undo the decentralization altogether and abolish the existing lower administrative bodies, or simply create new ones.

In light of the above, the unitary system of government in Africa—from independence to the massive decentralization of the 1990s—does not have the cultural currents of a nation-state, nor did it come into being through a political dynamic internal to it. The unitary system of government was first adopted in Africa at independence primarily as a French colonial inheritance, and later as part of the nation-state building project according to the European prototype.[63] The waves of decentralization we have seen since the 1990s have been informed more by federalist ideas and principles than by the unitary logic of decentralization.[64] While state efficiency remains an outstanding issue for the African state, regardless of its system of government, the main drives for decentralization have been the accommodation of ethno-linguistic and regional diversities and interests in the unitary states.[65] Even if there is a development and democratic imperative for these decentralizations, their institutional and normative configurations make the loci of power plural. Even though these states maintain some of the structures, principles, and discursive practices of a unitary system of government, the realities and conditions of legal syncretism transform their nature and operating principles, forcing them to deviate at least somewhat from the traditional unitary system of government. As these decentralizations are the results of a constitutional settlement, the reconceptualization of the unitary system of government aims

60 ibid 247–48.

61 ibid 243–44.

62 Yonatan Fessha and Coel Kirkby, 'A Critical Survey of Subnational Autonomy in African States' (2008) 38 Publius: The Journal of Federalism 248, 249; Aaron Schneider, 'Decentralization: Conceptualization and Measurement' (2003) 38 Studies in Comparative International Development 32, 34–35.

63 Dersso, *Taking Ethno-Cultural Diversity Seriously in Constitutional Design* (n 22) 62–70.

64 See also Rotimi T Suberu, 'Federalism and Decentralization' in David Anderson, Nicholas Cheeseman, and Andrea Scheibler (eds), *Routledge Handbook of African Politics* (Routledge 2013) 24.

65 Fessha and Kirkby, 'A Critical Survey of Subnational Autonomy in African States' (n 62) 251–52.

to strike some level of balance between the national and subnational actors, and, by extension, among the various ethno-linguistic and regional groups. Kenya, Uganda, and Cameroon are all fine examples that demonstrate the transformation of the unitary system as we know it, and its fusion with federalist ideas and principles.

The Kenyan Constitution entrenches the powers of county governments as part of its devolved government.[66] Forty-seven counties are established by the Constitution and they are each represented by a Senator in the Senate, the upper house of Parliament. Moreover, they are given political, administrative, and fiscal autonomy in their own domains.[67] County governments each have their own directly-elected Governor, a County Executive formed by the Governor, and a County Assembly, all of which draw heavily from the United States model of state government.[68] The County Governors cannot be removed by the President of the Republic, but only on constitutionally stipulated grounds, or on further grounds enacted by Parliament.[69] Even in times of emergency and exceptional circumstances, the President of the Republic can only suspend a county government with the investigation by an Independent Commission of Inquiry and with an Act of Parliament.[70] Furthermore, the Senate can terminate such suspensions at any time.[71] As the Senate is constituted of Senators from the counties, the bicameral parliamentary system has the objective and effect of protecting and ensuring the interests of the counties in the legislative processes, including in the impeachment of the President and Deputy President of the Republic, just like in federal states.[72]

Uganda, like Kenya, constitutionally decentralizes power by establishing districts as local political units. Districts have their own District Chairperson as a political head, a District Council as a deliberative body, and a District Executive Committee as an executive body. Districts have political,[73] administrative,[74] and fiscal autonomy[75] to perform local government functions. Like Kenya, the President of the Republic cannot dissolve the local government, nor can they remove the District Chairperson. The President of the Republic can exercise the powers of the district governments only in a state of emergency, or when it is difficult for the district government to function, or at the invitation of the District Council, and even then, only if two-thirds of all Members of Parliament approve the request.[76] Furthermore, the Constitution requires a two-thirds approval from the districts in order to amend the part of the Constitution that deals with local government.[77] The principle of constitutional unamendability by either level of government unilaterally is one of the essential

[66] The Constitution of Kenya 2010, Chapter 11.

[67] ibid arts 183, 185, 186, and 187.

[68] Nic Cheeseman, Gabrielle Lynch, and Justin Willis, 'Decentralisation in Kenya: The Governance of Governors' (2016) 54 The Journal of Modern African Studies 1, 13.

[69] The Constitution of Kenya, art 181.

[70] ibid art 192.

[71] ibid s 192(4).

[72] See also Cheeseman, Lynch, and Willis, 'Decentralisation in Kenya' (n 68) 13–16.

[73] See the Constitution of Uganda 1995, art 180.

[74] ibid arts 186 and 189.

[75] ibid art 190–95.

[76] ibid art 202.

[77] ibid art 260.

criteria of federal systems.[78] Unlike in Kenya, the Parliament of Uganda is unicameral.[79] Interestingly enough, Uganda tries to accommodate the interests of its districts by giving them a special quota in the Parliament and making that quota available to women only.[80] By doing so, women district parliamentarians can advance both the interests of their districts as well as their own as a vulnerable group in society.

Similarly, Cameroon constitutionally recognizes regional and local authorities as 'public law corporate bodies' in its decentralized unitary state.[81] Regions and local authorities have exclusive and concurrent powers with fiscal autonomy, although the national government is entitled to carry out supervision.[82] In line with this, ten regions headed by Presidents with Regional Councils as deliberative bodies are identified by the Constitution, and—unlike in Kenya and Uganda—the President of the Republic is given power to remove the Presidents of the regions and dissolve the Regional Councils.[83] However, as corporate bodies, the regions and local authorities themselves are constitutionally protected and immune from dissolution. Moreover, as the Senate—the upper house of Parliament—is constituted, like in Kenya, by representatives of regional and local authorities, they can influence the legislative process, just like in federal states.[84]

Thus, the unitary system of government in Kenya, Uganda, and Cameroon is a legal syncretic result of federalist ideas and principles along with unitary forms, principles, and discursive practices. Unlike their unsuccessful federal constitutional experiences of the past, the transformation and reconceptualization of the unitary system of government along these lines seems to be palatable both to national actors in their extension and consolidation of power as well as to subnational actors in the practice of self-government at the local level and shared rule at the national level.

Like with the unitary states, African federal states also reconfigured federalism with a new purpose or function and fused it with some unitarist principles and practices. Classic federal theory as typified by United States, Canada, Switzerland, and Australia has the aim of bringing together preexisting sovereign political units for the sake of collective security, democracy, and/or economic prosperity.[85] The institutional design of federalism in these states aims to combat majority tyranny, protect individual rights, safeguard democracy, and ensure government accountability.[86] Federal design is further guided by the ability to improve state efficiency by taking advantage of the benefits of unity as well as maintaining diversity by avoiding the costs of uniformity.[87]

[78] Ronald Watts, *Comparing Federal Systems* (3rd ed, McGill-Queen's University Press 2008) 9.
[79] The Constitution of Uganda, arts 77 and 78.
[80] ibid art 78(1)(b).
[81] The Constitution of Cameroon 1972, art 55.
[82] ibid art 55.
[83] ibid arts 56–60.
[84] For the practice see Ndiva Kofele-Kale, 'Local Governance under Cameroon's Decentralisation Regime: Is It All Sound and Fury Signifying Nothing?' (2011) 37 Commonwealth Law Bulletin 513, 513–30.
[85] Sujit Choudhry and Nathan Hume, 'Federalism, Devolution and Secession: From Classical to Post Conflict Federalism' in Tom Ginsburg and Rosalind Dixon, *Comparative Constitutional Law* (Edward Elgar Publishing 2011) 359.
[86] ibid 356.
[87] ibid.

Nonetheless, the federal theory as envisaged and experimented with in Africa has a different logic and purpose. As discussed in Chapter 4, federalism in Africa is primarily dictated by the quest to hold the postcolonial state together. Precisely because of this, the federal design in Africa mainly aims to achieve peace and territorial integrity by accommodating ethnic and regional diversity. Furthermore, whereas unitary states also have a federalist ambition, federal states have a unitarist impulse that either leads to the abolition of federalism, as we have seen in Cameroon and Uganda, or to extensive centralization, as witnessed in Nigeria, Ethiopia, and South Africa.[88]

The syncretic states in Africa design their systems of vertical organization of power by reforming and reconfiguring both unitary and federal systems of government, and by blending them together in order to address their peculiar needs and circumstances. Behind such experiments are the existence of a general commitment to the viability of the African state, the presence of ethno-linguistic and regional diversity, and the outstanding quest to legitimate the African state and, consequently, extend and consolidate its operation. These contexts, in turn, lead to the development of a syncretic system of government organization that mixes legal and political ideas, practices, and norms as manifested in the primordial public, civic public, and comparative liberal constitutional experiences. It is due to this syncretic condition that the system of vertical division of power hangs between federalism and unitarism in both federal and unitary states, despite their differences in name, form, and scope.

II. The African Government Architecture

As with the vertical division of power, the horizontal division of power in Africa is also animated by legal syncretism. The legislative branch draws from both the modern principle of democratic representation—one-person one-vote—as well as the traditional form of representation as symbolized in traditional leaders or chiefs, and then blends them together in its constitutional design. By doing so, the legislative branch becomes a dual house of representation based on both democratic and African principles of representation. In a similar vein, the executive branch is designed mainly through the adoption of presidential forms of government, with an additional blend of both the alleged African principles of government as well as the *modus operandi* of the Colonial Governor. As a result, executive power in Africa has an imperial and personal attribute that goes somewhat counter to the principle of separation of powers. Similarly, the judicial branch fuses laws and persons from both customary and/or religious laws as well as statutory laws. Consequently, the legislative, executive, and judicial branches in Africa are not only results of legal syncretism, but also spaces for the same. The following three sections explore and examine—in order—how legal syncretism animates the legislative, executive, and judicial branches of government in Africa.

[88] See also Rotimi Suberu, 'Federalism in Africa: The Nigerian Experience in Comparative Perspective' (2009) 8 Ethnopolitics 67, 68–69.

A. The Legislative: The Dual House of Representation

Until the third wave of democratization in the 1990s, the role and function of legislatures in Africa were to legitimize and support the executive branches. However, the adoption of democratic constitutions in the 1990s began to change the role of legislatures from that of being merely another arm of the executive to institutions with significant constitutional importance, particularly in taming the executive and consolidating constitutionalism.[89] While their constitutional roles and actual influence vary across states, the legislative as an institution has begun to matter in the practice of constitutionalism in Africa.[90]

In liberal constitutional systems, legislatures as institutions symbolize representative government and are the results of popular sovereignty as expressed in regular and periodic elections.[91] As people have diverse needs and interests, it forms and supports political parties for these purposes. Ultimately, while legislatures are composed of political parties with varied interests, the legislature as an institution is the reservoir of popular will, or popular sovereignty. This popular sovereignty resides undivided in the people.

However, a closer look at the legislatures of many African states reveals that they are not only representative bodies of the people as an expression of popular sovereignty, but are also representative bodies of the people as an expression of traditional forms of sovereignty. While the direct election of members of the legislature through regular elections embodies the notion of popular sovereignty, the incorporation and reconfiguration of traditional authorities into the legislature—in different degrees and forms,[92] as explained below—demonstrates the traditional conception of sovereignty, and such institutional configuration produces a syncretic legislative body. In this section, I explore how traditional authorities figure in the legislative bodies and how this, consequently, transforms the nature of these legislative bodies.

Traditional authorities are incorporated into the legislative branches in Africa in four major ways. The first is through direct incorporation into the legislature, the second is the institution of separate houses, the third is through inclusion as part of local government, and the fourth is the incorporation through an innovative institutional recreation. Lesotho, Eswatini (formerly Swaziland), and Sierra Leone are good examples of the first way, namely, by directly incorporating traditional chiefs into the legislative branch. While Lesotho and Eswatini are constitutional monarchies where traditional authorities and traditional conceptions of power animate the entire constitutional structure, Sierra Leone has established constitutional democracy, but has also chosen to represent traditional authorities in the legislature. In Lesotho, twenty-two out of thirty-three seats in the Senate, the upper house of Parliament, are allocated to chiefs,[93] while the National Assembly is composed of people's representatives.[94]

[89] MA Mohamed Salih, 'Introduction' in MA Mohamed Salih (ed), *African Parliaments: Between Governance and Government* (Springer 2005) 12–20.
[90] Joel D Barkan, 'African Legislatures and "the third wave" of Democratization' in Joel D Barkan (ed), *Legislative Power in Emerging African Democracies* (Lynne Rienner Publishers 2009) 1–3.
[91] András Sajó and Renáta Uitz, *The Constitution of Freedom: An Introduction to Legal Constitutionalism* (Oxford University Press 2017) 227–28.
[92] Englebert, *Africa* (n 29) 52–55.
[93] The Constitution of Lesotho 1993, art 55.
[94] ibid arts 56 and 57.

Eswatini also establishes constitutional systems for both traditional representation through chiefs as well as elected representation of peoples in the parliament, even though they have no clear nomenclature like 'Senate' or 'National Assembly' like they do in Lesotho.[95] Similarly, in Sierra Leone, the unicameral parliament is constituted of both Paramount Chiefs from each district as well as elected representatives.[96]

The preferred approach for the incorporation of traditional authorities into the legislature seems to be the second way: through the institution or establishment of separate houses—including a House of Chiefs—as a traditional conception of representation. In this respect, Ghana, Botswana, and Zambia are good examples of how Houses of Chiefs are established and to explicate their relationships with the legislature. In Ghana, customary laws and usage guide both the organization and tenure of the House of Chiefs at the national and regional levels.[97] To this end, the Parliament neither has the power to confer or withdraw the power of chieftaincy to anyone, nor to 'detract or derogate from the honour and dignity of the institution of chieftaincy'.[98] In addition, the election or removal of chiefs is entirely within the ambit of customary law and usage, with the role of Parliament being limited to making laws to this effect.[99] In Botswana, however, even though customary norms and practices are the normative basis for the institution of the Ntlo ya Dikgosi (House of Chiefs), there is a Regional Electoral College responsible for the election of chiefs and anyone who is a Botswanan national and reaches twenty-one years of age can run for the position.[100] In addition to being open to anyone, the tenure of the Ntlo ya Dikgosi is limited to five years.[101] By the same token, customary norms in Zambia are not the only sources of chieftainship, as the government can designate or select anyone as a chief and can appoint them to the House of Chiefs.[102] But unlike in Botswana, in Zambia it is the chiefs in the provinces who elect the members of the House of Chiefs.[103] However, their term of office is limited to three years with the possibility of re-election for one more term.[104]

The House of Chiefs participates to different degrees and levels—mostly as advisory organs, —in the business of the legislature. In Ghana, for example, the House of Chiefs plays a strong role in legislation primarily with respect to the institution of chieftaincy, customary law, and usage. This ranges from taking away the legislative power from the Parliament in making laws concerning the institution of chieftaincy

95 The Constitution of Swaziland 2005, arts 80, 81, and 84.

96 The Constitution of Sierra Leone 1991, s 74.

97 The Constitution of Ghana 1992, art 270.

98 ibid art 270(2); see Nicole Bonoff, 'Traditional Authority in the State: Chiefs, Elections and Taxation in Ghana' (PhD thesis, University of California, San Diego 2016). Bonoff discusses the influence and role of chiefs beyond their constitutionally recognized power.

99 The Constitution of Ghana, art 270(3)(a); for a details account of traditional authorities in Ghana's constitutional democracy see Irene K Odotei and AK Awedoba (eds), *Chieftaincy in Ghana: Culture, Governance and Development* (Sub-Saharan Publishers 2006).

100 The Constitution of Botswana 1966, ss 78(4) and 79(1); see Wazha G Morapedi, 'Demise or Resilience? Customary Law and Chieftaincy in Twenty-First Century Botswana' (2010) 28 Journal of Contemporary African Studies 215 (discussing how chiefs manage to secure their power and influences despite government interventions).

101 The Constitution of Botswana, s 80(1)(a); see also Ifezue (n 53).

102 The Constitution of Zambia 1991, art 128(c).

103 ibid art 132.

104 ibid art 133(1).

to a collaborative role in determining specific rules or procedures concerning chiefs and customary law.[105] Additionally, the House of Chiefs also plays an advisory role to the legislature and this advisory authority is not limited solely to matters of chieftaincy and customary law, but extends to any constitutional matter or law.[106] They particularly have the mandate and power to undertake progressive studies and evaluations on filtering out harmful customary practices and usages, and to codify customary laws.[107]

In Botswana and Zambia, however, the House of Chiefs only has an advisory role and the Parliaments have no constitutional limitations with regard to legislating on matters of chiefs or customary laws. And unlike in Ghana, where the constitution authorizes the House of Chiefs to be advisory organs for any person or authority, in Botswana and Zambia, the functions of the House of Chiefs are an advisory body solely for the legislature. For instance, the Botswanan Constitution provides that '[t]he Ntlo ya Dikgosi shall consider the copy of any Bill which has been referred to it under the provisions of section 88(2) of this Constitution and the Ntlo ya Dikgosi shall be entitled to submit resolutions thereon to the National Assembly.'[108] Furthermore, it states that:

> The Ntlo ya Dikgosi shall be entitled to discuss any matter within the executive or legislative authority of Botswana of which it considers it is desirable to take cognizance in the interests of the tribes and tribal organizations it represents and to make representations thereon to the President, or to send messages thereon to the National Assembly.[109]

By the same token, the Zambian Constitution stipulates that the House of Chiefs is an advisory body to the government on traditional, customary, or any other matter referred to it by the president.[110] In addition to this general advisory role, the House of Chiefs has the power to consider and discuss any bill concerning custom or tradition introduced by the National Assembly, or any other matter referred to it by the president, and submit resolutions to this effect to the National Assembly.[111]

The third way of incorporating traditional authorities into the legislative activities is by making them part of the local government. Local governments are corporate bodies in the devolved government system found in much of Africa, where they have their own legislative assemblies and executive organs subject to constitutional and legal limitations.[112] In Chad, the Democratic Republic of Congo, The Gambia, and South Africa, for instance, traditional authorities are either part of, or play a supportive role in, the functioning of the local government. In The Gambia, the constitution combines the local

105 The Constitution of Ghana, art 270.
106 ibid art 272(a) and (d), 274(3).
107 ibid art 272(b) and (c), 274(3).
108 The Constitution of Botswana, s 85(1).
109 ibid s 85(5).
110 The Constitution of Zambia, art 130.
111 ibid art 131.
112 For instance, see the Constitution of the Democratic Republic of Congo 2005, art 195.

government and traditional rulers and does not even make any distinction.[113] Traditional rulers, called *Seyfolu*, are represented in the local government and are, accordingly, responsible for local legislation and execution.[114] In Chad, unlike The Gambia, the constitution generally recognizes the institution of traditional and customary authority and makes them collaborators and supporters of the local government.[115] In the Democratic Republic of Congo, traditional authorities are recognized under the provinces, ie, the regional or local governments. While a future law determines the specific powers of traditional authorities in Congo as in Chad,[116] they assume the duty to promote national unity and cohesion.[117] In South Africa, traditional authorities assume a role in the local government on issues affecting local communities.[118]

The fourth and final approach to the inclusion of traditional authorities in the business of the legislature is through an innovative institutional recreation featuring a traditional logic and conception, but with a modern actor and participant. Rwanda is a good example of this: Rwanda does not follow the African trend of recognizing traditional authorities as noted above, but rather reinvents it in the form of the National Umushyikirano Council and the Abunzi Committee. The National Umushyikirano Council is composed of the President of the Republic and citizen representatives, whereas the Abunzi Committee is a conciliatory organ composed of persons of high integrity with skills of conciliation and dispute resolution.[119] The National Umushyikirano Council is relevant for our present purposes since the discussions of the Council lead to the adoption of resolutions as well as their submission to relevant institutions, including the legislature.[120] The organization, deliberations, and resolutions of the Council all resemble a traditional system of deliberation and governance—the exception being the President of the Republic who acts as a traditional leader, king, or chief with supreme power. In precolonial Africa, in which Rwanda was not an exception, people gathered around a traditional leader, king, or elder to discuss, deliberate, and solve issues of communal interest. In this National Umushyikirano Council, the President leads the discussion and deliberation along with citizen representatives that they invite. The Council can debate and adopt resolutions about any 'issues relating to the state of the nation and national unity'.[121] The President, through this Council, seems to exercise the powers of traditional authorities in influencing the legislature by submitting resolutions of the Council. The National Umushyikirano Council epitomizes the type of syncretic engineering of traditional conceptions of power and authority together with modern constitutional principles and institution, all of which make the leader of the Republic both a traditional leader or chief as well as

[113] The Constitution of Gambia 1996, chapter XV; the chapter on local government is titled as 'local government and traditional rulers'.
[114] ibid s 194(b).
[115] ibid ss 213–14.
[116] The Constitution of Chad 1996, art 216.
[117] The Constitution of Democratic Republic of Congo, art 207.
[118] The Constitution of South Africa 1996, s 212(1); For the political dynamics of traditional authorities see J Michael Williams, *Chieftaincy, the State, and Democracy: Political Legitimacy in Post-Apartheid South Africa* (Indiana University Press 2010).
[119] The Constitution of Rwanda 2003, arts 140 and 141.
[120] ibid art 140.
[121] ibid art 140.

a modern president. This ultimately strengthens both the executive power of the president as well as their leverage and influence on the legislature.

Beyond these four types of institutional recognitions, traditional authorities also engage in the business of law-making through customary laws, which are recognized as one source of law in many African states. In other words, the recognition of customary laws includes the recognition of the traditional institutions that produce these laws. In this regard, *Shilubana and Others v Nwamitwa*[122] affirms why the recognition of customary laws include the recognition of the legislative authority of traditional authorities to make and unmake customary laws.

In summary, there is incorporation and reconfiguration of traditional authorities and traditional conceptions of powers in the business of legislation and legislature in Africa.[123] While the national assemblies are usually houses of modern forms of representation, as they are composed of people who are popularly and democratically elected, the reconstitution and inclusion of traditional forms of representations is seen via membership of traditional authorities or chiefs in the Senate, the institution of separate Houses of Chiefs, the incorporation of traditional authorities in local government, the reinvention of traditional authorities, and the recognition of customary laws. Despite the differences in the precise degrees and levels of this incorporation and reconfiguration, the constitutions of many African states allow for the development of a syncretic legislative organ that appeals to both the modern and traditional political elite rather than a bifurcated one between the urban and the rural polity.[124] Even those countries which do not incorporate traditional authorities into the legislative branch, either recognize them as part of the state apparatus with clearly stipulated roles and functions, such as judicial roles,[125] or accept their role and function as a matter of constitutional practice within their own domains, as we see in Ethiopia.[126] As custodians of customary laws, traditional authorities engage in the making and unmaking of customary laws together with their constituencies, as customary laws evolve or change with time due to circumstances internal or external to it. These empirical realities illustrate the legislative role of traditional authorities, even when they are not formally incorporated into the legislative branch. This means that the legislative branch of

[122] *Shilubana and Others v Nwamitwa* [2009] (2) SA 66 (CC).

[123] See also Michaela Collord, 'The Legislature: Institutional Strengthening in Dominant-Party States,' in Nicholas Cheeseman (ed), *Institutions and Democracy in Africa: How the Rules of the Game Shape Political Developments* (Cambridge University Press 2017) 298–99.

[124] See also Charles Mwalimu, *Seeking Viable Grassroots Representation Mechanisms in African Constitutions: Integration of Indigenous and Modern Systems of Government in Sub-Saharan Africa* (Peter Lang 2009); Carolyn Logan, 'Selected Chiefs, Elected Councillors and Hybrid Democrats: Popular Perspectives on the Co-Existence of Democracy and Traditional Authority' (2009) 47 The Journal of Modern African Studies 101, 101–28.

[125] The Constitution of Federal Democratic Republic of Ethiopia 1995, arts 34(5) and 78(5).

[126] See Girmachew Alemu Aneme, 'Ethiopia: Legal and Judicial Plurality and the Incorporation of Traditional Dispute Resolution Mechanisms within the State Justice System' in Matthias Kötter and others (eds), *Non-State Justice Institutions and the Law: Decision-Making at the Interface of Tradition, Religion and the State* (Palgrave Macmillan 2015) 80–99; Dolores A Donovan and Getachew Assefa, 'Homicide in Ethiopia: Human Rights, Federalism, and Legal Pluralism' (2003) 51 The American Journal of Comparative Law 505, 505–52; Bahru Zewde, 'Introduction' in Bahru Zewde and Siegfried Pausewang (eds), *Ethiopia: The Challenge of Democracy from Below* (Nordic Africa Institute and Forum for Social Studies 2002) 7–14.

government in Africa incorporates both the modern and traditional mode of representation and lawmaking.

B. The Executive: Imperial and Personalized

In common parlance, the executive is a branch of government that gives effect to laws made by the legislature and performs other constitutionally allotted powers and functions, such as matters of foreign relations, national defense, and general welfare.[127] In a constitutional democracy, the executive is either headed by a president or a prime minster who, along with their cabinet, runs the executive branch of government. Informed by the principle of separation of powers, despite its wider prerogatives and powers as compared with the legislature and the judiciary in the administration of the state, the executive figurehead—be it a president or a prime minster—is expected to function and operate within the ambit of constitutional limitations and rules. Indeed, this is one of the main hallmarks of modern constitutionalism that distinguishes present day presidents or prime ministers from the ancient or medieval monarchs or kings. The functional division of government powers has been considered as 'a grand secret of liberty and good government' in Western constitutional thought.[128] The inbuilt system of checks and balances in the principle of separation of powers is supposed to keep the executive within its constitutional limits. The actual practice of the principle of separation of powers by the three branches of government in general, and the executive in particular, epitomizes the success of constitutional government.

However, this constitutional principle of separation of powers has been reinterpreted by African executives in a way that favors the executive and creates executive supremacy in the constitutional order. As discussed in Chapter 2, in the continuous negation and affirmation of liberal constitutionalism, the alleged African system of government under a strong king or chief has been used as a discursive practice to both legitimate the new leaders along with their styles of rule and to relegate the principle of separation of powers as a foreign and alien cultural imposition. By magnifying and universalizing that particular conception of the African system of government which concentrates political power in the person of the king or chief, while simultaneously deemphasizing the traditional systems of separation of powers and checks and balances, African executives have managed to accumulate much political power and, consequently, have personalized the executive power of government. Although the founding presidents of the African states admired the executive personas of the foreign leaders of their time, such as Charles de Gaulle, in reality they drew heavily from, and impliedly accepted, the theory of colonial government which knew no principle of separation of powers, but rather a politics of convenience.[129]

As discussed in Chapter 2, the colonial constitutions vested supreme legislative, executive, and judicial powers in the person of the colonial governor within their

[127] Sajó and Uitz, *The Constitution of Freedom* (n 91) 267–68.

[128] MJC Vile, *Constitutionalism and the Separation of Powers* (Liberty Fund 2012) 3.

[129] See also H Kwasi Prempeh, 'Presidential Power in Comparative Perspective: The Puzzling Persistence of Imperial Presidency in Post-Authoritarian Africa' (2007) 35 Hastings Const LQ 761, 802–04.

colonial territory. While there were forms of colonial administration and bureaucracy, the colonial governor trumped all of these colonial state institutions and practices at their pleasure. However, whether it was to advance their alleged projects of nation-building and development or to simply centralize and personalize their executive power, the colonial governor offered these African leaders an attractive theory of government which they tried to incorporate into their constitutions. The African constitutions have, thus, established an imperial executive and personalized executive power drawing from a selective incorporation and rejection of the traditional African theory of government, an implied acceptance of the colonial theory of government, and the principle of separation of powers.

By doing so, even if they maintained the government structures that channel the separation of powers, they significantly transformed the power allocations among these government structures and altered the relationships between them. As a result, in contrast with the principle of separation of powers, the African executive wields a wide range of powers.[130] The executive is usually symbolized and institutionalized around a president whose power is so strong that the other branches of government pay allegiance to it. The 'office of the president' becomes a sort of 'parallel government' with stronger executive powers than those of the cabinet ministers and with much more political influence than the legislative and judicial organs.[131] Even though executive hegemony and imperial presidency were common vernaculars used to describe the nature of African presidents in the past, they still recur in different forms and degrees to date.[132] While Chapter 5 discusses the constitutional design and practice of executive power with a particular focus on Nigeria, Ethiopia, and South Africa, for present purposes, I would like to explain the general nature of African executives and explain how this legal syncretism—ie, the selective incorporation and rejection of the traditional theory of government, an implied acceptance of the colonial theory of government, and the principle of separation of powers—brought an imperial executive and personalized executive power into the constitutional framework.

Indeed, the independence constitutions were able to put numerous constitutional limitations on the executive. In Anglophone Africa, the executive was divided in two: the head of state (run by a Governor General representing the Queen of England) and the head of government (run by a prime minister), mirroring the Westminster parliamentary system.[133] Accordingly, the prime minister and their cabinet were both answerable to, and depend on, the support of the parliament in order to continue in office. Furthermore, the constitutionalization of independent civil service, the police, and the judiciary on the one hand, and the recognition of a Bill of Rights with judicial review on the other, made the executive branches of Anglophone African states weak

[130] Charles M Fombad, 'An Overview of the Separation of Powers under Modern African Constitutions' in Charles M Fombad (ed) *Separation of Powers in African Constitutionalism* (Oxford University Press 2016) 70.

[131] Nicolas van de Walle, 'Presidentialism and Clientelism in Africa's Emerging Party Systems' (2003) 41 The Journal of Modern African Studies 297, 310.

[132] H Kwasi Prempeh, 'Africa's "Constitutionalism Revival": False Start or New Dawn?' (2007) 5 International Journal of Constitutional Law 469, 498.

[133] Robert B Seidman, 'Constitutions in Independent, Anglophonic, Sub-Saharan Africa: Form and Legitimacy' (1969) 1969 Wisconsin Law Review 83.

by design.[134] Under these constitutional arrangements, the executive had to receive the support of both the legislature and the judiciary in running the business of governance. In addition, the bifurcation of power into the head of state and head of government reduced the potential accumulation of power by any single individual. The incorporation of American constitutional ideas, such as a Bill of Rights and judicial review into a Westminster parliamentary model in Anglophone Africa was animated by the desire to prevent despotism, as political power was considered as an evil prone to corruption.[135] In retrospect, the successful practice—or effective implementation—of Anglophone independence constitutions would have avoided the emergence of imperial presidency and personal rule.[136] In Francophone Africa, however, the independence constitutions followed the French constitutional model by institutionalizing a strong executive president.[137] In particular, the sections dealing with presidential power were verbatim copies of the 1958 French Constitution.[138] Nevertheless, despite installing a strong executive president, the Francophone African independence constitutions also provided for a national legislature, judicial, and legal systems in order to ensure a French type of constitutionalism.[139]

Nonetheless, these constitutional limitations were either eroded or replaced by other constitutional rules from the late 1960s to the end of 1980s, as discussed in Chapter 2.[140] The pacesetter in this spectacle of imperial presidency and personal rule was Ghana, the first country to gain independence in sub-Saharan Africa, and its chief architect was Kwame Nkrumah.[141] Under Nkrumah's political engineering, the 1960 republican Constitution of Ghana abolished the previous independence constitution and established a single-party unitary state concentrating centralized government power under the unitary president—combining both the titular head of state and executive head of government into one.[142] Furthermore, the new republican Constitution granted the president strong powers which undermined the legislative and judicial branches of government.[143] For instance, the president was empowered to veto a bill without the possibility of a legislative override, to terminate or extend

[134] YP Ghai, 'Constitutions and the Political Order in East Africa' (1972) 21 The International and Comparative Law Quarterly 403, 412.

[135] ibid 413; See Francois Venter, 'Parliamentary Sovereignty or Presidential Imperialism? The Difficulties in Identifying the Sources of Constitutional Power from the Interaction Between Legislatures and Executives in Anglophone Africa' in Charles M Fombad (ed), *Separation of Powers in African Constitutionalism* (Oxford University Press 2016) 95–115.

[136] HWO Okoth-Ogendo, 'Constitutions without Constitutionalism: Reflections on an African Political Paradox' in Douglass Greenberg and others (eds), *Constitutionalism and Democracy: Transitions in the Contemporary World* (Oxford University Press 1993) 74 .

[137] Victor T Le Vine, 'The Fall and Rise of Constitutionalism in West Africa' (1997) 35 The Journal of Modern African Studies 181, 184.

[138] ibid.

[139] ibid.

[140] Young, *The Postcolonial State in Africa* (n 17) 16; Donald L Gordon, 'African Politics' in April A Gordon and Donald L Gordon (eds), *Understanding Contemporary Africa* (Lynne Rienner Publishers 2007) 76–80.

[141] Young, *The Postcolonial State in Africa* (n 17) 16.

[142] Prempeh, 'Presidential Power in Comparative Perspective' (n 129) 790.

[143] See also H Kwasi Prempeh, 'Progress and Retreat in Africa: Presidents Untamed' (2008) 19 Journal of Democracy 2, 109–25; H Kwasi Prempeh, 'Constitutional Autochthony and the Invention and Survival of "absolute Presidentialism" in Postcolonial Africa' in Gunter Frankenberk, *Order from Transfer Comparative Constitutional Design and Legal Culture Comparative Constitutional Design and Legal Culture* (Elgar 2013) 209–33.

the session of the parliament at any time, withdraw public funds outside of the approved budget, and unilaterally appoint or dismiss any number of cabinet members from the parliament.[144] The president was also entitled to appoint or dismiss the chief justice and judges of the superior courts, the auditor general, the attorney general, and members of the civil service—all of whom which were independent of the executive branch under the independence constitution.[145] In addition to allowing the president to run for re-election without limits and granting them the power to rule by decree, the republican constitution conferred *sui generis* powers on Nkrumah, as the first president 'to give directions by legislation whenever he [considered] it to be in the national interest to do so.'[146] Thus, his personal control of the one political party, which constituted the Parliament, as well as the abolishing of the regional assemblies and traditional chieftaincy powers, along with the aforementioned absolutist constitutional presidential powers, all turned Nkruma into a 'Presidential Monarch'.[147]

The rest of Africa, and Anglophone Africa in particular, soon followed Nkrumah's model of imperial presidency. For instance, Nkrumah's counterparts in Cote d' Ivoire, Guinea, Kenya, Malawi, Mali, Tanzania, Uganda, and Zambia, just to mention just a few, all installed imperial presidency and entrenched personal rule in their respective constitutions.[148] Common to the phenomenon of imperial presidency in postcolonial Africa were: the rejection of the separation of powers and the devolution of power and/or the (quasi) federal arrangement; the recentralization of power; the installation of single-party systems; the subordination of the political party and the state to the personal rule of the president; and, of course, the suppression of political dissent and human rights.[149] These have all resulted in the substitution of the rule of law and constitutionalism with the personal rule of the president, and the replacement of constitutional and legal rules with the informal rules of neopatrimonialism and its variants.[150] In this new configuration of government power, the legislature and the judiciary became rubber stamps for the executive, rather than being independent constitutional actors which could 'counteract ambition with ambition', in Madison's terms.[151]

[144] Prempeh, 'Presidential Power in Comparative Perspective' (n 129) 791–93.

[145] ibid 792.

[146] ibid.

[147] ibid 793.

[148] ibid 784, 794–95.

[149] ibid 794–95; Prempeh, 'Constitutional Autochthony and the Invention and Survival of "absolute Presidentialism" in Postcolonial Africa' (n 143) 210; Thomson (n 213) 109 and 132; Goran Hyden, *African Politics in Comparative Perspective* (Cambridge University Press 2005) Chapter 5 on Big Men.

[150] See Okoth-Ogendo, 'Constitutions without Constitutionalism' (n 136) 74; Michael Bratton and Nicholas van de Walle, 'Neopatrimonial Rule Regimes and Political Transitions in Africa' (1994) 46 World Politics 453; Paul Nugent, *Africa Since Independence: A Comparative History* (Palgrave Macmillan 2004) 204; Anne Pitcher, Mary H Moran, and Michael Johnston, 'Rethinking Patrimonialism and Neopatrimonialism in Africa' (2009) 52 African Studies Review 125, 129–30; Jean-François Bayart, *The State in Africa: The Politics of the Belly* (Longman 1993) 228–34; Pierre Englebert and Kevin C Dunn, *Inside African Politics* (Lynne Rienner Publishers 2013) 129–56.

[151] Salih, 'Introduction' (n 89) 11; H Kwasi Prempeh, 'Marbury in Africa: Judicial Review and the Challenge of Constitutionalism in Contemporary Africa' (2007) 80 Tulane Law Review 42–84; H Kwasi Prempeh, 'African Judges, in Their Own Cause: Reconstituting Independent Courts in Contemporary Africa' (2006) 4 International Journal of Constitutional Law 592; Robert B Seidman, 'Judicial Review and Fundamental Freedoms in Anglophonic Independent Africa' (1974) 35 Ohio St LJ 820, 820–50.

Although the return of multi-party systems and the introduction of term limits with the third wave of democratization have opened a space for plural political contestation and have limited the tenure of presidents, respectively, the substantive powers of presidents remain unaltered, or are not effectively limited.[152] Not only do these new constitutions remain committed to the presidential form of government, they also maintain the strong powers of the presidency by merely opening the office to multi-party competition and limiting its tenure without doing more to restrict its scope and power;[153] the imperial nature of the presidency doesn't seems to be a great problem for constitution-makers of the third wave. As in the *ancien régime*, the president still enjoys more powers than the legislature and the judiciary.[154] These powers range from the expression of the supremacy of the president over any other person or organ,[155] to wider appointment and emergency powers that can diminish the principle of separation of powers and checks and balances,[156] to presidential immunity.[157]

In a similar vein, in many of the constitutions, legislative and policy initiation—including those pertaining to national budgets—are the prerogatives of the executive, while the role of parliament remains limited to either passing or not passing the bills.[158] Even in this role, given the phenomenon of dominant or one-party systems coupled with wider presidential leverage, the parliaments are usually receptive to the executive bills and proposals.[159] The operating systems of these dominant or one-party systems is not significantly different from the one-party systems of the *ancien régime*.[160] Moreover, through subsidiary legislation, i.e., executive rule-making through delegation, the executive enjoys even wider discretion, thereby escaping both parliamentary

[152] Prempeh, 'Africa's "Constitutionalism Revival"' (n 132) 497.

[153] See Prempeh, 'Progress and Retreat in Africa' (n 143); Prempeh, 'Presidential Power in Comparative Perspective' (n 129).

[154] Muna Ndulo, 'Presidentialism in the Southern African States and Constitutional Restraint on Presidential Power' (2001) 26 Vt L Rev 769, 771.

[155] Article 98(2) of the Ugandan Constitution reads 'The President shall take precedence over all persons in Uganda, and in descending order, the Vice-President, the Speaker and the Chief Justice, shall take precedence over all other persons in Uganda'.

[156] Ndulo, 'Presidentialism in the Southern African States and Constitutional Restraint on Presidential Power' (n 154).

[157] Charles Manga Fombad and Enyinna Nwauche, 'Africa's Imperial Presidents: Immunity, Impunity and Accountability' (2012) 5 African Journal of Legal Studies 91, 91–118.

[158] Prempeh, 'Africa's "Constitutionalism Revival"' (n 132) 498.

[159] Salih, 'Introduction' (n 89) 13–18; R Doorenspleet and L Nijzink (eds), *One-Party Dominance in African Democracies* (Lynne Rienner 2013) (detailing the experiences of Namibia, South Africa, Tanzania, Zambia, Senegal, and Mali in particular); M Chege, *Political Parties in East Africa: Diversity in Political Party Systems* (International IDEA 2007) (exploring the one party dominant system in Ethiopia, Uganda, and Tanzania); G Erdmann and M Basedau, 'Party Systems in Africa: Problems of Categorizing and Explaining Party Systems' (2008) 26 Journal of Contemporary African Studies 3, 241–58; Matthijs Bogaards, 'Counting Parties and Identifying Dominant Party Systems in Africa' (2004) 43 European Journal of Political Research 173, 173–97.

[160] See de Walle, 'Presidentialism and Clientelism in Africa's Emerging Party Systems' (n 131); V Adefemi Isumonah, 'Imperial Presidency and Democratic Consolidation in Nigeria' (2012) 59 Africa Today 43, 43–68; Sarah Brierley, 'Party Unity and Presidential Dominance: Parliamentary Development in the Fourth Republic of Ghana' (2012) 30 Journal of Contemporary African Studies 419, 419–39; Andrew M Mwenda, 'Personalizing Power in Uganda' (2007) 18 Journal of Democracy 23, 23–37; Adem Kassie Abebe, 'From the "TPLF Constitution" to the "Constitution of the People of Ethiopia": Constitutionalism and Proposals for Constitutional Reform' in Morris Kiwinda Mbondenyi and Tom Ojienda (eds), *Constitutionalism and Democratic Governance in Africa: Contemporary Perspectives from Sub-Saharan Africa* (Pretoria University Law Press 2013) 71–74.

and judicial oversight.[161] Furthermore, these regressive constitutional designs have also helped to maintain executive hegemony.[162] For example, while terms limits have ended the tenure of some presidents, many others have managed to get constitutional amendments that either extend their tenure, or safely ignore the term limits.[163]

The phenomenon of imperial presidency also still persists—to various degrees and in different forms—in states that have recently adopted brand new constitutions. Kenya and South Sudan are good examples of how the imperial presidency persists and continues to figure in constitutional practice. While the 2010 Kenyan Constitution, in its design, limits executive hegemony and the recurring phenomenon of an imperial presidency,[164] the president continues to enjoy more powers from extra-constitutional sources.[165] From a constitutional design perspective[166] we have the following limitations: the president only nominates persons to different constitutional offices and their appointment and dismissal rests in the hands of the legislature;[167] the legislature not only controls the determination of the national revenue,[168] but must also approve any declaration of state of emergency and/or war;[169] the legislature not only calls and asks cabinet ministers,[170] but it can also impeach the president for violations of the constitution, national law, or international law;[171] the Constitution establishes an independent electoral commission,[172] and also positions the judiciary as the guardian of the Constitution and the 'people's will' by ensuring its institutional and functional independence.[173] Despite all of these constitutional designs, however, extra-constitutional sources manage to somehow maintain the impulses of an imperial presidency. Elite interests in the bureaucracy, real or alleged security threats, as well as the continuity of persons and their mode of engagement from the *ancien régime*,

161 Prempeh, 'Africa's "Constitutionalism Revival"' (n 132) 498.

162 ibid 498; Charles Manga Fombad, 'Constitutional Reforms and Constitutionalism in Africa: Reflections on Some Current Challenges and Future Prospects' (2011) 59 Buff L Rev 1007, 1024; Gedion T Hessebon, 'Some Major Themes in the Study of Constitutionalism and Democracy in Africa' (2013) 7 Vienna Journal on International Constitutional Law 28, 35–38.

163 Cheryl Hendricks and Gabriel Ngah Kiven, 'Presidential Term Limits: Slippery Slope Back to Authoritarianism in Africa' [2018] The Conversation <http://theconversationcom/presidential-term-limits-slippery-slope-back-to-authoritarianism-in-africa-96796> accessed 12 December 2018; Denis M Tull and Claudia Simons, 'The Institutionalisation of Power Revisited: Presidential Term Limits in Africa' (2017) 52 Africa Spectrum 79, 83–89 For instance, while Frederick Chiluba (2001) and Edgar Lungu (2015) of Zambia, Olusegun Obesanjo of Nigeria (2005), Mamadou Tandja of Niger (2010), and Blaise Compaore of Burkino Faso (2014) leave office as a result of term limits, the presidents of Burundi, Rwanda, Togo, Gabon, Uganda, Chad, Cameroon, Djibouti, Republic of Congo, Sudan, Senegal, Eritrea, and the Democratic Republic of the Congo amended or ignored terms limits to stay in office.

164 See Conrad M Bosire, 'Kenya's Budding Bicameralism and Legislative-Executive Relations' in Charles M Fombad (ed), *Separation of Powers in African Constitutionalism* (Oxford University Press 2016) 116–33.

165 See Mai Hassan, 'Continuity despite Change: Kenya's New Constitution and Executive Power' (2015) 22 Democratization 587, 587–609.

166 See also Gedion T Hessebon, 'The Fourth Constitution-Making Wave of Africa: Constitutions 40?' (2014) 28 Temple International & Comparative Law Journal 185, 212–13.

167 See for instance, the Constitution of Kenya, arts 132(2), 142(2), 152(2), 156(2), 166(1) (a), 233(2).

168 ibid arts 95(4) and 96(3).

169 ibid art 95(6).

170 ibid art 153(3).

171 ibid art 145.

172 ibid art 88.

173 ibid art 159.

all conspire to grant presidents extra-constitutional powers.[174] In South Sudan, however, the imperial impulses of the president are more explicit even in the constitutional design itself. For instance, the president is constitutionally empowered to unilaterally remove a state governor, dissolve a state legislative assembly, or appoint a caretaker governor in the event of a crises.[175] The presidential use of these powers has already led South Sudan to political turmoil, including civil war.[176]

Thus, such phenomena as imperial presidency and personal rule in Africa are neither a postcolonial governance big bang, nor are they attributes of the African traditional system of government, but are rather the result of blending diverse legal, political, and social norms and experiences—both from within and outside of Africa—into one constitutional order. Imperial presidency and personal rule are results of legal syncretism that is conditioned to serve the real or alleged interests of the African states and, concomitantly, entrench the power, role, and agency of its leaders. To this end, the African constitutional designs and practices incorporate and magnify the *power-enabling* aspects of the executive power from diverse legal and political rules and experiences, while relegating and deemphasizing the *power-limiting* aspects of the executive power from the very same diverse rules and experiences. The outcome of these processes is the institution of a hyperactive and imperial executive as well as highly-personalized executive power in which the executive controls the political party apparatus, the government institutions, and, ultimately, the state itself.

C. The Judiciary: The Fusion of Laws and Persons

As with the legislature, the judiciary in Africa had a limited role in the practice of constitutionalism.[177] Not only was 'Africa's first encounter with independent courts short lived', the role of courts was ignored altogether in discussions of African politics.[178] The predominance of imperial presidencies, one-party systems, military rules, and neopatrimonial politics from the 1960s to the 1980s placed courts and their role at the periphery of the experiment with constitutionalism.[179] Although the democratic constitutions of the 1990s grant courts the power of judicial review along with

[174] Mai Hassan, 'Continuity despite Change: Kenya's New Constitution and Executive Power' (2015) 22 Democratization 587, 598–604; Solomon Ayele Dersso, 'More Than Enacting a Just Constitution: Lessons from Kenya on the Challenges of Establishing a Rule-Based Democratic Politics' in Jaap de Visser, Nico Steytler, Derek Powell, and Ebenezer Durojaye (eds), *Constitution Building in Africa* (Nomos, Baden-Baden 2015) 271–92.

[175] The Constitution of South Sudan 2011, arts 101(r) and (s).

[176] See Mark AW Deng, 'Defining the Nature and Limits of Presidential Powers in the Transitional Constitution of South Sudan: A Politically Contentious Matter for the New Nation' (2017) Journal of African Law 1, 23–39.

[177] See for instance Seidman, 'Judicial Review and Fundamental Freedoms in Anglophonic Independent Africa' (n 151); Steven B Pfeiffer, 'The Role of the Judiciary in the Constitutional Systems of East Africa' (1978) 16 The Journal of Modern African Studies 33, 33–66; Le Vine, 'The Fall and Rise of Constitutionalism in West Africa' (n 137).

[178] Prempeh, 'African Judges' (n 151) 593–94; See Jennifer A Widner, *Building the Rule of Law: Francis Nyalali and the Road to Judicial Independence in Africa* (WW Norton and Company 2001), this being one of the works which examines the role of judges for constitutionalism in Africa .

[179] For why judiciaries are neglected in the scholarship, see Karen A Mingst, 'Judicial Systems of Sub-Saharan Africa: An Analysis of Neglect' (1988) 31 African Studies Review 135, 135–47.

institutional and functional independence, at least in principle, with few exceptions—such as in South Africa, many courts do not yet establish substantial jurisprudence.[180] In spite of this, the role of courts as legal and constitutional arbiters is emerging.[181] Even though there are differences with respect to the exact roles of these courts and their jurisprudence in specific countries,[182] there is a common theme in both their judicial organization and interpretation which unites judiciaries in Africa. This theme is the fusion of laws and persons from customary and/or Sharia laws along with those from constitutional and statutory laws. In this section, I show how these are all fused together in the works of the judiciary, and how adjudicators of these laws compose the institution of the judiciary. The aim of this discussion is to show how, like with the legislative and executive branches, the judiciary, too, is the product of legal syncretism as well as a space for the same.

As discussed elsewhere in this book, many African constitutions recognize customary laws in limited matters—subject to constitutional and legal conformity. While the scope of application of customary laws varies across constitutions,[183] they are predominantly applicable in personal and family matters, such as marriage, inheritance, and land.[184] They are also applicable in natural resource management and dispute resolution.[185] While the preferred approach is an express recognition of customary laws, some constitutions recognize them as part of the right to culture and/or minority rights, or a combination of both. Consider, for instance, South Africa and Cameroon. The South African Constitution expressly recognizes customary laws as well as the right to culture. Section 39 of their Constitution provides that '[w]hen interpreting any legislation, and when developing the common law or customary law, every court, tribunal or forum must promote the spirit, purport and objects of the Bill of Rights'. Moreover, section 211 stipulates that '[t]he institution, status and role of traditional leadership, according to customary law, are recognised, subject to the Constitution'. Additionally, the Constitution recognizes both the individual right to culture[186] and the right to culture of cultural, religious, and linguistic communities.[187] So, although customary law is expressly recognized on its own, the right to culture in general, and

[180] Prempeh, 'Marbury in Africa' (n 151); Fombad, 'Constitutional Reforms and Constitutionalism in Africa' (n 162).

[181] Prempeh, 'Africa's "Constitutionalism Revival"' (n 132); Yuhniwo Ngenge, 'Traditional and historical antecedents of constitutional justice in West Africa' in Markus Böckenförde and others (eds), *Judicial Review Systems in West Africa: A Comparative Analysis* (International IDEA 2016) 39–40; Josephine Dawuni, 'Gender and the Judiciary in Africa: An Introduction' in Gretchen Bauer and Josephine Dawuni (eds), *Gender and the Judiciary in Africa: From Obscurity to Parity?* (Routledge 2015) 5–6.

[182] See Rachel Ellett, *Pathways to Judicial Power in Transitional States: Perspectives from African Courts* (Routledge 2013). Discussing the various ways of judicial empowerment in Malawi, Uganda, and Tanzania.

[183] Katrina Cuskelly, 'Customs and Constitutions: State Recognition of Customary Law around the World' (International Union for Conservation of Nature and Natural Resources 2011) 6–11 <https://portalsiucnorg/library/efiles/documents/2011-101pdf> accessed 8 March 2017.

[184] See Anne Helium, 'Human Rights and Gender Relations in Postcolonial Africa: Options and Limits for the Subjects of Legal Pluralism' (2000) 25 Law & Social Inquiry 635, 635–55; Kuenyehia (n 405); Muna Ndulo, 'African Customary Law, Customs, and Women's Rights' (2011) 18 Indiana Journal of Global Legal Studies 87, 88–89; Jeanmarie Fenrich, Paolo Galizzi, and Tracy E Higgins (eds), *The Future of African Customary Law* (Cambridge University Press 2011).

[185] Cuskelly, 'Customs and Constitutions' (n 183) 6–11.

[186] The Constitution of South Africa, s 30.

[187] ibid s 31.

of cultural communities in particular, can help to consolidate more robust protection of customary law under the Constitution.[188]

Unlike in South Africa, however, one does not find any express recognition, or even mention, of customary law in the Constitution of Cameroon. The constitutional basis for customary law in Cameroon is found in the Preamble and Article 1(2). The Preamble states that 'the State shall ensure the protection of minorities and shall preserve the rights of indigenous populations in accordance with the law.' Article 1(2), among other principles, provides that '[i]t [the state] shall recognize and protect traditional values that conform to democratic principles, human rights and the law', and '[i]t shall ensure the equality of all citizens before the law'. Hence, the protection of minorities and indigenous peoples on the one hand, and the recognition and protection of traditional values on the other, provide a constitutional basis for the application of customary law in Cameroon. As with any other African country, customary law continues to apply in Cameroon—subject to constitutional and legal limitations.[189]

In addition to customary laws, Islamic law is also recognized in many African countries,[190] albeit to different degrees, ranging from predominantly Muslim countries, such as The Gambia, Djibouti, and Sudan, to countries where Muslims constitute almost half of the population, such as Ethiopia, Nigeria, and Ghana, to countries where Muslims constitute a minority, such as Kenya and Tanzania.[191] Even in Muslim-majority countries, the constitutional status of Islamic law varies. For example, Islam is the official state religion in Djibouti[192] and is a source of legislation in Sudan,[193] while it is only applicable in 'matters of marriage, divorce and inheritance among members of the communities to which it applies' in The Gambia.[194] The Gambian approach is typical of the recognition of Islamic law in Africa.[195] To be more precise, the typical

188 See TW Bennett, *Customary Law in South Africa* (Juta 2004). The current debate on the recognition of Muslim law in South Africa is along these lines. This is due to the fact that the claim for recognition of Muslim law rests on the right to religion and the possibility of legislative recognition of cultural and religious laws on personal matters according to ss 15(1) and 15(3)(a) of the Constitution. For details see Christa Rautenbach, 'Deep Legal Pluralism in South Africa: Judicial Accommodation of Non-State Law' (2010) 42 The Journal of Legal Pluralism and Unofficial Law 143, 143–77.

189 See Mikano Emmanuel Kiye, 'Conflict between Customary Law and Human Rights in Cameroon: The Role of the Courts in Fostering an Equitably Gendered Society' (2015) 36 African Study Monographs 75, 75–100; Lotsmart N Fonjong (ed), *Issues in Women's Land Rights in Cameroon* (African Books Collective 2012) (discussing how the land rights regime, including customary law, negatively affect women).

190 See Abdullahi Ahmed An-Na'im, *African Constitutionalism and the Role of Islam* (University of Pennsylvania Press 2006); Abdullahi Ahmed An-Na'im, *Islamic Family Law in A Changing World: A Global Resource Book* (Zed Books 2002) 37–62 (on East Africa), 187–98 (on Southern Africa), 281–306 (on West Africa).

191 See Shamil Jeppie, Ebrahim Moosa, and Richard L Roberts, *Muslim Family Law in Sub-Saharan Africa: Colonial Legacies and Post-Colonial Challenges* (Amsterdam University Press 2010).

192 The Constitution of Djibouti 1992, art 1.

193 The Constitution of Sudan 2005, art 5(1).

194 The Constitution of Gambia, s 7(f).

195 Nonetheless, there are differences in the practice of sharia law. For instance, despite the differences in the details the Ethiopian and Nigerian constitutions give to sharia law, they have similar substance that it is applicable in personal matters with the consent of parties. However, the actual application of sharia law in Nigeria extends to criminal law unlike Ethiopia. See Mamman Lawan, 'Islamic Law and Legal Hybridity in Nigeria' (2014) 58 Journal of African Law 303; Mohammed Abdo, 'Legal Pluralism, Sharia Courts and Constitutional Issues in Ethiopia' (2011) 5 Mizan Law Review 72, 72–106.

recognition of Islamic law in African constitutions goes as follows: 'The jurisdiction of a Kadhi's court shall be limited to the determination of questions of Muslim law relating to personal status, marriage, divorce or inheritance in proceedings in which all the parties profess the Muslim religion and submit to the jurisdiction of the Kadhi's courts.'[196] Thus, the application of Islamic law is limited in scope and is conditional upon the consent of all parties.

The constitutional recognition of customary and Islamic laws fuses together persons and laws from both indigenous and religious sources and constitutional and statutory sources. The recognition of customary and Islamic laws brings traditional, Islamic, and modern judges together in the business of adjudication. Unlike Islamic law, however, where Khadi or Islamic judges are primarily responsible for its adjudication in both first instance and appellate levels, there is no uniform body responsible for the adjudication of customary laws in Africa. However, there are three major institutional arrangements for the adjudication of customary laws. The first is the adjudication of customary laws through traditional authorities or rulers. These traditional authorities can either be duly constituted and established in the constitution, as is the case in Ghana,[197] or they may not have such constitutional institutionalization, but continue to judge on customary laws as traditional authorities, like in Kenya.[198] The second is adjudication through legal practitioners who have the necessary legal training and experience along with the necessary knowledge in customary laws, as is the case in Nigeria.[199] The third is adjudication through a combination of regular courts and traditional authorities or rulers, like we see in South Africa.[200] The mixture of these persons brings varied personal and professional experience and, concomitantly, produces diverse judicial reasoning and philosophy. Being placed within the hierarchy of courts, as is further discussed in Chapter 6, constitutional and/or apex courts are given the responsibility of ensuring a syncretic form of judicial practice and philosophy.

Like with the fusion of persons, the recognition of customary and Islamic laws blends them with constitutional and statutory laws, and, consequently, transforms them all in the business of adjudication. This is due to the fact that constitutional and statutory principles and values are used to filter exactly which customary and Islamic laws are to be recognized. In this process, the substantive and procedural aspects of these laws have to conform to constitutional and legal standards. The output of these processes is not simply one of customary and Islamic laws in their purest forms, but a transformed version of these laws as embedded within constitutional and legal principles and values.

In addition to the transformation of customary and Islamic laws at the level of normative recognition, they are also subject to further transformation in their

[196] The Constitution of Kenya, art 170(5).

[197] See the Constitution of Ghana, arts 273 and 274; where the National House of Chiefs and Regional House of chiefs are responsible for the judicial settlement of customary law.

[198] See the Constitution of Kenya, art 159(2)(c).

[199] See the Constitution of Nigeria, ss 266(1) and 277(1).

[200] See the Constitution of South Africa, s 211.

application. Such transformation happens at least at two levels. The first is the first instance/appellate application of customary and Islamic laws by customary and Islamic-specific adjudicatory bodies. The second is the application of these laws in higher and apex courts through appeal. While the transformation of customary and Islamic laws in customary and Islamic-specific adjudicatory bodies is less than in higher and apex courts, as is discussed in greater detail in Chapter 6, even just the possibility of applying other non-customary or non-Islamic laws or principles in cases involving customary and Islamic laws inevitably transforms them. At the same time, some constitutional and legal standards also have to give way—at least somewhat—for the application of customary and Islamic laws. Therefore, what we see in the constitutional recognition of customary and Islamic laws is the syncretism of these laws with constitutional and statutory laws and their transformation through judicial practice. The constitutional recognition and application of customary and Islamic laws brings the syncretism of laws and persons into the judiciary, which, in turn, transforms the institutional manifestation of the judiciary along with its guiding laws, practices, and philosophies.

III. The African Constitutional Rights Regime

Constitutional rights are one of the basic pillars of liberal constitutionalism. Along with the separation of powers, constitutional rights set a limit to government power and action. In their classic form, constitutional rights are shields against the government.[201] As such, they are constitutional entitlements of individuals against their states and, consequently, they limit the actions of the legislative, executive, and judicial branches of government—as well as other state organs—in their relationship with individuals. Equal treatment and equal concern for all individuals is the central edifice of constitutional rights.

The African constitutional rights regime, however, configures this liberal constitutional rights system with the African conception of rights. The incorporation of rights rooted in the African traditions and cultures into liberal constitutional rights transform the nature and identity of constitutional rights in Africa, as they become not only entitlements that limit the power of the state, but also duties that impose obligations onto the individual towards the state. In a similar vein, constitutional rights in Africa rest in a diverse normative universe that has plural senses of equal treatment and equal concern. As with the *constitution* and vertical organization of the state and its government architecture, as discussed above, legal syncretism animates the African constitutional rights regime, too. In this section, in order to demonstrate the nature of constitutional rights in Africa, I will explore and examine how legal syncretism combines constitutional duties with constitutional rights and produces a unique regime of women's rights.

201 Sajó and Uitz, *The Constitution of Freedom* (n 91) 377; Robert Alexy, *A Theory of Constitutional Rights* (Julian Rivers tr, Oxford University Press 2002) 365–96; Ronald Dworkin, *Taking Rights Seriously* (Harvard University Press 1978) 365.

A. The Duty-Rights Conception

The fusion of duties with rights is a fine example of the syncretism of the liberal account of rights and the African conception of rights. While the idea of individual duties is not unique to the African legal, cultural, and political experience,[202] duties do permeate all forms of social organization and the practice of rights in precolonial Africa. In this respect, the African Charter on Human and Peoples' Rights (the African Charter) is the pioneer legal instrument that introduces the notion of duties with rights on the continent. In his appeal for the recognition of duties in the African Charter, Leopold Senghor, the then President of Senegal, noted that:

> Room should be made for [the] African tradition in our Charter on Human and Peoples' Rights, while bathing in our philosophy, which consists in not alienating the subordination of the individual to the community, in co-existence, in giving everyone a certain number of rights and duties. In Europe, Human Rights are considered as a body of principles and rules placed in the hands of the individual, as a weapon, thus enabling him to defend himself against the group or entity representing it. In Africa, the individual and his rights are wrapped in the protection of the family and other communities ... If we want to build the *Homo africanus* of tomorrow, we should once again, assimilate without being assimilated. We should borrow from modernism only that which does not misrepresent our civilization and deep nature.[203]

Along similar lines, experts entrusted with the drafting of the African Charter proposed that '[t]he conception of an individual who is utterly free and utterly irresponsible and opposed to society is not consonant with African philosophy'.[204] The idea that the individual as an autonomous moral being is endowed with rights, but at the same time bound by duties, is held to be the quintessence of the human rights formulation in precolonial Africa.[205] Hence, the clear articulation of duties in the African Charter is the incorporation of the African conception of rights into the liberal notion of rights.[206]

Building on the African Charter, more than forty African constitutions incorporate the notion of individual duties along with rights.[207] However, the extent of these duties, and the places where they are stipulated, vary. In many of the constitutions, the

202 See the Universal Declaration of Human Rights 1948, art 29; the American Declaration of the Rights and Duties of Man 1948; Fatsah Ouguergouz, *The African Charter of Human and People's Rights: A Comprehensive Agenda for Human Dignity and Sustainable Democracy in Africa* (Martinus Nijhoff Publishers 2003) 381–400 (detailing the ethical, religious, and legal sources of the notion of duty beyond Africa).

203 Ouguergouz, *The African Charter of Human and People's Rights* (n 202) 377–78.

204 ibid.

205 Makau Mutua, *Human Rights: A Political and Cultural Critique* (University of Pennsylvania Press 2009) 84.

206 Vincent Obisienunwo Orlu Nmehielle, *The African Human Rights System: Its Laws, Practice, and Institutions* (Martinus Nijhoff Publishers 2001) 161–65; *Kofi Quashigah*, 'Scope of Individual Duties in the African Charter' in Manisuli Ssenyonjo (ed), *The African Regional Human Rights System: 30 Years After the African Charter on Human and Peoples' Rights* (Martinus Nijhoff Publishers 2011) 119–34.

207 See also Christof Heyns and Waruguru Kaguongo, 'Constitutional Human Rights Law in Africa' (2006) 22 S Afr J on Hum Rts 673, 712.

section on the Bill of Rights is entitled 'Fundamental Rights and Duties', while others either provide a separate section on duties, or duties are attached to the rights.[208] For instance, both Burundi and Angola entitled their Bill of Rights, 'Fundamental Rights and Duties', but they differ in the nature of the duties and their details. After declaring that citizens have rights and duties,[209] the Constitution of Burundi lists the duties individually and these include, among others, the responsibility to respect one's compatriots and to show them consideration without discrimination; responsibilities to the family, society, state and other public collectivities; to maintain national unity; to respect the laws and institutions of the state; to defend the country, etc.[210] The Angolan Constitution, however, mixes the duties in with the rights; in accordance with its principle of universality, it recognizes rights and freedoms, yet also imposes duties on the individual with regard to family, society, the state, and other legally recognized institutions. These include the particular duties to:

(a) To respect the rights, freedoms, and property of others, morals, acceptable behavior and the common good;
(b) To respect and be considerate of others without discrimination of any kind and to maintain relations that promote, safeguard and reinforce mutual respect and tolerance.[211]

The Constitution further imposes duties on the individual in the enjoyment of rights. For example, while the right to live in a heathy environment, the right to vote, and the right to work are all recognized, defending and preserving the environment, voting, and work are also individual duties.[212]

In addition to Bills of Rights, in some constitutions individual duties are found in the sections dealing with Directive Principles of State Policy as well as various Preambles. For instance, Section 24 of the Nigerian Constitution imposes duties on individuals requiring them to respect the Constitution, institutions, and legitimate authorities, defend the nation, respect the dignity and rights of other citizens, to pay taxes, and contribute to the wellbeing of the community.[213] By the same token, Section 63 of the Eswatini Constitution clearly stipulates that 'the exercise and enjoyment of rights is inseparable from the performance of duties and obligations' and, as a result, it imposes duties on individuals to respect the Constitution, defend the nation, further the national interest and ensure national unity, promote democracy and rule of law, work, and protect and safeguard the environment.[214] The Constitutions of Cameroon and Comoros, on the other hand, contain individual duties in their Preambles. The Constitution of Cameroon, for example, imposes duties on individuals to protect the environment, work, pay taxes, and defend the nation.[215] The Constitution of Comoros,

[208] ibid 712–13.
[209] The Constitution of Burundi 2005, art 20.
[210] ibid arts 62–74.
[211] The Constitution of Angola 2010, art 22(1) and (3).
[212] ibid arts 39(1), 54(3), and 76(1).
[213] See also the Constitution of Sierra Leone, s 13 which imposes similar duties on the individual.
[214] See also the Constitution of Zambia, art 113 and the Constitution of Uganda, art xxix which impose similar duties on individuals.
[215] See the Constitution of Cameroon, preamble paras 21–24.

on the other hand, emphasizes the corollary nature of rights and duties and makes the protection of the environment the duty of individuals.[216] Furthermore, the notion of duty is one of the basic constitutional principles in Ethiopia.[217] Along with the sovereignty of the people, human and democratic rights, the separation of state and religion, and the accountability of government, the 'duty to ensure the constitution and to obey it' constitutes the fundamental principle of the Ethiopian Constitution.[218]

Although these constitutional duties are not a subject of judicial or quasi-judicial litigation, unlike women's rights, the idea that individuals have duties to other individuals, their family, society, and the state in general, is deeply entrenched in the African social and cultural imagination.[219] By the same token, the notion that duties are express corollaries of rights also fits well with the conception of rights in precolonial Africa.[220] As with this syncretic normative articulation of the duty-rights conception, its constitutional practice will also surely lead to a syncretic notion of the constitutional rights regime, as Chapter 6 demonstrates with respect to women's rights. Regardless of the judicial or quasi-judicial practice, the normative design of the duty-rights conception in African constitutions is a clear manifestation of the syncretism between the liberal notion of rights with the African conception of rights.

B. Women's Constitutional Rights

Women's rights are another example of the syncretism in constitutional design between the liberal notion of rights and the communitarian vision of rights as embedded in African cultural conceptions. On the one hand, the right to equality of both women and men are guaranteed in every African constitution. However, women's rights are often tempered by the recognition of group rights in the form of the right to culture, customary and Islamic laws, and the powers of traditional authorities. Thus, women's rights are confluence points for the protection of individual rights mainly rooted in the liberal tradition on the one hand, and the quest for recognition of group rights in the African communitarian conception on the other. What we see in this experimentation is the fusion and configuration of the liberal and communitarian accounts of rights within constitutional rights.

As mentioned, the right to equality and non-discrimination is recognized in every constitution in Africa.[221] And despite differences in formulation, these rights form the core of the Bill of Rights. For instance, the Ethiopian Constitution contains a non-discrimination clause in its section on the right to equality. It provides that:

[216] Preamble of the Constitution of Comoros.

[217] The Constitution of the Federal Democratic Republic of Ethiopia, art 9(2).

[218] ibid arts 8–12.

[219] See Makau Wa Mutua, 'The Banjul Charter and the African Cultural Fingerprint: An Evaluation of the Language of Duties' (1995) 35 Virginia Journal of International Law, 339–80; Issa G Shivji, *The Concept of Human Rights in Africa* (African Books Collective 1989).

[220] Deng, *Identity, Diversity, and Constitutionalism in Africa* (n 17) 77–102; Josiah AM Cobbah, 'African Values and the Human Rights Debate: An African Perspective' (1987) 9 Human Rights Quarterly 309.

[221] Heyns and Kaguongo, 'Constitutional Human Rights Law in Africa' (n 206) 683.

> [a]ll persons are equal before the law and are entitled without any discrimination to the equal protection of the law. In this respect, the law shall guarantee to all persons equal and effective protection without discrimination on grounds of race, nation, nationality, or other social origin, colour, sex, language, religion, political or other opinion, property, birth or other status.[222]

The Ugandan Constitution, on the other hand, recognizes the right to equality and non-discrimination as follows:[223]

1. All persons are equal before and under the law in all spheres of political, economic, social and cultural life and in every other respect and shall enjoy equal protection of the law.
2. Without prejudice to clause (1) of this article, a person shall not be discriminated against on the ground of sex, race, colour, ethnic origin, tribe, birth, creed or religion, or social or economic standing, political opinion or disability.

Such constitutional rights to equality and non-discrimination guarantees and ensures—at least in principle—the rights of women, both as individuals and citizens.[224] Women can enjoy the rights protected in their respective constitutions, access the socio-economic and political opportunities available to them, and demand protection and safeguard in the event of discrimination based on sex. In addition to this general right to equality and non-discrimination, many constitutions contain specific rights under the title 'Women's Rights', or in the sections dealing with family and marriage,[225] and sometimes in the provisions for affirmative action.[226]

Without ignoring the empirical reality within which many African women lead their lives, the constitutional right to equality and non-discrimination in all facets of life seems to lay down a gender-sensitive rights framework.[227] However, the group rights conception of constitutions often brings back indigenous legal and political practices which are not always compatible with the rights of women. In this respect, the right to culture is one of the rights that presents a red light to the enjoyment of women's rights. More than forty constitutions in Africa recognize the right to culture.[228] For instance, Section 26 of the Ghanaian Constitution recognizes the right to culture as follows: 'Every person is entitled to enjoy, practice, profess, maintain and promote any culture, language, tradition or religion subject to the provisions of this Constitution.' Similarly, Section 44 of the Kenyan Constitution states that:

1. Every person has the right to use the language, and to participate in the cultural life, of the person's choice.

222 The Constitution of the Federal Democratic Republic of Ethiopia, art 25.

223 The Constitution of Uganda, art 21.

224 See Manisuli Ssenyonjo, 'Culture and the Human Rights of Women in Africa: Between Light and Shadow' (2007) 51 Journal of African Law 39.

225 The Constitution of Angola, art 35(3).

226 The Constitution of the Federal Democratic Republic of Ethiopia, art 35(3).

227 Ssenyonjo, 'Culture and the Human Rights of Women in Africa' (n 224); Fareda Banda, *Women, Law and Human Rights: An African Perspective* (Hart Publishing 2005).

228 Heyns and Kaguongo, 'Constitutional Human Rights Law in Africa' (n 207) 715.

2. A person belonging to a cultural or linguistic community has the right, with other members of that community—
   a. to enjoy the person's culture and use the person's language; or
   b. to form, join and maintain cultural and linguistic associations and other organs of civil society.

These constitutional stipulations represent how the right to culture is constitutionalized in Africa. While the individualistic formulation of the right to culture is the more dominant one, the addition of a group component, like in Kenya, shows the emphasis and attention given to groups.[229] Nonetheless, even in cases with a more individualistic formulation, the right to culture is also a collective right. As culture is 'a comprehensive way of life', an individual neither forms this way of life alone, nor can they enjoy it by themselves.[230] As such, the recognition of the right to culture presupposes the existence of a group and its peculiar way of life, and as a result, the choice available to the individual—in practice—is minimal as the group corporately controls the practice of a culture. Although women, like men, are cultural beings who identify and want to be identified with their own specific cultures,[231] there are numerous cultural practices in Africa which place women in an inferior position to men and continue to violate their rights and dignity.[232] While the right to culture should be practiced within the contours of an open and democratic society, and in line with the basic tenets of constitutions, the possibility of conflict with women's rights is not a stretch of the imagination, as demonstrated in Chapter 6.

More specifically, the recognition of customary and Islamic laws in constitutions channels the indigenous and religious laws and practices into the designs and practices of individual rights—and women's rights in particular—since, as noted elsewhere in this book, customary and Islamic laws are usually applicable in personal and family matters. Although there are customary laws which protect the rights and interests of women, there are also customary laws which discriminate against women on matters related to marriage, divorce, inheritance, land, and property, among others.[233] By the same token, Islamic law, on matters of marriage, divorce, and inheritance, discriminates against women in favor of men.[234] Thus, although the equality of women with men is guaranteed in the constitutions, the constitutional recognition of these customary and Islamic laws gives the normative basis for the abdication of gender

[229] See Hessebon, 'The Fourth Constitution-Making Wave of Africa' (n 166).

[230] Avishai Margalit and Moshe Halbertal, 'Liberalism and the Right to Culture' (2004) 71 Social Research 529, 535.

[231] Florence Butegwa, 'Mediating Culture and Human Rights in Favour of Land Rights for Women in Africa: A Framework for Community-level Action' in Abdullahi A An-Na'im (ed), *Cultural Transformation and Human Rights in Africa* (Zed Books 2002) 109.

[232] Ndulo, 'African Customary Law, Customs, and Women's Rights' (n 184).

[233] Manisuli Ssenyonjo, 'Culture and the Human Rights of Women in Africa: Between Light and Shadow' (2007) 51 Journal of African Law 39, 55; Dejene N Debsu, 'Gender and Culture in Southern Ethiopia: An Ethnographic Analysis of Guji-Oromo Women's Customary Rights' (2009) 30 African Study Monographs 15, 15–36; Fareda Banda, 'Women, Law and Human Rights in Southern Africa' (2006) 32 Journal of Southern African Studies 13, 13–27; Kuenyehia (n 405); Ndulo, 'African Customary Law, Customs, and Women's Rights' (n 184).

[234] See also Mashood A Baderin, *International Human Rights and Islamic Law* (Oxford University Press 2005).

equality, even though their application is conditioned upon the consent of all parties and practiced within the general framework of constitutional supremacy.[235]

Furthermore, the recognition of traditional authorities is almost akin to the constitutionalization of patriarchal institutions, which are usually not compatible with women's rights. As patriarchy permeates both the organization, rules, and operation of traditional authorities, the recognition of these institutions poses a severe danger to the provision of gender justice.[236] Not only are traditional authorities unaccountable to democratic processes, illiberal values and rules are their operating systems. As a result, as Chapter 6 demonstrates, the collision of these illiberal values and rules with the liberal constitutional rights of women is real and constitutionally tolerated. This means that women who find themselves within the powers of traditional authorities, in particular rural women who constitute the majority, are not in a position to enjoy and exercise their constitutional rights based on their liberal equality with men.[237]

Nonetheless, as discussed in Chapter 6, the incorporation of the communitarian vision of rights can actually advance and protect the rights of women, while the liberal notion of rights may in some ways limit the rights and interests of women. As is well known, customary and religious laws are neither static social phenomena nor are they homogeneous and uncontested; they are subject to change due to both internal dynamics as well as external cultural encounters. With respect to human rights, women have been claiming and asserting their rights within their customary and religious domains and, consequently, have managed to set more egalitarian customary and religious laws in line with the tenets of democratic principles and human rights.[238] Accordingly, the recognition of customary and Islamic laws in constitutions is not something to be contained or rejected in its entirety, but to be transformed in a more egalitarian way in order to benefit all subjects, including women. Along these lines, the Kwena women of Botswana have made creative use of the syncretic configuration of their rights—comprised of customary laws and liberal constitutional laws—to advance their best interests and rights.[239] Similarly, the Swahili Muslims of Kenya have been using the Khadi courts to protect and assert their rights in accordance with Islamic law.[240] Although the status of women and their position in society are huge factors in the dispensation of gender justice, the consciousness and awareness of women and women's rights activists themselves regarding the syncretic configuration of constitutional rights helps to assert women's rights within customary and Islamic laws and

[235] See the Constitution of the Federal Democratic Republic of Ethiopia, arts 9 and 34(5).

[236] Carolyn Logan, 'Selected Chiefs, Elected Councillors and Hybrid Democrats: Popular Perspectives on the Co-Existence of Democracy and Traditional Authority' (2009) 47 The Journal of Modern African Studies 101, 105.

[237] For instance see Haripriya Rangan and Mary Gilmartin, 'Gender, Traditional Authority, and the Politics of Rural Reform in South Africa' (2002) 33 Development & Change 633, 633–58; Millicent Odeny, 'Improving Access to Land and Strengthening Women's Land Rights in Africa', *Annual World Bank conference on land and poverty, The World Bank, Washington, DC* (2013) <http://weblawcolumbiaedu/sites/default/files/microsites/gendersexuality/odeny_improving_access_to_land_in_africapdf> accessed 7 June 2017.

[238] Madhavi Sunder, 'Piercing the Veil' (2002) 112 Yale LJ 1399, 1403.

[239] Anne Griffiths, *In the Shadow of Marriage: Gender and Justice in An African Community* (The University of Chicago Press 1997) 232–34.

[240] Susan F Hirsch, *Pronouncing and Persevering: Gender and the Discourses of Disputing in an African Islamic Court* (The University of Chicago Press 1998) 1–10.

modify the discriminatory ones.[241] On the other hand, the liberal notion of rights can limit the substantive equality of women by merely formally recognizing their right to equality and non-discrimination without fully accounting for their socio-economic and political circumstances.

Thus, the African constitutional rights regime incorporates both liberal and communitarian notions of rights into women's constitutional rights. While the normative syncretism in women's rights provides the framework and the operating orbit within which women can exercise their constitutional rights, the exact content and contour of these rights are determined by constitutional practices, and particularly judicial practices. In this respect, as discussed in Chapter 6, constitutional or apex courts determine the content and substance of women's rights through a judicial philosophy that maintains their syncretic ethos.

IV. Conclusion

This chapter demonstrates how *legal syncretism as a result* configures and brings a blend of constitutional ideas, principles, and practices into the African constitutional designs and practices. Legal syncretism animates the very *constitution* of the African state and its modalities of vertical organization, government architecture, and constitutional rights regime. Consequently, the legal syncretic constitutional designs and practices have led to a unique constitutional experiment, one that is different from both the precolonial and colonial constitutional systems, as well as from liberal constitutionalism, yet draws from each of these constitutional traditions to different degrees and in different forms. Through all this, the quest to establish an African theory of government that works best for the African state dictates the direction and dynamic of legal syncretism in the constitutional designs and practices. As will be further explored in the subsequent chapters focusing more specifically on federalism, the executive, and women's constitutional rights, legal syncretism clearly has a contingent role in advancing and fostering constitutionalism in Africa.

[241] Sunder, 'Piercing the Veil' (n 238) 1430–32; Helium, 'Human Rights and Gender Relations in Postcolonial Africa' (n 184) 638–46.

PART II
CASE STUDIES

4
Federalism

By taking federalism as one aspect of constitutional design and practice related to the vertical division of power, and using Nigeria, Ethiopia, and South Africa as comparative case studies, this chapter attempts to show in detail how legal syncretism figures in and permeates the federal systems of these countries. Classic federal theory[1] offers an explanation of the origin, formation, fundamental elements, and successes and failures of federalism. Drawing on the experiences of Nigeria, Ethiopia, and South Africa, this chapter aims to demonstrate how, on the one hand, federalism in Africa shares the forms, structures, and discursive practices of classic federal theory, while, on the other hand it also differs from classic federal theory in its normative articulations and institutional frameworks due to its syncretic configurations.

Due to legal syncretism, federalism transforms its purpose, fundamental elements, and operations in Nigeria, Ethiopia, and South Africa. This chapter shows how as federalism follows new pathways in these countries, its system of operation and standards of assessment take a similar course. In contrast to the central ethos of classic federal theory, federalism in these countries manages to operate and—to the extent possible—is able to serve its purpose mainly in the absence of liberal constitutionalism. By showing how legal syncretism structures the design and operation of federalism in these countries, this chapter demonstrates how federalism is reconceptualized and deployed to serve a different purpose than it does in classic federal states.

To identify and illuminate the syncretic features of federalism in Nigeria, Ethiopia, and South Africa, the first section of this chapter presents the original logic, formation, and fundamental elements of federalism as well as the reasons for its successes and failures as developed in classic federal theory. The second section proceeds to explore how federalism takes new pathways— in both its original purpose and formation—in Nigeria, Ethiopia, and South Africa. The third section examines how the fundamental elements of federalism in these countries are a blend of syncretic convergences, adaptations, and innovations. And building on this, the final section argues why it is necessary to rethink the classic standards for assessing the successes and failures of federalism and then proceeds to discuss how this can help to improve the performance of federalism in order to fostering constitutional democracy in these countries. The chapter then concludes by suggesting that if federalism is to ensure the practice of constitutional democracy in Africa, then democratic values, human rights, and constitutionalism should all animate its normative and institutional underpinnings of self-rule and shared rule, as they do in classic federal theory.

[1] Classic federal theory here refers to a constellation of federal theories that emerge from the experiences of established Western federal democracies.

A Theory of African Constitutionalism. Berihun Adugna Gebeye, Oxford University Press. © Berihun Adugna Gebeye 2021.
DOI: 10.1093/oso/9780192893925.003.0005

I. Federalism: A Conceptual Framework

To appreciate how legal syncretism features in the federal systems of Nigeria, Ethiopia, and South Africa, it is necessary to first adopt a conceptual framework of federalism within which these three systems are to be assessed. Therefore, this section only focuses on some aspects of federalism, namely, those that are relevant for the discussion of legal syncretism. Looking at the experiences of more established federal systems, such as the United States, Canada, Australia, and Switzerland, we can say that classic federal theory mainly concerns itself with understanding (a) what the fundamental elements of federalism are; (b) why states adopt federalism; (c) how federalism is formed; and (d) why federalism succeeds or fails. By investigating several federal theories as well as the literature on comparative federalism, this section develops a conceptual framework of federalism as a benchmark for the sections that follow.

The fundamental elements of federalism emanate from its very conceptions or meanings. In fact, although we are currently living in the age of federalism,[2] ie, more than half of the world population is currently living in systems that are considered as federal,[3] there is no unanimity as to its precise meaning.[4] The etymology of the word 'federal' is derived from the Latin word *foedus,* which means a covenant or pact among individuals and groups for mutual recognition and the promotion of unity among them.[5] While in the past federalism was equated with confederation or other forms of loose alliance between or among states,[6] since the introduction of federalism in the United States, it has been distinguished from similar arrangements and given a class of its own.[7] In spite of this, federalism still has no single, universally accepted definition.

Offering the definitions of the three towering figures in federalism should suffice for our present purposes. In this respect, William Riker defined federalism as an arrangement where the '(1) two levels of government rule the same land and people, (2) each level has at least one area of action in which it is autonomous, and (3) there is some guarantee ... of the autonomy of each level of government in its own sphere'.[8] Daniel Elazar defined federalism simply as 'self-rule plus shared rule' in a polity.[9] And Ronald Watts, like Elazar, defined federalism as 'the advocacy of multi-tiered government combining elements of shared rule and regional self-rule'.[10] From these definitions

2 William H Riker, *Federalism: Origin, Operation, Significance* (Little, Brown and Company 1964) 1.

3 Jenna Bednar, *The Robust Federation: Principles of Design* (Cambridge University Press 2008) 2.

4 Malcolm Feeley and Edward Rubin, *Federalism: Political Identity and Tragic Compromise* (University of Michigan Press 2009) 1–3.

5 Daniel J Elazar, *Exploring Federalism* (University of Alabama Press 1987) 5.

6 Montesquieu, 'Combining the Advantages of Small and Large States' in Dimitrios Karmis and Wayne Norman (eds), *Theories of Federalism: A Reader* (Palgrave Macmillan 2005) 55–57; Jean-Jacques Rousseau, 'A Lasting Peace Through the Federation of Europe: Exposition and Critique of St Pierre's Project' in Dimitrios Karmis and Wayne Norman (eds), *Theories of Federalism: A Reader* (Palgrave Macmillan 2005) 59–85; Immanuel Kant, 'Toward Perpetual Peace' in Dimitrios Karmis and Wayne Norman (eds), *Theories of Federalism: A Reader* (Palgrave Macmillan 2005) 87–99.

7 Dimitrios Karmis and Wayne Norman, 'Editors' Introduction' in Dimitrios Karmis and Wayne Norman (eds), *Theories of Federalism: A Reader* (Palgrave Macmillan 2005) 103–04.

8 Riker, *Federalism* (n 2) 11.

9 Elazar, *Exploring Federalism* (n 5) 12.

10 Ronald Watts, *Comparing Federal Systems* (3rd ed, McGill-Queen's University Press 2008) 98.

along with the wider scholarship on federalism,[11] we can draw the following fundamental elements: federalism at a minimum requires (a) at least two tiers of government endowed with sovereign power on some matters, (b) a non-unilateral amendable supreme written constitution with horizontal and vertical divisions of power, (c) representation mechanisms of self-rule and shared rule, and (d) an umpire.[12] Hence, these fundamental elements explain the meaning and essentials of federalism.

With respect to the original logic as to why states adopt federalism, scholars offer—among multiple others—at least four major explanations. The first is that provided by 'Publius', the pseudonym of the three authors of the *Federalist Papers* (Alexander Hamilton, John Jay, and James Madison), in connection with the ratification of the 1789 United States Constitution. According to the *Federalist Papers*, the Union should adopt federalism as it responds to military necessity and ensures security (Federalist Nos 2 and 15), provides individual liberty, prosperity, and freedom, and guarantees a democratic form of government (Federalist Nos 9, 10, and 17).[13] The *Federalists'* account is a widely accepted explanation as to why states should adopt a federal system. In this respect, Elazar further developed the democratic, liberty, equality, and freedom justifications for federalism. He argues that federalism maximizes individual liberty, equality, and freedom, and ensures and enhances democratic self-government in a polity.[14] He contends that federalism aims to institute a workable political arrangement based on a just moral order.[15] Hence, according to this view, the superiority of federalism—as a system of state organization—in bringing about a workable polity with a just moral order is the reason why states adopt, or should adopt, federalism.

The second theory focuses on the existence of external military or diplomatic threats as the origin of federalism. The chief architect of this theory is Riker, who rejects the assertion that states adopt federalism to protect liberty and ensure democracy. He posits that federalism is a result of a bargain between politicians who offer the bargain and those who accept it.[16] According to him, a federal bargain is possible when, on the one hand, those '[. . .] who offer the bargain desire to expand their territorial control, usually either to meet an external military or diplomatic threat or to prepare for military or diplomatic aggression or aggrandizement', and on the other hand, when those 'who accept the bargain, giving up some independence for the sake of union, are willing to do so because of some external military-diplomatic threat or opportunity'.[17] Thus, for Riker, it is the cumulative existence of these conditions—that is, 'the expansion' and 'the military condition'—that creates federalism.[18]

[11] See Kenneth Wheare, *Federal Government* (4th ed, Oxford University Press 1964); Thomas O Hueglin and Alan Fenna, *Comparative Federalism: A Systematic Inquiry* (2nd ed, University of Toronto Press 2015) 31–36; See also Michael Burgess, *In Search of the Federal Spirit: New Theoretical and Empirical Perspectives in Comparative Federalism* (Oxford University Press 2012); Burgess discusses the contributions of Kenneth Wheare, William S Livingston, William Riker, Carl J Friedrich, and Daniel Elazar with the view to discern the federal idea or spirit that animate the scholarship of these theorists of federalism.

[12] Watts, *Comparing Federal Systems* (n 10) 9.

[13] Alexander Hamilton, John Jay, and James Madison, 'Federal Theory' in Dimitrios Karmis and Wayne Norman (eds), *Theories of Federalism: A Reader (Palgrave Macmillan 2005)* 105–33.

[14] Elazar, *Exploring Federalism* (n 5) 83–91.

[15] ibid 104.

[16] Riker, *Federalism* (n 2) 12.

[17] ibid.

[18] ibid 13.

While the third theory, advanced by Malcolm Feeley and Edward Rubin, recognizes the relevance of Riker's theory of federal bargain, it primarily finds the origin of federalism in the disjuncture between the political identity and geography of a polity. According to this theory, states adopt federalism because of a 'tragic compromise' necessary for mediating the disjuncture between political identity and geographic governance. Unlike the first theory, which considers federalism as a means to minimizing human vice in a political community, Feeley and Rubin consider 'federalism as a tragic aspect of life' as it comes into being due to the misfortunes of 'conflicts in political identity'.[19] For them, the fundamental reason for the creation of federalism is 'to resolve conflicts among citizens that arise from the disjuncture between their geography based sense of political identity and the actual or potential geographic organization of their polity'.[20] In the absence of these conditions, they argue, federalism either cannot arise in the first place or, if arisen, it 'will become vestigial'.[21]

Unlike the third theory, the fourth theory attributes the origin of federalism to the level of institutionalization and infrastructural capacity of subunits for governance. Daniel Ziblatt argues that the origin of federalism is not so much related, as Riker argued, to the military power of those who offer the federal bargain, but rather to the state-society dynamics that the subunits find themselves in. For Ziblatt, 'federalism is possible only if state building is carried out in a context in which the preexisting units of a potential federation are highly institutionalized and are deeply embedded in their societies—and hence are capable of governance'.[22] This is due to the fact that '[o]nly subunits with high level of infrastructural capacity can deliver both to the core and the subunits the gains that were sought from state formation in the first place'.[23] Absent this, he argues, the political core will absorb all of the subunits to form a unitary state.[24]

Except for the theory advanced in the *Federalist Papers*, all of these theories are empirically grounded in comparative federalism; the authors of the *Federalist Papers* had no comparator for the system they were advocating for and the only available comparisons were confederations or other loose alliances. Aside from Ziblatt, they all draw inspiration from the federal experiences of the United States, Canada, Switzerland, Germany, and Australia, while they—particularly Elazar—also occasionally refer to the federal systems in Latin America, Asia, and Africa. Ziblatt, however, posits his theory by interrogating the state formation experiences of Germany and Italy, ie, through a comparison of state formation processes in both federal and unitary states. While each of them individually cannot adequately explain the origin of every federal system, they are all relevant justifications and, when taken together, build a robust theory as to why states adopt federalism.[25] Furthermore, given the socio-economic, cultural, historical, and political diversity and complexity within which federal

[19] Feeley and Rubin, *Federalism* (n 4) 39.

[20] ibid 38.

[21] ibid 38–39.

[22] Daniel Ziblatt, 'Rethinking the Origins of Federalism: Puzzle, Theory, and Evidence from Nineteenth-Century Europe' (2004) 57 World Politics 70, 71.

[23] ibid.

[24] See Daniel Ziblatt, *Structuring the State: The Formation of Italy and Germany and the Puzzle of Federalism* (Princeton University Press 2006); See also Wilfried Swenden, *Federalism and Regionalism in Western Europe: A Comparative and Thematic Analysis* (Palgrave Macmillan UK 2006) Chapter 2. Swenden explains the origins of federalism and regionalism in Europe.

[25] See also Watts, *Comparing Federal Systems* (n 10) 63–64.

systems arise and operate, formulating a unitary theory for federalism is a difficult task.[26]

Regardless of the different rationales for the origin of federalism, there are three major ways it is formed. As Watts observes, the first is through the aggregation of formerly-separate subunits, the second is through devolution from a former unitary state, and the third is through a combination of aggregation and devolution.[27] Alfred Stepan reduces these three processes of federal formation into two: *Coming together* and *Holding together* federalism.[28] While Coming together federalism refers to the formation of a federal state by uniting formerly sovereign states, Holding together federalism refers to the formation of a federal state from the preexisting subunits in a formerly unitary state.[29] The classic examples of Coming together federalism (or for those formed through aggregation) include the United States, Switzerland, and Australia, while many post-Second World War federal states, such as Nigeria and Belgium, are examples of Holding together federalism (or formed through devolution), and Canada and India combine the features of both Coming together and Holding together federalism.[30]

Another important theme of federalism studies is why federalism succeeds in some states while failing in others. Although approaching federalism in terms of success and failure is contested, the durability or longevity of the federal system itself, as well as the achievement of the original objectives for the creation of the federal system—or its *raison d'etre*—both stand out as major parameters with which success and failure are measured.[31] While durability can be relatively easy to measure, as its essential question is whether the federal system is still in operation or not, measuring the achievement of the original objectives is extremely complex and difficult, since not only may each federal system have had different objectives to achieve, but these objectives themselves—as well as the mechanisms for achieving them—are embedded in the particular socio-economic, cultural, and political contexts of their respective federal system.[32] Furthermore, these contexts are dynamic and the assessment of success and failure along these lines will always be relative and contingent upon time and place.[33] Bearing this in mind, scholars still offer some reasons for the successes and failures of federalism.[34] After a careful review of the comparative federalism scholarship, Michael Burgess lists the main conditions that must be present in a state in order for federalism to succeed.[35] These include:[36]

[26] See also Hueglin and Fenna, *Comparative Federalism* (n 11) 113–18.

[27] Watts, *Comparing Federal Systems* (n 10) 65.

[28] Alfred C Stepan, 'Federalism and Democracy: Beyond the US Model' (1999) 10 Journal of Democracy 19, 22.

[29] ibid.

[30] Watts, *Comparing Federal Systems* (n 10) 65.

[31] Michael Burgess, 'Success and Failure in Federation: Comparative Perspectives' in Thomas J Courchene and others, *The Federal Idea: Essays in Honour of Ronald L Watts* (The McGill-Queen's University Press 2011) 194–204.

[32] See Thomas M Franck, *Why Federations Fail: An Inquiry into the Requisites for Successful Federalism* (New York University Press 1968).

[33] Burgess, 'Success and Failure in Federation' (n 31) 194.

[34] See Riker, *Federalism* (n 2) Chapters 3 and 4.

[35] Michael Burgess, 'Asking the Same Question But Getting Different Answers: The Conditions of Success and Failure in Federal States' (2008) 16–17 <https://wwwkentacuk/politics/cfs/research/Conditions%20of%20Successpdf> accessed 23 August 2017.

[36] ibid 16.

A. a desire for the federal polity which is manifested by the dual loyalty of the political class and the citizenry to the federal union and constitute units at the same time;
B. the practice of constitutionalism along the federal spirit;
C. the existence of liberal democracy;
D. the commitment and capacity of political elites to work together;
E. the structure and vitality of the political party system to operate and function in a way to maintain federal unity while accommodating diversity;
F. the existence of fair and equitable resource allocation and redistribution; and
G. the existence of a commitment to keep 'the federal spirit' as an end in itself.

While the existence of these conditions contributes to the success of federalism, their absence may lead to its failure.[37] To give some examples of all these variables, the United States, Canada, Switzerland, and Australia, among others, are examples of successful federal states not only because their federal system endures, but also because their federal systems are able to deliver the original purposes for which they were adopted. In contrast, the Federation of the West Indies, Uganda, and Cameroon, among others, are examples of failed federal experiments as their federal systems no longer exists. And the Malaysian federal experiment shows how success and failure are complex variables, since while Malaysian federalism did not prevent Singapore from seceding the federation in 1965, it continues to hold the rest of its multi-ethnic and multi-cultural communities together. Indeed, as Burgess observes, it is also possible for federal states to succeed in some aspects and fail in others.[38]

Against this conceptual framework of federalism, the following sections examine and explore how legal syncretism animates and structures the original logic, fundamental elements, formation, and operation of federalism in Nigeria, Ethiopia, and South Africa. The aim of this discussion is to illuminate how legal syncretism explains the reasons and forms of convergence and divergence between classic federal theory and federalism in Africa—and the consequences thereof.

II. The Purpose and Formation of Federalism in Nigeria, Ethiopia, and South Africa

The original logic and ways of federal formation in Nigeria, Ethiopia, and South Africa differ significantly from those offered in classic federal theory. Why these countries adopted federalism in the first place and why they are committed to its continued operation, cannot be fully explained and captured by classic federal theory. Even though these countries aspire to have a democratic system that ensures individual liberty, freedom, and prosperity, as is evident from their constitutional histories, they do not consider federalism—unlike the authors of the *Federalist Papers*—as a superior

[37] See also Richard Simeon, 'Preconditions and Prerequisites: Can Anyone Make Federalism Work?' in Thomas J Courchene and others, *The Federal Idea: Essays in Honour of Ronald L Watts* (The McGill-Queen's University Press 2011) 207–23 .

[38] Burgess, 'Success and Failure in Federation' (n 31) 204.

government arrangement with which to achieve these purposes. By the same token, there were no external military threats or opportunities that set Riker's federal bargain into motion in these countries. Furthermore, although the theory of federalism as a tragic compromise due to the disjuncture between political identity and the geographical aspect of a polity has some relevance for these countries, it cannot explain why it was precisely these countries that adopted federalism, since this feature of disjuncture is common to the rest of Africa as well, as territories there were arbitrarily drawn by the colonial powers.

Similarly, the institutional infrastructure theory cannot be a helpful explanatory tool for these countries as the different ethnic groups that find themselves in territorial states have each had their own way of political organization before the advent of colonialism, in which the subunits in African federal states do not have a special institutional infrastructural capacity than any other state in the continent. The primary purpose for the adoption of federalism in these three countries was to accommodate the competing demands of ethnonational groups within a single state. The accommodation of diversity and the maintenance of territorial integrity were the twin justifications for federal formation, while the political strength of ethnonational groups during the constitution making processes was the determining factor.

With its new task of accommodation and integration of diverse ethnonational groups within a single state, federalism held new purposes and followed new pathways in Nigeria, Ethiopia, and South Africa. It was introduced and formed in these states to regulate and manage their *internal political dynamics*. Hence, federalism was formed through the devolution of power to both the center and the constituent units from formerly unitary states with the goal of holding these states together and concomitantly enabling the subnational units to broadcast their own respective ethnonational interests and ambitions through the channels of shared rule and self-rule. As a Holding together device—as the following section reveals—federalism in these countries enshrines unique normative and institutional configurations. Now I would like to explain in greater detail the original logic and ways of federal formation with respect to Nigeria, Ethiopia, and South Africa and demonstrate how federalism transformed its purposes and followed new pathways in the process.

A. Nigeria

Why Nigeria adopted federalism at independence and continues to commit to it can be understood from the way Nigeria came into being and continues to exist since independence. At the center of the original logic and ways of federal formation in Nigeria we find legal syncretism. To ascertain the reasons why Nigeria adopted federalism and how legal syncretism informed this choice, one has to briefly look at the formation of the Nigerian state and its operation from a historical perspective. Such examination reveals that the choice for federalism in the final years of colonial rule and the commitment to the federal idea since then is the result of a conscious effort to reconfigure, transform, and reinterpret both the precolonial and colonial systems of political and legal rules of organization into the postcolonial state. Thus, the federal idea has been a space for the experimentation with these institutional and legal reconfigurations and transformations.

Nigeria as a unified state came into being in 1914 as a result of British colonial conquest in the Scramble for Africa.[39] Although the British had already established colonies in West Africa before the Berlin Conference, it is only thereafter that their colonial conquest achieved sufficient strength and speed in the region known today as Nigeria.[40] In 1861, the British established the Lagos Colony in what is now Southern Nigeria.[41] After almost four decades, they penetrated further south and established the Southern Nigeria Protectorate. In 1906, the Lagos Colony and the Southern Nigeria Protectorate were amalgamated and named the Colony and the Southern Nigerian Protectorate.[42] At the beginning of the twentieth century, the Northern Nigeria Protectorate was created.[43] On 1 January 1914, under the leadership of Lord Lugard, the Colony and the Southern Nigeria Protectorate and the Northern Nigeria Protectorate were united to form present-day Nigeria.[44]

This amalgamation of the different parts of Nigeria into a unified state was mainly motivated by economic considerations.[45] This is due to the fact that the North, despite its huge landmass and population, was not able to cover its costs of administration.[46] The South, on the other hand, had a surplus of resources that could finance the administration of the North as well.[47] Thus, in order to efficiently use colonial resources to administer the colonies without spending imperial resources, the amalgamation of the Northern and Southern Protectorates became necessary for the colonial governors.[48] Aside from this economic and administrational rationale of the British, the Northern and Southern Nigeria Protectorates neither had any prior co-existence as members of a single political community, nor did they share similar cultural, ethnic, or political systems.[49] Thus, what brought them together was not their interest or will to build a nation called Nigeria;[50] the principal rationale for uniting Nigeria was to enable its administration with its own resources, and, consequently, enlarge the British colonial territory in West Africa.

Precisely because the aim of this amalgamation was economic, the British colonial rule did not develop any common institutions of governance nor did it allow for the integration of the people across Nigeria.[51] Separate governance regimes were put in

[39] Toyin Falola and Matthew M Heaton, *A History of Nigeria* (Cambridge University Press 2008) 117.

[40] Adegboyega Somide, 'Federalism, State Creation and Ethnic Management in Nigeria' in Bamidele A Ojo, *Problems and Prospects of Sustaining Democracy in Nigeria* (Nova Publishers 2001) 26.

[41] Toyin Falola, *The History of Nigeria* (Greenwood Press 1999) 55.

[42] ibid 56–58.

[43] ibid 59–60.

[44] Richard Bourne, *Nigeria: A New History of a Turbulent Century* (Zed Books 2015) 3.

[45] Falola and Heaton, *A History of Nigeria* (n 39) 68.

[46] Tekena Tamuno, 'Nigerian Federalism in Historical Perspective' in Kunle Amuwo and others, *Federalism and Political Restructuring in Nigeria* (Spectrum Books 1998) 15.

[47] ibid; Adiele E Afigbo, 'Background to Nigerian Federalism: Federal Features in the Colonial State' (1991) 21 Publius 13, 22.

[48] Falola, *The History of Nigeria* (n 41) 68.

[49] Ignatius Akaayar Ayua and Dakas Dakas, 'Federal Republic of Nigeria' in John Kincaid and George Alan Tarr (eds), *Constitutional Origins, Structure, and Change in Federal Countries* (McGill-Queen's Press 2005) 242.

[50] ibid.

[51] Falola, *The History of Nigeria* (n 41) 69.

place, and the people were kept apart. Instrumental in this was the philosophy of indirect rule, which gave birth to the system of Native Authority. The practice of Native Authority, as discussed in Chapter 2, required the acknowledgment of prior ethnic, cultural, and religious affiliations of people and their respective systems of traditional governance in a way that was suitable to the colonial state, and the creation of such a system in the case of its absence. In Northern Nigeria, where the Islamic emirates already had hierarchical systems of governance, the colonial administrators did not find it difficult to implant the system of indirect rule under the institution of Native Authority.[52] In a similar vein, the introduction of indirect rule to the southwest positioned the Yoruba kings on equal footing with the northern emirs.[53] In the southeast, the absence of any hierarchical traditional political institutions among the Igbo made the invention of the so-called 'warrant chiefs' necessary.[54] This colonial administration not only kept the people under the jurisdiction of the respective Native Authorities,[55] but also made formal cooperation among the native chiefs impossible as each native chief was directly responsible to a colonial governor or officer.[56]

Beyond this structural barrier, the differential approaches and treatments by the colonial state along ethnic, religious, regional, and educational lines have made the quest for national integration and unity difficult in the post-independence period. In the south, where the British started their colonial conquest, they were interested in putting their own systems of administration and laws in place. In the Lagos Colony, for example, in addition to the office of the colonial administrator, various institutions—such as the legislative council, judicial systems, and civil service mirroring the British tradition—were established.[57] Similarly, in the Southern Protectorate, British institutions and laws substituted the indigenous systems and laws. This is one of the reasons why education flourished in the south, since it was the key to holding lucrative positions in the colonial administration.[58] And this is also one of the reasons why the indigenous political institutions and laws were undermined.

In contrast, due to changes in colonial policy from direct rule to indirect rule, the British maintained the indigenous political institutions and laws in the Northern Protectorate. As the ally in the north for the British was the traditional elite, Western education found little place. After 1914, the system of indirect rule was extended to the south as well and this created a rivalry between the 'traditional elite', who derived

[52] Jonathan Reynolds, 'Good and Bad Muslims: Islam and Indirect Rule in Northern Nigeria' (2001) 34 The International Journal of African Historical Studies 601, 605–08.

[53] Falola, *The History of Nigeria* (n 41) 70; See also Joseph Adebowale Atanda, 'Indirect Rule in Yorubaland' (1970) 3 Tarikh 3, 16–28.

[54] See Afigbo, 'Background to Nigerian Federalism' (n 47) .

[55] Elizabeth Allo Isichei, *A History of Nigeria* (Longman 1983) 391–92; Toyin Falola, 'Neighbours at War: Conflicts over Boundaries in Colonial Nigeria' (2010) 19 Journal of the Historical Society of Nigeria 1, 1.

[56] Peter K Tibenderana, 'The Irony of Indirect Rule in Sokoto Emirate, Nigeria, 1903–1944' (1988) 31 African Studies Review 67, 74–79; See also Anthony Hamilton Millard Kirk-Greene, *The Principles of Native Administration in Nigeria: Selected Documents, 1900–1947* (Oxford University Press 1965).

[57] Afigbo, 'Background to Nigerian Federalism' (n 41) 18; FO Ogunlade, 'Education and Politics in Colonial Nigeria: The Case of King's College, Lagos (1906–1911)' (1974) 7 Journal of the Historical Society of Nigeria 325, 345.

[58] Larry Diamond, *Class, Ethnicity, and Democracy in Nigeria: The Failure of the First Republic* (Syracuse University Press 1988) 26–27.

authority and power from custom and/or religion, and 'the modern elite', who were schooled in the tradition of Western education. As both the conservation of indigenous practices and laws as well the governability of the masses were at the heart of indirect rule, the system pitted the traditional elite against the modern elite. As a result, the south, which, in turn, is largely populated by the Yoruba in the west and Igbo in the east, was more affected by the British colonial conquest than the north, which hosts the Hausa-Fulani.

While the south adhered to Christianity, the north adhered to Islam, so as with the regional, ethnic, and educational variables, the religion factor entered into Nigerian politics as well. The British maintained and recognized Islam and its rules of socio-economic and political organization—albeit only in the north—provided it did not go against the interests of the colonial state.[59]

The intersection of regionalism, ethnicity, religion, and economics shaped by the colonial experiences of direct and indirect rule all influenced the negotiation terms for the independence of Nigeria. The Hausa-Fulani, the Yoruba, and the Igbo—representing the main ethnic, regional, religious, and economic groups—all feared each other's domination as independence approached.[60] The Yoruba and Igbo advanced Nigerian nationalism and pushed for the independence of Nigeria, while the Hausa-Fulani were not yet ready for independence due to their fear of southern domination.[61] As a result, the Hausa-Fulani rejected the motion for the independence of Nigeria in 1956 in the House of Representatives.[62]

When the southern representatives were prepared to travel to the north to campaign for independence, the northern politicians not only mobilized their people against the campaign, but also revealed a plan for secession.[63] And although the southern politicians were advocates of Nigerian nationalism, they competed with each other as well for national dominance. The advantages the Igbo held in education, business, and civil service was of concern for the Yoruba, and vice versa.[64] These multi-layered dynamics brought about three regional political parties, all of which aimed to secure the interests of their own regions in the independence bargain and its aftermath. The Northern People's Congress with a political base amongst the Hausa-Fulani, the Action Group with a political base amongst the Yoruba, and the National Council of Nigeria and Cameroon with a political base amongst the Igbo all negotiated the terms of independence.[65]

[59] Somide, 'Federalism, State Creation and Ethnic Management in Nigeria' (n 40) 26–27; Olufemi Vaughan, 'Religion and State Formation' in Emmanuel Ike Udogu, Nigeria *in the Twenty-First Century: Strategies for Political Stability and Peaceful Coexistence* (Africa World Press 2005) 115.

[60] Olawale Albert, 'Federalism, Inter-ethnic Conflicts and the Northernisation Policy of the 1950s and 1960s' in Kunle Amuwo and others, *Federalism and Political Restructuring in Nigeria* (Spectrum Books 1998) 51.

[61] Larry R Jackson, 'Nigeria: The Politics of the First Republic' (1972) 2 Journal of Black Studies 277, 278; See also James Samuel Coleman and James Smoot Coleman, *Nigeria: Background to Nationalism* (University of California Press 1971).

[62] Diamond, *Class, Ethnicity, and Democracy in Nigeria* (n 58) 48–49.

[63] ibid 49.

[64] Albert, 'Federalism, Inter-ethnic Conflicts and the Northernisation Policy of the 1950s and 1960s' (n 60) 51.

[65] See Richard L Sklar, *Nigerian Political Parties: Power in an Emergent African Nation* (Africa World Press 2004) 87–140.

Within this atmosphere of mistrust, fear, and competition, the future of a unitary Nigerian state withered away and the adoption of a federal system, which could hold the three regions together, seemed like the only viable option to achieving independence and experiencing self-government.[66] Nonetheless, the asymmetry among the various regions and the concomitant effects on the structure and operation of the federal system posed further problems. The Hausa-Fulani, accounting for more than half of the population, demanded proportional representation in the federal government commensurate with their population, and this put the Yoruba and the Igbo in a disadvantageous position.[67] Moreover, other minority ethnic groups also demanded the creation of their own states within the federation in order to escape the domination of the three larger ethnic groups.[68] In the hope that these issues would be resolved after independence, the south agreed to the terms of the north, and the claims by minorities for the creation of other states were rejected as it was thought that they would delay independence.[69] On 1 October 1960, Nigeria achieved its independence with a federal constitution under the premiership of Abubakar Tafawa Balewa, a member of the Northern People's Congress.

Although the cumulative effects of the British colonial legacy, pre—and post-independence indigenous politics, and resource and opportunity allocation and distribution have not given federalism an easy ride, Nigeria remains committed to the federal idea to date.[70] Since 1960, Nigeria has adopted four republican federal constitutions that, in turn, governed the First Republic (1960–1966), the Second Republic (1979–1983), the Third Republic (1993–aborted), and the Fourth Republic (1999–present). During this period, Nigeria experienced military rule after the First Republic (from 1966 to 1979), after the Second Republic (from 1984 to 1999), and from 1967 to 1970, engaged in a civil war to stop the secessionist movements of Biafra. But despite changing constitutions, experiencing a bloody civil war, and having one military coup after another,[71] federalism is still relevant and appeals to many Nigerians who see it as their only hope for keeping their country united.[72] Although other systems of loose alliance—a confederation, for example—may still be on the table in the constitutional debates and discourse of Nigeria,[73] the idea of a unitary solution seems to have died with the Decree No 34 of 1966 which turned the country into a unitary state for a very brief period of time.[74]

Seen in this context, the choice of federalism and the allegiance to it in Nigeria is not due to it being considered—as a matter of principle—a superior system of state

[66] Sebastine Tar Hon, *Constitutional Law and Jurisprudence in Nigeria* (Pearl Publishers 2004) 7.

[67] Somide, 'Federalism, State Creation and Ethnic Management in Nigeria' (n 40) 28–29.

[68] ibid 28–29.

[69] Somide, 'Federalism, State Creation and Ethnic Management in Nigeria' (n 40) 29.

[70] Rotimi T Suberu, *Federalism and Ethnic Conflict in Nigeria* (United States Institute of Peace Press 2001) 45.

[71] See Richard A Joseph, *Democracy and Prebendal Politics in Nigeria* (Cambridge University Press 2014).

[72] Ladipo Adamolekun, 'The Nigerian Federation at the Crossroads: The Way Forward' (2005) 35 Publius: The Journal of Federalism 383, 398.

[73] Richard L Sklar, 'Unity or Regionalism: The Nationalities Question' in Robert I Rotberg (ed), *Crafting the New Nigeria: Confronting the Challenges* (Lynne Rienner Publishers 2004) 46.

[74] Tar Hon, *Constitutional Law and Jurisprudence in Nigeria* (n 66) 13; Dele Olowu, 'The Literature on Nigerian Federalism: A Critical Appraisal' (1991) 21 Publius: The Journal of Federalism 155; Suberu, *Federalism and Ethnic Conflict in Nigeria* (n 70).

organization for a workable and just polity, nor is it because it has brought about—in practical terms—good government, economic prosperity, and a culture of human rights; rather, it is primarily because federalism has offered a normative appeal and institutional framework for ethnonational and religious groups to channel and advocate their interests—regardless of the theory of government, be it civil/military or democratic/undemocratic. To this end, the idea of federalism as we know it in classic federal theory has been reconceptualized and deployed in Nigeria to serve new purposes in new realities.

B. Ethiopia

Although the history of Ethiopia and the processes by which the state was built are different from those of Nigeria, the original logic and ways of federal formation are quite similar. To appreciate the specific factors and historical processes which gave birth to the federal idea and continue to link Ethiopia's destiny with federalism, this section briefly explores and presents the history of the Ethiopian state-building project. The aim of this investigation is to demonstrate, like we did with Nigeria, how federalism follows new pathways in Ethiopia—both in its purpose and formation—from those we are accustomed to in classic federal states and how legal syncretism can explain the transformation from the original logic and formation of federalism into the variation we see in Ethiopia today.

Ethiopia is a country with ancient roots that date back millennia.[75] Despite the waxing and waning of its boundaries, Ethiopia's statehood has remained uninterrupted. Ethiopia successfully resisted waves of Italian aggression and is the only African country that was never colonized by a European power.[76] Its history can be classified into five stages for the study of its constitutional history: (a) pre-Christian times to the eighteenth century, (b) the *Zamana Mesafent* (the Era of Princes), (c) the modern monarchial period, (d) the military period usually known as *Derg*, and (e) the present federal period.[77] For our present purposes, a brief investigation of Ethiopia's modern history will suffice.

Ethiopia's modern history started with the restoration of monarchial rule by Emperor Tewodros II in 1855.[78] Tewodros defeated the regional *Rases* and recentralized power under his rule. After his coronation as king, Tewodros set into motion the modernization ambition of the Ethiopian Empire in which his successors advanced vigorously and skillfully. Among Ethiopia's modern monarchial kings, Emperor Menelik II was the one who gave the country its current form and texture. After maintaining Ethiopian sovereignty against European colonization at the battle

[75] Harold G Marcus, *A History of Ethiopia* (University of California Press 1994) 1; Sergew Hable Selassie, *Ancient and Medieval Ethiopian History to 1270* (Addis Ababa University Press 1972).

[76] See Raymond Jonas, *The Battle of Adwa: African Victory in the Age of Empire* (Harvard University Press 2011).

[77] See also Fasil Nahum, *Constitution for a Nation of Nations: The Ethiopian Prospect* (Red Sea Press 1997) 3.

[78] Bahru Zewde, *A History of Modern Ethiopia, 1855–1991* (2nd ed, James Currey 2001) 27; See also Teshale Tibebu, *The Making of Modern Ethiopia: 1896-1974* (The Red Sea Press 1995).

of Adwa in 1896, Menelik both negotiated and delimited the territorial frontiers of the empire and expanded and consolidated his power within the empire. As the regions that border Ethiopia were under British, French, and Italian colonial rule, the boundary delimitations were done with European powers. Menelik concluded boundary agreements with French Somaliland (now Djibouti) in 1897, with British Somaliland in 1899, with Italy for the severance of Eritrea in 1900, with the British for the territory with Sudan and Kenya in 1902 and 1907, respectively, and with Italian Somaliland in 1908.[79] About a decade after Adwa, Ethiopia took its present form territorially.[80] While Eritrea joined with Ethiopia through a federal arrangement in 1952 and united in 1962, its secession in 1991 rendered Menelik's original Ethiopia the enduring territorial limits of present-day Ethiopia.[81]

As with its territorial boundaries, the internal expansion and consolidation of Menelik's power gave Ethiopia its present ethnic and linguistic diversity and, concomitantly, gave birth to the center-periphery—or the north-south—political, social, economic, and ethnic relations and contestations that we have seen since the 1960s.[82] The north and its cultural and religious traditions were the core of the Ethiopian Empire,[83] and consisted of the provinces—or *kiflehager*, as they used to be called—of Tigray, Gonder, Gojjam, Wello, and Shewa. These provinces shared common cultural, religious, and linguistic traditions, although *Tigregna* is spoken in the province of Tigray. Orthodox Christianity and the Amharic language were the core of the empire. When Menelik made Addis Ababa the capital of his empire in 1886, not only did the political base of the empire move to the south, but it also heralded a further southern expansion.

Menelik's expansion took two forms.[84] The first was the recognition of existing traditional power structures upon a peaceful submission to the empire. Once a chief or king submitted to the empire, he would become the *Ras* of the province and would be part of the government machinery. The second was the use of force when provinces resisted the imperial request. After conquest, a new administration that included people from the north would be in charge.[85] The south was a mosaic of people with different ethnicities, languages, religions, and cultural identities. The triumph of Menelik's expansion in the south was also compounded by the hegemony of the Christian religion and the Amharic language. Menelik repeated his external success against Italy with an internal consolidation of power and territory. This makes Ethiopia exceptional as compared to its African peers.[86]

Menelik's expansion into the south is the most contested in Ethiopian history and has dominated much of the scholarly and political debate to date. There are three main theses on its historicity.[87] The first considers Menelik's expansion as part of

[79] Zewde, *A History of Modern Ethiopia* (n 78) 113.
[80] ibid.
[81] Tibebu, *The Making of Modern Ethiopia* (n 78) 180.
[82] See John Markakis, *Ethiopia: The Last Two Frontiers* (James Currey 2011).
[83] Tibebu, *The Making of Modern Ethiopia* (n 78).
[84] ibid 42.
[85] ibid 43–47.
[86] ibid 49.
[87] Merera Gudina 'Contradictory Interpretations of Ethiopian History: The Need for a New Consensus' in David Turton (ed), *Ethnic Federalism: The Ethiopian Experience in Comparative Perspective* (James Currey 2006) 120.

nation-building[88] and argues that the south was already part of the Ethiopian Empire and all Menelik did was simply reconfigure part of historic Ethiopia. The second thesis views Menelik's expansion as colonial conquest[89] and contends that what Menelik did in his southern expansion was akin to European colonialism—the only difference being that the colonizing empire was black. It is further claimed that in this process the distinct ethnic, linguistic, and religious makeup of the south had been subordinated, humiliated, and violated by the northern Amhara-Tigre culture and identity. And the third thesis holds that there was national oppression by the Ethiopian state[90] and that not only were Ethiopia's multi-ethnic groups discriminated against, but the Amhara-Tigre culture was considered as the official Ethiopian culture and all others were forced to assimilate. These competing and contradictory readings of Ethiopian history were critical in giving birth to many liberation movements and are still relevant in the political contestations of the country today.

Although the Solomonic monarchs, including Menelik, asserted absolute political power, they had to negotiate with the *Rases* or governors of the different provinces, in both the north and south, to ensure the smooth operation of the country. Regionalism relatively tempered the centralizing impulses of Ethiopian monarchs across time and place. This balance was fundamentally altered with the inauguration of Teferi Mekonnon as Emperor Haile Selassie I, the last monarch of the Solomonic dynasty, in 1930. Haile Selassie reconstructed feudalism in a way that enhanced the political power of the monarchy and guaranteed the economic privileges of the nobility.[91] To achieve this effect, Haile Selassie cemented his absolute rule with the adoption of the first written constitution of Ethiopia in 1931. The Constitution was both an expression of the emperor's absoluteness and evidence of his modernist ambitions, since, on the one hand, the Constitution unified political power in the person of the emperor—it rendered him the supreme lawmaker, executor, and adjudicator (as he was authorized to appoint members of the parliament, as well as the executive and judicial branches)—while also showing the international community that he ruled with a modern written constitution.[92] Not only did Haile Selassie dismantle the pre-existing regional powers of the *Rases* and governors of the provinces, but he also centralized their powers, and, in some places, appointed persons equipped with Western education.[93] Although the 1931 Constitution was revised in 1955 to include Eritrea with Ethiopia in a federation, in 1962 the federation was abolished to form a unitary Ethiopia.[94]

Haile Selassie is the only absolute monarch that Ethiopia ever had and the combined opposition from the progressive intelligentsia, the peasant rebellions, and the student movement, coupled with widespread social discontent and distress, ended his reign. The first critique came from his own circles, the Western-educated elite and

[88] ibid 120–22.

[89] ibid 124–26; see also Asafa Jalata, *Fighting Against the Injustice of the State and Globalization: Comparing the African American and Oromo Movements* (Springer 2002).

[90] Gudina, 'Contradictory Interpretations of Ethiopian History' (n 87) 122–23.

[91] Zewde, *A History of Modern Ethiopia* (n 78) 140.

[92] ibid 201; Gebru Tareke, *The Ethiopian Revolution: War in the Horn of Africa* (Yale University Press 2014) 17; the Constitution of Ethiopia 1931, Chapter II.

[93] Tareke, *The Ethiopian Revolution* (n 92) 16.

[94] Zewde, *A History of Modern Ethiopia* (n 78) 219.

members of his government, who held progressive ideas.[95] The attempted coup d'etat of 1960—the attempt to crown Asfawasan (the emperor's lawful heir) while the emperor was on a foreign visit—marked the violent expression of opposition from the progressive intelligentsia.[96] Additionally, aggrieved by land alienation, administrative inefficiency, and excessive taxes, peasants in Tigray, Bale, and Gojjam also rebelled against the central government.[97] Further, the spread of modern education and the enrollment of students from different corners of the country turned these students into critical opposition machines against Haile Selassie's rule. The pervasive backwardness, underdevelopment, and exploitation of the masses on the one hand, and the additional inequality and marginalization along ethnic, religious, and linguistic lines in national life on the other, made the students sworn enemies of Haile Selassie. A combination of all these forces eventually brought a revolution that led to the demise of the Solomonic monarchy and the inauguration of military socialism in 1974.[98]

The intellectual articulations and political actions in the final years of imperial rule, on the one hand, and the hijacking of the revolution by the military junta and its subsequent institutionalization of military socialism and the 'Ethiopia First' motto, on the other, were crucial to the birth of the federal idea in 1991. Although the military adopted Marxism-Leninism, the prevailing political ideology in Ethiopia at the time,[99] it was not able to deliver the dividends of Marxism-Leninism, nor was it able to respond to the outstanding questions of ethnic groups framed as 'the nationality question'. Even though there were a multitude of factors responsible for the outbreak of the revolution, such as questions of modernity, transformation, class, and ethnic relations, the last stands out as the center of Ethiopian politics and is responsible for the birth of the federal idea.

There is no person other than Wallelign Mekonnen, a student of the Haile Selassie I University (now Addis Ababa University), who has better articulated 'the nationality question' in Ethiopia and, consequently, shaped the terms of political discourse since then. He argues that:

> Ethiopia is made up of a dozen nationalities with their own languages, ways of dressing, history, social organization and territorial entity. [...] in Ethiopia there is the Oromo Nation, the Tigrai Nation, the Amhara Nation, the Gurage Nation, the Sidama Nation ... Ask anybody what Ethiopian culture is? Ask anybody what Ethiopian language is? Ask anybody what Ethiopian music is? Ask anybody what the "national dress" is? It is either Amhara or Amhara-Tigre!! To be a "genuine Ethiopian" one has to speak Amharic, to listen to Amharic music, to accept the Amhara-Tigre religion, Orthodox Christianity, and to wear the Amhara-Tigre Shamma in

[95] See also Bahru Zewde, *Pioneers of Change in Ethiopia: The Reformist Intellectuals of the Early Twentieth Century* (James Currey 2002).

[96] Zewde, *A History of Modern Ethiopia* (n 78) 213.

[97] See Tareke, *The Ethiopian Revolution* (n 92).

[98] See Andargachew Tiruneh, *The Ethiopian Revolution 1974–1987: A Transformation from an Aristocratic to a Totalitarian Autocracy* (Cambridge University Press 1993).

[99] See Donald L Donham, *Marxist Modern: An Ethnographic History of the Ethiopian Revolution* (University of California Press 1999).

> international conferences. In some cases, to be an "Ethiopian", you will even have to change your name. In short to be an Ethiopian, you will have to wear an Amhara mask ...[100]

Precisely because of this, the radical student movement considered Ethiopia as 'a prison house of nationalities', like Tsarist Russia.[101] Accordingly, the Stalinist account of self-determination, including secession of the nationalities, was considered as the primary means with which to transform and reconfigure the Ethiopian Empire.[102]

Armed with the ideological weapon of Marxism-Leninism, the ethnonational groups of Eritrea, Tigray, Oromo—and later the Somali—all started liberation movements for independence. Viewing the relationship of their ethnicities to the Ethiopian state through the prism of colonialism, the right to self-determination including secession became the overarching goal of their struggle. Although the Eritrean secession movement started even before the abolition of the federal arrangement, the unified struggle for liberation started in 1972 with the establishment of the Eritrean People's Liberation Front (EPLF).[103] The EPLF was also the inspiration for, and active supporters of, the establishment of the Tigray People's Liberation Front (TPLF). The EPLF and TPLF were the main armed forces that led to the removal of the military dictatorship of Mengistu Haile Mariam in 1991. Unlike the EPLF, however, the TPLF revised its political ideology from secession to internal self-determination before the final military victory.[104] As its political base was in Tigray, the TPLF needed a coalition of other ethnic groups representing the rest of the country to form the Ethiopian government after the defeat of the military. As a result, it established the Ethiopian People's Revolutionary Democratic Front (EPRDF) along with the Amhara National Democratic Movement (ANDM), the Oromo People's Democratic Organization (OPDO), and the Southern Ethiopia People's Democratic Movement (SEPDM).[105]

The triumph of ethnonational groups through military victory in 1991 not only introduced federalism as the only viable option for holding the country together, but it also helped to institutionalize the socialist account of the right to self-determination including secession as the fundamental principle that permeated both the origin and operation of the federal system.[106] As Ethiopia was considered 'the prison house of nationalities', any solution short of recognizing and assuring all ethnic groups the right to self-determination including secession would not have been accepted as a solution at all. The chief architect of the transition period, Meles Zenawi, unequivocally

[100] Wallelign Mekonnen, 'On the Question of Nationalities in Ethiopia' (Nov 17, 1969) <http://wwwethiopianforeignpolicycom/wallelign-mekonnen-and-his-article-on-the-question-of-nationalities-in-ethiopia/> accessed 13 November 2017.

[101] Semahagn Gashu Abebe, *The Last Post-Cold War Socialist Federation: Ethnicity, Ideology and Democracy in Ethiopia* (Ashgate 2014) 2.

[102] ibid.

[103] Zewde, *A History of Modern Ethiopia* (n 78) 220.

[104] Aregawi Berhe, *A Political History of the Tigray People's Liberation Front (1975–1991): Revolt, Ideology and Mobilisation in Ethiopia* (Tsehai Publishers 2009) 191.

[105] John Young, *Peasant Revolution in Ethiopia: The Tigray People's Liberation Front, 1975–1991* (Cambridge University Press 2006) 62. In 2018, ANDM changed its name to Amhara Democratic Party (ANP) and OPDO changed its name to Oromo Democratic Party following the recent waves of political transition in Ethiopia.

[106] See Abebe, *The Last Post-Cold War Socialist Federation* (n 101).

stated that '[t]he key cause of the war all over the country was the issue of nationalities ... Any solution that did not address them did not address the issue of peace and war'.[107] Committed to their respective ideologies, the ethnonational groups that won the military victory over the *Derg* proposed the right to self-determination including unconditional secession at the National Democratic Conference that adopted the Transitional Charter and inaugurated the Transitional Government of Ethiopia. In this process, while Eritrea chose independence from Ethiopia, the rest of the groups had to find an institutional mechanism that accommodated their right to self-determination including secession within the Ethiopian state—and federalism presented itself as the best choice.

Since then, like in Nigeria, the appropriateness of federalism for the Ethiopian state remains accepted across the political divide, although the precise type of federalism has been a point of contestation.[108] As federalism transformed its original logic, ethnonational groups find it appealing, for it enables them to broadcast their respective ethnonational interests and ambitions via the channels of shared rule and self-rule, regardless of the theory of government—be it authoritarian or democratic—as discussed in the following section.

C. South Africa

Although the history of South Africa and the socio-economic and political processes by which it came into being are different both from Nigeria and Ethiopia, the underlying rationale and purposes for adopting federalism in South Africa share a lot of commonalities with those countries. And like with Nigeria and Ethiopia, legal syncretism can explain the institutional choice for federalism in South Africa. This section illustrates how legal syncretism contributed to the origin of federalism in South Africa and how this, in turn, was situated within its socio-economic, political, and historical past.

The South Africa Act of 1909 brought together the settler colonies of the Cape, Free State, Transvaal, and Natal to form the Union of South Africa in 1910.[109] The creation of South Africa, when compared to Nigeria and Ethiopia, had two peculiar features. The first was the relationship between the settler populations—that is, the British and Afrikaners—and the question of whether a federal or unitary form of government should have been adopted for the newly established Union of South Africa. The second was the relationship between the settler and indigenous African populations in the union, that is, the 'Native question'.[110] As the British emerged victorious

[107] Meles Zenawil as quoted in Lovise Aalen, 'Ethnic Federalism in a Dominant Party State: The Ethiopian Experience 1991–2000' (2002) R 2002:2 CMI Report 40.

[108] See for instance Yonatan Tesfaye Fessha, 'The Original Sin of Ethiopian Federalism' (2017) 16 Ethnopolitics 232, 232–45; Jon Abbink, 'Ethnic-Based Federalism and Ethnicity in Ethiopia: Reassessing the Experiment after 20 Years' (2011) 5 Journal of Eastern African Studies 4, 596–618; Assefa Fiseha, 'Ethiopia's Experiment in Accommodating Diversity: 20 Years' Balance Sheet' (2012) 22 Regional & Federal Studies 4, 435–73.

[109] Heinz Klug, *The Constitution of South Africa: A Contextual Analysis* (Hart 2010) 8.

[110] Hassen Ebrahim, *The Soul of a Nation: Constitution-Making in South Africa* (Oxford University Press 1998) 6–7.

in the Boer War and the possibility of establishing a single political community became real, the Afrikaners demanded federalism where they could maintain autonomy within their own territorial hold.[111] Unlike the other settler colonies such as Canada and Australia, the British institutionalized a unitary state in South Africa.[112] In order to achieve unity and accommodate provincial interests, however, the South Africa Act 1909 established an upper house of parliament, called the Senate, which was made up of an equal number of senators from each province.[113] Furthermore, legislative and executive organs at the provincial level were also established, although the national organs were able to override their activities or actions.[114] Through such relatively inclusive institutional design, the Union of South Africa established the experiment of parliamentary democracy for the white minority in South Africa.

The South Africa Act 1909, however, excluded the black majority from participating in the newly inaugurated parliamentary democracy. Instead, a different governance regime was institutionalized for the black masses where the Governor-General in Council was the ultimate decision-maker. Unlike the practice in Nigeria and Ethiopia, the Union of South Africa—and from 1961, the Republic of South Africa through the Republic of South Africa Constitution Act of 1961—operated under two different constitutional systems that governed the white minority and black majority separately. Building on the race-based differentiated constitutional system pioneered in the Union of South Africa Act 1909, a series of statutes were enacted to further disenfranchise the black majority. The first series of legislative measures were aimed at segregating and discriminating against the black majority. These included, among others, the enactment of the 1911 Mines and Works Act which imposed the colour bar, the Natives Land Act of 1913 which dispossessed and disfranchised many blacks, the Native Affairs Act in 1920 which set up tribal councils and advisory councils for blacks in reserves and towns, respectively, the Native Urban Areas Act in 1923 which established the segregation of blacks in towns, the Industrial Conciliation Act in 1924 which excluded migrant black workers from employee protections, and the Native Administration Act in 1927 which retribalized the African natives. The ultimate goal of all of these legislative measures was to ensure continued white supremacy.

The rise of the National Party (NP) through electoral victory in 1948 inaugurated a special type of racial discrimination and segregation in South Africa known as apartheid. The quintessential feature of apartheid was the division of South Africa along racial lines. According to apartheid policy, South Africa was divided into four racial categories: white, colored, Asiatic (Indian and Pakistani), and Native (black Africans).[115] In order to keep these four categories of people apart, the parliament promulgated laws such as the Marriage Act (1949) and the Immorality Act (1950) which banned interracial marriage and sexual intercourse, the Group Areas Act

[111] ibid 7.

[112] Nico Steytler, 'South Africa' in John Kincaid and George Alan Tarr (eds), *Constitutional Origins, Structure, and Change in Federal Countries* (McGill-Queen's Press 2005) 313.

[113] ibid.

[114] ibid; Richard Simeon and Christina Murray, 'Multi-Sphere Governance in South Africa: An Interim Assessment' (2001) 31 Publius: The Journal of Federalism 65, 68.

[115] Nigel Worden, *The Making of Modern South Africa: Conquest, Apartheid, Democracy* (John Wiley & Sons 2012) 104–05.

(1950) for the separate residence of the races, the Separate Amenities Act (1953) which enforced the separate provision of public services such as transport, cinema, and restaurants, and the Natives Resettlement Act (1954) for the eviction of blacks to separate townships and separate educational systems.[116] Furthermore, the apartheid engineers created *homelands* for black South Africans with the objective of stripping them of their South African citizenship. For this purpose, nominal independent homelands such as Transkei (1976), Bophuthatswana (1977), Venda (1979), and Ciskei (1981) were created[117] and millions of black South Africans were forcefully relocated to them.

The notorious policy of apartheid brought both internal resistance and external exclusion to South Africa. As a result, the South African government adopted a constitution in 1983 with a tricameral parliament consisting of a (white) House of Assembly, a (Coloured) House of Representatives, and an (Indian) House of Delegates.[118] Although the coloured and Indians were given some form of representation to control their own affairs, such as education, health, and community administration, they were not equal partners with the whites in the constitutional dispensation.[119] And the black majority was not included or represented in this constitutional dispensation at all. Therefore, unlike in Nigeria and Ethiopia, the South African democratic constitutional dispensation came into being after more than nine decades of struggle by the black majority, the coloured, and the Indians, against white minority rule in their quest for equality, freedom, and dignity for all.

The main umbrella organization in the struggle against racial discrimination and apartheid was the African National Congress (ANC), established on January 12, 1912, soon after the inauguration of the Union of South Africa.[120] Unlike the ethnic-based regional parties that negotiated Nigerian independence or the ethnonational forces that restructured the Ethiopian state, the ANC provided the genesis for the unity of black South Africans and African nationalism that cut across tribal and linguistic differences.[121] Although there were other black organizations, as was evident during the constitutional negotiations for a democratic South Africa at the beginning of the 1990s, the ANC managed to mobilize and appeal to the black majority irrespective of tribal and linguistic affiliations in the struggle against racial discrimination and apartheid.

In addition to employing non-violent civil resistance, such as boycotts, strikes, and civil disobedience, as well as using the courtroom as a space of resistance against apartheid,[122] and later including armed struggle, with its ban, the ANC presented an inclusive political ideology—not only for black South Africans, but also for whites,

[116] ibid.

[117] ibid 119.

[118] Ebrahim, *The Soul of a Nation* (n 110) 18.

[119] Klug, *The Constitution of South Africa* (n 109) 13; Worden, *The Making of Modern South Africa* (n 115) 134.

[120] Leonard Monteath Thompson, *A History of South Africa* (Yale University Press 2001) 174; Ebrahim, *The Soul of a Nation* (n 110) 11.

[121] Richard Rive and Tim Couzens, *Seme: The Founder of the ANC* (Africa World Press 1993) 9–10; Peter Walshe, *The Rise of African Nationalism in South Africa: The African National Congress, 1912–1952* (C Hurst & Co Publishers 1970) 33.

[122] See Awol Allo (ed), *The Courtroom as a Space of Resistance: Reflections on the Legacy of the Rivonia Trial* (Ashgate Publishing 2015).

coloureds, and Indians. The 1955 Freedom Charter is the expression of the ANC's inclusive political ideology to all South Africans—irrespective of race—and a manifestation of its commitment to the ideals of human rights unmatched by any other political organization on the African continent at the time. The Freedom Charter in its opening clause stated that:

> [. . .] South Africa belongs to all who live in it, black and white, and that no government can justly claim authority unless it is based on the will of all the people; that our people have been robbed of their birthright to land, liberty and peace by a form of government founded on injustice and inequality; that our country will never be prosperous or free until all our people live in brotherhood, enjoying equal rights and opportunities; that only a democratic state, based on the will of all the people, can secure to all their birthright without distinction of colour, race, sex or belief.[123]

In pursuing this egalitarian and inclusive ideal, the Charter aimed to secure the right to equality before the law for men and women and all national groups, the right to share the country's wealth and land, the right to work, security, culture, education, and human rights, and it appealed to peace and friendship.[124]

When the apartheid system could no longer withstand the internal resistance and international exclusion, a negotiated transition became a sensible option. Before the official start of the negotiation in the formation of a Convention for a Democratic South Africa (CODESA) in 1991, bilateral negotiations between Botha's government and the ANC had already started in 1985 through the initiation of Nelsen Mandela.[125] From the first informal talks all throughout the formal negotiations, the position of the ANC was to establish a unitary state. Nonetheless, the NP was in favor of the devolution of power to the regional governments through the prism of federalism. Indeed, the ANC and the NP did reach consensus on the decentralization of power to the regional governments, although whether such decentralization should take a federal or unitary form was not agreed upon. In the multi-party negotiations, however, the issue of federalism provoked a heated debate and the political parties all held strong views. The NP, the Inkatha Freedom Party (IFP), the Conservative Party (CP), the Afrikaner Volksfront (AVF), the Freedom Front, and the Democratic Party all advocated for federalism, while the ANC and the Pan-Africanist Congress of Azania pushed a unitary state.[126]

Among the federalists, the IFP—with an ethnic base in KwaZulu-Natal—advocated for federalism in their territorial base, and the conservative Afrikaners proposed self-government in their own *Volkstaat*. Except for the IFP, the other federalist parties

[123] The Freedom Charter, adopted at the Congress of the People at Kliptown, Johannesburg (25–26 June, 1955) available at <http://wwwhistoricalpaperswitsacza/inventories/inv_pdfo/AD1137/AD1137-Ea6-1-001-jpegpdf> accessed on 14 September 2018.

[124] ibid; Worden, *The Making of Modern South Africa* (n 115) 115; Mary Benson, *The African Patriots: The Story of the African National Congress of South Africa* (Faber & Faber 1963) 214; Iris Berger, *South Africa in World History* (Oxford University Press 2009) 119.

[125] Ebrahim, *The Soul of a Nation* (n 110) 30.

[126] Nicholas Haysom, 'The Federal Features of the Final Constitution' in Penelope Andrews and Stephen Ellmann (eds), *The Post-Apartheid Constitutions: Perspectives on South Africa's Basic Law* (Witwatersrand University Press 2001) 506.

did not have a geographically concentrated base, but wanted federalism as a counter-majoritarian mechanism against the ANC's majority rule. The ANC saw the federalists' claim as an institutional configuration that could cripple majority rule, sustain the apartheid *homeland* systems, contribute to the creation of the *Volkstaat*, and be an obstacle to the South African transformation from a racially-based to a non-racial and inclusive society.[127]

Nonetheless, the secessionist moves of the IFP and the huge insecurity and anxiety of other federalist parties on the one hand, and the quest for inclusive and peaceful democratic transition necessary for the legitimacy of ANC's majority rule on the other, made concessions possible from both sides. The IFP, the CP, and the AVF formed a Freedom Alliance that demanded—amongst other things— for the creation of federal democracy, or else the IFP would opt for secession and the AVF for a civil war.[128] The open warfare in the KwaZulu-Natal between supporters of the ANC and IFP, as well as the loyalty and support of the AVF by both retired military generals and serving armed forces in the prevailing violence and disorder since the beginning of the transition, could not be ignored by all the actors of the transition, especially the ANC.[129] Thus, like in Nigeria and Ethiopia, the quest to accommodate ethnic and racial diversity, along with the urgency to secure peace, brought federalism to South Africa.

However, unlike in Nigeria and Ethiopia, federalism in South Africa is configured only in form and substance, but not in name. One cannot find the word federalism in the final Constitution. Indeed, the word federalism was avoided before the adoption of the final Constitution as it created an impasse between the federalists and unitarists.[130] Given South Africa's historical experience with racial segregation and apartheid, the term federalism was seen as a pejorative—particularly in the eyes of the ANC—and was considered an obstacle to the overall transformation of South Africa.[131] In order to facilitate meaningful debate, the constitutional negotiators dropped the term federalism and ultimately institutionalized the term 'Co-operative Government'.[132]

Unlike the ethnic, regional, and religious factors in the formative periods of the Nigerian political-party system, and the nationality question that conditioned political party organization in Ethiopia—all of which brought federalism as the first choice to these countries, the ANC's mobilization of the majority of black South Africans and others—including coloureds, Indians, and white liberals, and its commitment to liberal ideology as stated in the Freedom Charter, made a unitary form of government its first choice during the negotiations. Precisely because the ANC had inculcated African nationalism in the minds and hearts of black South Africans since 1912, and it managed to mainstream the ideals of freedom, human rights, equality, and dignity

[127] Steytler, 'South Africa' (n 112) 316; Karthy Govender, 'Federalism and Legal Unification in South Africa' in Daniel Halberstam and Mathias Reimann (eds), *Federalism and Legal Unification* (Springer 2014) 391–92.

[128] Nico Steytler and Johann Mettler, 'Federal Arrangements as a Peacemaking Device during South Africa's Transition to Democracy' (2001) 31 Publius: The Journal of Federalism 93, 95.

[129] ibid 95–96.

[130] Haysom, 'The Federal Features of the Final Constitution' (n 126) 505.

[131] Simeon and Murray (n 115) 68; Christina Murray, 'South Africa: Provincial Implementation of National Policies' in Raoul Blindenbacher and Abigail Ostien, *Dialogues on Legislative and Executive Governance in Federal Countries* (McGill-Queen's Press 2006) 29–30.

[132] Haysom, 'The Federal Features of the Final Constitution' (n 126) 504.

together with the struggle against racial discrimination and apartheid, it managed to propose a unitary state for a democratic South Africa. Thus, unlike in Nigeria and Ethiopia where the major political parties presented and advocated for federalism, the federalist idea in South Africa was a minority demand.[133] Not only did the ANC's unitary state proposal get acceptance by the majority because it syncretized the liberal ideology of human rights and inclusive politics with the democratic demands of the majority of South Africans, this syncretism, in turn, also led to the recognition of the minority demands for autonomy and self-government.

Accordingly, the way legal syncretism configured federalism in South Africa was significantly different than in Nigeria and Ethiopia. In South Africa, liberal constitutional ideas and principles were actually part of the struggle against apartheid and racial discrimination; even though liberalism was a Western export, the ANC accepted it as a mode of resistance and struggle against the South African state. Concomitantly, the ideals of equality, liberty, and dignity find their phenomenological similarity in the black South Africans quest for equal rights and concern in their country as fellow citizens. As a result, while the original purpose of federalism in Nigeria and Ethiopia was the accommodation of ethnic and racial demands—and even today the ethnonational groups only *use the forms and discursive practices* of federalism in order to channel their own corporate group interests—the general liberal constitutional vision of South Africa maintained the classic purposes of federalism, as discussed in greater detail in the following section.

III. The Fundamental Elements of Federalism in Nigeria, Ethiopia, and South Africa

As federalism followed new pathways in Nigeria, Ethiopia, and South Africa, some of the fundamental elements of federalism known to classic federal theory have been transformed and adapted along with non-federal principles and practices. As former unitary states, they draw heavily from the unitary theory of state organization and this is evident in the design and operation of their federal systems as well.[134] Furthermore, each state has blended federalism with its own unique experiences: while federalism has been fused with the military principles of administration in Nigeria, it has been blended with ethnic and socialist ideologies in Ethiopia, and configured with liberalism and *Ubuntu* in South Africa. Accordingly, the fundamental elements of federalism in these countries manifest convergences with classic federal theory with respect to forms, structures, and discursive practices, while also showing divergences related to the syncretic normative and institutional adaptations and innovations.

While Nigeria and South Africa have a three-tiered government arrangement, Ethiopia has a two-tiered system; each tier with some degree of sovereign power on

[133] See also Danie Brand and others, *South African Constitutional Law in Context* (Pierre De Vos and Warren Freedman eds, Oxford University Press 2015) 269–76.

[134] See also J Tyler Dickovick, 'Federalism in Africa: Origins, Operation and (In)Significance' (2014) 24 Regional & Federal Studies 5, 553–70.

some matters.[135] In all these states, the constitutions are unamendable unilaterally. In Nigeria, even if the National Assembly is empowered to amend the Constitution, it cannot do so without the approval of the House of Assembly and with no less than two-thirds of all states.[136] By the same token, in South Africa, the Constitution can mainly be amended by the National Assembly with the participation of the National Council of Provinces (NCOP) and requires approval by six of them.[137] In Ethiopia, constitutional amendment without the approval of a two-thirds majority vote by the states is impossible.[138]

Furthermore, there are representation mechanisms of both self-rule and shared rule in the multi-tiered government systems of these states. While states and local government areas (LGAs) in Nigeria, provinces and local government in South Africa, and states in Ethiopia are all avenues for the experiment of self-rule, the federal legislative, executive, and judicial branches are spaces for the practice of shared rule. Furthermore, the Supreme Court in Nigeria,[139] the Constitutional Court in South Africa,[140] and the House of Federation (HoF)—the upper house of parliament—in Ethiopia[141] are all federal umpires.

Moreover, the federalists in these states often invoke the benefits and rhetoric of federalism—building on the experiences of established federal states—in order to advance and safeguard their interests. To these extents, there is some convergence between classic federal theory and federalism in these states. Despite these formal convergences, however, several syncretic normative and institutional adaptations and innovations render the federal experiments in these states unique.

A. Nigeria: Centralized Federalism

Nigeria began experimenting with federalism at independence with three constituent units called regions. In the current Fourth Republic, Nigeria has thirty-six constituent units called states and 768 LGAs.[142] In addition to having many states and LGAs, the Fourth Republic operates within a system of centralized federalism, unlike in the First Republic. Not only are these states and LGAs the creation of the federal government, but the powers of the states are also taken away with the proliferation of states and LGAs. This is compounded by the distribution of resources and opportunities from the center to the states. In this section, I explain why and how the military logic of centralization transformed Nigerian federalism from decentralized or peripheral federalism to centralized federalism, and how legal syncretism explains this transformation.

135 The Constitution of Nigeria, ss 2(2) and 3(6); The Constitution of South African, s 40(1); The Constitution of the Federal Democratic Republic of Ethiopia, art 46(1).
136 The Constitution of Nigeria, s 9(1), (2), and (3).
137 The Constitution of South Africa, s 44(1)(a), (b), and 74.
138 The Constitution of the Federal Democratic Republic of Ethiopia, art 105.
139 The Constitution of Nigeria, s 232(1).
140 The Constitution of South Africa, s 167.
141 The Constitution of the Federal Democratic Republic of Ethiopia, art 62.
142 The Constitution of Nigeria, s 3(1) and (6).

The fragmentation of states in the Nigerian federation did not have a single explanation. Nevertheless, the military and civilian rulers present the original logic of federalism, ie, holding the country together, as a dominant rationale for the creation of new states.[143] In this regard, the official explanations given are: the demands of ethnic minorities, the need to correct population and territorial imbalances among the three dominant regions, economic development and its concomitant consequences of distribution, and the quest to bring governance nearer to the people.[144] Among other waves of state creation, the creation of the Mid-Western Region in 1963 out of the Western Region is the one most associated with minority ethnic demands for self-government;[145] indeed, minority ethnic groups in the Western Region wanted their own state.[146]

Nonetheless, such demands for statehood were present both in the Northern and Eastern Regions as well,[147] and out of the three regional political parties, the Action Group that was in charge of the Western Region was even in favor of creating new states for ethnic minorities.[148] The Northern People's Congress and National Council of Nigeria and Cameroon formed a coalition to diminish the political base of their rival—ie, the Western Region which was represented by the Action Group—by creating a fourth region out of it.[149] Thus, the real reason for the creation of the Mid-Western Region was more to destroy the Action Group than to recognize the ethnic minorities' right to self-government.[150]

The restructuring of Nigeria into twelve states was justified on grounds of avoiding the domination of any state by any other state due to the size of its population or territory.[151] By trying to address the asymmetry that was implanted in the Nigerian independence federal structure, the creation of new states was not only aimed at attracting support for the federation against the secessionist demands of the Igbo, but also aimed at reducing the southern fear of northern domination.[152] This restructuring was particularly fundamental in gaining the support of non-Igbo ethnic groups in the eastern region. The further fragmentation of the states was rationalized on grounds of economic development, social justice, interethnic balance, and bringing governance nearer to the people.[153] While these were the official explanations, the dual objectives of broadcasting the federal government into the states and LGAs along with the ambition of the governing regime to boost its political base throughout the federation were the real drivers of state creation in Nigeria. Put differently, the unitary impulse of the Nigerian state and the domination syndrome of the military and civilian elites were

143 Somide, 'Federalism, State Creation and Ethnic Management in Nigeria' (n 40) 33.

144 Rotimi T Suberu, 'The Struggle for New States in Nigeria, 1976–1990' (1991) 90 African Affairs 499, 499–503; Henry E Alapiki, 'State Creation in Nigeria: Failed Approaches to National Integration and Local Autonomy' (2005) 48 African Studies Review 49, 57–59.

145 See RT Akinyele, 'States Creation in Nigeria: The Willink Report in Retrospect' (1996) 39 African Studies Review 2, 71–94.

146 Suberu, *Federalism and Ethnic Conflict in Nigeria* (n 70) 82.

147 ibid.

148 Sklar, *Nigerian Political Parties* (n 65).

149 Diamond, *Class, Ethnicity, and Democracy in Nigeria* (n 58) 97.

150 Suberu, *Federalism and Ethnic Conflict in Nigeria* (n 70) 83.

151 ibid 86.

152 ibid 88–89.

153 ibid 90–103.

equally responsible for such fragmentation along with the growing demands for new states by various ethnic groups.[154]

Going against one of the fundamental elements of federalism, the federal government created states and LGAs single-handedly. One of the defining features of federalism is the absence of any unilateral amendment to the constitution or alteration of the structures and powers provided in the constitution; nevertheless, the federal military and civilian governments created states and LGAs unilaterally.[155] For instance, as noted above, the federal government created the Mid-Western Region as a fourth region in 1963; after the end of the First Republic, these were further divided into twelve regions by Lieutenant-Colonel Gowon's military administration;[156]Brigadier Murtala Mohammed increased the number of states to nineteen;[157] during the Ibrahim Babangida administration, the number of states reached thirty;[158]General Sani Abacha's regime added six new states and the number of states in the federation increased to the current thirty-six;[159] and like states, LGAs were created by the federal government, starting with 301 in 1976 and reaching 768 in 1999.[160] The manner of creating states and LGAs in Nigeria resembles the act of decentralization of a unitary state.

Beyond the centralized process of state and LGA creation, the federal government also centralized many of the powers of the states. A comparison of the powers of states in the First Republic and in the Fourth Republic shows how Nigerian federalism changed from decentralized federalism to centralized federalism. In the First Republic, the powers of the federal government were limited to national defense, foreign relations, the currency, mines and minerals, and the main transportation and communication services;[161] whereas higher education, industry and power development, the judiciary, the police, and the regulation of labor, among others, formed the concurrent powers of the federal government and the regions.[162] Not only did the regions have residual power, but they could also pursue their own socio-economic development policies.[163] Related to this, a 50 per cent revenue allocation formula was adopted which enabled regions to use half of the resources they mobilized and collected, while sharing the remaining half with others in the federation.[164] Moreover, they had their own regional constitutions and regional police forces.[165] Furthermore,

154 Rotimi T Suberu, 'States' Creation and the Political Economy of Nigerian Federalism' in Kunle Amuwo and others, *Federalism and Political Restructuring in Nigeria* (Spectrum Books 1998) 285.

155 See Alapiki, 'State Creation in Nigeria' (n 144).

156 Suberu, *Federalism and Ethnic Conflict in Nigeria* (n 70) 85.

157 ibid 90.

158 ibid 98.

159 ibid 101.

160 ibid 106.

161 Kalu Ezera, *Constitutional Developments in Nigeria* (2nd ed, Cambridge University Press 1964) 266–69; John P Mackintosh, 'Federalism in Nigeria' (1962) 10 Political Studies 3, 223–47.

162 Rotimi T Suberu, 'Federalism and Decentralization' in David Anderson, Nicholas Cheeseman, and Andrea Scheibler (eds), *Routledge Handbook of African Politics* (Routledge 2013) 26; Brian Smith, 'Federal-State Relations in Nigeria' (1981) 80 African Affairs 355, 362.

163 Adamolekun, 'The Nigerian Federation at the Crossroads' (n 72) 386.

164 ibid.

165 Eghosa E Osaghae, 'The Status of State Governments in Nigeria's Federalism: A Study of the Changing Phases' (1991) 52 The Indian Journal of Political Science 242, 244.

the regional bases of the political-party system made it crucial for political power to be in the regions rather than in the center.[166] Because of this constitutional and political configuration, the regions were stronger than the center in operating Nigerian federalism during the First Republic.[167]

In the Fourth Republic, however, the nucleus of power changed from the regions to the center. The 1999 Constitution confers legislative powers onto the National Assembly with regard to 68 broad items known as the Exclusive Legislative List (ELL).[168] Moreover, the Constitution also empowers the federal government to legislate on matters that are not included in the ELL, but which are incidental and supplementary to any of the matters listed.[169] Included on the ELL are the creation of states,[170] the regulation of police,[171] and political parties.[172] Most importantly, oil and natural gas exploration, the main engines of the Nigerian economy, are the exclusive domain of the federal government.[173] Moreover, not only do states operate under a single Constitution, they do not have Supreme Courts; states only have High Courts[174] and their appeals go to the Court of Appeal,[175] which is second to the Supreme Court of Nigeria.

Furthermore, the establishment of presidentially controlled federal institutions or commissions strengthens the powers of the federal government over the states.[176] For instance, the Independent National Electoral Commission has one Resident Electoral Commissioner in each state appointed by the president to organize, undertake, and supervise elections and monitor the operation of political parties in the states.[177] Additionally, the National Judicial Council recommends the governors of states on the appointment, removal, and disciplinary measures against state judges, in addition to collecting, controlling, and disbursing money for the judiciary throughout the federation.[178] In a similar vein, the Revenue Mobilization Allocation and Fiscal Commission, whose members are appointed by the president, determines the remuneration for political office holders at the state level and advises states on fiscal matters.[179]

Furthermore, the constitutionalization of the LGAs and the allocation of federal funds for their operation and function further diminish the autonomy of the states. LGAs have power with regard to, among others, 'the making of recommendations to a State commission on economic planning or any similar body on the economic development of a State, collection of rates, radio and television licenses, establishment and maintenance of slaughterhouses, construction and maintenance of public facilities

[166] ibid 186.
[167] Adamolekun, 'The Nigerian Federation at the Crossroads' (n 72) 387.
[168] The Constitution of Nigeria, s 4(2), (3), and (4).
[169] ibid Schedule II Part I Item 68.
[170] ibid Schedule II Part I Item 14.
[171] ibid Schedule II Part I Item 45.
[172] ibid Schedule II Part I Item 56.
[173] ibid Schedule II Part I Item 39.
[174] ibid s 270(1).
[175] ibid s 240.
[176] Rotimi Suberu, 'Managing Constitutional Change in the Nigerian Federation' (2015) 45 Publius: The Journal of Federalism 552, 558.
[177] The Constitution of Nigeria, Schedule III Part I 14.
[178] ibid Schedule III Part I 21(c) and (d).
[179] ibid Schedule III Part I 31 and 32.

such as roads, control and regulation of outdoor advertising, sale of liquors, shops and kiosks, restaurants and bakeries, provision and maintenance of public sewage and refuse disposal', and participate in the governance of the state on matters related to education, agriculture, natural resources, and health services.[180] For this purpose, the Constitution allocates a federal budget to them which is payable through the states from the State Joint Local Government Account.[181] The introduction of the three-tiered government structure reduced the power and autonomy of states from above and from below, although in practice, the LGAs struggle to maintain their constitutional standing from the states and the federal government.[182]

This centralized federalism is also accompanied by distributive federalism. The central logic of distributive federalism is to ensure 'equitable' sharing of resources and opportunities among the ethnonational and religious units of the federation. This is what is usually known as 'the cake sharing' syndrome in Nigerian politics.[183] Oil revenue sharing is the central orbit of distributive federalism. 90 per cent of public revenue and foreign exchange earnings of Nigeria is derived from the Niger Delta's oil wealth.[184] This revenue is distributed vertically among the three tiers of government and horizontally among the states and LGAs from the Federation Account.[185] Only 13 per cent of the revenue from oil or other natural resources goes to the states of derivation and is exempt from such distribution.[186]

Moreover, the 'federal character' principle is another means of distributive federalism in Nigeria. As one core of the Directive Principles of State Policy, this principle prescribes the following:

> The composition of the Government of the Federation or any of its agencies and the conduct of its affairs shall be carried out in such a manner as to reflect the federal character of Nigeria and the need to promote national unity, and also to command national loyalty, thereby ensuring that there shall be no predominance of persons from a few State[s] or from a few ethnic or other sectional groups in that Government or in any of its agencies.[187]

To this effect, a Federal Character Commission was established to look after the compliance of this principle.[188] The gist of the federal character principle is to ensure that

[180] ibid Schedule IV 1 and 2.

[181] ibid s 162(5), (6), and (7).

[182] Ozy B Orluwene, 'Constitutional Provisions and Challenges to Local Government Administration in Nigeria' (2008) 14 The Nigerian Academic Forum: A Multi-Disciplinary Journal 3, 67–69; Okey Marcellus Ikeanyibe, 'Uniformity in Local Government System and the Governance Model in Nigeria' (2016) Journal of Asian and African Studies, 1–15 (discussing how the centralization of the functions and forms of Local Government Areas affect their local performance).

[183] Felix Asogwa and FO Fagbohum, 'Revenue Determination and Political Conflict in a Federal State: The Nigerian Experience' in A Sat Obiyan and Kunle Amuwo, *Nigeria's Democratic Experience in the Fourth Republic Since 1999: Policies and Politics* (Rowman & Littlefield 2013) 210.

[184] Rotimi Suberu, 'The Nigerian Federal System: Performance, Problems and Prospects' (2010) 28 Journal of Contemporary African Studies 459, 467.

[185] The Constitution of Nigeria, s 162(3).

[186] ibid s 162(2).

[187] ibid s 14(3).

[188] ibid Third Schedule, Part I(c).

all Nigerians are equitably and proportionally represented in all posts and positions in government, such as public service, the army, the police, and bureaucracy. Beyond government posts and offices, the federal character principle obliges political parties to reflect the federal character of Nigeria in their executive committee or other governing bodies.[189] Not only does the Constitution ban ethnic-based political organizations, but it also enshrines the federal character principle in party organizations so that the form of political parties will also reflect the federal character of Nigeria. Thus, in addition to the government, the political-party system is also a distribution mechanism in the Nigerian style of federalism.[190]

Hence, the change from decentralized federalism to centralized federalism with a distributive feature is the result of legal syncretism. This is due to the fact that the federal idea is considered essential if the Nigerian state is to exist in its current form, but the practice of federalism as designed in the First Republic, or along the general practices of classic federalism like in the United States or Canada, did not work for—or interest—the Nigerian political and military elites. At the same time, the abrogation of the federal idea and the installation of a unitary state proved to be a failure. As a result, what the military and civilian leaders did was reinterpret the classic federal idea and reconfigure it to broadcast the ethnonational and religious interests through the systems of shared rule and self-rule. To this end, Nigerian federalism blends together—in both its design and operation—unitary principles and practices along with the military logic of centralization, all with the federal spirit at its core. Without accounting for these unique federal transformations and configurations, one would be hard pressed to understand and, at one's own peril, explain Nigerian federalism.

B. Ethiopia: Ethnic Federalism

Ethiopia, like Nigeria, albeit in a different context and form, configures federalism with the unitary impulse along with ethnic and socialist ideology. The uniqueness of the Ethiopian federal system lies in how legal syncretism animates and structures its design and operation. On the one hand, there is a need to maintain the unity of the Ethiopian state, and on the other, there is a commitment to channel ethnonational ambitions and interests in the state. Unlike classic federal states, this context places ethnicity at the center of the federal spirit in Ethiopia.

As noted in the previous discussion, the introduction of ethnic federalism in Ethiopia is, on the one hand, a metamorphosis of Marxist-Leninist political ideology to address the equal rights and concerns of Ethiopia's multi-ethnic and multi-lingual communities on its face, while on the other hand, it is a mechanism of broadcasting—in a seemingly liberal constitutional order—the political ambitions of the ethnonational forces that defeated the military regime. As the discussion here demonstrates, ethnic federalism is the syncretic result that combines socialist and indigenous Ethiopian

[189] ibid s 223(1)(b).

[190] JAA Ayoade, 'The Federal Character Principle and the Search for National Integration' in Kunle Amuwo and others, *Federalism and Political Restructuring in Nigeria* (Spectrum Books 1998) 101–17; Suberu, *Federalism and Ethnic Conflict in Nigeria* (n 70) 111–38.

norms of political organization into a constitutional framework. Although the adoption of ethnic federalism based on the recognition of the right to self-determination including the unconditional right of secession of ethnic groups—known as Nations, Nationalities and Peoples (NNPs)—is radical and has no comparator in Africa, its design reinforces centralized federalism. Moreover, the practice resembles unitary decentralization with an ethnic flavor.

The normative innovations and institutional configurations of the 1995 Ethiopian Constitution are shaped by the quest to address the issue of ethnicity.[191] Indeed, ethnicity animates the very foundation of the constitutional order.[192] Ranging from the Preamble to the basic principles of the Constitution including the Bill of Rights to the structural parts of the Constitution, it all speaks about the primacy of ethnicity. The Preamble of the Constitution begins with '[w]e, the Nations, Nationalities and Peoples of Ethiopia', which is different from the Nigerian Constitution, and many other constitutions around the word for that matter, that begin with '[w]e the people'. Not only does this articulation of the Constitution presuppose the existence of multiple *demoi*, but it also essentially requires every Ethiopian to be a member of one of the ethnic groups.[193] By using their right to self-determination, the various NNPs agreed to form one political and economic community known as the Federal Democratic Republic of Ethiopia that would be based on the ideals of rule of law, peace, and democracy.[194] The Preamble further provides that the achievement of these ideals by the NNPs requires 'the full respect for individual and people's fundamental freedoms and rights'. Unlike the Constitution of Nigeria, the Preamble of the Ethiopian Constitution envisions ethnic rather than territorial federalism, and multiple *demoi* rather than a *demos*.[195] This is because, as Nahum observes, ethnic groups are the founding units of the federation.[196]

NNPs are not only the authors of the Constitution, but they are also custodians of the sovereign power. Article 8 states that sovereignty resides in the NNPs and the 'Constitution is an expression of their sovereignty'. Although the NNPs are the authors of—and sovereigns in—the constitutional order, Article 39(5) defines them in the following way:

> A "Nation, Nationality or People" for the purpose of this Constitution, is a group of people who have or share a large measure of a common culture or similar customs, mutual intelligibility of language, belief in a common or related identities, a common psychological make-up, and who inhabit an identifiable, predominantly contiguous territory.

[191] See also Kidane Mengisteab, 'New Approaches to State Building in Africa: The Case of Ethiopia's Ethnic-Based Federalism' (1997) 40 African Studies Review 3, 111–32.

[192] See Jon Abbink, 'Ethnicity and Constitutionalism in Contemporary Ethiopia' (1997) 41 Journal of African Law 2, 159–74.

[193] Nahum, *Constitution for a Nation of Nations* (n 77) 51–52; See Berihun Adugna Gebeye, 'Toward Making a Proper Space for the Individual in the Ethiopian Constitution' (2017) 18 Human Rights Review 4, 439–58.

[194] The Constitution of the Federal Democratic Republic of Ethiopia, art 1.

[195] See also Jan Erk, '"Nations, Nationalities, and Peoples": The Ethnopolitics of Ethnofederalism in Ethiopia' (2017) 16 Ethnopolitics 3, 219–31.

[196] Nahum, *Constitution for a Nation of Nations* (n 77) 52.

Although there are no differences in meaning amongst the NNPs, nor do they have any type of hierarchy, they are indivisible corporate entities bestowed with equal sovereign power.[197] Moreover, they are endowed with a right of exit from the Ethiopian state whenever they wish so.[198] Article 39(1) states that '[e]very Nation, Nationality and People in Ethiopia has an unconditional right to self—determination, including the right to secession'. Although the procedure of secession is not easy,[199] no justification or rationale is required if any of the NNPs choose to secede. Unlike Nigeria, which built its federal system on the indivisibility of the state, Ethiopia established its federalism on the recognition of its potential disintegration if it is ever needed.[200] Although a solemn commitment to a federal union is usually the case for the establishment of democratic federal systems, Ethiopia opted to construct its federal system based on a pre-commitment to secession.[201]

Precisely because of this normative commitment, ethnicity is the primary means of delimiting the units of the federation. Article 46(1) stipulates that '[s]tates shall be delimited on the basis of settlement patterns, language, identity and consent of the people concerned'. Based on this formula, Article 47 lists the states of Tigray, Afar, Amhara, Oromia, Somalia, Benshangul/Gumuz, Southern Nations, Nationalities and Peoples, Gambela, and Harari as member states of the Federal Democratic Republic of Ethiopia. Except for the Southern Nations, Nationalities and Peoples Regional State, the rest of the states are named after the major ethnic groups they host. Accordingly, ethnic groups are expected to exercise self-government within their own respective states and participate in shared rule at the federal level.

Although Ethiopia is composed of more than eighty ethnic and linguistic groups, they were originally supposed to live within these nine states. This means that not every ethnic group got its own state. Indeed, many of the ethnic groups were lumped together under the Southern Nations, Nationalities and Peoples Region, and other states also host many minority ethnic groups together.[202] In recognition of this fact, Article 46(2) entitles every NNPs living in the nine states to establish their own states at any time if there should be a demand. Following this constitutional rule, Sidama has recently seceded from the Southern Nations, Nationalities and Peoples Region and has become the tenth state. Many of the other ethnic groups in this region are following the path of Sidama and they may likely also attain statehood in the near future.

Further, the NNPs are also umpires of the federal system. Unlike Nigeria, which bestows upon the Supreme Court the power of judicial review, or South Africa, which establishes a Constitutional Court, Ethiopia confers the power of constitutional

[197] Abbink, 'Ethnicity and Constitutionalism in Contemporary Ethiopia' (n 192) 166.

[198] For details see Alem Habtu, 'Multiethnic Federalism in Ethiopia: A Study of the Secession Clause in the Constitution' (2005) 35 Publius: The Journal of Federalism 2, 313–35.

[199] The Constitution of the Federal Democratic Republic of Ethiopia, art 39(4).

[200] See John M Cohen, '"Ethnic Federalism" in Ethiopia' (1995) 2 Northeast African Studies 157, 158. Because of the constitutional recognition of 'self-destruction', Cohen considers the Ethiopian system as one of confederation than a federation.

[201] Alemante G Selassie, 'Ethnic Identity and Constitutional Design for Africa' (1992) 29 Stan J Int'l L 1, 47–49; Cass R Sunstein, 'Constitutionalism and Secession' (1991) 58 The University of Chicago Law Review 633; Whittington (n 129) 281–98.

[202] The notable exception is the state of Harari that is named after the Harari ethnic group which constitutes 1/7 of the population of the Harari state.

interpretation on the HoF with the assistance of an expert legal body called the Council of Constitutional Inquiry (CCI).[203] Although there were proposals for judicial review and for the establishment of a constitutional court, the EPRDF rejected these proposals.[204] It was argued that as the main objective of the Constitution was to address the ethnicity issue, giving ultimate power to judges to decide on the fate of ethnic groups was not appropriate.[205] Accordingly, the HoF—which is composed of representatives of all ethnic groups plus one additional representative for each one million people—was considered best suited to perform constitutional interpretation.[206] Members of the HoF are chosen by the State Councils—the legislative bodies of the regional states—or directly by the ethnic groups concerned.[207] By establishing the CCI as an expert body that can give legal assistance to the HoF, Ethiopia chose an ethnic political body to umpire the operation of its federal system. As a result, the ethnic groups, via the HoF, are the ones who have final say on what the Constitution ultimately means.

Indeed, the configuration of ethnic federalism with the aforementioned normative and institutional setups gives the impression and façade that Ethiopia has been transformed from 'a prison house of nationalities' to 'a freedom house of nationalities'. Despite the laudable autonomy and freedom that can be heard from afar, ethnic federalism actually institutionalizes the centralizing impulses of the Ethiopian state in the design and operation of the federation. Although, unlike in Nigeria, states in Ethiopia do have their own constitution, Supreme Court, and regional police forces,[208] important government functions and prerogatives remain the mandates of the federal government. In addition to the list of twenty-one broad items—such as national defense, foreign affairs, financial and monetary matters, transportation, health, education, science and technology, and land and natural resources—that are considered as the exclusive legislative domain of the federal government,[209] the Constitution empowers the federal government to formulate and implement the country's overall socio-economic and development policies, plans, and strategies.[210] This gives the federal government wider power in implementing uniform socio-economic and development policies in the country and, consequently, shrinks the autonomy of the regional states in pursuing their own development policies. Even if states have residual powers and the Constitution specifically mentions the power of states to formulate and execute their own socio-economic and development policies, these cannot go against the

[203] The Constitution of the Federal Democratic Republic of Ethiopia, arts 62 and 82.

[204] Gedion Hessebon and Abduletif Idris, 'The Supreme Court of Ethiopia: Federalism's Bystander' in Nicholas Theodore Aroney and John Kincaid, *Courts in Federal Countries: Federalists or Unitarists?* (University of Toronto Press 2017) 181.

[205] See Getachew Assefa, 'All about Words: Discovering the Intention of the Makers of the Ethiopian Constitution on the Scope and Meaning of Constitutional Interpretation' (2010) 24 Journal of Ethiopian Law 139–69; Yonatan Tesfaye Fessha, 'Judicial Review and Democracy: A Normative Discourse on the (Novel) Ethiopian Approach to Constitutional Review' (2006) 14 African Journal of International and Comparative Law 53.

[206] The Constitution of the Federal Democratic Republic of Ethiopia, art 61(1) and (2).

[207] ibid art 61(3).

[208] ibid arts 50(7), 52(2)(b), (g), and 78(3).

[209] ibid art 51.

[210] ibid art 51(1).

policy framework of the federal government.[211] Moreover, states are only empowered to administer land—the key livelihood for more than 80 per cent of the Ethiopian population—and other natural resources in accordance with federal laws.[212] Thus, the division of power between the two tiers of government is not consistent with the laudable affirmation and recognition of the right to self-determination including secession.

The power and autonomy of the states are further diminished by the adoption of a unicameral legislative branch. The House of Peoples' Representatives (HPR), the lower house of parliament, is the sole legislative body of the federal government.[213] Unlike the case with federal legislature elsewhere,[214] which usually adopt a bicameral legislative body composed of the Senate, representing the interests of the states, and the House of Representatives, representing the interests of the general public, Ethiopia does not confer a legislative mandate to the HoF. As noted above, the main function of the HoF is merely constitutional interpretation. As the people in direct and universal suffrage elect members of the HPR, its members are responsible to their constituencies.[215] Although 20 out of 550 seats are allocated to minority nationalities, states as such do not have any representation in the legislative process.[216] Because of this, Article 8 of the Constitution which bestows sovereignty on the NNPs did not get any meaningful expression in the architecture of the legislative process. Moreover, the fact that the HPR, and not the HoF, is the highest authority in the federal government means that the *Ethiopian People*—in the singular—are the holders of the highest power.[217] Although the Constitution guarantees the equality of the states, the states of Amhara and Oromia, given their large population size, form a democratic majority in the HPR and put all others in a perpetual minority in the legislative process.[218] This, in turn, channels majority rule and an assimilationist legislative process in the operation of the federation.

In addition, the control of the major revenue sources by the federal government limits the autonomy of the states in executing their constitutionally allocated powers and responsibilities.[219] The major source of revenue for the states comes from low tax bases, such as from state and private employees, individual farmers, and cooperatives,[220] and thus, fiscal centralization makes states dependent on the

211 ibid art 52(1) and (2)(c).
212 ibid art 52(2)(d).
213 ibid art 55(1).
214 See Meg Russell, 'The Territorial Role of Second Chambers' (2001) 7 The Journal of Legislative Studies 105–18.
215 The Constitution of the Federal Democratic Republic of Ethiopia, art 54(1) and (2).
216 ibid art 54(3).
217 ibid art 50(3).
218 ibid art 47(4).
219 ibid art 96; Yonatan Fessha and Coel Kirkby, 'A Critical Survey of Subnational Autonomy in African States' (2008) 38 Publius: The Journal of Federalism 248, 262; See also Edmond Keller, 'Ethnic Federalism, Fiscal Reform, Development and Democracy in Ethiopia' (2002) 7 African Journal of Political Science / Revue Africaine de Science Politique 1, 21–50.
220 The Constitution of the Federal Democratic Republic of Ethiopia, art 97; See also Eshetu Chole, 'Opening Pandora's Box: Preliminary Notes on Fiscal Decentralization in Contemporary Ethiopia' (1994) 1 Northeast African Studies 1, 7–30.

federal government for their financial expenditures in operating their government and administration.[221]

When the constitutional design is seen in the light of the prevailing constitutional practice, the intermingling of socialist ideologies with the centralizing impulses and practices of the Ethiopian state become even more apparent.[222] The political ideologies and practices of the EPRDF cripple the autonomy of the states even more in practice:[223] the ideology of revolutionary democracy,[224] the principle of democratic centralism, the party rules on criticism and self-criticism (*gimgema*), and the ushering in of the developmental state[225] have all changed the federal state structure into a de facto unitary state. The EPRDF has been the primary producer of the country's socio-economic and political development policies, and the states have to then implement them as centrally planned.[226] In this respect, the inauguration of a new Growth and Transformation Plan every five years is a fine example of how the autonomy of states is limited in following and implementing their own development plans. The lack of appetite on the part of the EPRDF for different policy implementation, or even contextualization, coupled with the political cost to states (and their leaders) in pursuing their own policies make the constitutional right to self-determination including secession a mockery.[227] While we have yet to see how ethnic federalism works under the premiership of Abiy Ahmed, we have already seen early signs of centralization in the transformation of the EPRDF into the Prosperity Party and the substitution of revolutionary democracy with '*Medemer*' as the guiding ideology of the governing party and—by extension—the Ethiopian state.

Thus, the fundamental elements of federalism in Ethiopia are blended together with diverse normative sources. On the one hand, the concept of nationalities and their fundamental right of self-determination up to secession is the result of the migration of Marxist-Leninist ideologies to the Ethiopian political scene. On the other hand, building on the concept of nationalities, the Ethiopian Constitution adds the concept of 'nation and people' to describe and transform the country's multi-ethnic and multi-lingual communities into corporate democratic actors and homages of political identities.[228] Furthermore, inspired by the country's regional and provincial

[221] See Solomon Negussie, *Fiscal Federalism in the Ethiopian Ethnic-Based Federal System* (Wolf Legal Publishers 2006).

[222] See Abebe, *The Last Post-Cold War Socialist Federation* (n 101).

[223] See Abbink, 'Ethnic-Based Federalism and Ethnicity in Ethiopia' (n 108); Fiseha, 'The Original Sin of Ethiopian Federalism' (n 108).

[224] See Tobias Hagmann and Jon Abbink, 'Twenty Years of Revolutionary Democratic Ethiopia, 1991 to 2011' (2011) 5 Journal of Eastern African Studies 4, 579–95; Jean-Nicolas Bach, 'Abyotawi Democracy: Neither Revolutionary nor Democratic, a Critical Review of EPRDF's Conception of Revolutionary Democracy in Post-1991 Ethiopia' (2011) 5 Journal of Eastern African Studies 4, 641–63.

[225] See Christopher Clapham, 'The Ethiopian Developmental State' (2018) 39 Third World Quarterly 6, 1151–65.

[226] Aaron Tesfaye, *State and Economic Development in Africa: The Case of Ethiopia* (Palgrave Macmillan 2017) 54–59.

[227] See Theodore M Vestal, *Ethiopia: A Post-Cold War African State* (Praeger 1999); Bach (n 225).

[228] Jon Abbink, 'The Ethiopian Second Republic and the Fragile "Social Contract"' (2009) 44 Africa Spectrum 3, 10.

administrative setups, the Constitution grants 'a freedom house' to the ethnic groups in the specific places where they live.[229]

Although the current delimitation of states and other lower administrative units are not similar to the previous regional or provincial administrative organizations, its restructuring has not been entirely novel or devoid of influence from the past.[230] For the same reason, the reconfiguration of centralized federalism in design and, more importantly, in practice is also shaped by both the Ethiopian tradition of centralization as well as the influence of the Marxist-Leninist organization of the EPRDF. Like the former socialist federations of the USSR, Czechoslovakia, and Yugoslavia, which recognized the right of nationalities to self-determination up to secession, and seemingly even recognized the autonomy of subnational units in their constitutions, yet denied such autonomy in practice through the vanguard party rules and ideologies, the EPRDF also constitutionalizes centralized federalism in part, yet manages to somehow turn it into unitary decentralization in practice.[231] Thus, as with Nigeria, it is extremely difficult to fully understand and appreciate Ethiopian federalism without taking legal syncretism into account.

C. South Africa: Co-operative Government

South Africa establishes co-operative government drawing from the German experience of integrated federalism and building on the value systems of Ubuntu within the general unitary impulse, as we have seen in Nigeria and Ethiopia. The South African choice of co-operative government is the result of a compromise for a peaceful negotiated transition that aimed at accommodating ethnic and racial demands in the new democratic dispensation. Nonetheless, unlike in Nigeria and Ethiopia, once the institutional relevance of federalism was agreed upon by the negotiating parties, federalism was tasked with the purpose of ensuring democracy, development, and government efficiency. Inherent in the transformation of federalism from a peacemaking and accommodative device to a transformative and developmental tool in the final Constitution is some evidence of the acceptance of democratic and human rights ideals by the South African constitutional actors, particularly the ANC, which is unlike what we find in Nigeria and Ethiopia. As discussed above, in Nigeria and Ethiopia federalism was both *accepted* as an accommodative device and *maintained* for the same purpose. Precisely because of the change in the purpose of federalism in the final Constitution of South Africa, the debate there is over whether federalism has helped to advance the cause of democracy, development, and government efficiency. Nonetheless, like in Nigeria and Ethiopia, federalism in South Africa is also a blend of diverse normative values accompanied by a unitary impulse.

[229] See also Alem Habtu, 'Ethnic Pluralism as an Organizing Principle of the Ethiopian Federation' (2004) 28 Dialectical Anthropology 2, 91–123.

[230] Assefa Fiseha, *Federalism and the Accommodation of Diversity in Ethiopia: A Comparative Study* (Wolf Legal 2006) 11; Tareke (n 226) 36.

[231] Abebe, *The Last Post-Cold War Socialist Federation* (n 101) 52–54.

As the transformation of South Africa from a racial to a non-racial and inclusive society was the main driving force during the constitutional negotiations, the constitutional actors investigated various institutional mechanisms that could be deployed for this purpose. While their Ethiopian counterparts looked into former socialist federations to draw a lesson for the nationality question, the South Africans borrowed from the federal experience of Germany on how to use institutional mechanisms in a transformative way. The federal design in Germany institutionalizes consensus building and cooperative behavior within the multiple tiers of government.[232] For these purposes, it confers limited exclusive domains on any institution while leaving much of the governmental responsibilities to the shared and joint prerogatives of both the federal government and the Länder.[233] Further, federal laws prevail over the laws of the Länder to protect the interests of other Länder and to maintain the legal and economic unity of the federation.[234] This co-operative federalism made the constitutional negotiators interested—especially the ANC—in building a multilevel-government system that would work based on consensus and cooperation, and in times of conflict, would assure the primacy of the national government.

Drawing from the German experience of integrated federalism and building on the value systems of Ubuntu,[235] South Africa established a three-tiered sphere of co-operative government. Section 40(1) of the Constitution provides that '[i]n the Republic, government is constituted as national, provincial and local spheres of government which are distinctive, interdependent and interrelated'. Unlike Nigeria (in the First Republic) and Ethiopia, South Africa established nine provinces based on non-ethnic, non-racial, and non-linguistic grounds.[236] It founded the republic of South Africa based on the ideas of democratic values, social justice, and fundamental human rights 'to all who live in it', as stated in the Preamble of the Constitution. Section 41 outlines the principles of co-operative government which include the obligation 'to preserve peace, national unity, security, effective, transparent and coherent government as a whole' within their own sphere, as well as 'fostering friendly relations, assisting and supporting one another, cooperation on matters of common interest, and avoiding legal proceedings' in intergovernmental relations. There is a phenomenological similarity between Ubuntu and these principles of co-operative government, as consensus and cooperation are also the central ethos of Ubuntu.[237] Moreover, following the ethos of Ubuntu, Section 76(1)(d) of the Constitution requires the establishment of a Mediation Committee to solve intergovernmental disagreements.

The unitary impulse, as with Nigeria and Ethiopia, is evident in Schedules 4 and 5 of the Constitution that list, respectively, areas of concurrent and exclusive jurisdiction between the various spheres of government. The functional areas of concurrent

232 Richard Simeon, 'Considerations on the Design of Federations: The South African Constitution in Comparative Context' (1998) 13 South Africa Public Law 42, 56.

233 ibid 56–58.

234 ibid 56, see also the Basic Law of Germany 1949, art 31.

235 Simeon (n 233) 60.

236 South African Constitution, s 103(1); Christina Murray and Richard Simeon, 'Promises Unmet: Multilevel Government in South Africa' in Rekha Saxena (ed), *Varieties of Federal Governance: Major Contemporary Debates* (Cambridge University Press 2011) 238.

237 For the place and role of Ubuntu in the Constitution, see JY Makgoro, 'Ubuntu and the Law in South Africa' (1998) 1 Potchefstroom Electronic Law Journal 1, 1–11.

jurisdiction are numerous while the exclusive domains for the provinces and local government are limited. For instance, provinces are given exclusive jurisdiction only over 'abattoirs, ambulance services, archives, museums, libraries other than the national ones, liquor services, provincial planning, provincial roads, traffic, cultural, sport, recreation and amenities, and veterinary services excluding the regulation of the profession'.[238] South Africa, like Nigeria, centralizes judicial power and the police force. The limited legislative and administrative space for the provinces in South Africa makes its federal system very centralized, even more so than in Nigeria and Ethiopia.

While the Constitution establishes the NCOP as a guardian for provincial interests, its power and influence in the national legislative process are contingent upon the subject matter under consideration. Concerning bills that amend the Constitution and affect the interest of the provinces, the NCOP is given a significant power to defend provincial interests, as the support of two-thirds of the provinces is required,[239] while for bills affecting provincial interests to pass, the NCOP must agree.[240] Other than these, including money bills, the National Assembly can pass a bill on its own.[241] Also, the national legislature can override provincial legislatures even on matters exclusively assigned to the provinces.[242] Thus, unlike the Senate in Nigeria, the NCOP in South Africa has a differentiated role and influence in the national legislative process. As a result, the national legislature has an overriding power within the multi-sphere government system.

The limited legislative and administrative mandates for the provinces in South Africa are further reduced by the centralized fiscal federalism. Not only do provinces have limited tax bases with which to finance their operation, but these tax bases are also not immune from national regulation. For instance, provinces can impose 'taxes, levies and duties other than income tax, value-added tax, general sales tax, rates on property or customs duties' and 'flat-rate surcharges on any tax, levy or duty that is imposed by national legislation, other than on corporate income tax, value-added tax, rates on property or customs duties';[243] however, the national parliament is given the mandate to ensure that provinces legislate in a manner that does not materially and unreasonably affect national economic policies and activities.[244] The combination of limited legislative and administrative mandates coupled with financial dependability on the national government has reduced the capability of provinces to execute their prerogatives and hindered the experimentation of provincial policy choices in the scheme of multi-sphere government.[245] Indeed, this fact has ignited a debate on the role and utility of provinces in South African federalism, including by the ANC.[246]

238 The Constitution of South Africa, Schedule 5 Part A.

239 ibid s 74(1)(b).

240 ibid s 76(1)(a).

241 ibid ss 75(2) and 75(1)(c)(i).

242 ibid ss 146–48; see also Murray and Simeon, 'Promises Unmet' (n 237) 237; Ziyad Motala and Cyril Ramaphosa, *Constitutional Law: Analysis and Cases* (Oxford University Press 2002) 153–58.

243 The Constitution of South Africa, s 228(1).

244 ibid s 228(2).

245 Nico Steytler, 'Co-operative and Coercive Models of Intergovernmental Relations: A South African Case Study' in Thomas J Courchene and others, *The Federal Idea: Essays in Honour of Ronald L Watts* (The McGill-Queen's University Press 2011) 420–25.

246 See Tom Lodge, 'Provincial Government and State Authority in South Africa' (2005) 31 Journal of Southern African Studies 4, 737–53 (noting that despite their shortcomings, provinces proved to be helpful

The Constitution both enables local governments to share power with the national and provincial governments as stated in Part B of Schedules 4 and 5, and it also defines their purpose. Local governments are constitutionalized with the objective of providing democratic and accountable government, promoting socio-economic development, protecting the safety of the environment, and ensuring service delivery.[247] In addition to national financial support, the Constitution gives local governments taxing power 'on property and surcharges on fees for services provided by or on behalf of the municipality' and 'other taxes, levies and duties appropriate to local government or to the category of local government' when authorized by national legislation.[248] Although local governments are subject to supervision by both the national and provincial governments, the Constitution considers them as a transformative and developmental institutional setup.[249] However, as is the case with the provinces, the national government has the overriding power even on matters exclusively given to the local governments.[250] Thus, local governments can also be considered another arm of the national government, like in Nigeria.[251]

Hence, the blend of federalism with other diverse normative sources has transformed the identity of federalism in South Africa. Like in Nigeria and Ethiopia, some of the fundamental elements of federalism are transformed in the configuration of co-operative government. Although there are differences in the deployment of federalism at different stages of the constitution-making processes of South Africa on the one hand, and Nigeria and Ethiopia on the other, legal syncretism remains the central feature of all of them; the syncretic configurations have brought a unique institutional setup to the experimentation of federalism in South Africa, just as they did in Nigeria and Ethiopia. Without a proper understanding and appreciation of these unique features, it is difficult to understand and explain the South African federal experiment.

IV. The Performance of Federalism in Nigeria, Ethiopia, and South Africa

Without a doubt, the standards of assessment are equally as important as the assessment of federalism itself. As there are syncretic configurations between classic federal theory and federalism in Africa, the standards of assessment in classic federal theory

in exercising political authority at subnational level); Simeon and Murray, 'Promises Unmet' (n 237) (discussing the ANC's assessment on provinces and showing its preference to strengthening local government while questioning the relevance of provinces); Klug, *The Constitution of South Africa* (n 109) 282.

247 The Constitution of South Africa, ss 152 and 153.

248 ibid s 229(1).

249 See Rudolf Mastenbroek and Nico Steytler, 'Local Government and Development: The New Constitutional Enterprise' (1997) 1 Law, Democracy and Development 233–50; Christopher Pycroft, 'Democracy and Delivery: The Rationalization of Local Government in South Africa' (2000) 66 International Review of Administrative Sciences 1, 143–59.

250 Nico Steyler, 'Local Government in South Africa: Entrenching Decentralized Government' in Nico Steytler (ed), *The Place and Role of Local Government in Federal Systems* (Konrad-Adenauer-Stiftung 2005) 183–212.

251 See Murray and Simeon, 'Promises Unmet' (n 237).

are neither fully adequate nor totally irrelevant for Africa. To the extent that convergence exists in forms, structures, and discursive practices, these tools of assessment can be deployed. Accordingly, the standards of longevity or durability of the federal system as well as the desire of the citizenry and political class for the federal system itself can, indeed, be used as standards of assessment. On these counts, federalism in Nigeria, Ethiopia, and South Africa has been a success. After all, the federal system in Nigeria has existed since independence and there is a general desire for its continuity on the part of citizens and politicians alike. Similarly, the federal system in Ethiopia continues to exist since its first installation and will likely continue to do so for the foreseeable future, given the commitment of both citizens and politicians to the federal spirit. By the same token, South African federalism can be considered as a success not only because it still exists, but also because there is continued support for it.[252]

With respect to the achievements of the original objectives of federalism, however, the standards of assessment in classic federal theory will be of little help with regard to Africa. As the syncretic incorporations give federalism different purposes and functions here, these elements should be accounted for in its assessment. Consequently, the principal objective with which federalism is assessed in Africa should not be the achievement of democratic government, individual liberty, or economic prosperity, but rather the maintenance of territorial integrity and the accommodation of ethnonational and religious diversity. Democratic government, the respect for human rights, and economic development are all extra dividends rather than the original objectives of federalism in Africa. Precisely because of this, the continued viability of federalism is neither contingent upon the existence of a democratic system that respects human rights and delivers economic development, nor is the lack of practice of liberal democracy evidence of its failure. In these respects, the African experiment of federalism presents a paradox that cannot be explained by classic federal theory alone, for it holds that the existence of liberal democracy and constitutionalism are essential requirements for its success.

Nigeria is a fine example with which to demonstrate this paradox. Federalism has operated in Nigeria in both civil and military regimes. Indeed, much of Nigeria's post-independence period was under military rule and the military was the main architect of the present Constitution. By definition, military rule is in contradiction with constitutional government and liberal democracy as it installs itself through the displacement of constitutional rules and liberal democratic norms. Yet, Nigerian military rulers respected and protected the federal logic just like their civilian counterparts did. Thus, the difference between their rule and civilian governments was one of style and structure of administration.[253] Indeed, even after the transition to democracy, the performance of Nigeria with respect to democracy, human rights, and constitutionalism has been poor.[254]

[252] ibid 245–46.

[253] J Isawa Elaigwu, 'Nigerian Federalism under Civilian and Military Regimes' (1988) 18:1 Publius: The Journal of Federalism 173, 173.

[254] The Economist Intelligence Unit's Democracy Index, 'EIU Democracy Index 2017' <https://infographicseconomistcom/2018/DemocracyIndex/> accessed 28 December 2018.

By the same token, Ethiopia's federalism, in practical terms, has operated within a single-party system—run by the EPRDF—with a blatant disregard for the Constitution and a complete rejection of liberal democracy. While the Constitution has often been cited as a justification for the authoritarian and undemocratic actions of the EPRDF, it has been the leading ideology of revolutionary democracy and the party's practice of democratic centralism that have played the real constitutional role in the country. Since the introduction of ethnic federalism, multi-party democracy, respect for human rights, and constitutionalism have all been put aside and have given way to the emergence of the EPRDF as the only viable political party in the country. Unsurprisingly, Ethiopia scores very low with regard to democracy, human rights, and constitutionalism—even as compared to other African countries.[255] While years of protest movements against this type of authoritarian regime have brought change in the persons of the government, and recently even to the party, the practice of constitutionalism and liberal democracy have yet to be seen. Nevertheless, federalism will stay if the country is to remain united.

The paradox of federalism in Nigeria and Ethiopia has been its ability to operate in the absence of liberal constitutionalism. As long as the governance system accommodates ethnonational and religious interests at the national and subnational levels, the theories of government—be they civil/military or democratic/undemocratic—become secondary considerations, or matters of mere style or form informed by the dynamics of internal and international politics. Despite the existence of continued ethnonational and religious tensions and agitation, the governing elites in Nigeria and Ethiopia are aware of the benefits and costs of accommodation and integration and they try to be inclusive to the extent possible—albeit to different degrees—in order to make governmentality possible. Consequently, in Nigeria and Ethiopia federalism exists and performs its accommodative and integrative functions, but mainly without constitutionalism and liberal democracy.

In contrast, although South Africa introduced federalism as an accommodative and peacemaking device, it is part of a broader constitutional dispensation toward a post-apartheid and post-racial society. As such, like any other feature of the Constitution, federalism is fundamentally tied to the ideals of democratic values, social justice, and human rights. In particular, Sections 152 and 153 of the Constitution expressly specify the purposes of local government as the provision of democratic and accountable government, the promotion of socio-economic development, the protection of the safety of the environment, and the performance of service delivery. By doing so, South Africa, unlike Nigeria and Ethiopia, adds a democratic, human rights, and economic development task to federalism. As an accommodative and peacemaking device, federalism has enabled South Africa to transition from apartheid to democracy. In its classic tasks, federalism has also been able to bring government closer to the people and ensure public participation in government, while still being unable to improve the economic well-being of the poor majority.[256] For its good democratic and governance performance, the practice of constitutionalism and liberal democracy have been

[255] ibid.
[256] Murray and Simeon, 'Promises Unmet' (n 237) 240.

a great contribution, without which self-government and participation in local government would have been wishful thinking, like it is in Nigeria and Ethiopia.

Thus, the inability of federalism to deliver constitutional democracy to Nigeria and Ethiopia does not make it a failure. Indeed, federalism has succeeded in maintaining the unity and territorial integrity of these states. It has also provided the normative appeal and the institutional architecture with which to channel, accommodate, and integrate diverse interests and ambitions within a single state. Nonetheless, if federalism is to bring constitutional democracy as well, it should be given such tasks along with its holding-together function, as in South Africa and other classic federal states. To this end, in addition to the interests of the corporate ethnonational groups and the elites, democratic values, human rights, and constitutionalism should animate the normative and institutional frameworks of both self-rule and shared rule. As federalism in Africa is incorporated with syncretic elements, it is not primarily responsible for the constitutional and democratic deficits in Nigeria and Ethiopia, nor does associating such deficits with federalism help the diagnostic prescriptions for these states. The fundamental problem in this regard are the theories of government that accompany federalism, and it is these that require more serious consideration.

V. Conclusion

While federalism in Africa shares the forms, structures, and discursive practices with classic federal theory, its normative articulations and institutional frameworks are animated by syncretic configurations. These, in turn, transform the purposes, fundamental elements, and operation of federalism in Africa. As federalism followed new pathways in Africa, so do its systems of operation and standards of assessment. Contrary to the central tenets of classic federal theory, federalism sometimes manages to operate and—to the extent possible—is able to deliver its purposes without the existence of constitutionalism and liberal democracy, as is evident from the experiences of Nigeria and Ethiopia.

As the primary purpose of federalism in Africa is the accommodation of ethnonational diversity and territorial integrity, rather than the institution of constitutionalism and liberal democracy, it is not always incompatible with undemocratic—or even military—government, as long as the government maintains the aforementioned federal logic. It is precisely because of this that federalism in Nigeria and Ethiopia manages to operate and survive mainly without liberal constitutionalism. Hence, federalism is neither a failure nor prime suspect for the constitutional and democratic deficits in Nigeria and Ethiopia, for these are not its primary purposes there; indeed, it can be considered as a success as it holds these states together against the competing ethnonational interests.

If federalism is expected to ensure the practice of constitutional democracy in Nigeria and Ethiopia, it should be given such tasks explicitly, like in South Africa and other established federal states. In addition to the corporate ethnonational and elite interests, democratic values, human rights, and constitutionalism should animate the normative and institutional frameworks of both self-rule and shared rule.

5
The Executive

This chapter focuses on the executive branch, one of three branches of government in the horizontal division of power, in order to explain how legal syncretism influences the design and practice of executive power in Africa, and I will use—once again—Nigeria, Ethiopia, and South Africa as case studies. Like with federalism, legal syncretism in the institution of the executive varies between these states: while Nigeria has a popularly elected president, South Africa has an indirectly elected president, and Ethiopia chose to have a prime minister. As discussed below, these differences are crucial elements that make legal syncretism an important theory for understanding the nature of the different executive types in Africa.

As noted in Chapter 3, the African constitutional designs and practices incorporate and magnify the *power-enabling* aspects of executive power from diverse legal and political rules and experiences while relegating and deemphasizing the *power-limiting* aspects of executive power from these same diverse rules and experiences. The outcome of these processes is the establishment of a hyperactive and imperial executive and highly personalized executive power in which the executive controls the political party apparatus, the government institutions, and ultimately the state itself. Precisely because of this, the African executive has defied conventional vocabularies and requires an additional descriptor.[1]

To understand and appreciate the African type of executive, and how legal syncretism constitutes it, it is necessary to first present the standard notion of executive as conceived in liberal constitutional theory. To this end, this chapter first develops a conceptual framework for the design of the executive and the practice of executive power drawing from liberal constitutional theory. It then explores and examines the design of the executive and the practice of executive power in Nigeria, Ethiopia, and South Africa. The aim is to demonstrate how legal syncretism shapes the executives in these countries and how different configurations of legal syncretism have produced imperial executives in Nigeria and Ethiopia, but not in South Africa. By disentangling the discursive practices that bring about and sustain the imperial executives and by showing the pathologies of constitutional designs and practices related to the executive, this chapter defends the idea of a *limited executive* if constitutionalism is to prosper in Africa.

[1] H Kwasi Prempeh, 'Constitutional Autochthony and the Invention and Survival of "absolute Presidentialism" in Postcolonial Africa' in Gunter Frankenberk, *Order from Transfer Comparative Constitutional Design and Legal Culture Comparative Constitutional Design and Legal Culture* (Elgar 2013) 209.

A Theory of African Constitutionalism. Berihun Adugna Gebeye, Oxford University Press. © Berihun Adugna Gebeye 2021.
DOI: 10.1093/oso/9780192893925.003.0006

I. The Executive: A Conceptual Framework

Liberal constitutional theory concerns itself with defending individual liberty in a political community. On how to defend liberty, however, prescriptions differ. Thomas Hobbes thought the unity of sovereign power in a single man or assembly of men would secure and protect individual liberty. To this end, he proposed a social contract for the institution of a Commonwealth where individuals give up part of their rights and surrender their will to the sovereign.[2] Then individuals owe obedience and submission to the sovereign, as a custodian of public will, like a leviathan or a *mortal god*.[3] Nevertheless, as history has it, the leviathan has become the enemy of individual liberty, at worst, or an untrusted friend of liberty, at best. Hence, much of liberal constitutional theory grapples with taming Hobbes' leviathan, and it is in this quest that the executive is born in liberal constitutional theory.

The doctrine of separation of powers is one of the main inventions in limiting the powers of the sovereign. As developed in Montesquieu's *The Spirit of Laws*, this doctrine claims that for the sake of political liberty and the exclusion of tyranny or arbitrary power, government power should not be concentrated in one man or assembly of men.[4] Montesquieu argued that a government has three functions and, consequently, should have three separate bodies. As government has the power to make and repeal laws, the power to implement these laws, and the power to adjudicate and solve disputes based on these laws, a government should, accordingly, be structured into legislative, executive, and judicial branches that perform these functions, respectively. In addition to the functional separation of powers between these branches of government, they should not be manned by the same persons. In this way, as each branch of government is checked by the others, or in Madison's terms, 'as ambition will counteract ambition', the government will not encroach on individual liberty.[5]

Through this prism of separation of powers, liberal constitutions further specify the nature and powers of the executive. While some, closely following the tenets of separation of powers, establish a unitary executive, like the presidential system in the United States,[6] others institute a bifurcated executive, with one as the head of the state and the other as the head of the government, like the parliamentary system in the United Kingdom. Even when there are hybrid regimes that combine both presidential and parliamentary systems, the existence of a single figurehead of the executive and their cabinet represent the executive branch of government. To prevent arbitrary power, the executive has both enumerated and implied powers and it is within these strictures that the executive must function.[7] The idea of enumerated powers is another device for *limiting* the power of the executive as it cannot claim to have powers beyond what is expressly given to it by a constitution. However, prudence also requires that the

[2] Thomas Hobbes, *Hobbes: Leviathan* (Cambridge University Press 1996) 120.

[3] ibid 120–22.

[4] Charles de Secondat baron de Montesquieu, *The Spirit of Laws* (Batoche Books 2001) 173–74.

[5] Alexander Hamilton or James Madison, 'Federalist No 51' <https://wwwcongressgov/resources/display/content/The+Federalist+Papers#TheFederalistPapers-51> accessed 16 January 2018.

[6] See Steven G Calabresi and Christopher S Yoo, *The Unitary Executive: Presidential Power from Washington to Bush* (Yale University Press 2008).

[7] Louis Fisher, *The Law of the Executive Branch: Presidential Power* (Oxford University Press 2014) 1–2.

executive needs to have some additional powers that are essential or necessary for the execution of the enumerated powers.

Although there is a difference in the breadth and scope of executive power across liberal constitutional systems, there are limits to the duration and number of terms of office for the executive figurehead. The temporal limitation of executive power is as important as the limitation of substantive executive power for the purposes of taming the leviathan and defending political liberty. Term limits for the executive head are particularly the norm in presidential systems, like those of the United States and France, whereas the tenure of the prime minister rests on the confidence of the parliament in parliamentary systems, like that of the United Kingdom. Even so, although the powers of the executive are limited substantively and temporally in constitutions, the executive—as the successor to the absolute monarch—still dwarfs the legislative and the judicial branches of government due to its gigantic and complex bureaucracy and administrative apparatus.[8] Nonetheless, the executive still disposes its strong physical and financial resources, as well as its monopoly of coercion, within the framework of the rule of law.[9]

While the executive in liberal democracies looks less formidable in the constitutional designs, the rise of the modern regulatory and welfare state as well as the national security regime—among other things—have expanded the powers of the executives in practice.[10] The expansion of executive power beyond what the constitution allows has often been termed 'imperial power'.[11] The imperial executive in liberal democracies is usually associated with the exercise of presidential power in the United States. Even Webster's unabridged dictionary defines imperial presidency as 'a U.S. presidency that is characterized by greater power than the Constitution allows'.[12] In addition, an imperial presidency is said to exist in the French Constitution of the Fifth Republic.[13] Outside of Western democracies, the phenomenon of imperial presidency can be found in China and Russia, among others.[14] For present purposes, however, the focus will be on the United States, since the notion of imperial presidency emerged there, on France, because many post-colonial African presidents draw inspiration from the presidential power of the Constitution of the Fifth Republic, and on the United Kingdom, to show how imperial executive power can exist in parliamentary

[8] Eric Posner and Adrian Vermeule, *The Executive Unbound: After the Madisonian Republic* (Oxford University Press 2011) 5–6.

[9] András Sajó and Renáta Uitz, *The Constitution of Freedom: An Introduction to Legal Constitutionalism* (Oxford University Press 2017) 268.

[10] Renata Uitz, 'Courts and the Expansion of Executive Power: Making the Constitution Matter' in David Bilchitz and David Landau (eds), *The Evolution of the Separation of Powers Between the Global North and the Global South* (Edward Elgar 2018) 85–86.

[11] Posner and Vermeule, *The Executive Unbound* (n 8) 12.

[12] Webster's unabridged dictionary, <http://wwwdictionarycom/browse/imperial-presidency> accessed 23 December 2018.

[13] Ezra N Suleiman, 'Presidential Government in France' in Richard Rose and Ezra N Suleiman (eds), *Presidents and Prime Ministers* (American Enterprise Institute 1980) 103–04 Suleiman observes that the imperial presidency is more fitting to France than the United States.

[14] Elizabeth C Economy, 'China's Imperial President: Xi Jinping Tightens His Grip' (2014) 93 Foreign Aff 80; Luke Coffey, 'Putin Has Imperial (Not Soviet) Aspirations' The Daily Signal (13 June 2016) <https://wwwdailysignalcom/2016/06/13/putin-has-imperial-not-soviet-aspirations/> accessed 10 November 2018.

systems as well. A brief discussion of the practices of executive power in these three liberal democracies can shed some light on the nature of the executive in the practice of constitutional government.

In this regard, Arthur Schlesinger, in his seminal book *The Imperial Presidency*, offers a language and vocabulary to explain the practice and rise of presidential power in the United States under the pretext of an emergency.[15] As developed by Schlesinger, imperial presidency is an extra-constitutional phenomenon mainly concerning the sphere of foreign affairs, and particularly the power of declaration of war. His central argument is that although the United States Constitution divides war powers between Congress and the president, the former defers to the decisions and wisdom of the latter. Due to these developments since the founding of the Republic, the American president has become an absolute monarch on issues of war and peace, as he is unilaterally in charge contrary to the intended constitutional balance.[16] While Schlesinger attributes this imperial phenomenon to congressional abdication rather than presidential usurpation, he also notes that deference on the part of Congress towards the president is the result of an operational compulsion towards the belief that the executive has superior information and, thus, also has direct responsibility on these issues.[17]

Although imperial presidency in the United States is related to the dominance of the president in foreign policy and unilateral decision-making regarding declarations of war, its impact and influence on domestic policy have been growing ever since the 9/11 terrorist attack.[18] The transformation of the 'National Security State' into the 'National Surveillance State' has expanded the imperial presidency into domestic affairs as well.[19] Since protecting and guarding the United States from 'sudden attacks'—like that of 9/11—forms part of the inherent power of the president, it is argued that the imperial power based on the national security thesis with regard to foreign affairs is no less relevant when it comes to domestic affairs.[20] Based on this argument, President George W. Bush pursued a global war on terror which cut across foreign and domestic issues,[21] and which President Obama[22] then also pursued, albeit more carefully and less openly, in particular when it came to surveillance.[23] Furthermore, in this spectacle of imperial presidency, it isn't only Congress, but also the lower courts who have generally deferred to checking the executive through the doctrines of standing and political questions, while the Supreme Court has ordered *some* judicial supervision of the surveillance state.[24]

[15] Arthur Meier Schlesinger, *The Imperial Presidency* (Houghton Mifflin Harcourt 1973) ix.

[16] ibid.

[17] ibid 14.

[18] Mark Tushnet, 'The Presidential Empire' (2015) 62 Dissent 101, 102.

[19] ibid.

[20] See Charlie Savage, *Takeover: The Return of the Imperial Presidency and the Subversion of American Democracy* (Little, Brown and Company 2007).

[21] Franz-Josef Meiers, 'The Return of the Imperial Presidency? The President, Congress, and US Foreign Policy after 11 September 2001' (2010) 55 Amerikastudien / American Studies 249, 255; See also Andrew Rudalevige, *The New Imperial Presidency: Renewing Presidential Power After Watergate* (University of Michigan Press 2005).

[22] For details see Ryan C Hendrickson, *Obama at War: Congress and the Imperial Presidency* (University Press of Kentucky 2015).

[23] Tushnet, 'The Presidential Empire' (n 18) 103.

[24] ibid 105.

Imperial presidency in the United States, therefore, is not a general executive phenomenon like it is in Africa, but rather, as noted above, focuses exclusively on the specific executive powers of foreign affairs and/or national security. Moreover, not only is the president constitutionally empowered to wage war as the Commander-in-Chief of the army,[25] but they also perform this function after consultation with their Cabinet, Congress, the judiciary, the media, and public opinion, both at home and abroad.[26] Thus, the chief explanation for imperial presidency in the US is more one of emergency than normalcy. Presidents become imperial when the country faces some sort of emergency, either in foreign affairs and international relations or in the fight against terrorism, both abroad and at home.

Unlike the imperial presidency in Africa which bestows unlimited imperial executive power on the person of the president, the imperial presidency in the United States is constrained by both written and unwritten constitutional rules. Moreover, the separation of powers that animated the founding of the United States—and still permeates its operation—has made its presidents quite limited and constrained—more than any other leader in the Western world.[27] Furthermore, the United States is the pioneer and good example of a functioning limited government in the modern world. Thus, considering this context in which the notion of imperial presidency originated and manifested itself, using imperial presidency to describe executive dominance in the African context would be a misnomer without further contextualization and redefinition.

By combining various features of the presidency from both presidential and parliamentary systems, the French president, too, is like a 'republican monarch' who is less constrained in their power, unlike the president in the United States.[28] Beyond the charisma of presidents, which grants them extra-constitutional power and influence, the Constitution of the Fifth Republic explicitly bestows strong executive powers unto the president—probably more than any other head of executive in the Western world.[29] For instance, Article 5 of the Constitution expresses the place and function of the president as follows:

> The President of the Republic shall ensure due respect for the Constitution. He shall ensure, by his *arbitration*, the proper functioning of the public authorities and the continuity of the State. He shall be the *guarantor* of national independence, territorial integrity and due respect for Treaties [emphasis added].

Further, unlike the United States Constitution, the French Constitution enumerates the legislative powers of the parliament, in Article 34, and bestows all other residual legislative matters to the executive as stated in Article 37. Moreover, the President has the power to appoint and dismiss the Prime Minister,[30] preside over the Council of Ministers,[31] bypass Parliament and submits important issues for a

[25] The Constitution of the United States of America 1789, art II s 2.
[26] Schlesinger, *The Imperial Presidency* (n 15) ix.
[27] Louis W Koenig, 'Reassessing the "Imperial Presidency"' (1981) 34 Proceedings of the Academy of Political Science 31, 35.
[28] Sajó and Uitz, *The Constitution of Freedom* (n 9) 269.
[29] Suleiman, 'Presidential Government in France' (n 13) 103.
[30] The Constitution of France 1958, art 8.
[31] ibid art 9.

referendum,[32] dissolve Parliament,[33] and assumes emergency powers.[34] In addition to dividing law-making powers between Parliament and the executive, the Constitution establishes a Constitutional Council which checks Parliament in its legislative business.[35] Thus, the constitutional architecture engineered in the Fifth Republic ensures executive primacy under the leadership of a strong president.[36]

Because of this constitutional design of presidential power, many commentators consider the French presidency to be imperial.[37] But if we consider the French presidency to be imperial, given the strong executive powers conferred upon it by the Constitution, we must note that its nature, scope, rationale, and manifestations are all different from both the American imperial presidency and those prevalent in practice in Africa. Unlike in the United States, the imperial presidency in France is found in the text of the Constitution itself and its main rationale is not emergency but a response to a prior constitutional experiment. The Constitution of the Fifth Republic created a strong president to redeem the failures in the Fourth Republic where Parliament was strong and the president was a mere figurehead, in turn, led to government instability and weakness.[38] As such, imperial presidency is supposed to be a practice not only in cases of emergency but also in normalcy, and, consequently, the nature and manifestation of imperial presidency in France and the United States are different.

Nonetheless, like the United States, despite the variations in degree, the French presidency is constrained by constitutional and political rules and practices. Not only does the president seek the backing of a political party to run for election, but they also need to work with parliament to support their legislative proposals.[39] As a result, the president needs to take into consideration the interests of party and parliamentary politics throughout their presidency. Similarly, although the president can appoint and dismiss the prime minister, the Constitution institutionalizes built-in difficulties by composing the executive branch from the teams of both the president and the prime minister. This is particularly the case in times of cohabitation, where a different party than that of the president controls parliament.[40] In this scenario, the powers of the president are restricted while the powers of the prime minister are expanded[41] and the president is required and/or forced to co-operate with the prime minister.[42]

As a result, while loyalty to the president is expected from the prime minister, this is not always the case. Additionally, the functioning of *realpolitik* tames the president's influence and dismissal of his Prime Minister.[43] Furthermore, as presidents are

[32] ibid art 11.
[33] ibid art 12.
[34] ibid art 16.
[35] John Bell, *French Constitutional Law* (Clarendon Press 1994) 16–19.
[36] Sophie Boyron, *The Constitution of France: A Contextual Analysis* (Bloomsbury Publishing 2012) Chapter 3.
[37] See ibid 57–74; Suleiman, 'Presidential Government in France' (n 13).
[38] Bell, *French Constitutional Law* (n 35) 14.
[39] Suleiman, 'Presidential Government in France' (n 13) 98–103.
[40] Jean V Poulard, 'The French Double Executive and the Experience of Cohabitation' (1990) 105 Political Science Quarterly 243, 255–56.
[41] For the particular cases of cohabitation, see Martin A Rogoff, *French Constitutional Law: Cases and Materials* (Carolina Academic Press 2011) 70–78.
[42] Robert Elgie, '"Cohabitation": Divided Government French-Style' in Robert Elgie (ed), *Divided Government in Comparative Perspective* (Oxford University Press 2001) 118–19.
[43] Suleiman, 'Presidential Government in France' (n 13) 107–20.

popularly elected, the rejection of their referenda proposals usually ends their tenure. For instance, despite his charisma, de Gaulle stepped down from his presidency when he lost the 1969 referendum. Unlike the imperial phenomenon in Africa, French presidents work within the constitutional limits and submit to the will of the people.[44]

The prime minister in the UK, like the United States president, also enjoys a wide range of powers, in particular with respect to foreign affairs and declaration of war.[45] It is argued that parliament's deference to, or acceptance of, the prime minister's policies of foreign military interventions have transformed the prime minister into an imperial position, like happened in the United States.[46] Nonetheless, the political authority of the prime minister emanates from their position as a party leader and the confidence of the parliament in them. Indeed, the loss of support from one's party can oust a prime minister—even one as strong as Margaret Thatcher.[47]

Although the United States, French, and UK executives all have imperial characters and impulses, a commitment to the idea of limited government lies at the foundation of their operation. The heads of the executive, as well as their cabinets, submit to the rule of law and are neither above the state nor the political parties of which they are members. Further, they are neither president or prime minister for life, nor do they aspire to be so. Thus, the imperial executive phenomenon in these countries rests within their constitutional contours and choices.

Even though the type of president as found in the United States or France is the choice of many African states, their institution of the presidency and their practice of presidential power differ from both of these countries. As discussed in Chapter 3 and will be developed further in this chapter, the reading of presidential government by many African presidents undermines the notion of separation of powers and institutionalizes personal rule. While the origin of the executive and the allocation of executive power is related to the quest to *limit* government for the sake of liberty, the African executive has been preoccupied with *limiting the limitations* justified by the supposed quest to enlarge freedom in developmental terms. In this respect, there has been a near-universal adoption of the presidential system of government in Africa, and, consequently, there has been an acceptance of a regime-type modeled after Western democracies, or, to be more precise, after the United States and France. On the other hand, there has been a general distaste for, or even rejection of, the doctrines of separation of powers and judicial review that comes with the acceptance of such systems.

The following sections, building on the discussion on the executive in Chapter 3, explore and examine how legal syncretism has structured and instituted the executive branches in Nigeria, Ethiopia, and South Africa, and how different configurations of legal syncretism in these countries have contributed to the development of imperial presidency and premiership in Nigeria and Ethiopia, respectively, both of which are different from that of South Africa.

[44] David S Bell and John Gaffney, 'Introduction' in David S Bell and John Gaffney (eds), *Presidential Power in Fifth Republic France* (Palgrave Macmillan 2013) 1–5.

[45] Peter Leyland, *The Constitution of the United Kingdom: A Contextual Analysis* (Bloomsbury Publishing 2016) 158–60.

[46] See Sam Goodman, *The Imperial Premiership: The Role of the Modern Prime Minister in Foreign Policy Making, 1964–2015* (Manchester University Press 2016).

[47] Leyland, *The Constitution of the United Kingdom* (n 45) 162–63.

II. The Executive in Nigeria: 'Imperial Presidency'

As noted elsewhere, unlike in liberal constitutional systems where the origin of the executive is associated with the quest for limited government, the executive in Africa is the result of an imposed or imported constitutional design. The departing colonial powers imposed liberal constitutional systems that included the doctrine of separation of powers. As a result, the African executives mirror the executives of their former colonizers, although many former British colonies later adopted American-style presidential systems.[48] The independence constitutions were accepted by the African political elites not because they believed in the values of these liberal constitutional systems or in the separation of powers they were enshrined in, but simply because the acceptance of these constitutions was a condition precedent for independence. As discussed in Chapter 3, although the structural forms of the doctrine of separation of powers were accepted in the post-1990 constitutions, many of the constitutions have been preoccupied with *limiting the limitations* to the executive. The concentration of power in the executive has been the aim of both constitutions and constitutional practice in Africa. This section explores how legal syncretism has been used to *limit the limitations* to the executive in Nigeria.

Following the British colonial legacy, Nigeria adopted a parliamentary system at independence in 1960. Unlike much of Anglophone Africa, however, Nigeria did not have one national charismatic and mobilizing figure at the time of independence;[49] as discussed in Chapter 4, Nigeria was deeply divided across ethnic, regional, and religious lines. Furthermore, a three-party political system fashioned in light of these diversities was already in operation, and as a result, Nigeria even maintained the parliamentary system in the First Republican Constitution three years later. In this regard, Nigeria was among the few Anglophone African countries—along with Sierra Leone, Uganda, Lesotho, and Swaziland—to replace the British Queen as the head of the state with an indigenous president as head of state while still maintaining their parliamentary system.[50] The bifurcation of executive power into a titular head of state and executive head of government was not considered as un-African by then.[51] However, the real or alleged problems associated with the parliamentary system in the First Republic, coupled with the civil war experience, the quest for autochthony, and the prolonged military rule from 1966–1979 all conspired to bring about an American-style presidential system in 1979.[52]

Accordingly, the 1979 Constitution of Nigeria established an executive president for the federation, which the 1999 Constitution maintains to this day.[53] The shift from a parliamentary to a presidential system can be explained and rationalized on both

[48] Charles M Fombad, 'An Overview of Separation of Powers under Modern African Constitutions' in Charles M Fombad (ed), *Separation of Powers in African Constitutionalism* (Oxford University Press 2016) 69–88.

[49] Larry R Jackson, 'Nigeria: The Politics of the First Republic' (1972) 2 Journal of Black Studies 277, 278.

[50] BO Nwabueze, *Presidentialism in Commonwealth Africa* (St Martin's Press 1974) 70. Note that Lesotho and Swaziland have been kingdoms.

[51] Kalu Ezera, *Constitutional Developments in Nigeria* (2nd ed, Cambridge University Press 1964) 282–84.

[52] Benjamin Obi Nwabueze, *Military Rule and Constitutionalism in Nigeria* (Spectrum Law Pub 1992) 229.

[53] See also BO Nwabueze, *Nigeria's Presidential Constitution: The Second Experiment in Constitutional Democracy* (Longman 1984) 23–26.

cultural and institutional grounds.[54] From the perspective of culture, it was held that the bifurcation of power into a head of government and head of the state was foreign to the African conception and organization of power.[55] Accordingly, the friction, competition, and confusion between the office holders of the head of government and head of the state in exercising their constitutional powers was attributed to the lack of context and autochthony in the constitutional design;[56] despite the clear constitutional division of powers between the prime minister and the president, there was persistent competition between them.[57] A good example of this was the advice of the president to postpone the 1964 national election, advice that the prime minister rejected. The latter then carried out the election as initially planned—despite the boycott in the East, West, and Midwest regions—[58]which duly led to an election crisis that fermented the setting for prolonged military rule.[59] The argument went, that unifying the powers of the head of government and head of state into one person would not only avoid the competition and confusion of power between the president and prime minister, but would also place the constitutional design with the African cultural milieu, as such power had always resided in unitary kings, chiefs, or traditional leaders.[60]

The institutional explanations can be attributed to the advantages of the presidential system over the parliamentary system in the Nigerian setting.[61] In addition to the 1964 election crisis,[62] the theoretical challenge was that in this type of parliamentary system, Nigeria could clearly have a prime minister who has support only in their own region if their party controlled the majority of seats in parliament.[63] Obviously, this would go counter to the accommodative and holding-together nature of Nigerian federalism. It was held that the presidential system would provide the president with an opportunity to be a unifying figure in the federation, given their direct election. By fostering inter-ethnic and regional unity, it was argued, the president would be able to overcome the pressing national challenges by providing effective leadership.[64] To this

[54] Nwabueze, *Presidentialism in Commonwealth Africa* (n 50) 59–92; see also E Michael Joye and Kingsley Igweike, *Introduction to the 1979 Nigerian Constitution* (Macmillan Nigeria 1982) 119–31.

[55] JD Ojo, *The Development of the Executive Under the Nigerian Constitutions, 1960–81* (Ibadan, University Press 1989) 7–8.

[56] Rotimi T Suberu and Larry Diamond, 'Institutional Design, Ethnic Conflict Management, and Democracy in Nigeria' in Andrew Reynolds (ed), *The Architecture of Democracy: Constitutional Design, Conflict Management, and Democracy* (Oxford University Press 2002) 411; Nwabueze, *Presidentialism in Commonwealth Africa* (n 50) 59–69.

[57] Nwabueze, *Presidentialism in Commonwealth Africa* (n 50) 73–83.

[58] JD Ojo, 'The Executive under the Nigerian Constitutions, 1960–1995' in Kunle Amuwo and others, Federalism and Political Restructuring in Nigeria (Spectrum Books 1998) 300.

[59] Larry Diamond, *Class, Ethnicity, and Democracy in Nigeria: The Failure of the First Republic* (Syracuse University Press 1988) 190.

[60] See also Oyeleye Oyediran, *Nigerian Government and Politics under Military Rule, 1966-79* (Macmillan 1979) 247; Nwabueze, *Presidentialism in Commonwealth Africa* (n 50) 59–69.

[61] Nwabueze, *Military Rule and Constitutionalism in Nigeria* (n 52) 229–45 Nwabueze argues that presidential system ensures separation of legislative and executive powers, unity and stability of the political order, and effective leadership for economic development.

[62] Diamond, *Class, Ethnicity, and Democracy in Nigeria* (n 59) 190–247.

[63] Ojo, *The Development of the Executive Under the Nigerian Constitutions* (n 55) 300.

[64] See Suberu and Diamond, 'Institutional Design, Ethnic Conflict Management, and Democracy in Nigeria' (n 56) 411.

end, it was proposed, a clear separation of powers among the three branches of government was necessary.[65]

Although the military tradition of centralized rule had its own contributions to the shift from the parliamentary to the presidential system,[66] the choice for this type of system was the result of a conscious effort by the political and military elites of Nigeria to organize executive power.[67] In choosing presidentialism, the constitutional authors of the 1979 and 1999 constitutions selectively incorporated alleged indigenous norms of political organization along with a modern institutional setup of presidential power. By doing so, they absorbed a presidential regime based on real or imagined traits of commonality with the African notion of organization of power while rejecting a parliamentary regime based on claims of a lack of complementarity with the same. Evident in this constitutional act of absorption and rejection is the configuration of an American-style presidentialism. While the practical challenges of the parliamentary system in the First Republic informed the choice for presidentialism, the quest for autochthony and Africanism were used as a discursive practice to institute a strong executive president. In this regard, Benjamin Obi Nwabueze observes that '[p]residentialism may be regarded as the culmination in the constitutional field of the national struggle for emancipation from colonialism'.[68] Accordingly, it was believed that the presidential system should be further Africanized.[69] In this Africanization process, the authors of the Nigerian presidential constitutions selectively incorporated and reconfigured the *power-enabling* aspects of indigenous notions of power while relegating the *power-limiting* ones.

As noted elsewhere in this book, the concept of a unitary king or chief, or even a centralized political organization, is not a universal African experience. Even in the Nigerian context itself, the idea of a unitary king or chief is unknown to the Igbo, for example, as opposed to the Yoruba and Hausa-Fulani. Like with any other uncentralized political system, as discussed in Chapter 2, there was a general distaste for, and resistance to, political centralization among the Igbo. The claim of autochthony in establishing the executive was simply used as a discursive practice to centralize and personalize executive power. As a matter of fact, the Colonial Governor is a fine example of accumulating legislative, executive, and judicial powers in their person and this can be a huge inspiration for the creation of a strong president. Unlike the concept of a unitary king or chief, the practice of the colonial governor and its *modus operandi* was a universal African experience. As discussed in the previous chapters,

[65] W Alade Fawole, 'Executive-Legislative Relationship' in A Sat Obiyan and Kunle Amuwo (eds), *Nigeria's Democratic Experience in the Fourth Republic since 1999: Policies and Politics* (University Press of America 2012) 15–31.

[66] Nwabueze, *Military Rule and Constitutionalism in Nigeria* (n 52) 229.

[67] Suberu and Diamond, 'Institutional Design, Ethnic Conflict Management, and Democracy in Nigeria' (n 56) 415 (noting that despite its problems, the presidential system is preffered by the majority of Nigerians).

[68] Nwabueze, *Presidentialism in Commonwealth Africa* (n 50) 59.

[69] ibid 60, Nwabueze argues that autochthony has two aspects; the first is the source from which the constitution dervies its authority as law, and the second is the contents of the constitution. While the first has to do with the legitimacy of the constitution that who should make the constitution, the second has to do with the substantive contents of the constitution that it has to reflect the reality of the society and fit with its context.

even the alleged unitary king or chief in centralized political systems was limited by numerous institutional and customary practices and, consequently, may not provide the cultural background for the adoption of personal rule, unlike the practice of the Colonial Governor.

The constitutional design of presidential power in Nigeria shows how the doctrine of separation of powers has been used to both separate the executive from the other branches of government and how it has also been modified to ensure executive primacy, which is in direct contradiction to the central tenets of separation of powers. A closer look at the presidential powers and an assessment of the relationship between the executive and the other branches reveal that the president is granted enormous powers that challenge the doctrine of separation of powers.

Exclusive executive power is vested in the president and he is the chief executive officer of the federation in charge of the implementation of the Constitution and all laws enacted by the National Assembly.[70] All other executive organs of the federation do not have any constitutionally defined power or responsibility.[71] The vice president and the ministers of the federation only perform and execute such powers and responsibilities as given to them by the president at their own discretion.[72] In this respect, the Supreme Court also notes—in *AG Federation v Atiku Abubakar*—that although the Constitution created the office of the president and the vice president, all executive power is vested in the president alone.[73]

In addition, the president has very wide appointment, security, as well as emergency powers. Not only do they appoint the Chief of Defense Staff, the Chief of Army Staff, Chief of Naval Staff, Chief of Air Staff, and other heads of the armed forces,[74] they can also remove them all at their discretion.[75] The president can appoint and remove the Inspector General of the Nigerian Police Force upon consultation with the Nigeria Police Council.[76] They can also appoint and remove their own special advisors at their pleasure.[77] Subject to confirmation by the Senate, they can appoint Ministers of the Government,[78] the Attorney-General,[79] and other government officials.[80] Although the president cannot declare war without the resolution of the National Assembly, they can deploy the armed forces outside of Nigeria with the consultation of the National Defense Council for seven days if they think that the national security of the country is in danger.[81] They can also declare a state of emergency in any part of the federation.[82]

[70] The Constitution of Nigeria, s 5(1).
[71] Oyelowo Oyewo, 'Nigeria' in Baron André Alen and David Haljan (eds), *International Encyclopaedia for Constitutional Law* (Wolters Kluwer Law & Business 2012) 52–54.
[72] The Constitution of Nigeria s 148(1).
[73] *AG Federation v Atiku Abubakar* [2007] 4 S C 3 NWLR (PT II) 62.
[74] The Constitution of Nigeria s 218.
[75] Oyewo, 'Nigeria' (n 71) 55.
[76] The Constitution of Nigeria s 216(1).
[77] ibid s 151.
[78] ibid s 147.
[79] ibid s 150.
[80] ibid ss 154(1) and 171.
[81] ibid s 5(5).
[82] ibid s 305(1); AA Idowu, 'Emergency Powers, Political Instability, and the Nigerian Constitution: The Plateau State Experience of Year 2004 Revisited' in A Sat Obiyan and Kunle Amuwo, *Nigeria's Democratic Experience in the Fourth Republic Since 1999: Policies and Politics* (Rowman & Littlefield 2013) 82, the

The executive also participates in law-making by initiating bills and in the appointment of judicial functionaries.[83] Further, the president, through the veto power, controls the law-making process.[84] Even though there is veto override procedure,[85] the president still possesses enormous power to influence the legislative process. Along these lines, although the control of the public revenue resides primarily within the ambits of the National Assembly,[86] it is the president who decides how the revenue is distributed or disbursed, since it is the president who has the power to put forth proposals on revenue allocation or utilization on which the National Assembly then has to decide.[87] Moreover, the president's proposal is a condition precedent for the National Assembly to exercise its power in this respect.[88] And, finally, with the confirmation by the Senate, the president also appoints justices to the Supreme Court.[89] Hence, as is clear from all of the aforementioned examples, the executive holds enormous powers that can dwarf the legislative and judicial branches even further.[90]

The practice of presidential powers in the Fourth Republic has shown that not only can an executive President be a source of ethno-regional anxiety and suspicion, but it can also lead to the emergence of personal rule and imperial executive power.[91] Since the transition back to civilian democratic rule in 1999, the office of the presidency has become a preeminent office to which other branches of the government pay deference.[92] Abuse of incumbency has become a feature in Nigerian political life which makes accessing the office of the presidency a difficult task for the opposition.[93] In this respect, Olusengun Obasanjo's presidency was a good example of the practice of imperial presidency in the Fourth Republic.[94] Like the other imperial presidents in Africa discussed in Chapter 3, Obasanjo started institutionalizing his personal rule by controlling his party—the People's Democratic Party (PDP)—as well as the state apparatus.[95] This, in turn, helped him to secure his two-term presidency. Although he was not able to secure a constitutional amendment to run for a third term, he was

president by using his emergency powers suspend and disband the Governor and State House of Assembly respectively.

[83] See also Sylvester Shikyil, 'Legislative-Executive Relations in Presidential Democracies: The Case of Nigeria' in Charles M Fombad (ed), *Separation of Powers in African Constitutionalism* (Oxford University Press 2016) 142–43.

[84] The Constitution of Nigeria, s 58(4).

[85] ibid s 58(5).

[86] ibid ss 162–68.

[87] ibid s 162(2).

[88] Oyewo, 'Nigeria' (n 71) 64.

[89] The Constitution of Nigeria s 231(1) and (2).

[90] Eugene N Nweke, 'The Principle and Practice of Separation of Power in Nigeria: A Study of Olusengun Obasanjo's Civilian Regime (1999–2007)' in Obiyan and Amuwo, *Nigeria's Democratic Experience in the Fourth Republic Since 1999* 63–67.

[91] Suberu and Diamond, 'Institutional Design, Ethnic Conflict Management, and Democracy in Nigeria' (n 56) 412.

[92] V Adefemi Isumonah, 'Imperial Presidency and Democratic Consolidation in Nigeria' (2012) 59 Africa Today 43.

[93] Gedion Timothewos Hessebon, *Contextualizing Constitutionalism: Multiparty Democracy in the African Political Matrix* (Eleven International Publishing 2017) 57–62.

[94] A Sat Obiyan, "The Federal State in Obasanjo's Nigeria: Coordinate Relationship or Imperial Order?" in Obiyan and Amuwo, *Nigeria's Democratic Experience in the Fourth Republic Since 1999* 97–103.

[95] Isumonah, 'Imperial Presidency and Democratic Consolidation in Nigeria' (n 92) 53–65.

successful in making a person of his choice, Goodluck Jonathan, become his successor in 2007.[96]

During his tenure, Obasanjo subordinated the legislature and the judicial branches to his rule. For instance, with respect to the legislature, even though the Constitution requires parliamentary approval for expenditure by the executive, Obasanjo spent the budget on numerous occasions without such approval.[97] The presidential dominance of the legislative process continues in the Fourth Republic as a legacy of colonial and postcolonial military traditions.[98] In a similar vein, Obasanjo often either disregarded or altered the decisions of the Supreme Court. Even in 2019, only three weeks away from the sixth presidential election since 1999, President Muhammadu Buhari suspended the Chief Justice of the Supreme Court, Justice Walter Nkanu Samuel Onnoghen, on allegations of corruption,[99] even though according to the Nigerian Constitution, the president cannot suspend or remove a justice of the Supreme Court without two-thirds support from the Senate.[100] This suspension of the justice was said to be linked to the expected contestation of the February 2019 presidential election in the Supreme Court.[101] In addition to the abuse of incumbency and the imperial presidency which secured Obasanjo's presidency and his personal clientelistic networks in his party and state apparatus,[102] the federal government under his leadership was actively involved in the impeachment processes of state governors, in which the federal government has no constitutional mandate.[103]

Thus, unlike in liberal constitutional democracies, the establishment of a unitary executive under a presidential system in Nigeria was intended to unify and concentrate executive power. As Ali Mazrui observed of much of Africa, at the core of presidential power and practice in Nigeria is the 'personalization' and 'sacralization' of authority.[104] While the justification for such 'personalization' and 'sacralization' of authority is advanced on cultural grounds, it is the colonial theory of government and the postcolonial military tradition that are the prime culprits in this regard. In summary, when we locate the Nigerian executive within the country's broader constitutional history, design, and practice, its phenomenon of imperial presidency is clearly in sharp contrast with those of the United States and France. This is primarily because, as mentioned, the executive in Nigeria is created through the syncretism of the *power-enabling* aspects of diverse legal and political traditions on the one hand, and the relegation or displacement of the *power-limiting* ones on the other.

[96] Christian Purefoy, 'Goodluck Jonathan: By Name and Nature?' (2011) <http://wwwcnncom/2010/WORLD/africa/05/06/nigeriajonathan/indexhtml> accessed 1 October 2017.

[97] Nweke (n 90) 66.

[98] Shikyil, 'Legislative-Executive Relations in Presidential Democracies' (n 83) 150–52.

[99] Paul Wallace, 'Nigeria Leader Sparks Pre-Vote Crisis by Replacing Top Judge' (25 January 2019), Bloomberg, <https://wwwbloombergcom/news/articles/2019-01-25/buhari-suspends-nigeria-s-top-judge-ahead-of-election-aide-says-jrcau3pn> accessed 28 January 2019.

[100] Nigerian Constitution s 291(1)(a)(i).

[101] ibid.

[102] See Andrew C Okolie, 'The 2007 General Elections in Nigeria: An Account of the Politics of Personal Rule in an African Country by a Former Presidential Aide' (2010) 37 The Review of Black Political Economy 2, 153–72.

[103] Mamman Lawan, 'Abuse of Powers of Impeachment in Nigeria' (2010) 48 The Journal of Modern African Studies 311, 323–27.

[104] Ali A Mazrui, 'The Monarchical Tendency in African Political Culture' (1967) 18 The British Journal of Sociology 231, 231.

III. The Executive in Ethiopia: 'Imperial Premiership'

The executive in Ethiopia, unlike in Nigeria, is a successor to an absolute monarch. For much of its history, Ethiopia was under monarchial rule where the monarch was the custodian of all government power. Under its unwritten constitution, the monarch was the sovereign and acted as it wished mainly within the intricate power relationship involving the Ethiopian Orthodox Church and the nobility.[105] With the adoption of the first written Constitution of Ethiopia in 1931, however, the monarchy emerged as a 'superpower' by subordinating both the nobility and the Church.[106] On claims of modernization, Emperor Haile Selassie established an absolute monarchy in a written constitutional framework. In this respect, by disregarding centuries-old unwritten constitutional rules, Article 4 of the 1931 Constitution limited the throne and crown of the empire exclusively to the decedents of Emperor Haile Selassie. Such constitutional arrangements excluded the right of other members of the nobility who could have had equal opportunity to access the throne if they had had what it required. In a similar vein, by displacing an old tradition of bringing in an *Abun* (a head of the Ethiopian Orthodox Church) from the Coptic Church of Alexandria as a means of maintaining the neutrality of the Church in throne politics, Haile Selassie became the final authority to approve an Ethiopian *Abun* to head the Church. Further, while the 1931 Constitution did establish a parliament, ministerial positions, and judiciary, all legislative, executive, and judicial power ultimately rested in the person of the Emperor. Hence, the modernization rationale and the adoption of a written constitution were not meant to limit the power of the government for the sake of individual liberty, but were used as opportunities to further centralize and enlarge the power of the Emperor.

The military regime, which came after the collapse of the monarchy, did not even pretend to rule the country with a constitution; Colonel Mengistu Haile Mariam, president of the military regime, ruled the country with mighty brutal force—without a constitution—for thirteen years. It is only in 1987 that the military adopted a constitution to legitimate its rule and to appease opposition forces in the country. Even in the 1987 Constitution, the military centralized ultimate government power in the National Shengo and its standing organ, the Council of State, where the president controlled all governmental functions.[107] By making the Workers' Party of Ethiopia the only political party in the country, the military regime fused this party and the government into the same political group, and, ultimately, in the same person, ie the leader of the party and the government, Colonel Mengistu Haile Mariam. Thus, the adoption of a written constitution by the military regime was yet another occasion for the centralization of power. Just like the 1931 Constitution established monarchical absolutism, the 1987 Constitution tried to replicate and consolidate absolutism within a socialist military system.[108]

[105] Fasil Nahum, *Constitution for a Nation of Nations: The Ethiopian Prospect* (Red Sea Press 1997) 17; Messay Kebede, *Survival and Modernization, Ethiopia's Enigmatic Present: A Philosophical Discourse* (Red Sea Press 1999) Chapter Two.

[106] Kebede, *Survival and Modernization* (n 105) 21.

[107] See the Constitution of Ethiopia 1987, Chapter, 9–11.

[108] Nahum, *Constitution for a Nation of Nations* (n 105) 30.

In sharp contrast to Ethiopia's tradition of centralized rule under one person—and, indeed, the prevailing practice in Africa—the Tigray People's Liberation Front (TPLF)/the Ethiopian People's Revolutionary Democratic Front (EPRDF) established a parliamentary system to effectuate a strong executive in 1995. Given Ethiopia's political tradition, a presidential system should have been the first choice of the TPLF/EPRDF; nonetheless, the move towards a parliamentary system was dictated by the desire for centralization. The power configuration within the EPRDF and the politics of ethnic federalism made a presidential system unappealing at the time. Put differently, a presidential system could not offer a strong enough executive under the leadership of the TPLF. Precisely because of this, the TPLF had to turn to a parliamentary system in order to effectively centralize and control executive power. Unlike many other African countries, Ethiopia seems to have been successful in keeping the president as head of the state with ceremonial powers and the prime minister as head of government with executive powers. Thus far, there has been neither competition nor conflict between the two office holders.

Indeed, the Constitutional Commission, which was in charge of drafting the Constitution, did not give any special preference to either a semi-presidential or a parliamentary system of government when the first draft proposal on the form of government was being discussed, as long as the design would have fit within the Ethiopian context.[109] The first draft proposal was to establish a semi-presidential system where the president would be elected from the majority party controlling parliament, and the president, in turn, would choose the prime minister, but both would have a constitutionally defined power. While there was no opposition from members of the Commission, Dawit Yohannes, the Secretary of the Commission and the presiding Chairperson of this meeting, opined and proposed that unifying the head of the state and the head of government in the president, and replacing the prime minister with a vice president, would be more appropriate for Ethiopia as it would ensure political stability.[110] The second proposal was to establish a parliamentary system where the president would have ceremonial powers as the head of state, and would be indirectly elected, while the prime minister would have executive powers and would head the government.[111] Without much contestation and debate on this matter, the Commission adopted a parliamentary system in its draft,[112] which the final Constitution maintained.

Given the tightly controlled constitution-making process,[113] the choice for a parliamentary system was made by the TPLF/EPRDF.[114] The TPLF comes from

[109] See Minutes of the Ethiopian Constitutional Commission, 78th regular session, *Megabit* 5, 1986 (in *Ethiopian Colander*).

[110] ibid.

[111] See Minutes of the Ethiopian Constitutional Commission, 82nd regular session, *Megabit* 14, 1986 (in *Ethiopian Colander*).

[112] See ibid 88th regular session, *Megabit* 29, 1986.

[113] Tsegaye Regassa, 'The Making and Legitimacy of the Ethiopian Constitution: Towards Bridging the Gap between Constitutional Design and Constitutional Practice' (2010) 23 Afrika focus 1, 85–118.

[114] See Theodore M Vestal, 'An Analysis of the New Constitution of Ethiopia and the Process of Its Adoption' (1996) 3 Northeast African Studies 2, 21–38; Semahagn Gashu Abebe, *The Last Post-Cold War Socialist Federation: Ethnicity, Ideology and Democracy in Ethiopia* (Ashgate 2014) 51–87.

a minority ethnic group consisting of around 6 per cent of the population, which makes their choice for a parliamentary system quite rational. With a minority democratic base where ethnic federalism is the primary means and ultimate end of channeling and advancing the right to self-determination of each ethnic group, the installation of a presidential system would have been a suicidal constitutional act for the TPLF. Under ethnic federalism, which the ethnonational forces established, it is reasonable to expect that many ethnic groups would want to see persons from their own group run for the presidency and control presidential power. In this respect, persons from the major ethnic groups, such as the Amhara and the Oromo, would always have an electoral advantage in winning the office of the presidency as they account for more than 60% of the population. It is no wonder, then, that the Oromo Federalist Democratic Movement (OFDM), an opposition party, supports constitutional reform in favor of a presidential system[115] (even though as it is all of the presidents of Ethiopia since 1995 have been from Oromo ethnic group).[116] Hence, the adoption of a parliamentary system to operate Ethiopia's ethnic federalism was a conscious choice by the TPLF, as it is the type of government best suited to broadcast and channel their interests in the country.

After the choice for a parliamentary system was made, the Constitution almost crowned the prime minister by granting him a wide range of powers. Like the president in Nigeria, the prime minister in Ethiopia is the chief executive, chairperson of the Council of Ministers, and Commander-in-Chief of the national armed forces.[117] The prime minister selects and appoints ministers, commissioners, federal officers, and presidents and vice presidents of the Federal Supreme Court,[118] the auditor general,[119] the National Election Board,[120] and the Population Census Commission[121] with the approval of the House of Peoples Representatives (HPR). Like the vice president in Nigeria, the vice prime minister in Ethiopia does not have any constitutionally defined powers, but carries out such responsibilities as entrusted by the prime minister and is, in turn, responsible to him.[122] The prime minister not only oversees the implementation of the Constitution and all the laws, policies, and directives adopted by the HPR,[123] but can also declare a state of emergency with the support of the Council of Ministers which the prime minister also composes and heads.[124] In performing this wide range of powers, the Constitution does not consider that the prime minister could make errors or be impeached; nor does it limit the term limits of the prime minister. While it can be argued that in a parliamentary system, the prime minister's stay in office depends upon the confidence of parliament and their party, the

[115] Abebe, *The Last Post-Cold War Socialist Federation* (n 114) 80.

[116] Dr Negasso Gidada from 1995–2001, Ato Girma Wolde-Giorgis from 2001–2013, and Dr Mulatu Tesheme from 2013–2018. Sahle-Work Zewde who is appointed as President of Ethiopia in October 2018 is a non-Oromo.

[117] The Constitution of the Federal Democratic Republic of Ethiopia, art 74(1).

[118] ibid art 74(2) and (7).

[119] ibid art 101(1).

[120] ibid art 102(2).

[121] ibid art 103(2).

[122] ibid art 75.

[123] ibid art 74(3), (4), (5), (6) and (8).

[124] ibid art 93.

failure to provide term limits and grounds of impeachment in the Constitution, in a country that is rich with the tradition of one-man rule, is ill-advised, at best, and institutionalizing personal rule, at worst.[125]

The design of prime ministerial power and its practice are not very different from the prevailing practice of presidentialism in other African countries, including Nigeria. While presidentialism has led to the emergence of imperial presidency in many African countries, the Ethiopian experiment of parliamentarianism has produced imperial premiership; the parliamentary experiment since 1995 has confirmed the prevailing phenomena of imperial presidency in Africa in the form of imperial premiership in Ethiopia. As elsewhere in Africa, for instance Nkrumah of Ghana or Obasanjo of Nigeria, Meles Zenawi, the transitional-period president of Ethiopia from 1991–1994 and prime minister from 1995–2012, started his imperial premiership by establishing and consolidating his power within his party, the TPLF, and his coalition party, the EPRDF, and these ultimately conferred upon him 'imperial power' in Ethiopia until his death in 2012.

In fact, Zenawi started consolidating his power within the TPLF by establishing the Marxist-Leninist League of Tigray (MLLT) in 1985 with the alleged objective of guiding the TPLF in the right direction by being the party's intellectual and political hub.[126] Not only did Zenawi assumed the leadership position within the MLLT, but he also managed to exclude some of the prominent members of the TPLF.[127] He continued to consolidate his power within the TPLF after becoming the prime minister of Ethiopia in 1995. When he faced strong opposition from his party; in 2001, he managed to dismiss his comrades and high-ranking ministers—both from their party as well as their government posts.[128] After 2001, Zenawi was the chief socio-economic and political architect of the EPRDF and of Ethiopia.[129] Zenawi, the person, became the institutional embodiment of the federal system. Not only did the federal legislature[130] and judiciary[131] follow his directions, state presidents and institutions were also subservient to Zenawi.[132] Due to the immense power and influence he accumulated in the party and state apparatus, it was customary for individuals and groups alike to petition and appeal their grievances directly to him, bypassing other institutions such as

125 See also Gedion Timothewos, 'Tackling the Imperial Premiership and Abuse of Incumbency: Ideas for Constitutional Reform in Ethiopia' in Gedion Timothewos and Helen Fikre (eds), *The FDRE Constitution: Some Perspectives on the Institutional Dimension* (Addis Ababa University Press 2014).

126 Aregawi Berhe, *A Political History of the Tigray People's Liberation Front (1975-1991): Revolt, Ideology and Mobilisation in Ethiopia* (Tsehai Publishers 2009) 209.

127 ibid.

128 Medhane Tadesse, 'The Tigray People's Liberation Front (TPLF)' in Gérard Prunier and Éloi Ficquet (eds), *Understanding Contemporary Ethiopia: Monarchy, Revolution and the Legacy of Meles Zenawi* (Hurst & Company 2015) 279–80.

129 Gérard Prunier, 'The Meles Zenawi Era: From Revolutionary Marxism to State Developemntalism' in Gérard Prunier and Éloi Ficquet (eds), *Understanding Contemporary Ethiopia: Monarchy, Revolution and the Legacy of Meles Zenawi* (Hurst & Company 2015) 426.

130 Kassahun Berhanu, 'Parliament and Dominant Party System in Ethiopia' in MA Mohamed Salih (ed), *African Parliaments: Between Governance and Government* (Palgrave Macmillan 2005) 162–81.

131 See Assefa Fiseha, 'Separation of Powers and Its Implications for the Judiciary in Ethiopia' (2011) 5 Journal of Eastern African Studies 4, 702–15; Siye Abraha, *Nestanet ena dagninet be Ethiopia* (ZA Printing 2002) (in Amharic).

132 See also Prunier, 'The Meles Zenawi Era' (n 129) 415–36.

the courts and other administrative organs.[133] A combination of wide constitutional powers and party domination enabled Zenawi to be the first Ethiopian imperial Prime Minister unconstrained by the federal arrangement.

However, prime minister Hailemariam Desalegn, the successor of Zenawi, was not able to maintain the imperial premiership and his tenure was ended abruptly. Deselagn, handpicked by Zenawi, even struggled to be a prime minister at all, let alone an imperial one. As even admitted by the EPRDF, Desalegn was a puppet without executive power. This was not because the powers of the prime minister under the Constitution or the power of a party leader in the EPRDF had changed, but simply because Desalegn lacked the extra-constitutional and extra-party influence that Zenawi possessed; Desalegn belonged to the Southern Ethiopia People's Democratic Movement (SEPDM), which is a marginal party in the EPRDF power architecture, and comes from the south which lacks influence in the political dynamics of the country.[134] As a result, Desalegn acted as the TPLF/EPRDF wanted him to act, and as he was not able to control the EPRDF, the coalition began to have multiple sites of power. This led to the development of assertive state presidents—particularly in the regional states of Amhara, Oromia, Tigray, and Somali—who started to influence politics at the federal level, which would have been unthinkable under Zenawi. Finally, the waves of protest movements that had shaken the EPRDF from 2015 onward abruptly ended Deselagn's tenure in April 2018.

Even though it is too early to tell what kind of Prime Minister Abiy Ahmed—who assumed office in April 2018—will become, all the factors that can make him imperial are in his hands. In contrast to Zenawi, who was an ardent ethnonationalist, Ahmed emerged as a pan-Ethiopianist, or even Pan-Africanist. His idea of *medemer*—synergy or unity—appeals to many people regardless of ethnic, religious or other differences. Like *Ujamma* of Julius Nyerere or *Harambee* of Jomo Kenyatta, Ahmed's *medemer* posits the necessity of unity, synergy, and cohesion among Ethiopians, and even sheds light on the necessity of co-operation and integration of the wider Horn of African region. In addition to his unifying ideology, Ahmed's ethnic affiliation with the Oromo, one of the largest ethnic groups in Ethiopia, gives him a strong democratic base, which was not the case for Zenawi and Desalegn. And unlike Desalegn, since his ascent to power, Ahmed seems to be in charge of both the EPRDF and the executive arm of government. Moreover, he seems to be hyperactive in 'transforming and democratizing Ethiopia' by reforming the judiciary and parliamentary rules and practices. Most importantly, he transformed the EPRDF into the Prosperity Party and replaced revolutionary democracy with *meder* as the guiding ideology, or philosophy, of his party, the government, and, by extension, the entire Ethiopian state. While these are much-needed and welcome reforms, how his premiership unfolds will reveal his democratic or imperial impulses.

Hence, although Ethiopia chose parliamentarism over presidentialism, unlike Nigeria, the underlying rationale for their choice was the same. The establishment of a strong executive was the main justification for the rejection of presidentialism and the absorption

[133] Timothewos, 'Tackling the Imperial Premiership and Abuse of Incumbency' (n 125).

[134] BBC News, 'Ethiopia Profile Leaders—Prime Minister: Hailemariam Desalegn' *BBC News* (30 July 2015) <http://wwwbbccom/news/world-africa-13349400> accessed 23 November 2017.

of parliamentarism. As discussed above, a strong executive under a directly elected president was untenable for the Ethiopian constitutional authors for the simple reason that the TPLF does not have a democratic base to support this system. As a result, rather than unifying the head of state and the head of government into one, it was believed that bifurcating the same would ensure a strong executive. By controlling the party and state apparatus, it is possible for the TPLF to maintain the premiership either within its own members or within the coalition.[135] On the other hand, a direct presidential election, in addition to bringing multiple competitors to the presidency,[136] would further make the presidential outcome costly even if the TPLF/EPRDF nominee could win. Thus, the adoption of parliamentarism with strong premiership powers does the same job as presidentialism.

The Ethiopian parliamentary experiment shows how legal syncretism informs its design and, perhaps even more so, shapes its practice. In contrast to liberal constitutional theory, the adoption of a written constitution was aimed at centralizing and enlarging the executive power rather than limiting it for the sake of individual liberty. Even if there are striking differences in the constitutional and political theories that brought about Ethiopia's monarchial, military, and federal constitutions, they essentially share the similar ambition of centralizing executive power. When we pierce the veil of executive power in the modern Ethiopian constitutions, we find an imperial executive both in the military and civilian regimes, just like in the monarchy. In this respect, all of the modern constitutions have been used as a centralizing, rather than a limiting, device for the executive. And like in Nigeria, the introduction of written constitutions in Ethiopia has been used as a means of enabling, rather than limiting, the executive.

IV. The Executive in South Africa: 'Constrained Presidency'

South Africa, unlike Nigeria and Ethiopia, has had an experience of parliamentary democracy for the white minority since its establishment.[137] Deviating from the British tradition, South Africa provided the powers and functions of government in a written constitution. From the Union of South Africa to the Republic of South Africa, limited government was instituted for the benefit of the white minority.[138] The powers and functions of the executive were expressly stated in the constitution and democratic elections were the only means to assume government power. With respect to the white minority, the executive had limited power and could not act as it wished;[139] it had to follow constitutional rules and conventions in its operation and engagement with the white minority. As such, unlike in Nigeria and Ethiopia, the introduction of

[135] See also Abebe, *The Last Post-Cold War Socialist Federation* (n 114).

[136] As a matter of fact, the Prime Minister is simply elected with nominal competitor who has to resign from the outset.

[137] Lauren Segal and Sharon Cort, *One Law, One Nation: The Making of the South African Constitution* (Jacana Media 2011) 14–21.

[138] Leonard Thompson and Andrew Prior, *South African Politics* (Yale University Press 1982) 71–83.

[139] LM Thompson, 'Constitutionalism in the South African Republics' (1954) 1954 Butterworths South African Law Review 49, 49–72.

a written constitution in South Africa was not to centralize and enlarge the executive power of government in opposition to political liberty for all. Instead, it aimed to establish a democratic republic for the white minority and this, in turn, required a limited government.

As noted in Chapter 4, the struggle of the black majority was to extend the range of this limited government to all who live in South Africa. The quest for democracy, human rights, and equal citizenship were at the root of the nine-decade struggle by those disfranchised by white-minority rule.[140] Put differently, the idea of constitutionalism, ie, limited government, individual rights, and the rule of law, was at the heart of the South African struggle against racial segregation and apartheid.[141] As a result, the plan of the ANC during the constitutional negotiations was the establishment of a democratic South Africa that respected the equal rights of everyone, regardless of race or other status.[142] Accordingly, unlike in Nigeria and Ethiopia, the adoption of the new Constitution in South Africa in 1996 was not considered as an occasion to further centralize and enlarge the power of the executive; rather, all of the actors in the constitution-making process agreed upon the establishment of a limited executive. Moreover, instead of *limiting the limitations* to executive power, the Constitution introduced novel institutional mechanisms to ensure and safeguard the practice of limited government. The acceptance of the idea of limited government by the South African constitutional actors, mainly by the ANC, brought a limited or constrained executive.

Due to this acceptance of limited government, the rationale and substance of executive power in South Africa are both different from those in Nigeria and Ethiopia. As noted above, this has to do with the constitution-making processes and the nature of the constitutional actors.[143] Unlike in Nigeria and Ethiopia, the constitution-making process in South Africa was inclusive of all of the competing interests and the final Constitution is the result of a negotiated settlement. At the beginning of the negotiation, the ANC proposed a French-style presidency—strong enough to execute the transformative ambitions of post-apartheid South Africa, yet limited enough not to trump minority rights and interests.[144] The NP, for its part, proposed a collective presidency where each member would hold veto power in order to ensure government by consensus.[145] As a matter of fact, in order to advance and protect their own interests, the ANC had to defend the liberal notion of majority rule, while the NP had to defend the African notion of decision by consensus. The common ground for both

[140] Hassen Ebrahim, *The Soul of a Nation: Constitution-Making in South Africa* (Oxford University Press 1998) 31–32 and 429–36.

[141] Stu Woolman, *The Selfless Constitution: Experimentalism and Flourishing as Foundations of South Africa's Basic Law* (Juta 2013) 505–08.

[142] See David Chidester, Cassius Lubisi, and Kader Asmal, *Legacy of Freedom: The ANC's Human Rights Tradition* (Jonathan Ball Publishers 2005).

[143] See Steven Friedman and Doreen Atkinson, *The Small Miracle: South Africa's Negotiated Settlement* (Ravan Press 1994).

[144] Roger Southall, 'The South African Presidency in Comparative African Context' in Catherine Jenkins and Max du Plessis (eds), *Law, Nation-Building & Transformation: The South African Experience in Perspective* (Intersentia 2014) 263.

[145] ibid 262.

sides was to structure a limited executive where majority rule would prevail while minority rights would still be respected. In addition to co-operative government, a Bill of Rights, and judicial review, the proper organization of the executive were deemed necessary in order to channel all these interests in a proper equilibrium. Hence, unlike Nigeria, which sees strong executive power in presidentialism, or Ethiopia, which adopted parliamentarism in order to establish a strong executive, South Africa, engineered a unique type of limited executive government.

In fact, the executive of post-apartheid South Africa shares some common features with the executive of the 1983 Constitution in form, but differs in substance. The 1983 Constitution unified the head of state and the head of government in one person without altering the parliamentary system. When the Tricameral Parliament was inaugurated to include Indian and Colored communities, the centralization and consolidation of executive power were deemed important to maintaining white supremacy.[146] By unifying the bifurcation of power into one State President, South Africa departed from its Westminster parliamentary tradition. The State President of the 1983 Constitution assumed extensive powers in both the legislative and executive fields.[147] For instance, during PW Botha's presidency, the state was militarized, other institutions were subordinated to the executive, and some form of imperial presidency was in reign.[148] The unification of the head of state and the head of government into a State President in the 1983 Constitution, was motivated by the quest to centralize and consolidate executive power in order to suppress government opposition and dissent—just like in Nigeria, or in Ethiopia's choice for parliamentarism.[149] The post-apartheid Constitution, like the 1983 Constitution, also eliminated the office of the prime minister and made the president both the head of state and the head of the executive.

Nonetheless, the substance of executive power and its form of organization under the new Constitution was different from the 1983 Constitution. As a result of a negotiated settlement,[150] it is fair to assume that the prime purpose of unifying the head of state and the head of government in the president was not to centralize and consolidate executive power.[151] Further, as stated in Constitutional Principle VI, within the broader ambit of separation of powers, the structuring of the executive is meant to ensure government 'accountability, responsiveness and openness'.[152] In the South African quest for a democratic transition, the executive power is structured differently from both an American—or French-style presidency as well as a Westminster parliamentary system.[153] Further, the South African Constitution, by going beyond the

146 I Currie and J De Waal (eds), *The New Constitutional and Administrative Law: Constitutional Law Vol 1* (5th edn, Juta Legal and Academic Publishers 2005) 56.

147 ibid.

148 Southall, 'The South African Presidency in Comparative African Context' (n 144) 262.

149 See D Basson and H Viljoen (eds), *South African Constitutional Law* (Juta Legal and Academic Publishers 1988) 46–61.

150 See Patti Waldmeir, *Anatomy of a Miracle: The End of Apartheid and the Birth of the New South Africa* (Rutgers University Press 1998).

151 See also Albert Venter, 'The Executive: A Critical Evaluation' in Bertus De Villiers (ed), *Birth of a Constitution* (1st edn, Juta Legal and Academic Publishers 1994) 172–88.

152 Annex to the Interim Constitution of South Africa 1993.

153 Christina Murray and Richard Stacey, 'The President and the National Executive' in Stu Woolman and Michael Bishop (eds), *Constitutional Law of South Africa Vol 1* (Juta & Company Ltd 2013) 18-2-18-3; DA Basson, *South Africa's Interim Constitution: Text and Notes* (Juta & Co 1994) 112–13.

traditional notions of separation of powers among the three branches of government, introduces a new institutional architecture so as to disperse the executive power itself and insulate some decisions from ordinary politics.[154] The objective of this new institutional architecture was to protect human rights and advance good governance in post-apartheid South Africa.[155]

In terms of substantive structure, the South African executive is shaped by the hybridization of presidential and parliamentary systems.[156] Like in Nigeria, the president in South Africa is both the head of state and government but is elected by the National Assembly from amongst its members and is dependent on the support of parliament for their office.[157] Additionally, unlike in Nigeria, with the exception of two Cabinet ministers, the president in South Africa appoints his Cabinet ministers from the members of the National Assembly.[158] Since the president is elected from amongst the members of the National Assembly, they have to vacate their seat, unlike in Ethiopia. Most importantly, the president has a differentiated authority or power when acting as the head of state as opposed to the head of government. As head of the state, the president's responsibilities include—among others—assenting to and signing bills, referring bills back to the National Assembly for reconsideration or to the Constitutional Court for confirmation of constitutionality, as well as appointing ambassadors and diplomatic representatives.[159] In exercising these head of state powers as stated in Section 84(2), the president is autonomous and acts alone, as it is considered that other institutions make these decisions and the president's decision is merely one of formalization.[160] However, it does not mean that the president cannot consult his advisors or Cabinet members in exercising these powers, nor does it mean that the head of state and head of government powers are clearly separated;[161] it means that the president is the final decision-maker and is more autonomous when acting on behalf of the state.

As the head of the executive, the President has the power of:[162]

(a) *implementing national legislation except where the Constitution or an Act of Parliament provides otherwise;*
(b) *developing and implementing national policy;*
(c) *co-ordinating the functions of state departments and administrations;*
(d) *preparing and initiating legislation; and*
(e) *performing any other executive function provided for in the Constitution or in national legislation.*

[154] Heinz Klug, *The Constitution of South Africa: A Contextual Analysis* (Hart 2010) 188.

[155] ibid.

[156] Romano Orru, 'South African 'Quasi-Parliementariansim' in Hugh Corder and Veronica Federico, *The Quest for Constitutionalism: South Africa since 1994* (Routledge 2014) 28.

[157] The Constitution of South Africa, ss 83(a), 86(1), and 102(2). See also Danie Brand and others, *South African Constitutional Law in Context* (Pierre De Vos and Warren Freedman eds, Oxford University Press 2015) 173–76.

[158] ibid s 91(3).

[159] ibid s 84(2).

[160] Murray and Stacey, 'The President and the National Executive' (n 153) 18-5.

[161] See Brand and others, *South African Constitutional Law in Context* (n 157) 177; Murray and Stacey, 'The President and the National Executive' (n 153) 18-6.

[162] The Constitution of South Africa, s 85(2).

In performing these executive functions, the president has to act with their cabinet which includes the deputy president and ministers.[163] Although the Constitution vests executive power in the president, its exercise is the joint domain of the cabinet.[164] In order to ensure joint executive action, the Constitution requires a decision made by the president to be written and 'countersigned by another cabinet member if that decision concerns a function assigned to that cabinet member'.[165] While presidents appoint their deputies and ministers by themselves,[166] they appoint judges with the consultation of the Judicial Service Commission and/or the leaders of parties represented in the National Assembly;[167] independent constitutional institutions such as the Public Protector, the Auditor General; and members of the South African Human Rights Commission, the Commission for Gender Equality, and the Electoral Commission—all with the recommendation of the National Assembly.[168] And presidents also appoint the members of the Financial and Fiscal Commission.[169] Although presidents can dismiss their deputies or ministers,[170] they have no power of removing judges or appointed persons of the independent constitutional institutions.[171]

Moreover, unlike in Nigeria and Ethiopia, South African presidents and their cabinets have no power of declaration of state emergency; this power rests within the domain of parliament.[172] Although the South African president has the power to declare national defense emergencies as the Commander-in-Chief of the army, this declaration will lapse after seven days if not approved by parliament.[173] The emergency power of the president is considered a key power in many African countries, including Nigeria and Ethiopia, for maintaining incumbency.

Furthermore, unlike in Nigeria and Ethiopia, the establishment of institutions that support constitutional democracy, such as the Public Protector, the South African Human Rights Commission, the Commission for the Promotion and Protection of the Rights of Cultural, Religious and Linguistic Minorities, the Commission for Gender Equality, the Auditor General, and the Electoral Commission all insulate some decisions from the discretions of the executive.[174] These institutions enjoy constitutionally guaranteed independence in advancing constitutional democracy by executing tasks specifically assigned by the Constitution and legislation.[175] Through their oversight, supervision, and enforcement of their specific tasks, these constitutional institutions keep the executive within its constitutional limit.[176] In addition, legislative oversight

[163] ibid ss 85(2) and 91(1).
[164] ibid s 85(1).
[165] ibid s 101(2).
[166] ibid s 91(2).
[167] ibid s 174(3), (4), and (6).
[168] ibid s 194(4).
[169] ibid s 221(1).
[170] See also Brand and others, *South African Constitutional Law in Context* (n 157) 194–95; Stating that the president has to consult the leadership of the majority party to remove the deputy or one of his ministers.
[171] The Constitution of South Africa, ss 91(2), 177, and 194.
[172] ibid s 37.
[173] ibid ss 202 and 203.
[174] ibid s 181.
[175] For the mandates of these institutions and organizational structure, see South African Constitution Chapter 9.
[176] See Fombad, 'Constitutional Reforms and Constitutionalism in Africa' (n 16) 1019.

and judicial review of the exercise of presidential power in South Africa has successfully limited and constrained the power of the presidency, unlike in Nigeria and Ethiopia.[177]

Thus, in contrast with Nigeria and Ethiopia, the post-apartheid practice of presidential power in South Africa is one of constraint rather than imperial. This is not only related to substantive executive power but also to the resources available to the presidency. Nelson Mandela, South Africa's first democratically elected president, not only had fewer administrative resources than his predecessor FW de Klerk, but he had to share his office with his two deputies, Klerk and Thabo Mbeki, and had to consult with them on all issues.[178] Although the administrative and financial resources of the office of the presidency expanded through time, presidential power has remained within the contours of the Constitution.[179] Mandela, in sharp contrast with Obasanjo, Zenawi, and other postcolonial African leaders, not only stepped down from his presidency after one term, but also submitted to the decision of the judiciary when it invalidated his executive actions—and he even acted as a court witness.[180]

Although Mbeki enlarged the capacity of the presidency more than Mandela, he did not control the state and party apparatus, unlike Obasanjo and Zenawi.[181] When he lost the internal party election, he resigned from his presidency before the expiry of his second term although he could have challenged it in the National Assembly following Constitutional procedures.[182] Following his predecessor Mbeki, Jacob Zuma also resigned before the end of his second term, since the ANC wanted him to step down.[183] Although corruption was alleged to be rampant in the Zuma presidency, almost every legislation and executive action of the government was challenged in the Constitutional Court—another indicator of the practice of checks and balances.[184] So far, the presidents in South Africa have not personally controlled their political party nor the state. Unlike Obasanjo of Nigeria, South African presidents have respected the constitutional rule of terms limits and they did not reign over their political parties; they have been constrained by both political party and constitutional rules. Beyond respecting term limits, they have also been constrained by, and operated within, the strictures of executive government as provided in the Constitution.[185]

[177] See Ziyad Motala and Cyril Ramaphosa, *Constitutional Law: Analysis and Cases* (Oxford University Press 2002) (n 916) 177–91; Brand and others, *South African Constitutional Law in Context* (n 157) 174–96; Murray and Stacey, 'The President and the National Executive' (n 153) 18-12 and 18-22.

[178] Klug, *The Constitution of South Africa* (n 154) 201.

[179] Brand and others, *South African Constitutional Law in Context* (n 157) 180–81.

[180] Klug, *The Constitution of South Africa* (n 154) 192; Diana Kapiszewski, Gordon Silverstein, and Robert A Kagan, 'Introduction' in Diana Kapiszewski, Gordon Silverstein and Robert A Kagan *Consequential Courts: Judicial Roles in Global Perspective* (Cambridge University Press 2013) 26–27; Nelson Mandela and Mandla Langa, *Dare Not Linger: The Presidential Years* (Pan Macmillan 2017).

[181] See also Shane Mac Giollabhuí, 'The Fall of an African President: How and Why Did the ANC Unseat Thabo Mbeki?' (2017) 116 African Affairs 464, 395–404; Sean Jacobs and Richard Calland, *Thabo Mbeki's World: The Politics and Ideology of the South African President* (University of Natal 2002).

[182] Klug, *The Constitution of South Africa* (n 154) 192.

[183] See Richard Calland, *The Zuma Years: South Africa's Changing Face of Power* (Random House Struik 2014); 'South Africa's President Zuma Resigns' *BBC News* (14 February 2018) <http://www.bbc.com/news/world-africa-43066443> accessed 14 February 2018.

[184] Heinz Klug, 'Challenging Constitutionalism in Post-Apartheid South Africa' (2016) 1 Constitutional Studies 41, 50.

[185] Southall (n 144) 263–72; Motala and Ramaphosa (n 916) 179–200; Brand and others, *South African Constitutional Law in Context* (n 157) 182–94.

The chief explanation for this constrained presidency is to be found in the syncretism of the idea of limited government amongst the main constitutional actors, particularly the ANC as the main actor during the transition and post-apartheid South Africa.[186] The creation of a limited executive was not only a necessary condition for the transition from apartheid, but it was also essential in transforming South Africa into a non-racial state that would be hospitable to all people living in it. Unlike in Nigeria and Ethiopia, the *power-limiting* aspects of indigenous and liberal constitutional ideas were deployed in South Africa. Although the ANC had majority support, it agreed to form a Government of National Unity in the interim Constitution in order to ensure inclusivity, co-operation, and consensus among a wide range of political parties. While this was, in fact, part of a deal in a two-step constitution-making process, consensus in decision-making—which has animated traditional African notions of power—was at the service of South Africa's transition from apartheid to democracy. As discussed above, the creation of executive power in a personally and institutionally dispersed and diffused way attests to the syncretism of the more *power-limiting* aspects of both liberal and indigenous notions of power in South Africa.

V. Conclusion

Legal syncretism animates both the power and structure of the executive in Nigeria, Ethiopia, and South Africa—albeit differently in each country. While presidentialism in Nigeria and parliamentarism in Ethiopia are adopted with the objective of centralizing and consolidating power in the person of the executive, South Africa's unique regime is motivated by placing effective constraints on the power of the executive. Nigeria and Ethiopia have consciously configured the *power-enabling* aspects of presidential and parliamentary systems as well as traditional notions of political power, and the result is the establishment of a strong executive with imperial tendencies that trumps other constitutional organs. Nonetheless, the nature, rationale, scope, and manifestations of imperial presidency and premiership in Nigeria and Ethiopia, respectively, are different from the American or French imperial presidency, since the former two rest in the conscious act of absorption and rejection of liberal and indigenous constitutional ideas. South Africa, in contrast, constructed its executive mainly from the *power-limiting* aspects of both the liberal and indigenous notions of political power. Consequently, its executive is more limited, or constrained, and operates within the strictures provided by the Constitution. Because of this syncretic logic, presidential power in South Africa is also different from the United States and France. Thus, despite the differences in the powers of the executive in Nigeria, Ethiopia, and South Africa, legal syncretism captures and explains the nature, organization, and practice of executive power in all three of them. The experiences of these countries show the contingent role of legal syncretism for constitutionalism in Africa.

[186] See also Chidester, Lubisi, and Asmal (n 142); Jens Meierhenrich, *The Legacies of Law: Long-Run Consequences of Legal Development in South Africa, 1652–2000* (Cambridge University Press 2008).

6
Women's Constitutional Rights

The previous chapters demonstrated how legal syncretism features in the vertical and horizontal divisions of power with a focus on federalism and the executive. Following a similar path, this chapter explains how legal syncretism influences and manifests itself in the designs and practices of the Bill of Rights—with a particular focus on women's rights—in the constitutional systems of Nigeria, South Africa, and Ethiopia. By taking women's rights as one aspect of the Bill of Rights, this chapter aims to demonstrate how the interaction between the liberal notion of rights and the indigenous conception of rights in a constitutional space produce unique regimes of women's rights in these countries.

Women's rights are one of the main intersection points in the universalism versus cultural relativism debate regarding human rights. On the one hand, universalists claim that culture poses a serious challenge to the enjoyment of women's rights as such cultures are produced by, and operated in, patriarchal systems. Hence, to protect and ensure the rights and interests of women, human rights should have primacy over cultural systems.[1] On the other hand, cultural relativists contend that human rights are only part of the overall cultural experience of any particular society and, consequently, culture should inform the substantive content and enforcement of human rights;[2] and as a result, the theory and practice of human rights should not be judged simply by the cultural understanding of the Western societies that brought about the so-called 'universal human rights'.[3]

However, the universal account of human rights is not without problems for women, and the cultural relativist view is not without its advantages. Many feminist scholars reveal how the human rights discourse and structure often place women in a disadvantaged position.[4] In a similar vein, some scholars also demonstrate how cultural systems often protect the rights and interests of women[5] and how women are changing their cultures from *within* these cultures in order to create more egalitarian value systems.[6] Therefore, despite the universalism versus cultural relativism debate,

[1] Susan Moller Okin, 'Is Multiculturalism Bad for Women?' in Joshua Cohen, Mattew Howard and Martha C Nussbaum (eds), *Is Multiculturalism Bad for Women?: Susan Moller Okin with Respondents* (Princeton University Press 1999) 22–24.

[2] Makau Mutua, *Human Rights: A Political and Cultural Critique* (University of Pennsylvania Press 2009) 74–81.

[3] Abdullahi Ahmed An-Na'im, 'Toward a Cross-Cultural Approach to Defining International Standards of Human Rights: The Meaning of Cruel, Inhuman, or Degrading Treatment or Punishment' in Abdullahi Ahmed An-Na'im (ed), *Human Rights in Cross-Cultural Perspectives: A Quest for Consensus* (University of Pennsylvania Press 1999) 25–29 .

[4] See Gayle Binion, 'Human Rights: A Feminist Perspective' (1995) 17 Human Rights Quarterly 509, 509–26.

[5] Anne Helium, 'Human Rights and Gender Relations in Postcolonial Africa: Options and Limits for the Subjects of Legal Pluralism' (2000) 25 Law & Social Inquiry 635, 635–55.

[6] Madhavi Sunder, 'Piercing the Veil' (2002) 112 Yale LJ 1399, 1402–04.

A Theory of African Constitutionalism. Berihun Adugna Gebeye, Oxford University Press.
DOI: 10.1093/oso/9780192893925.003.0007

culture influences the structure, perception, adjudication, and enforcement of human rights, and human rights, in turn, influence and shape the development of culture.[7] Furthermore, as Sally Engle Merry observes, the cultural translation of human rights localizes the so-called universal human rights, which concomitantly transforms both culture and universal human rights.[8]

In the African context, the idea of women's rights broadcasts and channels its universality both in the sense that women are entitled to the same rights available to men on the basis of equality as well as their claim to those specific rights available to women internationally as the special circumstances of women warrant it. At the same time, as these women's rights are exercised within a cultural and religious setting, their universality is set in motion along with cultural relativism. In this regard, constitutions are spaces within which the universality and cultural relativity of women's rights are fused. This constitutional design offers women unique opportunities to claim their rights and advance their interests within their cultural universes, while also carrying over old problems that challenge these very rights. Further, in such constitutional designs and practices, women's rights are neither a Western export nor an indigenous product: they are the results of legal syncretism, ie, a conscious constitutional craft which aims to channel the seemingly opposite and diverse notions of rights within a constitutional plane.

In order to show how women's rights in these countries are the results of legal syncretism, this chapter first presents a brief theory of women's rights as a standard of comparison and evaluation; this is done through a more general investigation of women's rights in international law. This is then followed by a discussion of women's constitutional rights in Nigeria, South Africa, and Ethiopia. Such discussion explores the substantive content and the way in which women's rights are constitutionalized, along with their practical and judicial applications. The syncretic nature of women's rights in these countries sheds some light on the importance of looking beyond the universalism versus cultural relativism debate when trying to enforce human rights.

I. Women's Rights as Human Rights

It is conventional wisdom that human rights are the rights one has by the simple fact of being a human. However, it is neither self-evident that human rights were available to women, nor that women could enjoy human rights on the basis of equality with men.[9] Both the French Declaration on the Rights of Man and Citizen and the American Declaration of Independence, the precursors to international human rights law, did not extend what they declared as self-evident truths about rights to women.[10] The

[7] Federico Lenzerini, *The Culturalization of Human Rights Law* (Oxford University Press 2014) 213–17.

[8] See Sally Engle Merry, *Human Rights and Gender Violence: Translating International Law to Local Justice* (The University of Chicago Press 2006).

[9] Catharine A MacKinnon, *Are Women Human?: And Other International Dialogues* (Harvard University Press 2006) 1–7.

[10] Eileen Hunt Botting, *Wollstonecraft, Mill, and Women's Human Rights* (Yale University Press 2016) 6; Sally McMillen, *Seneca Falls and the Origins of the Women's Rights Movement* (Oxford University Press 2009).

extension of human rights to women in the Universal Declaration of Human Rights (UDHR) and all of the subsequent conventions are the results of women's struggle for equality and the subsequent recognition of women as an equal part of humanity in liberal thought.[11] Although international human rights law now plays a significant role in protecting and advancing the rights and interests of women, the deeply embedded socio-economic, cultural, and political barriers that still exist continue to set a huge obstacle for women to enjoy their rights on an equal basis with men.

Against this backdrop, this section briefly introduces the concept of women's rights in general as a frame of reference with which to evaluate and examine women's rights in South Africa, Nigeria, and Ethiopia. Fundamental to the discussion of women's rights are women's rights to equality and non-discrimination in the enjoyment of all the human rights available to men, the protection of women from structural power imbalances and violence, enabling women to enjoy their rights in a meaningful and substantive way, and understanding and incorporating women's world view in the theory and practice of human rights. This section discusses these issues in light of international human rights law in general, with some added feminist and African insights. As there are clear international and regional standards with regard to women's rights—unlike with regard to federalism or imperial presidency—a discussion of women's rights in specifically non-African jurisdictions are not necessary here. Moreover, as the UDHR inspired the constitutional rights that we find in Africa, including our case studies here, it is appropriate to evaluate the question of women's constitutional rights using international standards.[12]

The International Bill of Human Rights recognizes the equal rights of women and men and unequivocally prohibits discrimination on the grounds of sex. The pioneer in this regard is the UDHR which declares that '[a]ll human beings are born free and equal in dignity and rights'.[13] It continues, '[e]veryone is entitled to all the rights and freedoms set forth in this Declaration, without distinction of any kind, such as […] sex'.[14] Even though the UDHR does not completely avoid sexist terms and understandings,[15] it does introduce gender-neutral terms such as 'everyone, no one, all, and human beings' in its framing of the subject of human rights. By doing so, the UDHR makes both women and men subjects of the civil, political, economic, and social rights it recognizes. Further, by taking the traditional position and role of women into account, it recognizes the equality of women and men in marriage[16] and provides for special care and assistance in motherhood.[17]

Building on the UDHR, the International Covenant on Civil and Political Rights (ICCPR) reaffirms the equality of women and men in the enjoyment of civil and political rights[18] and prohibits discrimination on the grounds of sex.[19] In a similar

[11] Johannes Morsink, 'Women's Rights in the Universal Declaration' (1991) 13 Human Rights Quarterly 229, 231–32.

[12] See Hurst Hannum, 'The Status of the Universal Declaration of Human Rights in National and International Law' (1995) 25 Ga J Int'l & Comp L 287, 289–312.

[13] The Universal Declaration of Human Rights 1948, art 1.

[14] ibid art 2.

[15] See ibid art 13(2) and 25(1).

[16] ibid art 16(1).

[17] ibid art 25(2).

[18] The International Covenant on Civil and Political Rights 1966, arts 23(2) and 26.

[19] ibid art 2(1).

vein, the International Covenant on Economic, Social and Cultural Rights (ICESCR) recognizes the equal rights of women and men in the enjoyment of economic, social, and cultural rights[20] and prohibits any discrimination based on sex.[21] These international human rights instruments legally guarantee the equality of women and men in the enjoyment of, and access to, human rights.

Although the recognition of women's rights in these instruments has played a significant practical and symbolic role in the improvement of women's lives, these instruments have not fully put women on equal footing with men in the enjoyment of human rights, nor have they completely eliminated discrimination based on sex. This generally has to do with the lack of participation of women in the making and monitoring of human rights, the way in which human rights are legalized, as well as the special circumstances of women in society and the understanding and translation of this phenomenon by human rights norms.

Along these lines, feminist scholars present four major critiques of international human rights law that explain why human rights as recognized in the International Bill of Human Rights are not able to adequately improve the situation of women and ensure their equality with men.[22] The first is the absence of women and their voices in the process of international human rights norm-making.[23] They argue that as it is predominantly men who make these norms, it is the perspectives of men and how men see women's rights that shape the kind of equality and non-discrimination that these norms envision.[24] As a result, some argue, even the very language of human rights can become a structural barrier, just like the other socio-economic and political structures.[25] The second critique is that international human rights as a whole are shaped by the realities of men and, consequently, marginalize women's concerns and experiences. Despite the recognition of formal equality, feminist scholars contend that 'human rights are men's rights'.[26] The privilege of patriarchy, the standardization of men, and the primacy of civil and political rights over economic and social rights are all considered as the manifestation of human rights as men's rights.[27]

The third critique points to the distinction between the public and the private spheres in international human rights law.[28] While the public sphere is considered as the space for reason, culture, and intellectual endeavor, the private sphere is considered as the site for 'nature, nurture and non-rationality'.[29] By intervening only in the public sphere, international human rights law protects men, as they are the main

[20] The International Covenant on Economic, Social and Cultural Rights 1966, art 3.

[21] ibid art 2(2).

[22] Alice Edwards, *Violence against Women under International Human Rights Law* (Cambridge University Press 2010) 36.

[23] ibid 43.

[24] See also Hilary Charlesworth, 'Alienating Oscar—Feminist Analysis of International Law' (1993) 25 Studies in Transnational Legal Policy 1, 1–18.

[25] Hilary Charlesworth, 'What are "Women's International Human Rights"?' in Rebecca J Cook (ed), *Human Rights of Women: National and International Perspectives* (University of Pennsylvania Press 1994) 60–61.

[26] Edwards (n 22) 51.

[27] ibid 51–64.

[28] ibid 64.

[29] Margaret Thornton, 'The cartography of Public and Private' in Margaret Thornton (ed), *Public and Private: Feminist Legal Debates* (Oxford University Press 1995) 11–12.

actors there, while alienating women.[30] Hence, some feminists argue, international human rights law marginalizes women's interests and subordinates their world in its very conceptualization.

The fourth and final critique is that even though international human rights law recognizes women's rights, it considers women as homogeneous groups who all essentially share the same feminine identity.[31] Although women share some similar structural and social problems in every society, they also have different experiences and problems across the world due to differences in ethnicity, race, religion, culture, class, and other similar attributes. These feminist scholars contend that by essentializing women to their feminine identity, international human rights law fails to consider their particular needs and circumstances.

In order to tackle 'the extensive discrimination against women'[32] despite numerous human rights instruments recognizing their equality and prohibiting discrimination on the grounds of sex, and partly to respond to some of the feminist critiques of international human rights law, the Convention on the Elimination of All Forms of Discrimination against Women (CEDAW) was adopted. CEDAW, going beyond the International Bill of Human Rights, prohibits any discrimination against women 'in the political, economic, social, cultural, civil or any other field'.[33] Not only does it require states to take all appropriate measures 'to eliminate discrimination against women by any person, organization or enterprise',[34] it also obligates states to take 'temporary special measures' to ensure the de facto equality of women and men.[35] CEDAW directly deals with the social and cultural contexts women lead their lives in and prohibits discrimination in these fields. It specifically stipulates that states should:

> [. . .] modify the social and cultural patterns of conduct of men and women, with a view to achieving the elimination of prejudices and customary and all other practices which are based on the idea of the inferiority or the superiority of either of the sexes or on stereotyped roles for men and women.[36]

In addition to reaffirming the equal rights of women in all aspects of life, from the socio-economic and political fields to the domains of personal and family matters,[37] CEDAW pays particular attention to the trafficking of women, prostitution, and rural women.[38] Furthermore, the CEDAW Committee, the body overviewing the implementation of this convention, has explained via its general recommendations on the various provisions of CEDAW by relating them to the specific circumstances of women

[30] Celina Romany, 'State Responsibility Goes Private: A Feminist Critique of Public/private Distinction in International Human Rights Law' in Rebecca J Cook (ed), *Human Rights of Women: National and International Perspectives* (University of Pennsylvania Press 1994) 87.

[31] Edwards, *Violence against Women under International Human Rights Law* (n 22) 71.

[32] See Convention on the Elimination of All Forms of Discrimination against Women 1979, preamble.

[33] ibid art 1.

[34] ibid art 2(e).

[35] ibid art 4.

[36] ibid art 5(1).

[37] ibid arts 3, 7–13, 15 and 16.

[38] ibid arts 6 and 14.

around the world, such as violence against women,[39] the practice of female circumcision,[40] AIDS,[41] unpaid women workers in family enterprises,[42] disabled women,[43] older women,[44] women in conflict and post-conflict situations,[45] and refuge and asylum seeker women.[46] Although many have expressed reservations to CEDAW,[47] particularly predominantly Muslim states, it remains the most transformative and progressive women's rights convention at the international level;[48] it provides the case for formal and substantive equality for women in all aspects of life, unconstrained by cultural, religious, customary, or any other explanations, and, consequently, makes women's rights universal human rights.[49]

Even though CEDAW recognizes the equal rights of women and men in all fields at the international level and the African Charter on Human and Peoples' Rights affirms the equal rights of women and men at the regional level,[50] African women continue to face discrimination, marginalization, and violence in a wide range of spheres.[51] In order to address the specific needs of women in Africa, the African Union (AU) adopted the Protocol to the African Charter on Human and Peoples' Rights on the Rights of Women in Africa (African Women's Rights Protocol) in 2003.[52] In addition to reaffirming the women's rights recognized by other human rights instruments, the African Women's Rights Protocol defines and prohibits harmful cultural practices,[53] violence against women,[54] recognizes women's sexual and reproductive rights including the right to abortion in some instances,[55] and prohibits female genital

[39] United Nations Committee on the Elimination of Discrimination Against Women, 'General Recommendation No 19' <https://wwwohchrorg/en/hrbodies/cedaw/pages/recommendationsaspx> accessed 17 January 2019; See also United Nations Committee on the Elimination of Discrimination Against Women, 'General Recommendation No. 35' <https://wwwohchrorg/en/hrbodies/cedaw/pages/recommendationsaspx> accessed 17 January 2019.

[40] ibid General Recommendation No 14.

[41] ibid General Recommendation No 15.

[42] ibid General Recommendation No 16.

[43] ibid General Recommendation No 18.

[44] ibid General Recommendation No 27.

[45] ibid General Recommendation No 30.

[46] ibid General Recommendation No 32.

[47] See Rebecca J Cook, 'Reservations to the Convention on the Elimination of All Forms of Discrimination against Women' (1989) 30 Virginia Journal of International Law 643, 643–716.

[48] Frances Raday, 'Gender and Democratic Citizenship: The Impact of CEDAW' (2012) 10 International Journal of Constitutional Law 512, 529.

[49] See Marsha A Freeman, Christine Chinkin, Beate Rudolf, 'Introduction' in Marsha A Freeman, Christine Chinkin, and Beate Rudolf (eds), *The UN Convention on the Elimination of All Forms of Discrimination Against Women: A Commentary* (Oxford University Press 2012) 2.

[50] African Charter on Human and Peoples' Rights 1981, Arts 2, 3, and 18(3).

[51] Claude E Welch, 'Human Rights and African Women: A Comparison of Protection under Two Major Treaties' (1993) 15 Human Rights Quarterly 549, 550–53; Fareda Banda, 'Blazing a Trail: The African Protocol on Women's Rights Comes into Force' (2006) 50 Journal of African Law 72, 72–74; See also African Women's protocol, Preamble.

[52] For the protocol's comparison with other human rights instruments see Frans Viljoen, 'An Introduction to the Protocol to the African Charter on Human and Peoples Rights on the Rights of Women in Africa' (2009) 16 Washington and Lee Journal of Civil Rights and Social Justice 11.

[53] The Protocol to the African Charter on Human and Peoples' Rights on the Rights of Women in Africa 2003, art 1(g) and 5.

[54] ibid art 1(j).

[55] ibid art 14, 14(2(c)).

mutilation.[56] Furthermore, it recognizes women's right to a positive cultural context. This right is defined as women's '[...] right to live in a positive cultural context and to participate at all levels in the determination of cultural policies'.[57] By recognizing culture as a site for women's rights and by appreciating the agency of women in culture and its development and transformation, the African Women's Rights Protocol extends the reach of human rights into the province of culture.[58]

In summary, the nature and substance of women's rights in Africa emanate from these international and regional human rights instruments. Equality, non-discrimination, and temporary special measures or affirmative action on the one hand, and the prohibition and elimination of all legal, social, cultural, religious, customary, or other harmful practices against women on the other, characterize the nature of women's rights. In terms of substance, women's rights include (a) those civil, political, economic, social, environmental, and developmental rights recognized to every human being, and (b) those specific women's rights recognized by CEDAW and the African Women's Rights Protocol.

While it is a truism that the ideals of human rights are embedded—in one form or another—in all the different cultural, social, and religious contexts around the world,[59] the advancement of human rights in their current shape and form is the result of the triumph of liberalism since the end of the Second World War.[60] And women's rights as part of the human rights regime and movement are not an exception. Against this backdrop, the following sections explore and examine the constitutional designs and practices of women's rights in Nigeria, South Africa, and Ethiopia. Like the chapters dealing with federalism and the executive, the aim of these sections is to demonstrate how women's constitutional rights in Africa are the result of legal syncretism and how this phenomenon concomitantly shapes women's constitutional rights to equality and non-discrimination.

II. Women's Constitutional Rights in Nigeria

A cursory reading of the Bill of Rights under the Constitution of Nigeria shows that women and men are equal in enjoying and accessing rights. However, a closer look at the constitutional normative and institutional configurations reveals that the scope and nature of women's rights in Nigeria are not as clear as they seem. On the one hand, the Constitution reaffirms the liberal account of human rights by extending them to everyone including women without any discrimination based on sex. On the other hand, it incorporates the notion of rights as found in religious and customary

[56] ibid art 5(b); See also Fareda Banda, *Women, Law and Human Rights: An African Perspective* (Hart Publishing 2005) 80–82; Rose Gawaya and Rosemary Semafumu Mukasa, 'The African Women's Protocol: A New Dimension for Women's Rights in Africa' (2005) 13 Gender and Development 42, 48.

[57] The Protocol to the African Charter on Human and Peoples' Rights on the Rights of Women in Africa, art 17(1).

[58] See also Sylvia Tamale, 'The Right to Culture and the Culture of Rights: A Critical Perspective on Women's Sexual Rights in Africa' (2008) 16 Feminist Legal Studies 47, 57–58.

[59] See Mutua, *Human Rights* (n 2).

[60] See Jack Donnelly, *Universal Human Rights in Theory and Practice* (3rd edn, Cornell University Press 2013).

practices by recognizing Sharia and customary laws. By transcending the dichotomy between universalism and cultural relativism found in the wider human rights debate, the Constitution of Nigeria considers Sharia and customary laws as both manifestations of freedom of religion and the right to culture as well as avenues for the enforcement of human rights—including women's rights. As a result, the exact contents of women's rights in Nigeria are determined by the normative, institutional, and practical interactions set out by the Constitution. In this respect, courts play a crucial role in defining women's rights and shaping their contours. The following section outlines the substance of women's rights under the Constitution of Nigeria and, more specifically, investigates women's right to equality and non-discrimination under Sharia and customary laws.

A. Constitutional Design

Unlike South Africa and Ethiopia, as discussed below, Nigeria recognized socio-economic rights in Chapter II of their constitution which deals with the Directive Principles of State Policy (DPSP) and civil and political rights in Chapter IV which covers fundamental rights. While the DPSP are general guidelines for the implementation of the Constitution and other laws, they may not be justiciable before a court of law,[61] whereas fundamental rights are justiciable and, accordingly, can be enforced by the judiciary. Like with the International Bill of Human Rights, feminist criticism can also be levelled with regard to the different levels of recognition and protection towards socio-economic rights and civil and political rights under the Nigerian Constitution. Nonetheless, the discussion here is limited to ascertaining women's rights in general—and particularly their right to equality and non-discrimination—at the formal level.

The DPSP chapter makes it clear that the fundamental objectives and directives of state policy in the socio-economic, cultural, and political fields should include and take into account every Nigerian. Moreover, it explicitly emphasizes the equality of women and men and prohibits discrimination based on sex within the DPSP framework. For instance, Section 17(2(a)) states that 'every citizen shall have equality of rights, obligations and opportunities before the law'; thus, women—as Nigerian citizens[62]—are entitled to the same equal rights, responsibilities, and opportunities as men. Conscious of the prevalence of discrimination, including based on sex, Section 17(3)(a) commands the state to direct its policies to ensure that 'all citizens, without discrimination on any group whatsoever, have the opportunity for securing adequate means of livelihood as well as adequate opportunity to secure suitable employment'. In particular, Section 17(3)(e) recognizes equal pay for equal work without discrimination on account of sex.

Following similar trends in international human rights standards, the DPSP chapter encourages the state to direct its policies to the 'evolution and promotion of family

[61] The Constitution of Nigeria, s 13; see also Atudiwe P Atupare, 'Reconciling Socioeconomic Rights and Directive Principles with a Fundamental Law of Reason in Ghana and Nigeria' (2014) 27 Harv Hum Rts J 71, 90–91.

[62] See the Constitution of Nigeria, s 25(1).

life'[63] and the development and promotion of positive cultural practices. In this regard, Section 21(a) provides that the state shall 'protect, preserve and promote the Nigerian cultures which enhance human dignity and are consistent with the fundamental objectives as provided in this Chapter'. This 'cultural right' formulation is important when seen in light of women's rights. First, women, like men, are cultural beings and want to participate in the cultural life of their communities. Second, in as much as there are cultural practices that channel and reinforce discrimination against women, there are cultural practices that protect and advance women's rights.[64] Moreover, even those cultural practices that are discriminatory are subject to change due to various internal and/or external reasons.[65] Hence, the recognition and rejection of cultural practices opens multiple possibilities and contestations for women's rights.[66]

Within the general context of equality and non-discrimination, the DPSP Chapter specifically entitles women to—among other things—the right to human dignity,[67] the right to adequate standard of living,[68] the right to health,[69] the right to work,[70] the right to rest and leisure,[71] the right to education,[72] and the right to culture.[73] And beyond rights, the DPSP chapter enshrines principles that advance the causes of social justice, development, national integration, and constitutionalism, and it positions women and men on an equal plane.

The fundamental rights chapter contains the classic civil and political rights and makes them available to women. Among these civil and political rights, freedom of religion and equality before the law are given special mention due to their impact on women's rights in the domain of Sharia law. Section 38(1) of the Constitution states that:

> Every person shall be entitled to freedom of thought, conscience and religion, including freedom to change his religion or belief, and freedom (either alone or in community with others, and in public or in private) to manifest and propagate his religion or belief in worship, teaching, practice and observance.

This article is almost a verbatim copy of Article 18(1) of the ICCPR and does not pose any danger to women's rights in itself.[74] Furthermore, Section 42 explicitly guarantees

[63] ibid s 17(3)(h).

[64] See Sunder, 'Piercing the Veil' (n 6).

[65] See also Susanne Zwingel, 'How Do Norms Travel? Theorizing International Women's Rights in Transnational Perspective' (2012) 56 International Studies Quarterly 1, 115–29.

[66] See also Bonny Ibhawoh, 'Between Culture and Constitution: Evaluating the Cultural Legitimacy of Human Rights in the African State' (2000) 22 Human Rights Quarterly 838, 842; Manisuli Ssenyonjo, 'Culture and the Human Rights of Women in Africa: Between Light and Shadow' (2007) 51 Journal of African Law 39, 66.

[67] The Constitution of Nigeria, s 17(2) (b).

[68] ibid s 17(3).

[69] ibid s 17(3)(d).

[70] ibid s 17(3)(a), (b), and (c).

[71] ibid s 17(3)(b).

[72] ibid s 18(3).

[73] ibid s 21(a).

[74] See also Human Rights Committee, General Comment No 22 <https://tbinternetohchrorg/_layouts/treatybodyexternal/Downloadaspx?symbolno=CCPR%2fC%2f21%2fRev1%2fAdd4&Lang=en> accessed 17 January 2019 When we see General Comment No 22 on freedom of thought, conscience and religion, it is clear that freedom of religion does not enlarge religious freedom to the public sphere (ie criminal law).

equality and prohibits any discrimination based on sex, among other grounds. Thus, while the Constitution of Nigeria did not recognize any special rights for women, unlike CEDAW or the African Women's Rights Protocol, it does recognize the equality of women and men in enjoying and accessing rights and performing duties and responsibilities.

This description of women's rights under the Constitution of Nigeria is just the tip of the iceberg. The complex terrain of women's rights in Nigeria can be unraveled through a more thorough investigation of the judicial structure, the applicable laws, and the judicial practice. As a federal state, Nigeria has a decentralized judicial system and there are three major types of courts in Nigeria. For lack of a better description, the first type of courts are those that predominantly apply statutory and common law, and these include the Supreme Court, the Court of Appeal, the Federal High Court, the Federal High Court of the Federal Capital Territory, the High Courts of States, and other lower courts of a similar type. The second type of courts are those that predominantly apply Sharia law and include the Sharia Court of Appeal of the Federal Capital Territory, the Sharia Court of Appeal of states, and other lower Sharia courts. The third type of courts are those that predominantly apply customary laws and include the Customary Court of Appeal of the Federal Capital Territory, the Customary Court of Appeal of states, and other lower customary courts. While there is a three-tiered court system at both the Federal Capital Territory and state levels, there is also a unified court system at the federal level having appellate jurisdiction on Sharia and customary laws.

As with the nature of the judiciary in Africa in general, as discussed in Chapter 3, the judiciary in Nigeria is also syncretic as there is a fusion of diverse laws and persons. For instance, Sharia and customary court judges need to have standard legal training in addition to having proven expertise in Sharia and customary laws,[75] as the jurisdiction of Sharia and customary courts are not limited to Sharia or customary laws.[76]Additionally, the appointment of Sharia and customary court judges and their rules of procedure are regulated by statutory laws.[77] Moreover, the higher federal courts have appellate jurisdiction to review the decisions of Sharia and customary courts.[78] Seen in this syncretic judicial framework, the court system in Nigeria is set out in a unified and harmonious manner despite the seemingly diverse, and perhaps competing, judicial design.[79]

In addition to the formal recognition of women's right to equality and non-discrimination in the Constitution, this syncretic judicial design, with its diverse bodies of laws, determines the substance of women's rights and their level of actual protection in practice. In this respect, it is of particular importance to look at women's rights—and particularly their right to equality and non-discrimination—in light of Sharia and customary laws. The Constitution simply mentions that Sharia and customary courts have jurisdiction on issues involving Islamic personal law and

[75] See the Constitution of Nigeria, ss 260(3) and 266(3).
[76] See ibid ss 262(1) and 267.
[77] See ibid ss 261(1) and (2) and 266(1) and (2).
[78] See ibid s 247.
[79] See also Abdulmumini A Oba, 'Judicial Practice in Islamic Family Law and Its Relation to 'Urf (Custom) in Northern Nigeria' (2013) 20 Islamic Law and Society 272, 279.

customary laws; as a result, it is necessary to consult extra-constitutional sources to ascertain the content of these laws in order to assess their compatibility—or lack thereof—with the constitutional recognition of women's rights. As Sharia and customary laws are applicable in personal matters, I will now focus on what these laws say about marriage and inheritance and examine women's rights as expressed therein in order to demonstrate the range of these rights in the constitutional design of Nigeria.

B. Islamic and Customary Laws on Marriage and Inheritance

It should be noted from the outset that Islamic law was considered as customary law for Northern Nigeria during the colonial period.[80] Moreover, while the current Constitution simply says Islamic personal law, the Maliki school has been the official school of Islamic law applicable in Nigeria.[81] One of the features of the Maliki school is the strong consideration of 'custom' as a source of Islamic law.[82] As long as custom is not contrary to the law and spirit of Islamic law, it is applicable in Islamic courts.[83] This means that what is considered as Islamic law for the purposes of judicial application may include a complex combination of Islamic laws and local customs. Being as it may, the canonical Islamic laws on marriage and inheritance are well-known. What follows here is a brief restatement of the main contents of these laws related to women's rights to equality and non-discrimination.

Marriage under Islamic law, as practiced in Nigeria, requires the consent of both future spouses in principle, while the consent of the guardian (often the father) suffices if the woman or girl is a virgin.[84] Although she is entitled to revoke the consent of her guardian after attaining the age of majority, the guardian has a legal right to give her in marriage even against her will. For the marriage to be valid, the future husband must pay a dowry to the future wife. Once the marriage is concluded, the husband has an obligation to support his wife and family. As a matter of law, the wife has no obligation to pay a dowry, nor to assume the duty of supporting the family during marriage. After the first marriage, the man is entitled to marry up to three or four wives, while the wife cannot marry again. A validly concluded marriage can be dissolved either through *talaq* (a declaration of divorce on the part of the husband alone, where he repeats three times that he would like to divorce her), *khul* (a divorce by the wife after

[80] See AA Oba, 'Islamic Law as Customary Law: The Changing Perspective in Nigeria' (2002) 51 The International and Comparative Law Quarterly 4, 817–50.

[81] ibid 275–76. See the Supreme Court in *Abdulsalam v Salawu* [2002] 6 SCNJ, 388–403 holding that the official Islamic law is the Maliki school.

[82] Oba, 'Judicial Practice in Islamic Family Law and Its Relation to 'Urf (Custom) in Northern Nigeria' (n 79) 277.

[83] Ibid; Mohammad Hashim Kamali, *Principles of Islamic Jurisprudence* (3rd revised edition, The Islamic Texts Society 2003) 283; see also Khaleel Mohammed, 'The Islamic Law Maxims' (2005) 44 Islamic Studies 2, 191–207.

[84] Jamila M Nasir, 'Sharia Implementation and Female Muslims in Nigeria's Sharia States' in Philip Ostien (ed), *Sharia Implementation in Northern Nigeria 1999-2006: The Sharia Penal and Criminal Procedure Codes* (Spectrum Books 2007) 76–118.

paying compensation—returning the dowry to the husband—and with the intervention of the Qadi/judge), or mutual consent through the courts.[85]

With respect to inheritance under Islamic law, both women and men are entitled to inheritance. However, regarding the share of women and men, the Quran says: 'Allah commands you as regards your children's [inheritance]: to the male, a portion equal to that of two females; if only daughters, two or more, their share is two thirds of the inheritance; if only one, her share is half (4:11).'[86] Thus, under Islamic law, women and girls are only entitled to half the share of inheritance that men and boys are entitled to.

Unlike Islamic law, there are numerous customary laws in Nigeria and it is difficult— and unnecessary for present purposes—to list every customary law of marriage and inheritance here. While there are differences among these customary laws, there are some common features among all of them in Nigeria. A recent study by the Nigerian Institute of Advanced Legal Studies documents some of the common features of customary laws.[87] For instance, for the conclusion of a customary marriage, the consent of the families of the future spouses is required.[88] This consent is gained through intermediary persons well known to both families. While the consent of the man to the marriage is assumed, as it is often initiated by him or in consultation with him, the same could not be said for the woman; consent to marriage is the right of her family.[89] Like in Islamic law, the man is required to pay the bride price to the family of the woman, and this has to be effected in the presence of witnesses.[90] Unlike in Islamic law, however, the bride price is not paid to the woman. However, as in Islamic law, the woman has no such obligation.

After the conclusion of a customary marriage, the husband and wife assume rights and duties to each other and to their families. The rights of the husband include, among others, 'the right to be respected and obeyed by his wife, the right to claim ownership of property belonging to his wife, the right not to be denied conjugal relations by his wife, and the right to the status of headship of the home'.[91] While his main duties are 'to love and cherish his wife and to provide for her needs, to consummate the marriage, to avoid maltreating his wife (but this does not preclude him from disciplining her occasionally for her misbehaviors[*sic*]), and to support his children and the family'.[92] Although the wife has the right to be loved and cherished by her husband, she neither has equal decision-making power with her husband, nor can she discipline him in the event of his misbehavior.[93] Even if the wife has similar duties to those of her husband, her main duty is confined to domestic matters.[94] During a

[85] Judith E Tucker, *Women, Family, and Gender in Islamic Law* (Cambridge University Press 2008) 84–100.

[86] See also Jamal J Ahmad Nasir, *The Status of Women under Islamic Law and Modern Islamic Legislation* (3rd revised edition, Brill 2009) 19; Tucker, *Women, Family, and Gender in Islamic Law* (n 85) 26.

[87] Epiphany Azinge (eds), *Restatement of Customary Law of Nigeria* (Nigerian Institute of Advanced Legal Studies 2013).

[88] ibid 254.

[89] ibid 265.

[90] ibid 268–70.

[91] ibid 289.

[92] ibid 290.

[93] ibid 295.

[94] ibid 296.

divorce, the family of the wife is obliged to return the dowry to the husband, without which—in some communities—children from subsequent marriages belong to the former husband.[95] Once the marriage is dissolved, the wife loses custody of her children to the husband, with the exception of the very little ones, and she loses her property rights in marriage.[96]

Customary law with regard to inheritance also treats women and men differently. The predominant principle in customary inheritance is the rule of male primogeniture, where succession goes along the male line and entitles the eldest son to be the successor of his deceased father or male relative.[97] In this rule of inheritance, women are completely absent in the equation.[98] Even in those communities that allow female inheritance, a distinction is made between those 'who remain in the house and procreate to further the family lineage' who are entitled to inherit landed property, and others whose entitlement is limited to movable property if their deceased fathers gave it to them as gifts.[99]

From a formal legalistic perspective, therefore, some aspects of these Islamic and customary laws on marriage and inheritance are apparently discriminatory against women. Women do not have equal rights in the conclusion, duration, and dissolution of marriage. Similarly, they do not enjoy equal rights with men in inheritance; they either have no inheritance rights at all, or if they have them, their shares are significantly lower than those of men. A plethora of scholarship is available on how these laws violate women's rights in Nigeria;[100] however, much of the focus is on how Islamic and customary laws contradict women's constitutional rights. Nonetheless, while such criticism is appropriate on its own, the more interesting point of analysis in this respect is not Islamic and customary laws, but rather constitutional law, since Islamic and customary laws are not applicable in Nigeria because religion or custom commands them to be, but because the Constitution itself authorizes their application on its own terms; as discussed above, the Constitution even established its own Sharia and customary courts at different levels in order to adjudicate matters concerning Islamic and customary laws. While the religious and customary basis of these laws is very clear, the Constitution transforms them into positive law, and consequently, they are no longer only Islamic and customary laws. This transformation and configuration of Islamic and customary laws into positive law changes the frames of reference for analyzing women's rights under these laws. In this context, it is the Constitution, not the body of Islamic and customary laws, that should be the principal unit of analysis for women's

[95] ibid 332.

[96] ibid 348; MOA Ashiru, 'Gender Discrimination in the Division of Property on Divorce in Nigeria' (2007) 51 Journal of African Law 316, 321; Ebenezer Durojaye, '"Woman, But Not Human": Widowhood Practices and Human Rights Violations in Nigeria' (2013) 27 International Journal of Law, Policy and the Family 2, 176–96.

[97] ibid 113.

[98] See also Mary Adebola Ajayi and Abiodun Olukayode Olotuah, 'Violation of Women's Property Rights within the Family' (2005) 1 Agenda: Empowering Women for Gender Equity 1, 58–63; Ikechukwu Olueze, 'Women's Right to Inheritance under Customary Laws in Nigeria' (2004) 29 International Legal Practitioner 135–38; Christopher E Ukhun and Nathaniel A Inegbedion, 'Cultural Authoritarianism, Women and Human Rights Issues among the Esan People of Nigeria' (2005) 5 African Human Rights Law Journal 129, 135.

[99] Azinge, *Restatement of Customary Law of Nigeria* (n 87) 114.

[100] Ajayi and Olotuah, 'Violation of Women's Property Rights within the Family' (n 98).

rights. As a result, it is the notion of women's rights under these transformed Islamic and customary laws, along with the notion of women's right as expressed in the chapters on DPSP and fundamental rights, that together compose the full women's rights regime under the Nigerian Constitution. This constitutional design makes women's constitutional rights in Nigeria syncretic, as it incorporates both the liberal account of women's rights as well as an account of women's rights as rooted in religion and custom.

The following analysis of the judicial practice and adjudication regarding issues of women's rights in light of Islamic and customarily laws can shed further light on this syncretic feature: the feature of recognition, interpenetration, and resistance between the liberal account of women's rights and Islamic and customary conceptions of women's rights.

C. Judicial Practice

In order to show the judicial practice with regard to women's rights in the field of Islamic and customary laws, I will focus on Islamic marriage and customary laws of inheritance. As the following cases demonstrate, women's rights in Nigeria are the syncretic results of liberal, Islamic and customary notions of rights and their specific content is determined by their interactions in a given time and place. For instance, in the case of *Karimatu Yakubu and Alhaji Mahmoud Ndatsu v Alhaji Yakubu Tafida Paiko and Alhaji Umaru Gwagwada* the issue was who exactly is entitled to give consent for the conclusion of marriage.[101] Under liberal constitutional standards, it is obvious that marriage is concluded by the free and full consent of both spouses. However, according to the laws of Islamic marriage, within which the parties in this case concluded their marriage, the father as a guardian of his daughter can marry her off against her will. This itself is a violation of the constitutional right to equality and, consequently, should render this law unconstitutional. Indeed, the Area Court that first received the case found no difficulty in making the marriage invalid as it was concluded between Karimatu's father and her husband without her consent.[102] However, the Sharia Court of Appeal in Sokoto reversed the decision of the Area Court by arguing that Karimatu's father had the right to compel his daughter to marriage under Islamic law.[103] Although the Federal Court of Appeal in Kaduna reversed the decision of the Sharia Court of Appeal, it did so on different grounds[104] and, indeed, reaffirmed the father's right to compulsion (*ijbar*) in marriage.[105]

In the case of *Hasana Gbaguda v Muhammadu Gbaguda*, Hasana filed an application to divorce her husband, Muhammadu, in the Area Court alleging that he beat her while he got drunk.[106] Although Muhammadu admitted the allegations, the court

[101] Yushau Sodiq, *A History of the Application of Islamic Law in Nigeria* (Springer International Publishing 2017) 79.
[102] ibid 80.
[103] ibid 81.
[104] Once the father gave his daughter a choice to marry in the first place, he cannot revoke his promise.
[105] Sodiq, *A History of the Application of Islamic Law in Nigeria* (n 101) 81–82.
[106] ibid 88.

denied Hasana's claim for divorce and further noted that if she wanted a divorce she would have to pay compensation (*khul*).[107] Unhappy with the decision of the Area Court, she appealed to the Sharia Court of Appeal for divorce which, in turn, decided in her favor by reasoning that her husband had beaten and abused her and, accordingly, did not deserve any compensation.[108] The fact that men can divorce through *talaq* (without compensation) and women can only divorce through *khul* (with compensation) was not considered as discriminatory against women—nor was it even contested —in this case. Furthermore, in the case of *Habiba Sarkin Fulani v Alhaji Dahiru Dayi*, the appellant's right to divorce through *khul* was denied as she could not find any evidence that showed that she had been mistreated by her husband.[109]

In addition to the application of Islamic law in personal matters, as seen in the above cases, its application in the field of criminal law is extended in the twelve northern states. The extension of Islamic law to all aspects of life in these states is a highly contested issue in Nigeria. Nevertheless, the Supreme Court has neither given a decision about the constitutionality of the application of Sharia in criminal law, nor has an application for its constitutionality been made yet. The famous Amina Lawal case, *Amina Lawal v the State*,[110] is a classic example that demonstrates the (in)compatibilities of the Islamic mode of punishment with international human rights standards. For the crime of adultery, which Lawal was charged with, death by stoning is the punishment under Islamic law. The man whom Lawal alleged to have committed adultery with her was not prosecuted due to a lack of evidence—and no DNA tests were even considered—while her pregnancy was the single concrete evidence for the crime. The lower Sharia Court sentenced Lawal to death by stoning, but the Sharia Court of Appeal set her free on procedural grounds.[111] Thus, just like Islamic personal law, Islamic criminal law also has a gender discriminatory dimension, which brings an additional element to the women's rights regime in Nigeria and, consequently, broadens the syncretic range of women's rights.

With respect to customary laws, courts are generally progressive and ensure the formal equality of women and men in accessing rights, while the Supreme Court takes a more tempered approach and counsels lower courts on their far-reaching decisions. In the case of *Mojekwu v Mojekwu*,[112] women's inheritance rights under customary law was at issue. Under the *oli-Ekpe* custom of Southeastern Nigeria (Ibo), women do not have a right to inheritance. The appellant, Mr Augustine Mojekwu, instituted a claim—based on this customary law—against Mrs Caroline Mojekwu to inherit her deceased husband's property. The appellant argued that as the deceased had no son or brother, the deceased's property should go to him as the deceased was his paternal uncle and he was the closest male relative. The Court of Appeal, based on the facts and

[107] ibid.
[108] ibid 89.
[109] ibid 90–91.
[110] *Amina Lawal v The State* [2002] USC FT/CRA/1/02.
[111] Sodiq, *A History of the Application of Islamic Law in Nigeria* (n 101) 97. Indeed, there are some persons (both men and women) who are sentenced to death by stoning for adultery; see Harvard Law Review, 'Saving Amina Lawal: Human Rights Symbolism and the Dangers of Colonialism' (2004) 117 Harvard Law Review 2365, 2366.
[112] *Mojekwu v Mojekwu* [1997] 7 NWLR 283.

evidence produced, decided that another customary law, called *Kola Tenancy*, was the applicable law in this case and under this law women are entitled to inherit the property of the deceased as men. The court further observed that the *oli-Ekpe* custom that excludes women from inheritance is not only contrary to public policy and repugnant to natural justice, equity and good conscience, but is also against the Constitution and the international human rights standards that Nigeria had ratified. This decision was welcomed by the human rights and legal community of Nigeria as a landmark case in fine-tuning discriminatory customary laws with human rights standards.[113]

However, the pronouncement of the Court of Appeal was watered-down by the Supreme Court in its appellate judgment of *Mojekwu v Iwuchukwu*.[114] While the Supreme Court upheld the decision and holding of the Court of Appeal, it reversed the opinion on the *oli-Ekpe* custom of inheritance. Justice SO Uwaifo, on behalf of the Supreme Court, stated that:

> I cannot see any justification for the court below to pronounce that the Nnewi native custom of '[o]li-ekpe' was repugnant to natural justice, equity and good conscience ... the learned justice of appeal was no doubt concerned about the perceived discrimination directed against women by the said Nnewi 'oli-ekpe' custom and that is quite understandable. But the language used made the pronouncement so general and far[-]reaching that it seems to cavil at, and is capable of causing strong feelings against, all customs which fail to recognise a role for women. For instance, the custom and traditions of some communities which do not permit women to be natural rulers or family heads. The import is that those communities stand to be condemned without a hearing for such fundamental custom and tradition they practice by the system by which they run their native communities.[115]

As seen from this comment of the Supreme Court, the fact that some customary laws discriminate against women does not ipso facto lead to the conclusion of unconstitutionality of such laws. Further, it also alludes to the fact that the exact substance and contours of women's rights in relation to customary laws will be determined and delimited on a case-by-case basis after consideration of all competing interests.

Following this approach, the Supreme Court reaffirmed women's rights of inheritance by declaring Igbo customary inheritance law discriminatory and unconstitutional in the case of *Ukeje v Ukeje*.[116] In its decision, the court notes that:

> No matter the circumstances of the birth of a female child, such a child is entitled to an inheritance from her late father's estate. Consequently, the Igbo customary law which disentitles a female child from partaking, in the sharing of her deceased father's estate is in breach of section 42(1) and (2) of the Constitution, a fundamental

[113] IN Eme Worugji and RO Ugbe, 'Judicial Protection of Women's Rights in Nigeria: The Regrettable Decision in Mojekwu v Iwuchukwu Note' (2013) 16 University of Botswana Law Journal 59, 59–72.

[114] *Mojekwu v Iwuchukwu* [2004] 4 SC (Pt II) Mrs Iwuchukwu, the daughter of Mrs Caroline Mojekwu substituted as a party to the case as her mother died.

[115] *Mojekwu v Iwuchukwu* [2004] 4 SC (Pt II) as cited by Azinge, *Restatement of Customary Law of Nigeria* (n 87) 125.

[116] *Mrs Lois Chituru Ukeje & Anor v Mrs Gladys Ada Ukeje* [2001] 27 WRN 127.

> rights provision guaranteed to every Nigerian. The said discriminatory customary law is void as it conflicts with section 42(1) and (2) of the Constitution.[117]

In a similar case of *Anekwe v Nweke*,[118] the Supreme Court declared a customary law that denies a widow and her female child from inheriting her husband's property as repugnant to national justice, equity, and conscience, and—accordingly—void. Unlike the previous case that relied on the Constitutional provisions of equality, in this case the Court applied a public policy test in outlawing the customary law pertaining to widow's and women's disinheritance.[119] Although both cases ensure the equal rights of women and men in inheriting property, the specific accounts of women's rights in customary laws had to be judicially litigated in order to ascertain their substance and delimit their contour's within the constitutional framework.[120]

Thus, in light of such constitutional design and judicial practice, the women's rights regime in Nigeria is different from the women's rights regime discussed in the first section of this chapter. The primary difference emanates from the recognition of Islamic and customary laws as applicable laws in the Nigerian judiciary in general, and the establishment of Sharia and customary courts as avenues for rights enforcement in particular.[121] There is a constant dialectic between the rights rooted in Islamic and customary laws and the rights rooted in the liberal human rights tradition.[122] As a result, women's rights are the syncretic result of this dialectic at both the levels of constitutional design of rights as well as their judicial practice.

Indeed, the syncretism of women's rights unfolds differently—in practice—with respect to Islamic law and customary laws. Regarding Islamic law, there is mainly a symbiotic relationship with respect to the liberal tenet of the Constitution. This is because the rights rooted in Islamic law seem to co-exist with the rights found in liberalism within the same constitutional space. This constitutional state of affairs is comparable to the idea of religious syncretism we see in China which enables Confucianism, Taoism, and Buddhism to co-exist in the same social field. In such symbiotic relationships, mutual recognition and tolerance are the predominant courses of action in the constitutional matrix. In the case of customary law, however, there is a relationship of adoption, fusion, and transformation with the liberal tenet of the Constitution. As a result, the relationship is characterized by changes within the customary law and the outcome is one of assimilation to the liberal notion of rights. Like with federalism and the executive, as discussed in earlier chapters, the syncretic constitutional designs and practices of women's rights is a conscious choice made by constitutional actors.

117 *Mrs Lois Chituru Ukeje & Anor v Mrs Gladys Ada Ukeje* [2001] 27 WRN 127, paras 32–33.

118 *Anekwe v Nweke* [2014] 234 LRCN 34.

119 ibid paras 64–65.

120 See also Oba, 'Islamic Law as Customary Law' (n 80) 894.

121 See also Phil E Okeke, 'Reconfiguring Tradition: Women's Rights and Social Status in Contemporary Nigeria' (2000) 47 Africa Today 49, 55.

122 See also Abdullahi Ahmed An-Na'im, 'The Compatibility Dialectic: Mediating the Legitimate Coexistence of Islamic Law and State Law' (2010) 73 The Modern Law Review 1, 1–29.

III. Women's Constitutional Rights in South Africa

Beyond the formal recognition of women's right to equality, the Constitution of South Africa provides a framework for the advancement of the substantive equality of women with men. Unlike the Constitution of Nigeria, it does not differentiate the levels of protection between civil and political rights and socio-economic and cultural rights, nor does it limit the application of the Bill of Rights to the state. Furthermore, not only does it found the state based on 'human dignity, the achievement of equality and the advancement of human rights and freedoms', but also on 'non-racialism and non-sexism'.[123] Moreover, it established a constitutional institution that works solely on the issues of gender equality. Thus, the normative and institutional architecture for women's rights in South Africa is more robust than in Nigeria. Nonetheless, like Nigeria, the Constitution of South Africa recognizes the right to culture and the application of customary laws which often challenge the equal rights of women. Additionally, it recognizes the power of traditional authorities whose basic pillar is patriarchy. The women's rights regime in South Africa, like in Nigeria, can best be understood through an investigation of both the liberal account of rights and the notion of rights as rooted in African culture. In this process, the judiciary plays a significant role in defining the contours of women's rights within the constitutional framework. The aim of this section, therefore, is to explore the women's rights regime in South Africa in general, with a particular focus on women's rights to equality and non-discrimination under customary laws, in order to demonstrate how legal syncretism animates women's rights there and permeates their application in practice. For this purpose, I first look at the constitutional design for women's rights, explore the official customary laws on marriage and inheritance, and then examine the judicial practice on women's rights under customary laws.

A. Constitutional Design

Post-apartheid South Africa is as much informed by the prevalence of discrimination based on sex and gender as it is by discrimination on account of race. The issue of women's rights permeates the founding values of the new democratic republic, its Bill of Rights, and its constitutional institutions. For example, while human dignity, equality, human rights, and freedoms are inclusive enough to herald the foundation of an inclusive society, the Constitution specifically mentions that 'non-sexism' should also be one of the foundational values of the new constitutional order. Although there are no specific constitutional rights exclusively for women unlike CEDAW or the African Women's Rights Protocol, the way the Bill of Rights is designed does favor women's rights.

By positioning the Bill of Rights as the cornerstone of democracy in South Africa,[124] the Constitution expands the reach of the Bill of Rights beyond the sphere of the state in order to include natural or juristic persons as well—to the extent that they

[123] The Constitution of South Africa, s 1(a) and (b).
[124] ibid s 7(1).

are applicable.[125] Unlike the International Bill of Human Rights, the South African Bill of Rights transcends the public-private dichotomy in its application of human rights;[126] by extending the Bill of Rights to the private sphere,[127] it protects and safeguards the interests and activities of women in that sphere as well. In this regard, the South African Bill of Rights adopts the philosophy behind CEDAW and the African Women's Rights Protocol in mainstreaming human rights in both the public and private spheres. Similarly, the South African Bill of Rights recognizes the indivisibility and interdependence of both civil and political rights as well as socio-economic and cultural rights. Since much of women's interests and activities rest in the field of socio-economic rights, the constitutional recognition of the latter has the potential of advancing women's interests and rights. For instance, the right to heath includes the right to access to reproductive health care, for which many women have an outstanding need.[128]

The Constitution not only makes the Bill of Rights available to every person, but also pays particular attention to equality irrespective of sex and gender.[129] Equality, in addition to being a value in the foundation and operation of the republic, is a fundamental value that should be considered in the interpretation and application of the Bill of Rights. Section 39(1) of the Constitution makes it mandatory for a court, tribunal, or forum that interprets the Bill of Rights to 'promote the values that underlie an open and democratic society based on human dignity, equality and freedom'.[130] In addition, equality is one of the values considered when limiting constitutional rights: Section 36(1) provides that 'the rights in the Bill of Rights may be limited only in terms of law of general application to the extent that the limitation is reasonable and justifiable in an open and democratic society based on human dignity, equality and freedom'.[131] Moreover, freedom of expression is also limited if it includes advocacy of hatred on grounds of gender.[132]

On the content of equality, the Constitution of South Africa recognizes—unlike the Constitution of Nigeria—both formal and substantive equality. Section 9(1) provides for formal equality and reads: '[e]veryone is equal before the law and has the right to equal protection and benefit of the law.' Formal equality operates in very general circumstances and contexts and may not capture the specific needs or demands of individuals in different circumstances and contexts. While the recognition of this formal equality is indeed a big deal in situations where this was previously lacking, eg, in apartheid, it has limited capacity to truly enable everyone to have and access rights. This is particularly true for women who have faced ages of discrimination and

[125] ibid s 8(1) and (2).

[126] See Deeksha Bhana, 'The Horizontal Application of the Bill of Rights: A Reconciliation of Sections 8 and 39 of the Constitution' (2013) 29 South African Journal on Human Rights 2, 351–75.

[127] See Delisa Futch, 'Du Plessis v De Klerk: South Africa's Bill of Rights and the Issue of Horizontal Application' (1996) 22 NC J Int'l L & Com Reg 1009–33.

[128] South African Constitution, s 27(1) (a).

[129] Joan Small and Evadne Grant, 'Equality and Non-Discrimination in the South African Constitution' (2000) 4 International Journal of Discrimination and the Law 47.

[130] Emphasis added.

[131] Emphasis added.

[132] The constitution of South Africa, s 16(2)(c).

marginalization in all walks of life.[133] In recognition of this fact, the Constitution also recognizes substantive equality in section 9(2) as follows:

> [e]quality includes the full and equal enjoyment of all rights and freedoms. To promote the achievement of equality, legislative and other measures designed to protect or advance persons, or categories of persons, disadvantaged by unfair discrimination may be taken.

One example of this is the fact that the Constitution recognizes affirmative action as a mechanism of equalizing those who have suffered past discrimination and marginalization. Obviously, the provision of affirmative action can be a helpful constitutional tool for the advancement of women's rights and interests as disadvantaged groups. Furthermore, the Constitution prohibits direct or indirect unfair discrimination by either the state or any person on the grounds of— among others—'sex, gender, pregnancy, and marital status'.[134] On top of this, any discrimination based on these grounds is presumed to be unfair and the burden of proof is on the one who performed the discrimination to prove that it was fair.[135] The Constitution does not simply see sex and/or gender as potential grounds for discrimination, but it also takes into account the specific circumstances of women, such as those who are pregnant, married, unmarried, and widowed. The recognition of these diverse needs and contexts of women is of great importance in designing a women's rights regime.

In addition to equality, the Constitution of South Africa recognizes human dignity as both a foundational value and a right that have a huge impact in transforming the world of women from one of discrimination and marginalization to that of equal concern, respect, and rights. Within the biosphere of equality and human dignity, both as foundational values as well as substantive rights, women are entitled to enjoy the civil, political, economic, social, and cultural rights recognized in the Constitution, ranging from the right to life, reproductive health care, and education, to a clean and healthy environment.

Beyond the Bill of Rights, the Constitution also mainstreams the issue of gender in the composition of constitutional institutions. Perhaps most importantly, it established a constitutional commission on gender: the Commission for Gender Equality (CGE).[136] The CGE works for the attainment of gender equality through monitoring, investigating, researching, educating, and lobbying on matters concerning gender equality.[137] Moreover, all Chapter Nine institutions that are established to support constitutional democracy are required to consider gender in the appointment of their members.[138] Similarly, gender is a prominent consideration in the appointment of judicial officers.[139]

[133] Catherine Albertyn and Beth Goldblatt, 'Equality' in Stu Woolman and Michael Bishop (eds), *Constitutional Law of South Africa Vol 3* (Juta & Company Ltd 2012) 35-3-35-4.
[134] The Constitution of South Africa, s 9(3) and (4).
[135] ibid s 9(5).
[136] ibid s 181 (1) (d).
[137] ibid s 187.
[138] ibid s 193(2).
[139] ibid s 174(2).

Although the normative commitment in the Bill of Rights and the mainstreaming of gender in different constitutional institutions herald a robust protection of women's rights in South Africa, the recognition of the right to culture and religion pose some tensions to the liberal notions of women's rights as discussed above. For instance, as part of freedom of religion, the Constitution allows for the recognition of various personal and family laws from different religions and traditions, subject to the Constitution.[140] Similarly, the Constitution recognizes everyone's right to culture and the right to participate in the cultural life of one's community.[141] By the same token, not only are customary laws and the rights that emanate from those laws recognized,[142] but the institution of traditional authority in accordance with customary laws is also constitutionalized.[143] In addition to traditional authorities, courts are obligated to apply customary laws when applicable.[144]

Even though the Constitution allows for the application of customary laws only as subject to constitutional conformity, its practical application is much more complex than this. This complexity arises not only due to the nature of customary laws as such, but also due to the approach that South Africa takes regarding them. Unlike Nigeria, South Africa codifies customary laws, and this is usually referred to as 'official customary law'. Nonetheless, the customary law in the legislation is not always similar to the one that applies in practice, which is usually referred to as 'living customary law'. In order to properly illustrate women's rights to equality and non-discrimination under customary laws,[145] I will now briefly discuss the official customary laws on marriage and inheritance and proceed to examine how courts adjudicate these customary laws in light of the Constitution and legislative frameworks.

B. Official Customary Laws on Marriage and Inheritance

Unlike Nigeria, South Africa codifies some customary laws on marriage and inheritance; as such, customary laws on marriage and inheritance can be found in statutes. Nonetheless, the fact that customary laws are codified does not mean that the content of these laws is uncontested or settled. As judicial practice shows, and will be discussed below, there is some contestation between the nature and substance of customary laws as they exist in statutes and how they are practiced in society.[146] Bearing this in mind, I will explore some of these official customary laws on marriage and inheritance with the objective of examining women's rights to equality and non-discrimination under these laws.

[140] ibid s 15(3).
[141] ibid ss 30 and 31.
[142] ibid s 39(2) and (3).
[143] ibid s 211(1).
[144] ibid s 211(3).
[145] I focus on customary laws here as it is a dominant law with a broad application in South Africa unlike sharia law.
[146] See also TW Bennett, 'Re-Introducing African Customary Law to the South African Legal System' (2009) 57 The American Journal of Comparative Law 1, 10–12.

The Recognition of Customary Marriages Act (RCMA), in line with the constitutional commitment to ensuring equality, aims to ensure the equal status of women and men before, during, and after the conclusion of marriage, as well as upon its dissolution.[147] While it recognizes customary marriages concluded before the commencement of the RCMA, it provides essential validity requirements for the conclusion of marriage under customary laws after its commencement. Section 3(1) provides that:

> For a customary marriage entered into after the commencement of this act to be valid
> The prospective spouses—
> (a) Must be above the ages of 18 years; and
> (b) Must be both consent to be married to each other under customary law; and
> (c) The marriage must be negotiated and entered into or celebrated in accordance with customary law.

These requirements somewhat modified some of the customary laws of marriage in South Africa as the payment of *lobolo, a bride price,* is no longer deemed the essential requirement for the commencement of marriage.[148] The age restrictions as well as the requirement of spousal consent are also additions to the customary requirements of marriage.[149] Nonetheless, the third requirement that 'the marriage must be negotiated and entered into or celebrated in accordance with customary law' leave open many avenues for the application of numerous customary practices with respect to marriage;[150] and the diversity of these practices continues to make their precise ascertainment a difficult task. In this regard, the RCMA defines customary marriage simply as 'a marriage concluded in accordance with customary law',[151] and it defines customary law as 'the customs and usages traditionally observed among the indigenous African peoples of South Africa and which form part of the culture of those people'.[152] This legislative design brings what customary laws consider to be necessary requirements for the conclusion of marriage into contestation with the other RCMA requirements provided in section 3(1).

Although the RCMA requires the registration of customary marriages, it also states that failure to register will not affect its legal validity.[153] Unlike the position of the wife under customary law, which considers her as a perpetual minor under the power of her husband, the RCMA equalizes the wife with her husband with respect to status, property acquisition and disposal, or any other matter under customary law.[154] However, the RCMA maintains the practice of polygamy while trying to protect the interests and rights of women within it.[155] Finally, it introduces judicial divorce as the

[147] IP Maithufi and others (eds), *African Customary Law in South Africa* (Oxford University Press 2015) 91–92.
[148] TW Bennett, *Customary Law in South Africa* (Juta 2004) 234.
[149] Ann Skelton and others, *Family Law in South Africa* (Oxford University Press Southern Africa 2010) 180–84.
[150] Maithufi and others, *African Customary Law in South Africa* (n 147) 103–04.
[151] The Recognition of Customary Marriages Act of South Africa 1998, s 1.
[152] ibid.
[153] ibid s 4.
[154] ibid s 6.
[155] ibid s 7.

only mechanism for dissolving marriage under customary law, on the condition of its irretrievable breakdown.[156]

The overall objective of the RCMA is to tame the patriarchy that animates customary marriages by uplifting the low status and positions of women. Yet, while it does proclaim the equality of women and men in marriage, it also maintains some customary practices that adversely affect women's equality, such as polygamy and other customary practices necessary for the conclusion of the marriage. Setting aside the issue of whether the RCMA is really 'customary law', given its modifications of the substance of customary law and its mode of production, as it is an Act of Parliament, it maintains the constitutional ethos of both equality as well as the accommodation of cultural practices.[157] In this dual pursuit, women's rights remain the main subjects of contestation.

Like the RCMA does for marriage, the Reform of Customary Law of Succession and Regulation of Related Matters Act (RCLSA) regulates the customary laws on succession and inheritance.[158] Similar to the customary laws of inheritance in Nigeria, the rule of male primogeniture has been the dominant customary law in South Africa.[159] The eldest son—to the exclusion of the female family members and younger males—succeeds the status of the deceased father and inherits his property as the new family head. Even when women are allowed to inherit the deceased's property, they only inherit the domestic utensils and other goods used by females, while men inherit all the cattle and other property used by males.[160] With the objective of protecting widows and children born outside of customary marriages in cases of intestate succession, as well as to reconcile the rule of male primogeniture with the constitutional notions of equality and human dignity,[161] the RCLSA considers widows of customary marriages and children of the deceased— regardless of sex, age, gender, and status—to be heirs.[162] Thus, the RCLSA fundamentally transformed the African customary laws of inheritance in South Africa. The big question is whether the customary laws on marriage and inheritance as codified in the RCMA and RCLSA are also the customary laws that are applied in the everyday life of society in South Africa. For further insight and nuance on this, I now turn to judicial practice.

C. Judicial Practice

The Constitution already establishes a syncretic approach to women's rights in South Africa. On the one hand, it recognizes the liberal notion of rights based on the values of equality, human dignity, and freedom, yet on the other hand, it incorporates the indigenous notion of rights rooted in the cultural milieu of Africans in South Africa—all

[156] ibid s 8(1).

[157] Maithufi and others, *African Customary Law in South Africa* (n 147) 100.

[158] ibid 176.

[159] Bennett, *Customary Law in South Africa* (n 148) 334–45.

[160] Maithufi and others, *African Customary Law in South Africa* (n 147) 165.

[161] The Reform of Customary Law of Succession and Regulation of Related Matters Act of South Africa 2009, preamble.

[162] ibid ss 2, 3, and 4.

in the same constitutional space. While the official customary law is mainly equality-friendly, it still accommodates some cultural practices that are incompatible with the liberal notion of equality, such as polygamy which only entitles men to have more than one spouse. Judicial practice regarding customary law offers additional insight into not only its nature, substance, and application, but also its relation to women's rights in line with the ethos of the Constitution. Despite the contestations between official and living customary laws, judicial practice further entrenches the syncretic theory of women's rights in South Africa.[163]

The Constitutional Court of South Africa (CC) authoritatively described the status, nature, and application of customary law in the case of *Alexkor Ltd and Another v Richtersveld Community and Others*.[164] In this case, the CC recognized customary law on its own terms in light of the Constitution. The CC captured the essence of customary law in democratic South Africa as follows:

> [. . .] the Constitution acknowledges the originality and distinctiveness of indigenous law [customary law] as an independent source of norms within the legal system. At the same time the Constitution, while giving force to indigenous law, makes it clear that such law is subject to the Constitution and has to be interpreted in the light of its values. Furthermore, like the common law, indigenous law is subject to any legislation, consistent with the Constitution, that specifically deals with it. In the result, indigenous law feeds into, nourishes, fuses with and becomes part of the amalgam of South African law.[165]
>
> . . .
>
> In applying indigenous law, it is important to bear in mind that, unlike common law, indigenous law is not written. It is a system of law that was known to the community, practiced and passed on from generation to generation. It is a system of law that has its own values and norms. Throughout its history it has evolved and developed to meet the changing needs of the community. And it will continue to evolve within the context of its values and norms consistently with the Constitution.[166]

This judicial pronouncement reinforces the constitutional vision of integrating, fusing, and reconfiguring customary laws with constitutional law and vice versa for a transformative South Africa.

Accordingly, women's rights are in a continuum of contestation and fusion between the liberal vision of rights and the cultural account of rights—whose exact content is determined by the courts.[167] As discussed below, the constitutionality test for the application of customary law is not a silver bullet that solves all the incongruences

[163] See also Lee Stone, 'Two Decades of Jurisprudence on Substantive Gender Equality: What the Constitutional Court Got Right and Wrong' (2016) 30 Agenda: Empowering Women for Gender Equity 10, 12–13.

[164] *Alexkor Ltd and Another v Richtersveld Community and Others*.

[165] ibid para 51.

[166] ibid para 53.

[167] See also the Traditional Courts Bill of South Africa 2016 and the Traditional Leadership Bill of South Africa 2015 For instance, for the impact of the traditional Courts Bill see Jennifer Williams and Judith Klusener, 'The Traditional Courts Bill: A Woman's Perspective' (2013) 29 South African Journal on Human Rights 2, 276–93.

between the liberal notion of rights and the cultural one; rather there is a normative constitutional commitment to keeping these incongruences alive which the courts then maintain in their adjudication.[168] As a result, the decision whether to have a statutory law about customary law, ie, official customary law, or to rely on the practical experiences of people in different times and places, ie, living customary law, will always be a question of technicality and efficacy. This is because both official and living customary laws are permeated by the legally syncretic vision of the Constitution. In recognition of this fact, courts apply both official and living customary laws when it comes to women's rights, depending on the circumstances. In the following paragraphs, I discuss some of the landmark cases of the CC concerning women's rights to inheritance, succession to chieftainship, and polygamy.

In the case of *Bhe and Others v The Magistrate, Khayelitsha and Others,*[169] considered with *Shibi v Sithole and Others* and *South African Human Rights Commission and Another v President of the Republic of South Africa and Another,* the constitutionality of the customary law of male primogeniture[170] and Section 23 of the Black Administration Act 38 of 1927[171] were at issue. The high courts that saw the cases of *Bhe* and *Shibi* declared these laws as unconstitutional and sent it to the CC for confirmation. The *South African Human Rights Commission and Another* joined these cases at the CC in the public interest of all women and children who are denied their right of inheritance under these laws. In the *Bhe* case, the two daughters of the deceased were prevented from inheriting their father's estate, and in the *Shibi* case, the sister was prevented from inheriting her deceased brother's estate. The reason was that both the Black Administration Act of 1927 and the customary law of male primogeniture did not recognize women's right of inheritance. While Section 23 of the former provides succession to women according to 'black law and custom' in the majority of instances, including in cases such as these, the latter only allows men to inherit the status and property of the deceased. Both the official and living customary laws on this issue were found to be incompatible with the constitutional vision of human dignity and equality.[172] Consequently, the CC found them both to be unconstitutional and ordered the application of the Intestate Succession Act until the legislature would take action.[173]

Both the development of customary law and the recognition of living customary law were found to be unnecessary in this case as the CC considered that the rule of male primogeniture was the essential element of the customary law of inheritance and it did not have sufficient information and evidence to ascertain the content of living customary law on this issue.[174] The solution was, therefore, to substitute the common law rule of inheritance, ie, the Intestate Succession Act, in lieu of customary law so as

[168] Thandabantu Nhlapo, 'Customary Law in Post-Apartheid South Africa: Constitutional Confrontations in Culture, Gender and "Living Law"' (2017) 33 South African Journal on Human Rights 1, 1–24.

[169] *Bhe and Others v Khayelitsha Magistrate and Others* (CCT 49/03) [2004] ZACC 17; 2005 (1) SA 580 (CC); 2005 (1) BCLR 1 (CC).

[170] This was the living customary law.

[171] This was official customary law.

[172] *Bhe and Others v Khayelitsha Magistrate and Others,* para 100.

[173] ibid para 117.

[174] ibid para 109.

to ensure human dignity and equality.[175] Following the vision of the CC, the legislature later enacted the RCLSA, as discussed above, in order to regulate the customary law of succession by enshrining the values of liberal equality into it.

Nonetheless, the dynamism and flexibility of customary laws continue to present challenges to the official version of customary law. The case of *Shilubana and Others v Nwamitwa*[176] is an excellent example which shows how statutory customary law, ie official customary law, and living customary law diverge and pose challenges for the ascertainment of customary law at any given time and place. In this case, Ms. Shilubana was not allowed to succeed her father as *Hosi* (chief), despite being the eldest child, as women were not allowed to be *Hosi* under the customary law of the time. Accordingly, her father's brother, Richard Nwamitwa, became *Hosi*. Following the democratic transition in South Africa, the traditional authorities in the community adopted a resolution to the succession of *Hosi* based on the equality of women and men, and, consequently, installed Ms. Shilubana as *Hosi* as a successor to Richard Nwamitwa. However, Nwamitwa's eldest son claimed that he was the rightful successor to his father and the traditional authorities acted illegally by installing Ms. Shilubana as *Hosi*. Both the High Court and the Supreme Court of Appeal decided in his favor by noting that the traditional authorities acted illegally in changing the customary laws of succession. The CC, however, reversed the decision and noted that:

> [...] where there is a dispute over the legal position under customary law, a court must consider both the traditions and the present practice of the community. If development happens within the community, the court must strive to recognise and give effect to that development, to the extent consistent with adequately upholding the protection of rights. In addition, the imperative of section 39(2) must be acted on when necessary, and deference should be paid to the development by a customary community of its own laws and customs where this is possible, consistent with the continuing effective operation of the law.[177]
>
> Customary law must be permitted to develop, and the enquiry must be rooted in the contemporary practice of the community in question. Section 211(2) of the Constitution requires this. The legal status of customary law norms cannot depend simply on their having been consistently applied in the past, because that is a test which any new development must necessarily fail. Development implies some departure from past practice. A rule that requires absolute consistency with past practice before a court will recognise the existence of a customary norm would therefore prevent the recognition of new developments as customary law. This would result in the courts applying laws which communities themselves no longer follow, and would stifle the recognition of the new rules adopted by the communities in response to the changing face of South African society. This result would be contrary to the Constitution and cannot be accepted.[178]

[175] Rita Ozoemena, 'Living Customary Law: A Truly Transformative Tool?' (2016) 6 Constitutioanal Court Review 147, 149.

[176] *Shilubana and Others v Nwamitwa* [2009] (2) SA 66 (CC).

[177] ibid para 49.

[178] ibid para 55.

This case of *Shilubana* sheds light on the treatment of official and living customary law by the courts and how the essential factor in considering both official or living customary law is the existence of syncretism which advances the constitutional vision. In this case, living customary law on succession to chieftainship prevailed over official customary law because the former converged with the constitutional ethos of equality.

In the case of *Mayelane v Ngwenyama and Another*,[179] however, as neither the official customary law nor the living customary law was helpful, the CC had to develop the customary law on its own in order to adjudicate on the issues before it. The issue in *Mayelane* was whether the consent of the first wife was necessary for the conclusion of a second marriage under customary law. As the RCMA is silent on this issue—it only deals with the consent of the contracting spouses—the CC resorted to investigating living customary law. Unable to find a uniform practice surrounding this issue, the CC developed the rule of consent of the first wife for the conclusion of subsequent customary marriages.[180] The CC argued that a subsequent marriage without the consent of the first wife is against the equality and human dignity envisioned in the Constitution.[181] It particularly states that:

> [. . .] where subsequent customary marriages are entered into without the knowledge or consent of the first wife, she is unable to consider or protect her own position. She cannot take an informed decision on her personal life, her sexual or reproductive health, or on the possibly adverse proprietary consequences of a subsequent customary marriage. Any notion of the first wife's equality with her husband would be completely undermined if he were able to introduce a new marriage partner to their domestic life without her consent . . .[182] Given that marriage is a highly personal and private contract, it would be a blatant intrusion on the dignity of one partner to introduce a new member to that union without obtaining that partner's consent.[183]

Even if the CC considers polygamy under customary laws subject to the consent of the first wife with the objective of protecting her equality and human dignity, it does not substantively deal with the compatibility of polygamy with women's rights to equality and human dignity; it prefers to continue to work within the ambit of polygamy.[184] Surely, the arguments made for the introduction of consent of the first wife can be deployed to challenge polygamy itself, or to extend it to women as well so that they can have more than one husband. Nonetheless, as the Constitution enshrines a syncretic theory of women's rights, the practice of polygamy continues to be tolerated by the CC.

Thus, the constitutional design of women's rights and subsequent judicial practice in South Africa—just like in Nigeria—show that women's rights are enshrined within the spectrum of both the liberal notion of rights and rights rooted in the African cultural milieu. And within this spectrum, courts give content and substance to women's

179 *Mayelane v Ngwenyama and Another* (CCT 57/12) [2013] ZACC 14; 2013 (4) SA 415 (CC); 2013 (8) BCLR 918 (CC).

180 ibid para 75.

181 ibid para 71.

182 ibid para 72.

183 ibid para 74.

184 ibid para 70.

rights. Following the syncretic design of rights in the Constitution, courts give it life through recognition and interpretation of customary laws in light of the Constitution. In this judicial process—unlike Nigeria which opts for a more symbiotic relationship between the rights rooted in Islamic law and those found in liberalism—fusion, integration, rejection, convergence, and innovation between the liberal and African accounts of rights inform women's rights in South Africa. While much of the syncretism happens *from above*, ie, constitutional design and judicial practice from apex courts, just like in Nigeria, there is also syncretism *from below*, and the case of *Shilubana* is a fine example of the latter. In syncretism *from below*, the local community is the main driver of change and transformation of the customary towards the liberal notion of equality between women and men.

IV. Women's Constitutional Rights in Ethiopia

Women's rights under the Constitution of Ethiopia are syncretic by design and practice. The Constitution recognizes women's rights as human and democratic rights in themselves. Within the framework of equality and non-discrimination, the Constitution recognizes all generations of human rights without any distinction. In addition to the Bill of Rights, the Constitution incorporates the idea of women's equality in its Preamble and the DPSP. At the same time, it recognizes the right to culture and religion as well as the application of customary and religious laws with regard to family and personal matters upon the consent of all parties. Even if the constitutional review system in Ethiopia is different from those in Nigeria and South Africa, the House of Federation (HoF) still determines the syncretic outcomes of women's rights. An examination of the constitutional design of women's rights and the constitutional review practice shows that women's rights in Ethiopia are configured through syncretism that combines the liberal notion of rights and the notion of rights as they manifest themselves in cultural and religious practices. The result is the transformation of both the liberal and cultural accounts of rights of women's constitutional rights. Following a similar approach as with Nigeria and South Africa, this section explores and examines the constitutional design of women's rights, Sharia and customary laws regarding marriage and inheritance, and, finally, actual judicial practice pertaining to women's rights as it relates to these laws. The objective of this exploration is to demonstrate how legal syncretism informs both the design and practice of women's constitutional rights in Ethiopia.

A. Constitutional Design

The Constitution of Ethiopia is quite generous in its recognition of women's rights. It incorporates the conception of women's rights as found both under the International Bill of Human Rights as well as CEDAW. Nonetheless, the Constitution sees the recognition and enforcement of human rights, including women's rights, as merely a means for fulfilling of a 'larger objective': the realization of the right to self-determination for Nations, Nationalities and Peoples (NNPs) within one economic and political community.[185] As discussed in Chapter 4, the primary goal of the Constitution is to ensure the right to self-determination of ethnic groups and not the individual rights and liberties of their members.[186] Against this socialist backdrop, the Constitution recognizes the rights of women in numerous ways, ranging from making equality and non-discrimination based on sex a constitutional aspiration, to the substantive formulation of women's rights as 'democratic rights', to the recognition of women's participation in the economic and social development endeavors of the state. The Constitution presents women right upfront as equal human beings and citizens.

Not only does the Constitution recognize the indivisibility and interdependence of rights by according similar treatment to civil, political, economic, social, and developmental rights, it also makes a case for the horizontal application of human rights. The recognition of the indivisibility and interdependence of human rights is of great importance to women as it brings their worlds and spaces to the attention of the state. Furthermore, their horizontal application can shield women from oppression and discrimination in the private sphere as well. Indeed, the Bill of Rights Chapter imposes a human rights duty onto state organs at both the federal and state levels, thereby establishing the vertical application of human rights.[187] However, the chapter on the Fundamental Principles of the Constitution goes even further, making it compulsory for all physical and juristic persons to obey and enforce the Constitution. Article 9(2) provides that '[a]ll citizens, organs of state, political organizations, other associations as well as their officials have the duty to ensure observance of the Constitution and to obey it'. Hence, this provision imposes both a vertical and horizontal duty for everyone to ensure the enforcement of the Bill of Rights.[188] As a result, women can claim their constitutional rights both in the public and private spheres.

In addition, the Constitution makes the interpretation of the Bill of Rights, including women's rights, in light of various international human rights instruments.[189] Article 13(2) states that '[t]he fundamental rights and freedoms specified in this Chapter shall be interpreted in a manner conforming to the principles of the Universal Declaration of Human Rights, International Covenants on Human Rights and international instruments adopted by Ethiopia'. A combined reading of Article 13(2) and Article 9(4)—which makes ratified international agreements an integral part of Ethiopian law—provides human rights with special protected status under the Constitution.[190] Accordingly, the interpretation of women's rights in Ethiopia must be

[185] The Constitution of the Federal Democratic Republic of Ethiopia, preamble.

[186] Alem Habtu, 'Ethnic Pluralism as an Organizing Principle of the Ethiopian Federation' (2004) 28 Dialectical Anthropology 2, 92.

[187] The Constitution of the Federal Democratic Republic of Ethiopia, art 13(1).

[188] Adem Kassie Abebe, 'Human Rights under the Ethiopian Constitution: A Descriptive Overview' (2011) 5 Mizan Law Review 1, 45–46.

[189] See Theresa Rouger, 'The Impact of International Human Rights Law on the National Laws of Ethiopia from a Gender Rights and Disability Rights Perspective' in Malcolm Maclachlan and Leslie Swartz, *Disability & International Development* (Springer 2009) 31–49.

[190] Ibrahim Idris, 'The place of International Human Rights Conventions in the 1994 Federal Democratic Republic of Ethiopia Constitution' (2000) 20 Journal of Ethiopian Law 113. Although the status of international instruments under the Ethiopian Constitution is a subject of debate, in *Miss Tsedale Demissie v Mr Kifle Demissie* [2007] Federal Supreme Court Cassation Division, File 23632, Judgment 6 November 2007, the Federal Supreme Court applied the Convention on the Rights of the Child to protect the child's best interest.

in line with international human rights standards, such as those of CEDAW. This enables the channeling and mainstreaming of women's human rights in the application and interpretation of women's constitutional rights.

Within these enabling normative designs, in addition to recognizing the rights to equality and non-discrimination on grounds of sex,[191] the Constitution recognizes some special rights of women.[192] Under the article on women's rights, the Constitution reiterates the formal equality of women and men in the enjoyment of rights and available protections, the equality of women and men in marriage, the right to maternity leave with full pay, and the right to access family planning services.[193] Furthermore, it recognizes the rights of women to full consultation concerning national development programs, the right to property, and the right to employment on the basis of equality with men.[194] These women's rights can already be found in the provisions dealing with the right to property,[195] the right to labor,[196] and the right to development,[197] so their restatement under the article on women's rights seems to emphasize their relevance for women and shows appreciation for the outstanding quests of women in these fields. Additionally, in its bid to enforce women's rights, the Constitution also prohibits customs and practices that oppress or harm women.[198]

Furthermore, in order to create an enabling condition for women to enjoy their rights, the Constitution provides women the right to affirmative action. In this respect, article 35(3) stipulates that:

> The historical legacy of inequality and discrimination suffered by women in Ethiopia taken into account, women, in order to remedy this legacy, are entitled to affirmative measures. The purpose of such measures shall be to provide special attention to women so as to enable them to compete and participate on the basis of equality with men in political, social and economic life as well as in *public* and *private* institutions.[199]

With a particular emphasis on equality, non-discrimination, and special women's rights including affirmative action, the Constitution spreads the idea of women's rights over the entire Bill of Rights as well as the economic objectives of the DPSP. By doing so, the Constitution incorporates the liberal notion of women's rights in Ethiopia.

However, like in Nigeria and South Africa, the liberal notion of rights in Ethiopia is also configured with the notion of rights rooted in religion and custom. In addition to the recognition of freedom of religion[200] and the right to culture,[201] the Constitution specifically allows for the application of religious and customary laws with regard to personal and family matters, and for the establishment of religious and customary

[191] The Constitution of the Federal Democratic Republic of Ethiopia, art 25.
[192] ibid art 35.
[193] ibid art 35(1), (2), (5), and (9); see also art 34(1).
[194] ibid art 35(6), (7), and (8).
[195] ibid art 40(1).
[196] ibid art 42(1)(d).
[197] ibid art 43(2).
[198] ibid art 35(4).
[199] Emphasis added.
[200] The Constitution of the Federal Democratic Republic of Ethiopia, art 27.
[201] ibid arts 41(9) and 39(2).

courts.[202] As noted at the beginning of this chapter, while religious and customary laws offer potential spaces and forums for the implementation of women's rights, there are well-known practices that are incompatible with the liberal notion of rights.[203] In order to ascertain the notion of rights rooted in religious and customary laws, I will now briefly discuss these laws on marriage and inheritance as they relate to women.

B. Islamic and Customary Laws on Marriage and Inheritance

Following the constitutional recognition of the application of religious law regarding personal and family matters, Parliament enacted a proclamation that consolidated the jurisdictions of the federal Sharia courts.[204] In addition to regulating the appointment and operation of Sharia courts by the states, this proclamation further introduced a syncretic form of law to be applied in these courts. On the one hand, the proclamation authorized the application of Islamic law on matters related to marriage, family relationships, and inheritance, among other personal and family matters.[205] On the other hand, it obliged Sharia courts to apply general civil procedure law.[206] Although the application of Islamic law is subject to constitutional conformity, Ethiopia does not adopt a specific Islamic school of law—unlike Nigeria—and Sharia judges are at liberty to apply the law of the Islamic school they are familiar with, or choose. In this regard, while the Shafi'I school is predominant in Ethiopia, followers of the Hanafi and Maliki schools can also found.[207] As a result, identifying the applicable substantive Islamic law for any given time and case is extremely difficult.

Although the different Islamic schools in Ethiopia have variations in their applications and interpretations of Islamic law, they have some common approaches towards marriage and inheritance. For example, there are some essential requirements for a valid conclusion of Islamic marriage that all schools in Ethiopia recognize. For instance: while the consent of the woman is requested, her guardian can marry her off even without her consent, while the consent of the man is a mandatory requirement;[208] although there is no consensus on the marriageable age, puberty is considered as a manifestation of capacity for a woman to marry;[209] the payment of a dowry (*mahr*) by the man to the woman is required for the conclusion of Islamic marriage;[210] once the marriage is concluded, the husband assumes the obligation to support the wife and children, while the wife has no such obligation even if she is rich;[211] after the first marriage, the husband can marry two, three or four wives while the wife

[202] ibid arts 34(4), (5), and 78(5).

[203] See also Gemma Lucy Burgess, 'When the Personal Becomes Political: Using Legal Reform to Combat Violence against Women in Ethiopia' (2012) 19 Gender, Place & Culture 153, 163–64.

[204] There are sharia courts at the federal and regional levels consisting of first instance, high, and supreme sharia courts.

[205] Federal Courts of Sharia Consolidation Proclamation of Ethiopia 1999, art 4.

[206] ibid art 6.

[207] See J Spencer Trimingham, *Islam in Ethiopia* (Oxford University Press 1952) 232–33.

[208] Abdulmalik Abubaker, Islamic Law (Ethiopian Justice and Legal Systems Institute 2009) 25.

[209] ibid 30–32.

[210] ibid 30.

[211] ibid 37.

cannot marry again;[212] if the husband wants to end the marriage, he can use *talaq*, but the wife has to use *khul*, or they can terminate the marriage through *mubarh* (mutual consent).[213] Regarding inheritance, Islamic law provides the right of inheritance to both women and men—albeit with different shares. While a wife can inherit a fourth of her deceased husband's estate, a husband can inherit half of his deceased wife's estate. Similarly, women and girls are only entitled to half the share of inheritance that men and boys are entitled to.[214]

Unlike with Sharia courts, Parliament did not enact a law for the operation and establishment of customary courts that apply customary laws. As the Constitution conditioned the application of religious and customary laws upon the future enactment of statutory laws that would grant them authority, the continued absence of any enabling law in this regard means that there is still no practical official recognition to customary laws. Despite this, however, customary laws continue to apply in Ethiopia—in real, everyday life—even beyond what is constitutionally permissible.[215] Although there are numerous customary laws on marriage and inheritance in Ethiopia, patriarchy is a common theme that runs across all these laws:[216] women are not considered as equal partners in marriage and are often discriminated against in inheritance.[217] Despite many improvements in recent years, early and forced marriage are routine practices in rural Ethiopia, and polygamy and widow inheritance are still the prevailing customary practices among the Afar, Oromo, Somali, and other ethnic groups.[218]

Under typical customary law in Ethiopia, marriage is a family affair and is concluded with the consent and agreement of the two families. Nonetheless, the consent of the man is usually given due consideration, unlike that of the woman. While the consent of the woman is requested, it is not always essential for the conclusion of the marriage, and marriage against the express will of the girl, or even through abduction, is also practiced in some places.[219] Once the marriage is concluded, there are a set of gender roles that the spouses have to perform, with the husband being the head of the family and assuming huge decision-making power.[220] By the same token, given

[212] ibid 34–35.

[213] ibid 41–49.

[214] ibid 85–88.

[215] Dolores A Donovan and Getachew Assefa, 'Homicide in Ethiopia: Human Rights, Federalism, and Legal Pluralism' (2003) 51 The American Journal of Comparative Law 505; Exploring how different customary laws are applicable in the domain of criminal law.

[216] Seyoum Worku Telila, '"Irra Dhaaba": A Customary Marriage among the Gelan Oromo of Caaffee Tumaa in Ada'a Disrict, East Shewa, Ethiopia' (Master Thesis, Addis Ababa University 2016).

[217] Meaza Ashenafi and Zenebeworke Tadesse, 'Women, HIV/AIDS, Property and Inheritance Rights: The Case of Ethiopia' (UNDP 2005) 23–24.

[218] For instance see Tilahun Seyoum, 'Widow Inheritance and Women's Rights: The Case of the Boro-Shinasha in Bullen Woreda, Benishangule Gumuz Regional State' (Master Thesis, Addis Ababa University 2015).

[219] Gemechu Beyene, 'Marriage Practices Among The Gidda Oromo, Northern Wollega, Ethiopia' (2006) 15 Nordic Journal of African Studies 240, 250–51.

[220] Nasser B Ebrahim and Madhu S Atteraya, 'Women's Decision-Making Autonomy and Their Attitude towards Wife-Beating: Findings from the 2011 Ethiopia's Demographic and Health Survey' (2018) 20 Journal of Immigrant and Minority Health 3, 603–11; Eshetu Gurmu and Senait Endale, 'Wife Beating Refusal among Women of Reproductive Age in Urban and Rural Ethiopia' (2017) 17 BMC International Health and Human Rights 6, 1–12.

the social structure and the role and position of women,[221] the customary inheritance practices also perpetuate discriminatory practices against women.[222] For example, since women move out of their families and join the families of their husbands—unlike men who stay with their own families—they are viewed with suspicion with respect to property allocation and inheritance.[223] Due to their continued physical proximity and higher role in society, men are considered to be 'genuine' family members with much more access to family property, including land, while women are seen with suspicion by both their families as well as their husbands' families, and, consequently, are left with limited access to property, including in inheritance.[224]

Hence, the recognition of both the liberal notion of women's rights and Islamic and customary laws in the same constitutional space heralded the establishment of a syncretic women's rights regime. Even if Islamic and customary laws are applicable only subject to the Constitution, determining the constitutionality of Islamic and customary laws related to marriage and inheritance is not an easy task. Furthermore, when the Constitution recognizes these laws, it opens accommodative spaces for them in the constitutional order; the question is what type of accommodation is constitutionally permissible, and what type is not. The above description of women's rights as rooted in both the liberal tradition and Islamic and customary laws only provides the normative framework, but its actual application can only be determined through an investigation of actual judicial practice with regard to these issues.

C. Judicial Practice

The HoF has decided some cases on issues related to the syncretic regime of women's rights. As these cases demonstrate, the HoF gives effect to this syncretic nature of women's rights. In the case of *Kedija Bashir*,[225] the HoF reversed the decisions of the Sharia courts, as well as the Federal Supreme Court, based on preliminary objections rather than on substantive merits with the intention of protecting the rights of women. In this case, the inheritance of a house that belonged to an alleged common grandfather was at issue.[226] When the applicants instituted a claim against the defendants in a Sharia court, the defendants submitted a preliminary objection that they did not consent to the jurisdiction of the Sharia court. While article 34(5) of the Constitution clearly provides for the consent of all parties as an essential requirement for setting the

221 Jeylan W Hussein, 'A Cultural Representation of Women in the Oromo Society' (2004) 25 African Study Monographs 3, 103–47.

222 Burgess, When the Personal Becomes Political' (n 203) 158.

223 Kuma Beyene Fita, 'The Inheritance Rights of Women: The Case of Yaa"aa Yaaboo" Customary Court in Ambo' (Master Thesis, Addis Ababa University 2017).

224 See also Åsa Torkelsson and Bekele Tassew, 'Quantifying Women's and Men's Rural Resource Portfolios—Empirical Evidence from Western Shoa in Ethiopia' (2008) 20 The European Journal of Development Research 3, 462–81.

225 Kedija Bashir case [2004] the House of Federation of FDRE (May 2008), 1 Journal of Constitutional Decisions 35–41.

226 Girmachew Alemu Aneme, 'Ethiopia: Legal and Judicial Plurality and the Incorporation of Traditional Dispute Resolution Mechanisms within the State Justice System' in Matthias Kötter and others (eds), *Non-State Justice Institutions and the Law: Decision-Making at the Interface of Tradition, Religion and the State* (Palgrave Macmillan 2015) 95.

Sharia courts in motion, the proclamation for the consolidation of Sharia courts was not yet in force at the time of the application, and based on this reasoning, the court dismissed the preliminary objection and went on to rule on the merits. The reason why the defendants, who were women, did not want to consent is because they knew that litigation based on Sharia law would put them at a disadvantageous and unequal position. As the defendants feared, the Sharia court decided based on Sharia law and they were unhappy with the decision and appealed to the Federal Supreme Court. But the Federal Supreme Court also confirmed the decision of the Sharia court. The Ethiopian Women Lawyers Association filed an application to the HoF challenging the constitutionality of the decision. The HoF reversed the decision, arguing that Sharia courts do not have jurisdiction without the consent of the parties;[227] as the defendants did not want to litigate in Sharia courts, the courts should have simply followed Article 34(5) of the Constitution even though the aforementioned proclamation was not in force at the time of application. However, the HoF did not examine the compatibility of the decision with constitutional standards. Its failure to engage with the merits of the case may either be due to strategy, or simply presumption of compatibility with the constitutional framework had the litigation been based on consent. Either way, this decision by the HoF reinforces the syncretic philosophy of rights in Ethiopia.

In contrast, in the case of *Halima Mehamed v Adem Abdi*,[228] the HoF did focus on the substance of the case in order to defend the rights of women. As noted above, although the Constitution provides for the application of customary law, it did not yet enact legislation that would enable its application. In this case, Adem Abdi inherited Halima Mehamed and her property through the customary practice of widow inheritance. Accordingly, Adem Abdi possessed the land that Halima Mehamed and her three children inherited from her deceased husband as common property, while he also possessed other land that he had acquired through his other marriage. Halima Mehamed, on behalf of herself and her children, instituted a suit against Adem Abdi. While the lower and higher courts of the regional state of Oromia decided in her favor, arguing that the land belonged to them as it was private property gained through inheritance before her second marriage to Adem Abdi, the Oromia Supreme Court reversed the decision of the lower courts on the grounds that rural land cannot be considered as private property gained before marriage. Consequently, the Oromia Supreme Court decided that the husband had a right to share half of the land, in addition to retaining the possession of the other land that he already had through the other marriage. The HoF then reversed this decision, noting that women have the right to equality with men in marriage in accordance with article 35(2), and also have the right to acquire, control, and administer property—including land—in accordance with Article 35(7). As the contested land was acquired before marriage through inheritance, it was a personal possession and the husband had no right to share this personal property.[229] Although the HoF's decision secures the women's right to property, it also alludes to

[227] See also *Raniya Ahmed Ibrahim v Dr Ibrahim Mohamed Hasen* [2008] House of Federation /2/160 (2008) where the HoF found that the decision of the sharia courts unconstitutional for lack of adequate consent.

[228] *Halima Mehamed v Adem Abdi* [2007] House of Federation /5/163/ (2007).

[229] ibid 3.

confirm the constitutionality of widow inheritance and bigamy within which the case was situated. As a result, this decision mainstreamed the liberal notion of rights while also maintaining some notions of rights rooted in customary laws.

Thus, like in Nigeria and South Africa, women's constitutional rights in Ethiopia are syncretic. Constitutional practice in this respect unfolds towards the fusion and transformation of the religious and customary-based rights along with rights rooted in liberalism, and, consequently, the former is assimilated into the liberal tenet of the Constitution. Such syncretism predominantly comes *from above,* and the HoF plays a crucial role in this respect. As in Nigeria and South Africa, the Constitution of Ethiopia establishes a syncretic constitutional adjudication system that further complicates the practice of constitutional rights rather than issuing simple declarations of (un)constitutionality simply because Islamic and customary laws are incompatible with the liberal half of the Constitution.

V. Conclusion

As is evident from the preceding discussion, women's constitutional rights in Nigeria, South Africa, and Ethiopia are the result of legal syncretism. However, the syncretic nature of women's rights does not come in a single form or shape. For instance, while there is a general blend and transformation of women's rights rooted in both the liberal and customary systems in all three countries, there is more of a symbiotic relationship between women's rights rooted in the liberal tradition and Islamic law in Nigeria. Furthermore, beyond the constitutional design, the syncretism between women's rights rooted in the liberal tradition and customary laws comes mainly *from above*, that is from apex judicial or quasi-judicial organs. However, such syncretism can also arise *from below,* as the South African experience demonstrates.

Despite these different forms of syncretism, the women's rights regimes in these countries share the liberal notion of women's rights as incorporated in international human (and/or women's) rights instruments, but also diverge from them somewhat, as they include the notion of rights rooted in customary and religious laws. Precisely because these women's rights regimes are syncretic, the universalist ambitions and supremacy of these countries' constitutions do not override any particular conception of women's rights simply because they are incompatible with the liberal notion of rights. They establish a jurisgenerative approach—an approach which will be further explored in the following chapter—to the design and practice of women's rights.[230] The result is the creation of spaces and interactions for the enforcement of women's rights in multiple, overlapping, and contestable avenues through creative procedural innovation and normative commitments to syncretism.[231]

[230] See Robert M Cover, 'The Supreme Court, 1982 Term—Foreword: Nomos and Narrative' (1983) 97 Harvard Law Review 4, 4–68. For a detail account of jurisgenerative constitutionalism in Africa see Berihun Adugna Gebeye, 'Global Constitutionalism and Cultural Diversity: The Emergence of Jurisgenerative Constitutionalism in Africa' (2020) Global Constitutionalism, 1–32.

[231] See also Paul Schiff Berman, 'Jurisgenerative Constitutionalism: Procedural Principles for Managing Global Legal Pluralism' (2013) 20 Indiana Journal of Global Legal Studies 665, 668–69.

However, it does not mean that the syncretic constitutional approach to women's rights and the concomitant jurisgenerative approach to women's rights adjudication offer the best protection to women. It merely means that the women's rights regimes are the results of conscious acts of acceptance, rejection, and reinterpretation of both the liberal and indigenous notions of rights within a constitutional space. Surely, this type of constitutional designs and practices offer better options to women than what either the universalists or cultural relativists prescribe. However, as the case studies here demonstrate, the optimal service of legal syncretism for women is contingent upon several considerations at any given time and place.

PART III
FUTURE APPLICATION

7

The Future of African Constitutional Design and Practice

So far, I have presented how the unique constellation of international law, colonial laws, African indigenous laws, and liberal constitutional norms have transformed African constitutionalism from precolonial times to the present and undergird the attendant syncretic constitutional designs and practices with a particular focus on federalism, the executive, and women's constitutional rights. It is clear from the discussion that there is a mismatch between what African constitutionalism actually is and what scholars and policymakers consider it to be. Improving the designs and practices of African constitutionalism, as noted in Chapter 1, rests on a clear understanding of its true nature, texture, and structure. Not only does legal syncretism offer us a new perspective for understanding the nature and structure of African constitutionalism, but it also supplies us with the theoretical and practical tools for its diagnosis, improvement, and consolidation. Building on the theses and analyses of the previous chapters, this chapter attempts to bring the elements of legal syncretism to the attention of future African constitutional designs and practices. With this objective, the first section discusses why African constitutional design should take sovereignty seriously and underscores why sovereignty is—and must be—an important aspect of any African constitutional theory. The second section presents some of the major limits or shortcomings of postcolonial constitutional reforms and draws attention to possible future constitutional reform areas. The third and final section highlights the potential of an aspect of African constitutional design and practice that can mediate and operationalize the practice and application of plural constitutional values—something that future constitutional designs and practices should attempt to consolidate.

I. Taking Sovereignty Seriously in Constitutional Design

The idea of a state being externally immune from interference and internally autonomous in its course of action permeates conventional constitutional theory.[1] This is precisely why founding moments that give birth to states, and the idea of 'we the people' that inaugurates states, hold huge significance and play important roles both in constitutional theory and practice as well as in the popular imagination.[2] Despite the contestations around the nature and structure of the constitution-making power

[1] Martin Loughlin, *Foundations of Public Law* (Oxford University Press 2012) 208; Martin Loughlin, 'The State: Conditio Sine qua Non' (2018) 16 International Journal of Constitutional Law 1156.

[2] See also Richard Albert, Menaka Guruswamy and Nishchal Basnyat (eds), *Founding Moments in Constitutionalism* (Hart Publishing 2019).

A Theory of African Constitutionalism. Berihun Adugna Gebeye, Oxford University Press. © Berihun Adugna Gebeye 2021.
DOI: 10.1093/oso/9780192893925.003.0008

of the people,[3] *pouvoir constituent* or constituent power, 'the principle that political power belongs to the people' is the foundation of the modern state.[4] The power of the people inherent in the exercise of constituent power provides legitimacy to the constituted power, that is, to the state, its institutions, and laws. Liberal constitutional theory takes sovereignty for granted and ushers in either legal constitutionalism[5] that bestows ultimate power on the courts, or political constitutionalism[6] that confers on parliament the final decision-making power in a polity, or a combination of both as in Canada.[7]

African constitutional theory, however, cannot take such sovereignty for granted. As discussed in Chapter 3, the legal, rather than the empirical, origin of the state in Africa has brought about syncretic sovereignty. In a departure from classic theories of state, the state in Africa first comes into being and takes root in society through the technology of law. Firstly, in as much as international law bestowed on African states internal autonomy and external protection through the doctrine of sovereignty on the eve of independence from colonial rule, it also continues to meddle in their socio-economic, cultural, and political self-determination. A strong characterization of this international meddling is what Nkrumah called neocolonialism, which is essentially when 'the State which is subject to it is, in theory, independent and has all the outward trappings of international sovereignty ... [but] in reality its economic system and thus its political policy is directed from outside'.[8] The international support for civilian and military dictatorships during the Cold War and the 'end of history' politics of democracy and rule of law promotion have significantly influenced the socio-economic, cultural, and political practice and vision of African states and societies.[9] Due to the international legal (ie, colonial) origin of the state, for better or worse, African governments have assumed a sort of dual accountability to both their people and 'the international community' at the end of colonialism. Externally, postcolonial sovereignty in its very establishment is prone to the interference of international political and economic actors, and, therefore, one cannot take the existence of full sovereignty—like that of the Western states—for granted in one's constitutional thinking.[10]

Second, the indigenous legal or political order is a constitutive part of the African state that provides the state with the necessary institutional infrastructure and

[3] See Andrew Arato, *The Adventures of the Constituent Power: Beyond Revolutions?* (Cambridge University Press 2017); Martin Loughlin and Neil Walker (eds), *The Paradox of Constitutionalism: Constituent Power and Constitutional Form* (Oxford University Press, USA 2008).

[4] Lucia Rubinelli, *Constituent Power: A History* (Cambridge University Press 2020) 1–2.

[5] András Sajó and Renáta Uitz, *The Constitution of Freedom: An Introduction to Legal Constitutionalism* (Oxford University Press 2017).

[6] Richard Bellamy, *Political Constitutionalism: A Republican Defence of the Constitutionality of Democracy* (Cambridge University Press 2007).

[7] See Adam Dodek, 'The Canadian Override: Constitutional Model or Bête Noire of Constitutional Politics?' (2016) 49 Israel Law Review 45.

[8] Kwame Nkrumah, *Neo-Colonialism: The Last Stage of Imperialism* (Thomas Nelson & Sons Ltd 1965) ix.

[9] Berihun Adugna Gebeye, 'The Janus Face of Legal Pluralism for the Rule of Law Promotion in Sub-Saharan Africa' (2019) 53 Canadian Journal of African Studies / Revue canadienne des études africaines 337, 337–53.

[10] It must be noted that due to global and transnational actors and institutions, the way states (including Western states) exercise their sovereignty has been changing. See Ran Hirschl and Ayelet Shachar, 'Spatial Statism' (2019) 17 International Journal of Constitutional Law 387.

resources for its internal operation. In as much as the indigenous legal order plays a crucial role in the maintenance of law and order in much of the territory of the state through the device of legal pluralism,[11] it channels different rationalities and senses of justice in the operation of the state. Accordingly, unlike the Weberian state, the African state cannot simply enforce its uniform laws and will throughout its territory through its 'modern machinery' but has to work and negotiate with various indigenous legal and/or political institutions. Internally, postcolonial sovereignty in its design (as a successor to colonial sovereignty) is open to accommodating indigenous legal and political actors although the nature of accommodation may vary from place to place within a state, or from state to state. If anything, therefore, postcolonial sovereignty is something that 'we are expounding', to borrow from Chief Justice Marshall's powerful statement about the US Constitution in *McCulloch v Maryland*.[12] Taking sovereignty for granted in African constitutional design limits later constitutional enforcement or practice as there is a mismatch between the assumed and the actual existence of sovereignty. What African constitutional design can do is take this syncretic sovereignty seriously in both its institutional and normative considerations.

African constitutional design can take syncretic sovereignty seriously by paying more attention to Africa's past and present predicaments. Despite differences in degree, history and context are always important elements and factors in constitutional design. Indeed, much of liberal constitutional theory also builds on some historical and contextual experiences; needless to say, constitutional theory and design are not merely exercises in the abstract. More generally, the theory of limited government in liberal constitutional theory was a reaction to royal or monarchial absolutism in Western societies.[13] For instance, consider the American and French constitutional responses after their respective revolutions. The American revolutionaries won their war of independence against Great Britain and proclaimed:

> We hold these Truths to be self-evident, that all Men are created equal, that they are endowed by their Creator with certain unalienable Rights, that among these are Life, Liberty, and the Pursuit of Happiness—That to secure these Rights, Governments are instituted among Men, deriving their just Powers from the Consent of the Governed, that whenever any form of Government becomes destructive of these Ends, it is the Right of the People to alter or to abolish it, and to institute new Government, laying its Foundation on such Principles, and organizing its Powers in such form, as to them shall seem most likely to effect their Safety and Happiness.[14]

To effectuate these ideals, they established a system of government based on the principle of separation of powers and federalism. The French revolutionaries, on the other hand, overthrew a monarchy 'believing that [...] contempt of the rights of man are

[11] Berihun Adugna Gebeye, 'Decoding Legal Pluralism in Africa' (2017) 49 The Journal of Legal Pluralism and Unofficial Law 228, 228-249.

[12] For details see AIL Campbell, '"It Is a Constitution We Are Expounding": Chief Justice Marshall and the "Necessary and Proper" Clause' (1991) 12 The Journal of Legal History 190.

[13] Sajó and Uitz, *The Constitution of Freedom* (n 5) 13.

[14] The American Declaration of Independence, July 4, 1776, preamble para 2.

the sole cause of public calamities and of the corruption of governments'.[15] To cure this ill, they proclaimed and instituted a system of government based on the recognition of the rights of man as expressed in the 1789 Declaration of the Rights of Man and of the Citizen. While the American founding fathers paid more attention to the structural aspects of constitutionalism, their French counterparts paid more attention to the rights of man and the citizen in the institution of their respective republican governments, and their successful experiments emanate, in large part, from the proper reflection and choices they made in inaugurating their new republics.

African constitutional design, however, has mainly been unreflective and unreactive to the historical development of the state and its syncretic sovereignty. As discussed earlier in the book, the reaction has mainly been to the cultural attributes of the state and its system of government, and not to its historical and colonial underpinnings. While it is difficult to clearly distinguish cultural reactions from historical ones, historicizing constitutional developments and transformations across time and place opens new possibilities and perspectives for constitutional thought and practice. So far, much of African constitutional design has taken the state in its Weberian conception for granted—even though it is not truly Weberian—and has focused on reforming state or government institutions. One-party systems, personal rule, and multi-party systems all have been experimented with since independence. While the search for a workable theory of government is an important undertaking and a project that should continue in African constitutional thought and practice, constitutional experimentations based exclusively on the Weberian assumptions have limited the constitutional development of the continent.

Accordingly, African constitutional design should, first of all, be reactive to the historical development of the state and the ways in which the state was incorporated into world society as a colony in the late nineteenth century, and later as an equal sovereign into the community of nations in the mid-twentieth century. As discussed earlier in the book, African states were born in the graveyard of African sovereignty and the founding moments of African states (with few exceptions) was that of a *founding violence* channeled in the form of territorial states and mainstreamed into their *body politic*.[16] Through the aid of international law, the Berlin African Conference brought together the 'international community' that was assembled in Berlin in 1884/1885 as a constituent power for the *constitution* of Africa. This created an inherent and apparent disjuncture between the identities and political visions of the constituent power and the constituted people of the colonies. Even if independence transferred government power from the colonial powers to African political elites, it kept the colonial state intact. Building on the principles of the United Nations Charter, the heads of states and governments of the newly independent African states assembled in Addis Ababa in 1963 reaffirmed and further convinced to safeguard and consolidate the sovereignty and continuity of colonial states as they established the Organization of African Unity (OAU). Just like the Berlin Act helped with the *constitution* of colonial Africa, the OAU Charter helped with the *constitution* of postcolonial Africa, although it can be considered as an act of self-determination. Although African states can still redeem

[15] The 1789 French Declaration on the Rights of Man and Citizen, preamble.
[16] See also Achille Mbembe, *On the Postcolony* (University of California Press 2001) 25.

their *founding violence* through the institutionalization and practice of popular or democratic sovereignty, they remain externally vulnerable to the interference of international economic and political actors due to their unequal and onerous membership in the international community.[17] This means that African governments have some fundamental limitations in fully executing their constitutions and exercising popular or democratic sovereignty, even when they have the political will and are fully committed.

Secondly, African constitutional design should also consider the configuration of the state along with the societies living in it through indigenous legal and political institutions. As discussed in Chapters 2 and 3, the African geography—ie, low population densities, large territories, and difficult physical environments—has made the task of state building more difficult here than in any other region of the world.[18] This political geography leads to the imagination of alternative forms of sovereignty and methods of broadcasting of power in Africa. As a result, precolonial leaders asserted their sovereignty and exercised power not based on territory or land but based on people.[19] As land was abundant, unlike people, precolonial leaders did not have the interest to broadcast power throughout their territory, nor did they have the resources to do so. Similarly, the colonial state run by Europeans did not have empirical sovereignty over the whole of their colonies, nor were they endowed with the resources, the will, or capacity to do so.[20] Although the postcolonial state has a more-enhanced state capacity than its predecessor, it hasn't become the Weberian state—at least not yet; it still depends on the indigenous legal and/or political orders for the provision of 'indigenous rule of law' for much of its rural population. Although postcolonial constitutional design tries to incorporate indigenous legal and political institutions into the legislative, executive, and judicial branches of government at different levels and to different degrees, as discussed in Chapter 3, it does not give the attention and refection that these indigenous institutions deserve and hold in the actual establishment and operation of the states. As Prempeh rightly observed, 'capital-city constitutionalism, a constitutionalism whose forms, priorities, and rhetoric, centered around the interests of competing elites in the national capital city, [that] do not speak—except abstractly—to the realities of Africa's largely rural citizenry' dominates postcolonial constitutional design.[21] Taking into account the rural polity (the democratic majority), and using its institutional and normative resources, would not only enrich the African constitutional design, but it could also help consolidate the power, legitimacy, and accountability of the state.

Aligning African constitutional design with syncretic sovereignty may take many forms and shapes, and it is neither necessary, nor is the space sufficient, to detail all the nuts and bolts of the process here. For present purposes, it will suffice to indicate

[17] See Adom Getachew, *Worldmaking after Empire: The Rise and Fall of Self-Determination* (Princeton University Press 2019).

[18] Jeffrey Herbst, *States and Power in Africa: Comparative Lessons in Authority and Control* (Princeton University Press 2000) 12–13.

[19] ibid 35–36.

[20] Herbst, *States and Power in Africa* (n 18) 78.

[21] H Kwasi Prempeh, 'Africa's "Constitutionalism Revival": False Start or New Dawn?' (2007) 5 International Journal of Constitutional Law 469, 469–70.

two general directions that African constitutional design can take in order to (a) mitigate the vulnerability of states before international economic and political actors, and (b) help include the rural polity in the constitutional imagination. The first is for African states to recognize that international institutional and normative architectures can limit (although they can also help) their practice of constitutionalism and sovereignty—including the use of their natural resources—even when they are genuinely committed to the principles of constitutionalism and democracy. As Nkrumah observed:

> If we are to remain free, if we are to enjoy the full benefits of Africa's rich resources, we must unite to plan for our total defense and the full exploitation of our material and human means, in the full interests of our peoples. 'To get it alone' will limit our horizons, curtail our expectations, and threaten our liberty.[22]

African states can overcome their international vulnerability through political and economic integration at different levels. The political and constitutional developments in the East African Community (EAC), which includes Burundi, Kenya, Rwanda, South Sudan, Tanzania, and Uganda, are good examples in this regard. In 2010, Kenya adopted a brand-new constitution after many years of its constitutional reform process. As noted in Chapter 3, the Constitution of Kenya sets in motion a limited and devolved government and promises to make Kenya a constitutional democracy. In 2017, the various EAC heads of state—including Kenya—adopted a new political confederation as the EAC transitions to the East African Political Federation 'to widen and deepen economic, political, social and cultural integration in order to improve the quality of life of the people of East Africa through increased competitiveness, value added production, trade and investments'.[23] Some current members of the EAC, such as South Sudan, are in crises and one may wonder how the East African Political Federation can meaningfully operate and contribute to the peoples of the EAC under such dynamics. True, the road is a bumpy one with complex socio-economic and political challenges that may conspire against meaningful political integration, but it is the right way forward. Once South Sudan solves its internal constitutional crises, as Kenya was able to do, the East African Political Federation can create more suitable conditions for the enforcement of its national constitutional choices. Burundi, Kenya, Rwanda, South Sudan, Tanzania, and Uganda working together—with a total of 117 million people under one federation (the second largest group in Africa after Nigeria)—can create better socio-economic and political conditions for constitutionalism and full self-determination than each of them working separately.

At the continental level, in recognition of Africa's common historical past, future, and destiny, the African Union put forth the *Agenda 2063* at the 50th anniversary of the foundation of the OAU in 1963 with the aim of establishing a united and integrated Africa with common African citizenship and free movement of goods and persons to 'build an integrated, prosperous and peaceful Africa, driven and managed

22 Kwame Nkrumah, *Africa Must Unite* (FA Praeger 1963) xvii.

23 See the vision and mission of the EAC <https://www.eac.int/overview-of-eac> accessed 20 August 2020.

by its own citizens and representing a dynamic force in the international arena'.[24] In this integration process, *Agenda 2063* considers the merger and integration of the Regional Economic Communities such as the EAC as one of the building blocks of the Union.[25] The EAC's march towards a federation not only advances the African Union's *Agenda 2063*, but can also inspire other sub-regional economic communities to form a more integrated political and economic union. Moreover, the establishment and operation of the African Continental Free Trade Area, which aims to create a single market for goods and services and free movement of persons, has huge potential for African states to realize their constitutional promises, by and for themselves. Although intra-African trade increased from 10% in 1995 to 17% in 2017, it is the lowest when compared to Europe (69%), Asia (59%), and North America (31%).[26] In light of global political and economic forces, only a united Africa can offer better socio-economic, political, and cultural conditions for the complete self-determination and sovereignty of a continent that will host 2.5 billion people by 2050 (ie, more than a quarter of the world's population).[27]

One may think that the idea of African unity and integration is simply an illusion driven more by passion than by reason; however, in addition to the above analysis and recent African integration initiatives, comparative experience shows that reason, more than passion, guides regional political integration. Just to give one example, in the late eighteenth century, the newly independent American colonies faced an unequal international system dominated by European empires that could have made their independence fragile. As Aziz Rana argued in the *Two Faces of American Freedom*, the American founding fathers faced a postcolonial condition that could have perpetuated dependence, limited freedom, and constrained their sovereignty and full self-determination.[28] Without addressing this threat posed by the foreign powers, the founders feared that they could have been bound to the European powers and that their independence would have remained partial. This postcolonial condition motivated the American founders to invent a *structural constitutional theory* that *maintained* and *enhanced* their sovereignty and enabled them to fully exercise their right of self-determination, and Federalism, as discussed in Chapter 4, offered the former American colonies this ability. Although settler colonialism has had its own impact on postcolonial development, African constitutional design can and should also take a *sovereignty maintaining and enhancing* approach like the American colonies did. In this regard, the EAC's march towards a federation and the AU's *Agenda 2063* can be both seen as constitutional design exercises—or experiments—in *sovereignty maintaining and enhancing*, as they both go beyond the territorial and political boundaries of each state.

[24] African Union 50th Anniversary Solemn Declaration, <https://au.int/sites/default/files/documents/36205-doc-50th_anniversary_solemn_declaration_en.pdf> accessed 17 September 2020.

[25] ibid, C(ii)

[26] Vera Songwe, 'Intra-African Trade: A Path to Economic Diversification and Inclusion' (*Brookings*, 11 January 2019) <https://www.brookings.edu/research/intra-african-trade-a-path-to-economic-diversification-and-inclusion/> accessed 25 August 2020.

[27] The Economist, 'Africa's Population Will Double by 2050' *The Economist Special Report* <https://www.economist.com/special-report/2020/03/26/africas-population-will-double-by-2050> accessed 4 August 2020.

[28] Aziz Rana, *The Two Faces of American Freedom* (Harvard University Press 2014) 131–40.

The second general direction that African constitutional design can take is inward; in as much as African constitutional design looks beyond the state, it should also look within itself. In this regard, as discussed in Chapter 3, there are promising developments in including indigenous political institutions in the design of the legislative, executive, and judicial branches of government. However, African constitutional design does not give much thought to the place and role of indigenous legal and political institutions within the state and society. Many of the indigenous legal and political institutions operate under the realm of informality that colonialism introduced. This means that these institutions perform some of the state duties mainly without the necessary financial and technical support from the state. Although these institutions are one of the constitutive elements of the state, there is either a lack of understanding about this fact or there is a willful ignorance of this empirical reality on the part of African constitution-builders. Accordingly, the rural polity (the democratic majority) has been at the periphery of the constitutional imagination. Without accounting for the rural polity in national constitution design, and without appreciating the institutional and normative resources of indigenous legal and political systems in restructuring state and government institutions, African states may not really establish a sustainable national constitutional order, and that can also meaningfully contribute to African integration in larger sovereignty.

II. The Limits of Postcolonial Constitutional Reforms

Beyond the broader issues of sovereignty, postcolonial constitutional reforms have at least three major limitations that future constitutional designs and practices should take into consideration. The first is the turn to centralized authority in order to address the postcolonial condition and mitigate the specter of neocolonialism, which also ends up entrenching personal rule and authoritarianism. As the independence constitutions were ill-equipped to address the postcolonial challenges of external imperial interference and internal socio-economic and political dynamics, the turn to centralized authority is somehow understandable.[29] The independence leaders' concern about internal division as well as the potential of previous colonial powers regaining control through other means may have, indeed, necessitated the centralization of power in the establishment of unitary presidential republics in the first republican constitutions of many African states. However, as discussed earlier in the book, the territorial (vertical) concentration of power in the center and the horizontal concentration of power in the executive neither safeguarded the state from external interference nor did it save it from internal division. Moreover, the personalization of state power around the presidency and at the center further weakened the capacity of the state and deepened the fragmentation of the people along ethnic, religious, and regional lines.

[29] Aziz Rana, 'Constitutionalism and the Predicament of Postcolonial Independence' in Richard Albert (ed), *Revolutionary Constitutionalism: Law, Legitimacy, Power* (Hart Publishing 2020) 80. (Comparing the kind of worries the Article of Confederation caused to the American founders with the worries independence constitutions generated to the African states such as Kenya).

Although the democratic constitutions of the 1990s have tried to decentralize power territorially, either through federalism or various other forms of decentralization, as discussed in Chapters 3 and 4, important powers have remained at the center—both as a matter of constitutional design and, perhaps even more so, as a matter of actual constitutional practice. Even in the federal systems, where a strong vertical division of power would be expected, important political and financial powers still belong to the national governments, as the case studies of Nigeria, Ethiopia, and South Africa have shown. Even if many of the unitary states have decentralized power, they either do not decentralize it enough or do not give it a chance to function as constitutionally designed.[30] Kenya, however, provides a good example of decentralizing power through devolution, and, with some additional measures,[31] its experience shows that a territorially decentralized power can provide useful structural checks and balances in the exercise of political power at the center.[32]

In addition to addressing the outstanding issue of vertical decentralization of power, such as to municipalities and localities, with the intention of both extending and consolidating the power of the state as well as putting necessary checks and balances in the exercise of political power, future constitutional design and practice should also pay particular attention to the rural polity and big cities. Decentralization certainly has to account for the institutional and normative resources of the rural polity. Indigenous legal and political institutions play a fundamental role (even with all their weaknesses) in the operation of the rural polity and the African constitutional project can build on these institutions and norms in decentralizing power by going beyond colonial rationales of governmentality and accepting and working with the indigenous legal and political institutions—not as 'informal institutions' but as part of the formal *body politic*, as they truly are. By going beyond mere recognition in constitutional texts, as Muna Ndulo observed, '[c]onstitutional arrangements designed to implement the devolution of power to local communities in Africa must, therefore, address the place of traditional institutions of governance in modern political systems', even though this may take different forms and shapes within and among states.[33]

Likewise, decentralization also should recognize the place of big cities as important actors and spaces in the contemporary constitutional project. Today, many big African cities such as Lagos, Kinshasa, Nairobi, and Addis Ababa, just to mention a few, host many millions of people in an expanded territory with little political power to administer their own affairs. In fact, 'Africa's urban population increased from 53 million in 1960 to 548 million in 2018—more than a tenfold increase within half a century. And it is projected to further increase to 1.34 billion by 2050—an increase of nearly 1.3 billion urban dwellers within less than a century.'[34] As Ran Hirschl argued, we cannot

[30] Prempeh, 'Africa's "Constitutionalism Revival"' (n 21) 495. Nico Stytler, 'Local Multiparty Democracy in Africa', in Nico Stytler and Charles Fombad (eds), Democracy, *Elections and Constitutionalism in Africa* (Oxford University Press 2021).

[31] See Ken Ochieng' Opalo, 'Citizen Political Knowledge and Accountability: Survey Evidence on Devolution in Kenya' (2020) 33 Governance 4: 849-869.

[32] See Hannah Waddilove, 'Support or Subvert? Assessing Devolution's Effect on Central Power during Kenya's 2017 Presidential Rerun' (2019) 13 Journal of Eastern African Studies 334.

[33] Muna Ndulo, 'Constitutions and Constitutional Reforms in African Politics' in *Oxford Research Encyclopedia of Politics* (Oxford University Press 2019) 18.

[34] Ran Hirschl, *City, State: Constitutionalism and the Megacity* (Oxford University Press 2020) 4.

simply ignore big cities in our constitutional thinking and imagination, nor can we address the socio-economic, demographic, cultural, political, and spatial dynamics of cities merely through 'the constitutional structures, doctrines, perceptions, and expectations that were conceived along with the modern nation-state'.[35]

In a similar vein, while the democratic constitutions of the 1990s introduced some cosmetic changes to the powers of the executive, they did not sufficiently change the substantive allocation of power between the various branches of government, nor did they change the practice of executive power. As discussed in Chapters 3 and 5, in addition to the near-universal reaffirmation of the presidential system, these constitutions only opened the political office to plural political contestation through the reintroduction of multi-party politics and limited the tenure of presidents for life through term limits; but the nature of the office itself remained unchanged. Centralization of power was the motivation even for those states that adopted a parliamentary system, such as Ethiopia. As Prempeh observed, '[o]nce installed in office and for the duration of his term, the contemporary African president generally retains within the constitutional and political orbit the essential attributes of imperium long associated with presidential power in postcolonial Africa'.[36] Even in the best of times, respect for term limits and commitment to multi-party democracy can only help to replace one strong executive with another strong executive that operates with the same *modus operandi* of the *ancien régime* while in office. At the worst of times, the president can simply amend the term limit provision and remain in office.

In addition to opening up the office to plural political competition and limiting the tenure of presidents, future constitutional design and practice has to limit the substantive powers of the executive, both to enhance its efficiency and to minimize, if not to avoid, the abuse or misuse of power. This requires rethinking the current power allocation among the various branches of government and introducing new institutional frameworks that facilitate and constrain executive power. In this regard, as discussed in Chapters 3 and 5, Kenya and South Africa offer some good lessons in designing a limited executive. Consider, for instance, how the Constitution of Kenya limited the power of its president: the president only nominates persons to different constitutional offices and their appointment and dismissal rests on the legislature. The legislature not only controls the determination of the national revenue, but also must approve declarations of state of emergency and war. Moreover, the legislature not only calls and asks cabinet ministers but also can impeach the president for violations of the constitution, national law, or international law. Furthermore, the Constitution establishes an independent electoral commission, and positions the judiciary as the guardian of the Constitution and the 'people's will' by ensuring its institutional and functional independence. Due to these changes in constitutional design, the Supreme Court has been playing an important role in defending the Constitution, including by annulling the 2017 presidential election results due to some election irregularities—a first of its kind in Africa.[37] In addition, bringing the South African type of 'state

[35] ibid 9.

[36] Prempeh, 'Africa's "Constitutionalism Revival"' (n 21) 497.

[37] *Raila Amolo Odinga and other v independent Electoral and Boundaries Commission and others* [2017] Supreme Court of Kenya, Presidential Petition No 1 of 2017.

institutions supporting constitutional democracy' into the equation of distributing and dispersing government power—beyond the traditional horizontal separation of powers framework—may open new avenues and opportunities with which to facilitate and limit the exercise of political power. Ultimately, there is no one magic formula for the design of institutions that can work everywhere. However, unlimited government is always inefficient, expensive, and corrupt, while limited government is more efficient, less expensive, and less corrupt and can enable government by the very act of limiting it.[38]

The second limitation that future constitutional designs and practices should take into consideration is the almost singular focus on reforming or revising the written constitutions while retaining much of the legal systems that provide the government and public administration with their significant and untamed political power. The independence constitutions retained the colonial legal systems—which were inherently coercive, exploitative, and discretionary—as the foundation of public administration in postcolonial Africa.[39] And the republican constitutions, rather than reforming these legal systems, added some other statutes and decrees that give even more power to the government as well as to the administrative apparatus or bureaucracy. Similarly, the constitutional reforms of the 1990s focused on the written constitutions while reaffirming the continuity of the legal systems. These constitutional reforms regulate their own relationship with the legal systems through the principle of constitutional supremacy, namely, that '[a]ny law, including customary law, that is inconsistent with this Constitution is void to the extent of the inconsistency, and any act or omission in contravention of this Constitution is invalid'.[40] According to this constitutional principle, change to the repressive parts of the legal systems can only happen either through the courts (if there is a challenge to their constitutionality) or through the parliament, and absent such interventions, these laws may continue to apply. The low levels of constitutional literacy[41] as well as the general lack of legal awareness on the part of the citizenry limit the constitutional challenges in courts.[42] As these laws offer the government an 'awesome' political power, to use Okoth-Ogendo's words,[43] the dominant or single-party parliaments may not be motivated to ever change these repressive laws. For instance, Yoweri Museveni not only refused to reform the repressive laws that were in force, but he even reinforced them.[44] Even in Ghana, a state which currently has one of the promising democratic experiments on the continent, '[t]he influence of the colonial militaristic orientation to policing, with its quintessential lack of accountability and respect for the fundamental rights of citizens, remains

[38] For the paradox of limited government see Stephen Holmes, *Passions and Constraint: On the Theory of Liberal Democracy* (University of Chicago Press 1995).

[39] See HWO Okoth-Ogendo, 'Constitutions without Constitutionalism: Reflections on an African Political Paradox' in Douglass Greenberg and others (eds), *Constitutionalism and Democracy: Transitions in the Contemporary World* (Oxford University Press 1993) 69.

[40] 2010 Kenyan Constitution, art 2(4), which is a standard provision in all African constitutions.

[41] See Charles Manga Fombad, 'Constitutional Literacy in Africa: Challenges and Prospects' (2018) 44 Commonwealth Law Bulletin 492.

[42] Prempeh, 'Africa's "Constitutionalism Revival"' (n 21) 502–03.

[43] Ogendo, 'Constitutions without Constitutionalism' (n 39) 69.

[44] Migai Akech, 'Constraining Government Power in Africa' (2011) 22 Journal of Democracy 96, 100.

strong and visible'.[45] Despite the many constitutional reforms, the repressive parts of the legal systems continue with little alteration across the continent.

The continuity of the repressive parts of the legal systems maintains the power of the executive (as the executive controls the public administration) as both a matter of law and practice despite some progressive constitutional changes. By operating within the domain of the legal systems, the executives can reclaim the powers that the constitutional reforms took away. The constitutional reforms, thus far, take away some powers of the executive at the constitutional level, but they maintain the executive and administrative powers at the sub-constitutional level by '[grandfathering] all preexisting legislation and sub legislative laws' into the new constitutional order.[46] As noted in Chapter 3, even though the Constitution of Kenya introduces a much more limited or constrained president, the legal and administrative system of the *ancien régime* have granted the president some extra-constitutional power that upsets the constitutional allocation of power between the different branches of government. Moreover, in many cases:

> [t]he faces of "abuse of public power" most intimately familiar to the African are not necessarily those of the president or a minister of state; they are often those of the police sergeant manning the checkpoint or roadblock; the midlevel tax assessor at the district tax office; the customs official at the port of entry or border post; the clerk at the land-title office; the municipal clerk in charge of allocating market stalls; the official at the local vehicle registration or drivers' licensing office; and the principal determining admission to the local high school. The public's recurring encounters with these public officers are characterized by spur-of-the-moment "rule making," unjustified discrimination, opportunistic delays, and plain extortion ... To the average African, then, the constitutionalism that would seem to matter the most is not always or necessarily the high constitutionalism of the political elites ... but a low constitutionalism ... that would address the rampant impunity and abuse of power by officials at the most basic level of the public administration.[47]

Therefore, without reforming the repressive parts of the legal systems, constitutional reforms may not effectively limit the power of the executive and, perhaps most importantly, the administrative or bureaucratic apparatus that is in close contact with the people in everyday life. One way of reforming these laws is like what was done in Rwanda, which identified and repealed more than 1,000 colonial laws through legislation in 2020.[48] Obviously, there are also other ways of reforming colonial and

[45] Justice Tankebe, 'Colonialism, Legitimation, and Policing in Ghana' (2008) 36 International Journal of Law, Crime and Justice 67, 82.

[46] Prempeh, 'Africa's "Constitutionalism Revival"' (n 21) 502.

[47] ibid 500.

[48] Rwanda Law Reform Commission, 'There Is No Legal Gap Left by Repealed Colonial Laws' <https://www.rlrc.gov.rw/index.php?id=82&L=0&tx_news_pi1%5Bnews%5D=102&tx_news_pi1%5Bcontroller%5D=News&tx_news_pi1%5Baction%5D=detail&cHash=850a96f5d5058a2eb05afcbd3b3fa66f> accessed 30 August 2020; See also Agnes Binagwaho, Richard Freeman, and Gabriela Sarriera, 'The Persistence of Colonial Laws: Why Rwanda Is Ready to Remove Outdated Legal Barriers to Health, Human Rights, and Development' <https://harvardilj.org/2018/06/the-persistence-of-colonial-laws-why-rwanda-is-ready-to-remove-outdated-legal-barriers-to-health-human-rights-and-development/> accessed 29 August 2020.

repressive postcolonial laws. The crux of the argument here is that without effective legal system reform, constitutional reform may not bring the desired change in limiting the power of the government precisely because, as discussed in Chapter 2, the legal system is as constitutive of political power as the written constitutions are.

The third limitation that should be taken into consideration —which actually follows from the above two—is the *structural deficit* of postcolonial constitutional reforms and the heavy reliance on 'rights-based constitutionalism' without a clear articulation of the broader postcolonial constitutional vision and the constitutional structure that such vision requires. The main challenge of the postcolonial African state is structural, ranging from broader issues of sovereignty (national, popular, and empirical) to organizing political power and establishing legitimate political authority. This requires, as discussed above, addressing the issue of syncretic sovereignty and outlining a political power map that structures political power both vertically and horizontally, and that includes, of course, fundamental rights and liberties. However, the post-1990s constitutional reforms have a limited purview as they mainly react to the first two or three decades of postcolonial constitutional experience, with one-party systems and military dictatorships, and the associated gross violations of human rights. As noted earlier in the book, these constitutional reforms mainly open up the political space for multi-party competition, recognize a range of human rights including free media, and establish systems of judicial review. In so doing, they rely heavily on the rights revolutions of the mid-twentieth century and the international human rights system, rather than drawing from and building on the postcolonial African condition, in their effort to institute constitutional democracy anew.[49] They put too much faith in rights as a limit to political power and they rely on the courts for their enforcement. Surely, the recognition of rights and the institution of judicial review are important undertakings in actually establishing a constitutionally limited government, despite the different motivating factors such as Hirschl's 'hegemonic preservation thesis',[50] Tom Ginsburg's 'insurance model',[51] or Stephen Holmes' 'cognitive constitutionalism' thesis.[52] However, without the wider necessary constitutional structures, rights may have a limited role in limiting political power and the courts alone may not do much in fostering the culture of constitutionalism, as the constitutional practices of many African states have shown.

The issue here is not why the constitutional reforms include rights as an important part of the constitutions, or why they establish systems of judicial review, but rather why they make the idea and practice of rights 'the central and primary function' of the constitutions,[53] and why they make 'the burden of promoting and sustaining constitutionalism to fall, disproportionately, on the third branch of

[49] Michael Ignatieff, *The Rights Revolution* (House of Anansi 2007); Bruce Ackerman, 'The Rise of World Constitutionalism' (1997) 83 Virginia Law Review 771.

[50] See Ran Hirschl, *Towards Juristocracy: The Origins and Consequences of the New Constitutionalism* (Harvard University Press 2007).

[51] See Tom Ginsburg, *Judicial Review in New Democracies: Constitutional Courts in Asian Cases* (Cambridge University Press 2003).

[52] Stephen Holmes, 'Constitutions and Constitutionalism', in Michel Rosenfeld and András Sajó (eds), *The Oxford Handbook of Comparative Constitutional Law* (Oxford University Press 2012) 189–214.

[53] For a detail discussion on the limits of the rights discourse see Makau Mutua, *Human Rights: A Political and Cultural Critique* (University of Pennsylvania Press 2002) Chapter 6.

government: the judiciary'.[54] Obviously, constitutions have many important functions other than protecting rights, and the structure of government (including law-making, law enforcement, and administrative practice) plays a fundamental role in promoting and sustaining constitutionalism.[55] In addition to the narrow vision of the constitutional reforms, rights-based constitutionalism has some major limitations in fulfilling its promises. First, rights in their constitutive function (that is, in encoding and projecting 'a certain vision of political community, in particular the idea of a political community as consisting of rights-bearing citizens of equal status') have limitations in ushering in a shared national identity around the norms and values that underpin them; this is true even in consolidated democracies such as Canada, and how much more so on a continent like Africa that grapples with establishing a legitimate political order in an environment of much more constitutive cultural diversity.[56] Second, and perhaps most importantly and concretely, rights in their regulative function (that is, in serving as 'credible commitments against future abuses of human rights') have inherent limitations due to the existence of politicized judiciaries, constitutional underenforcement, and the ex post nature of judicial review in non-established democracies, including in Africa.[57]

Furthermore, as history and experience have it, even within an environment of judicial independence, judicial philosophy and reasoning not only grant the judiciary a checking function with regard to legislative and executive excesses but also a legitimating function to the same.[58] Contemporary constitutional experience also shows that as governments 'use mechanism of constitutional change to erode the democratic order', a phenomenon that David Landau called 'abusive constitutionalism',[59] courts can issue decisions that 'intentionally attack the core of electoral democracy', a phenomenon that David Landau and Rosalind Dixon called 'abusive judicial review'.[60] Moreover, Tom Gerald Daly, in *The Alchemists: Questioning Our faith in Courts as Democracy-Builders*, shows how a court-centered model for constitutionalism and democracy actually limits the viability and effectiveness of the constitutional project in post-authoritarian states, to which the African continent certainly belongs.[61] This is because, unlike courts in established democracies that operate within the universe of the structural and normative frameworks of a democratic government, courts in non-established democracies are expected to both *judge* and *facilitate* the democratization process, that is, to 'both assess what is required to support the democratization process at any given point and to judge when the democratization context requires a different

[54] Prempeh, 'Africa's "Constitutionalism Revival"' (n 21) 502; Stephen Gardbaum, 'The Place of Constitutional Law in the Legal System', in Michel Rosenfeld and András Sajó (eds), *The Oxford Handbook of Comparative Constitutional Law* (Oxford University Press 2012)) 177.

[55] Bellamy, *Political Constitutionalism* (n 6) 15.

[56] Sujit Choudhry, 'After the Rights Revolution: Bills of Rights in the Postconflict State' (2010) 6 Annual Review of Law and Social Science 301, 316–18.

[57] ibid 311–16.

[58] Alexander M Bickel, *The Least Dangerous Branch: The Supreme Court at the Bar of Politics* (2nd ed, Yale University Press 1986).

[59] David Landau, 'Abusive Constitutionalism' (2013) 47 University of California, Davis 189.

[60] David Landau and Rosalind Dixon, 'Abusive Judicial Review: Courts Against Democracy' (2020) 53 University of California, Davis 1315.

[61] Tom Daly, *The Alchemists: Questioning Our Faith in Courts as Democracy-Builders* (Cambridge University Press 2018).

approach', a task that is simply too onerous for courts to execute.[62] Hence, while rights and judicial review play a fundamental role in the practice of constitutionalism, they need a structural framework that can share the burden of promoting constitutionalism and can make them effective.

III. The Potential of Constitutional Jurisgenesis

Postcolonial African constitutional experiences also have some potential that future constitutional designs and practices should build on and consolidate. One of the major strengths of postcolonial constitutional experiences is the dual commitment to liberal constitutionalism and cultural diversity. As discussed in Chapter 3, the African state, government architecture, and constitutional rights regime have ushered in—at different levels and to different extents—tenets of liberal constitutionalism as well as cultural diversity in the designs and practices of constitutionalism. The dual commitment to liberal constitutional values and African cultures manifests itself most strongly in the field of constitutional rights. As discussed extensively in Chapter 6, African constitutions reject the jurispathic claims of both the universalist and cultural relativist accounts of human rights and set constitutional jurisgensis in motion.[63] By constitutional jurisgensis, I mean a constitutional design and practice committed to both liberal constitutional values and cultural diversity.[64] In such constitutional systems, what is constitutionally permissible and what is not cannot be simply determined by an attachment to either liberal constitutional values or cultural diversity; it is the interaction of these plural constitutional values in time and place that dictates what the constitutional practice or outcome should look like. The singularity of the constitutional order, therefore, lies not in having a singular conception of justice, rights, and values, but in its ability to provide a framework within which various pluralities can exist and operate within the polity. As such, the constitutional order is procedurally and normatively open to accommodating seemingly competing plural constitutional values.

Precisely because of this, as discussed in Chapter 6, the universalist ambition and the supremacy of the constitutions do not override a certain conception of women's rights, for example, simply because it is incompatible with the liberal notion of rights. Rather, the constitutional systems have created spaces and possibilities for the practice of women's rights in multiple, overlapping, competing, and contestable avenues through procedural innovation and normative openness. Through constitutional jurisgensis, African constitutionalism has created better options for the practice of human rights than what the universalists and cultural relativists can offer. As the experiences of Nigeria, Ethiopia, and South Africa demonstrate, rather than alienating

[62] ibid 1.

[63] For a detail discussion on the jurispathic and jurisgenesis approaches see Robert M Cover, 'The Supreme Court 1982 Term—Foreword: Nomos and Narrative' (1983) 97 Harvard Law Review 65; Paul Schiff Berman, 'Jurisgenerative Constitutionalism: Procedural Principles for Managing Global Legal Pluralism' (2013) 20 Indiana Journal of Global Legal Studies 665; Ming-Sung Kuo, 'Politics and Constitutional Jurisgenesis: A Cautionary Note on Political Constitutionalism' (2018) 7 Global Constitutionalism 75.

[64] See also Berihun Adugna Gebeye, 'Global Constitutionalism and Cultural Diversity: The Emergence of Jurisgenerative Constitutionalism in Africa' (2020) 10 Global Constitutionalism 1, 40-71.

Africans from their cultural values and resources and imposing sole obligations on states for human rights promotion, constitutional jurisgensis brings the state and society together in the practice of human rights and, consequently, gives the society the necessary agency and structure to engage with the broader constitutional universe in light of its cultural understanding. Such human rights practice—by translating and localizing the abstract and universal ideas of human rights into culturally accessible and legally and politically meaningful ways—transforms both the cultural practices and universal human rights, and not only *from above* (particularly through apex court decisions), but also *from below* (through change in the cultural understanding of society).[65]

And beyond just rights, constitutional jurisgenesis also mediates between *system-threatening* or competing constitutional systems—such as constitutional theocracy and constitutional democracy—within a specific constitutional order. Constitutional theocracy is a constitutional system that adopts a state religion and uses that religion as a—or the—main source of legislation and adjudication, while constitutional democracy is a secular constitutional system that takes the democratic will of the people as the foundation of the constitutional order.[66] While constitutional theocracy is the dominant constitutional system of the non-secular world, constitutional democracy is the constitutional system of the secular world. But can constitutional theocracy and constitutional democracy co-exist in a single polity? The answer is yes—if the constitutional system of that polity operates in the system of constitutional jurisgenesis, and Nigeria is a good example of that.

The Nigerian constitutional order contains both theocratic, in the form of Shariacracy, and democratic constitutional systems. Shariacracy is the adoption of Sharia as the foundation of governance in a constitutional democracy.[67] The practice of constitutional jurisgensis makes it possible for Shariacracy to emerge through, and operate in, the realm of constitutional democracy.[68]

Shariacracy is not a twenty-first century constitutional and political 'big bang' in Nigeria; it is embedded in the socio-political and religious experience of Northern Nigeria as well as the national and international order in which it is situated. With the establishment of the Sokoto Caliphate by Jihadist Sheikh Usman Dan Fodio in 1804, Sharia was fully operational in the Northern Region until the British limited its application to civil matters subject to the repugnancy clause.[69] Despite demands for Sharia in the public domain after independence, the political and military elites of Northern Nigeria who dominated the national politics did not allow it any official expression.[70]

[65] See also Sally Engle Merry, *Human Rights and Gender Violence: Translating International Law to Local Justice* (The University of Chicago Press 2006).

[66] Ran Hirschl, *Constitutional Theocracy* (Harvard University Press 2010) 2–16.

[67] Ali A Mazrui, 'Shariacracy and Federal Models in the Era of Globalization: Nigeria in Comparative Perspective', in Edward R McMahon and Thomas Sinclair, *Democratic Institution Performance: Research and Policy Perspectives* (Greenwood Publishing Group 2002) 66.

[68] Brandon Kendhammer, 'The Sharia Controversy in Northern Nigeria and the Politics of Islamic Law in New and Uncertain Democracies' (2013) 45 Comparative Politics 291, 297.

[69] Mohammed HA Bolaji, 'Between Democracy and Federalism: Shari'ah in Northern Nigeria and the Paradox of Institutional Impetuses' (2013) 59 Africa Today 92, 98; for details see Anthony Stephens Johnston, *The Fulani Empire of Sokoto* (Oxford University Press 1967).

[70] Rotimi T Suberu, 'Religion and Institutions: Federalism and the Management of Conflicts over Sharia in Nigeria' (2009) 21 Journal of International Development 547, 548–52; See also Andrew Ubaka Iwobi,

This has changed with a turn to civilian rule in 1999 under the leadership of Olusegun Obasanjo, a Southern Christian and the first non-Muslim popularly elected president of Nigeria.[71] One of the reasons for the rise of Shariacracy was the shift of power from the North to the South and the concomitant feeling of marginalization in the North caused by Obasanjo's presidency. In this respect, bringing Sharia into the public domain in the North was considered to be a 'political bargaining chip' in the federation.[72] The other reason was related to the revival of cultural self-determination that has accompanied waves of centralization since independence.[73] The inauguration of the Fourth Republic in 1999 has brought about Yoruba nationalism and Igbo confederal demands which have pushed the North to advance Shariacracy as a cultural and religious identity. The forces of globalization at the international level, with the South as its vanguard at the national level, coupled with the 'North's inability' to compete within globalization, have all forced the North to resort to Sharia as a mode of resistance, both at home and abroad. The official reasons for Shariacracy, however, are related to practicing religious rights and addressing corruption of the morals of both the government and the governed through Sharia, thereby delivering development, social justice, and good government.[74]

Although Nigeria has the largest Muslim population in Africa (more than any other Arab country),[75] Sharia has been reintroduced within the framework of a liberal democratic constitutional system.[76] Ahmed Sani Yerima ran for the governorship of Zamfara state promising to implement Sharia through the state's legislature.[77] Two months after his inauguration, he set up a law review committee and, based on its recommendations, he put forth a bill to fully implement Sharia penal law in the state through the adoption of Sharia penal and procedure codes, and to reorganize the judiciary in line with the tenets of Sharia. And the State House of Assembly adopted the law.[78] Following Zamfara, eleven other Northern states adopted Sharia into their criminal law domain, including: Kano, Katsina, Niger, Bauchi, Kaduna, Sokoto, Borno, Gombe, Kebbi, Jigawa, and Yobe.[79] In addition to the extension of Sharia into the criminal justice system, Sharia has also been central in the public policy priorities

'Tiptoeing through a Constitutional Minefield: The Great Sharia Controversy in Nigeria' (2004) 48 Journal of African Law 111.

[71] Mazrui, 'Shariacracy and Federal Models in the Era of Globalization' (n 67) 63.

[72] ibid.

[73] ibid.

[74] Kendhammer, 'The Sharia Controversy in Northern Nigeria and the Politics of Islamic Law in New and Uncertain Democracies' (n 68) 297–98; Bolaji, 'Between Democracy and Federalism: Shari'ah in Northern Nigeria and the Paradox of Institutional Impetuses' (n 68) 111; See also Matthias Krings, 'Conversion on Screen: A Glimpse at Popular Islamic Imaginations in Northern Nigeria' (2008) 54 Africa Today 45.

[75] Mazrui, 'Shariacracy and Federal Models in the Era of Globalization' (n 67) 63.

[76] Suberu, 'Religion and Institutions' (n 70) 552.

[77] Kendhammer, 'The Sharia Controversy in Northern Nigeria and the Politics of Islamic Law in New and Uncertain Democracies' (n 68) 294; Greg Mills and others, *Making Africa Work: A Handbook for Economic Success* (Tafelberg 2017) 234. Obasanjo notes that the governors wish in introducing sharia was to consolidate his power and secure his legitimacy.

[78] Mamman Lawan, 'Islamic Law and Legal Hybridity in Nigeria' (2014) 58 Journal of African Law 303, 310.

[79] Bolaji, 'Between Democracy and Federalism: Shari'ah in Northern Nigeria and the Paradox of Institutional Impetuses' (n 69) 93–94.

of the North with respect to the enforcement of rights, delivery of social justice and economic development, and in holding government officials accountable.[80] Equal to the right to practice religion according to the dictates of Islam as well as the appeal of Sharia for the welfare of Muslims and their just development, Sharia's power in disciplining the conduct of leaders and containing corruption has been no less fundamental in its reintroduction.[81] In order to shape the culture and principles of governance in light of the tenets of Sharia, institutions such as Shari'ah, Zakkah, and Hubusi Commissions, as well as a Hisbah Board, have been established in these states.[82]

Not only is Shariacracy advanced in a liberal constitutional system, it also accepts the supremacy of the Constitution. The twelve Sharia-implementing states justify the reintroduction of Sharia into their states based on different Sections of the Constitution itself, not by rejecting its existence or supremacy.[83] For instance, they defend Shariacracy with reference to Sections 2(2) (which proclaims that Nigeria shall be a federation), 4(7) (the legislative powers of the State House of Assembly), 6(2&4) (the power of the State House of Assembly to establish courts), 38 (freedom of religion), and 277 (the jurisdiction of the Sharia Court of Appeal). Although the constitutionality of Shariacracy is a contentious matter in Nigerian political and public life, its advancement is claimed to have a constitutional basis.[84] Furthermore, all of these states affirm the supremacy of the Constitution along with their Sharia reforms.[85] While it would be problematic, to say the least, to claim that the full implementation of Sharia would be compatible with some aspects of the Constitution, Shariacracy is not advanced on the premise that Sharia is a supreme form of law and not subject to the standards of positive law.

Moreover, the proponents of Sharia are not radical Muslims like Boko Haram (who reject the constitutional system and want to create an Islamic state of Nigeria),[86] but rather politicians who rely on the democratic votes of the people for their access to, and time in, government office.[87] Furthermore, governors such as Ahmed Sani Yerima of Zamfara and his counterparts in the eleven Sharia-implementing states proposed Shariacracy within the prism of the federal structure; they did not demand Shariacracy for the whole of Nigeria, or even for all of Northern Nigeria. Further, even if Zamfara inspired some other Northern states to adopt Shariacracy, not all of the Northern states have implemented Sharia reforms, nor have those which have implemented these reforms always followed the Zamfara model.[88] Out of the nineteen

[80] Kendhammer, 'The Sharia Controversy in Northern Nigeria and the Politics of Islamic Law in New and Uncertain Democracies' (n 68) 298.

[81] ibid.

[82] Lawan, 'Islamic Law and Legal Hybridity in Nigeria' (n 78) 312–13; Rasheed Oyewole Olaniyi, 'Hisbah and Sharia Law Enforcement in Metropolitan Kano' (2011) 57 Africa Today 70.

[83] Vincent O Nmehielle, 'Sharia Law in the Northern States of Nigeria: To Implement or Not to Implement, the Constitutionality Is the Question' (2004) 26 Human Rights Quarterly 730.

[84] Ibid; Lawan, 'Islamic Law and Legal Hybridity in Nigeria' (n 78); Iwobi, 'Tiptoeing through a Constitutional Minefield' (n 70); Suberu, 'Religion and Institutions' (n 70); Bolaji, 'Between Democracy and Federalism: Shari'ah in Northern Nigeria and the Paradox of Institutional Impetuses' (n 69).

[85] Nmehielle, 'Sharia Law in the Northern States of Nigeria' (n 83) 310.

[86] Roman Loimeier, 'Boko Haram: The Development of a Militant Religious Movement in Nigeria' (2012) 47 Africa Spectrum 137.

[87] Suberu, 'Religion and Institutions' (n 70) 553.

[88] Daniel Plang, 'Sharia penal laws in northern Nigeria: a review', in Etannibi EO Alemika (ed), *Human Rights and Shariah Penal Code in Northern Nigeria* (Human Rights Monitor 2005) 69–136; Mohammed

Northern states, twelve have chosen to implement Sharia reforms and they have taken one of three approaches.[89] The first is the Zamfara model, which was followed by the majority of states and reintroduces Sharia and its court system by abolishing Area Courts. The second is the Kaduna/Gombe model which establishes Sharia and customary courts—for Muslims and non-Muslims, respectively—by abolishing Area courts.[90] The third is the Niger/Kebbi model which maintains Area Courts which have jurisdiction on persons who profess Islamic religion or consenting non-Muslims.[91] Thus, Shariacracy has been implemented fully with the federal structure.

Equally with its advancement, Shariacracy has been practiced within the institutional frameworks of the federation. In addition to the federal character principle which permeates the legislative and executive composition of the states, including the political party system, the federal allocation of resources for the implementation of Shariacracy is further evidence that it is implemented within the constitutional framework. The Sharia-implementing states rely on the Nigeria Police Force, the single police force of the federation, for the implementation of their Sharia criminal justice systems. Further, the Sharia-implementing states submit their legislative undertakings and judicial practices to higher courts of the federation. Although the position of the federal government on the constitutionality of Shariacracy is not consistent[92]—sometimes saying it is constitutional while at other times saying it is not—it neither asked the Nigerian Supreme Court to rule on the constitutionality of such measures, nor will it ask so in the foreseeable future.[93] In light of these circumstances, the practice of Shariacracy is presumed to be consistent with the constitutional system of Nigeria. On normative grounds, however, the practice of Shariacracy is not consistent with some of the constitutional rights enshrined under the Nigerian Constitution.[94] A series of Sharia cases affirm that Shariacracy cannot exist without violating some human rights.[95] For instance, Buba Jangebei was amputated for stealing a cow in 2000 in Zamfara state, and Amina Lawal was sentenced to death by stoning for adultery in 2002 in Katsina state (although the decision was later reversed on procedural grounds)—both according to Sharia law.[96]

The existence of Shariacracy along with constitutional democracy within a single constitutional order, and the former's advancement through the latter, are possible through the *practice, if not the design,* of constitutional jurisgenesis; the practice of constitutional jurisgenesis, not jurispathic constitutionalism, makes this possible.

Laden, 'Legal pluralism and the development of the rule of law in Nigeria: issues and challenges in the development and application of the Sharia', in Jibrin Ibrahim (ed), *Sharia Penal and Family Laws in Nigeria and in the Muslim World: Rights Based Approach* (Global Rights 2004) 57–113.

89 Suberu, 'Religion and Institutions' (n 70) 553.
90 ibid 553–54.
91 ibid 554.
92 See Iwobi, 'Tiptoeing through a Constitutional Minefield' (n 70).
93 See Lawan, 'Islamic Law and Legal Hybridity in Nigeria' (n 78).
94 See Nmehielle, 'Sharia Law in the Northern States of Nigeria' (n 83).
95 See also Abdulmumini Adebayo Oba, 'The Sharia Court of Appeal in Northern Nigeria: The Continuing Crises of Jurisdiction' (2004) 52 The American Journal of Comparative Law 859.
96 J Isawa Elaigwu and Habu Galadima, 'The Shadow of Sharia over Nigerian Federalism' (2003) 33 Publius: The Journal of Federalism 123, 123; Iwobi, 'Tiptoeing through a Constitutional Minefield' (n 70) 143.

Consider, for instance, the jurispathic constitutional alternative: the federal government or the Supreme Court rejects Shariacracy as unconstitutional. Such a declaration of unconstitutionality would probably either bring about prolonged conflict and chaos that would make the practice of constitutional theocracy and constitutional democracy difficult, or it would lead to the disintegration of Nigeria which would, in turn, make the rise of a pure constitutional theocracy in the North possible and would also weaken the socio-economic and political conditions of both the North and the South. It is not by accident that Nigeria is the African giant, both in terms of its economy (ranked 26th in the world with a GDP of 448,120 USD) and its demography (ranked 7th in the world with a population of more than 206 million).[97] Its territorial integrity and its social unity are worth protecting in larger sovereignty and self-determination through the accommodation of some variants of constitutional theocracy.

Thus, constitutional jurisgenesis not only mediates liberal constitutional values with African cultures, but also makes it possible for different African cultures and worldviews to co-exist within a particular polity. Future constitutional designs and practices can build upon and consolidate this experience of constitutional jurisgenesis.

However, one should make a clear distinction between the potential of constitutional jurisgenesis in mediating the liberal account of rights with the African notion of rights on the one hand, and in mediating *system-threatening* constitutional systems, such as Shariacracy, and constitutional democracy on the other. In mediating different notions of rights, constitutional jurisgenesis has huge potential and can work in almost any part of the continent, as discussed in Chapter 6—although obviously working differently according to different circumstances. In mediating between *system-threatening* constitutional systems, however, constitutional jurisgenesis should only be a constitutional design and practice of *last resort*. To begin with, the Nigerian experience with Shariacracy is the exception rather than the norm in sub-Saharan Africa; furthermore, one should only resort to constitutional jurisgenesis in the most unlikely scenario that some *system-threatening* constitutional systems arise as an empirical matter.

IV. Conclusion

This chapter presented a general theory or meta-framework for future African constitutional designs and practices. Within such a framework, each African state has to address its peculiar challenges that arise from its national socio-economic, cultural, and political contexts. The future constitutional design and practice areas discussed in this chapter, therefore, constitute a *minimum core* in each African state. African states have to take sovereignty seriously in their constitutional design and they have to look both beyond and within themselves in order to create suitable conditions for the practice of constitutionalism. They have to restructure political power vertically and horizontally in a way that both *limits* and *facilitates* state action so that the constitutional systems

[97] See World Bank, 'Gross domestic product 2019' <https://databank.worldbank.org/data/download/GDP.pdf>; World Population Review, <https://worldpopulationreview.com/countries> accessed 2 December 2020.

can be more self-executing and self-correcting. In their attempts to establish functional and sustainable constitutional governments, African states need not take refuge in the homeland of cultural authenticity, nor should they rely solely on Western ideas of universality; understanding and appreciating the syncretic nature of their states and constitutional systems will help African states to pass such an impasse. The procedural and normative openness inherent in constitutional jurisgenesis arms them with the constitutional tools necessary to mediate plural and competing constitutional values and systems. Through such constitutional designs and practices, African states can better realize their full self-determination and execute their constitutional promises, for and by themselves.

Conclusion

This book began its exploration of African constitutionalism with two questions: Why we need a new theoretical framework for African constitutionalism and how this framework could offer us better theoretical and practical tools with which to understand, improve, and assess African constitutionalism on its own terms. To answer these questions, the book developed and presented *legal syncretism* as a theory of African constitutionalism in epistemologically conscious, theoretically defensible, and methodologically sound ways. Legal syncretism offers a better theoretical framework than both legal centralism and legal pluralism for understanding the processes and dynamics of African constitutional change and transformation from precolonial times to the present, and for capturing and explaining the identity, nature, and structure of the resultant constitutional designs and practices across time and space. By decoding the African constitutional matrix that triggers and produces constitutional change and transformation while simultaneously informing constitutional designs and practices, legal syncretism enables us to better understand African constitutionalism in all its normative configurations and empirical manifestations.

The first step in understanding African constitutionalism is to unearth its roots and trace the constitutive elements of the constitutional matrix. As colonial and postcolonial African states and their corresponding constitutional systems did not come into being *ex nihilo*, the study of the constitutional systems in precolonial Africa becomes necessary for understanding how constitutionalism has unfolded throughout the continent. In this respect, the genealogical orientation of legal syncretism provides the analytical tools and resources we need to retrieve and register the African experience of constitutionalism in precolonial times as the first element of the constitutional matrix. This, in turn, rectifies one of the epistemological problems associated with legal centralism, namely, the belief that Africa was pre-constitution before European colonialism. Additionally, legal syncretism creates the opportunity to study the identity and nature of precolonial constitutionalism. As the idea and practice of precolonial constitutionalism—in all its many variants—feature in the design, practice, and discourse of postcolonial constitutionalism, a critical study and construction of the former opens a window of opportunity for testing the validity of some of the widely held assumptions, or myths, about 'the African political culture'.

The second element of the African constitutional matrix which legal syncretism identifies is international law. One can, at one's own peril, explain and understand African constitutionalism without appreciating the broader international system within which Africa has been situated since the late nineteenth century. International law played the role of constitutional law—or basic law—in both the establishment of African colonial states in the late nineteenth century as well as in their independence

A Theory of African Constitutionalism. Berihun Adugna Gebeye, Oxford University Press. © Berihun Adugna Gebeye 2021.
DOI: 10.1093/oso/9780192893925.003.0009

in the mid-twentieth century. In the establishment of colonial states, international law—of which the 1885 General Act of the Berlin Conference is a classic expression—not only denied recognition to the constitutional systems and sovereignty of precolonial Africa, but it also considered Africa *terra nullius* and, hence, a legitimate *object* of European colonialism. At the end of colonialism, however, post-World War II international law—including the right to self-determination and the principle of sovereignty—created possibilities for the inauguration and incorporation of colonial African states into the community of nations as independent states. In both ways, it was international law that created the necessary external conditions for the existence and operation of colonial and postcolonial states, and it should not be missing from any analysis of African constitutionalism. By presenting international law into the African constitutional matrix, legal syncretism captures many theoretical and practical insights that escaped the attention of both legal centralism, which considers the birth of the state as an empirical—not legal—matter and assumes the state as externally immune from interference and internally autonomous in its course of action, and legal pluralism, which focuses on the dynamics of customary, religious, and imported European laws within colonial and postcolonial states.

The third element of the constitutional matrix is imported colonial laws. Within the general spirit of international law, colonial laws gave African states their own forms and textures. During colonialism, the primary occupation of these laws was the legitimation and maintenance of colonial states and, consequently, they were devoid of the constitutional morality, justice, and rationality inherent in the laws of the colonizers back home. More often than not, the Colonial Governor was the chief legislator, executive, and justice of the colony. At independence, however, the colonial powers imposed a liberal constitutional system modeled after their own historical experience as a condition for exercising the right to self-determination. Accordingly, the newly independent African states still have to operate with a system of liberal constitutional democracy.

Finally, along with the triumph of liberal democracy in the 1990s, liberal constitutional norms and practices feature as the fourth element of the African constitutional matrix. In this regard, the influence of the American constitutional system and comparative constitutional law looms large in the African constitutional experiment. The migration of liberal constitutional norms and practices such as judicial review, the Bills of Rights, presidentialism, and federalism are all good examples of this phenomenon.

The encounters and contacts in the late nineteenth and mid-twentieth centuries between international law, colonial laws, and liberal constitutional norms and practices, on the one hand, and the African indigenous constitutional systems and practices, on the other, led to conflict, resistance, acceptance, and exchange at different levels and in different ways. These syncretic processes changed and transformed the nature and identity of the four constitutive elements of the African constitutional matrix. Accordingly, the indigenous constitutional systems of precolonial Africa were dissolved, but their various elements were accepted, modified, and even invented by the colonial laws. Similarly, international law altered one of its fundamental principles—from empirical sovereignty to juridical sovereignty—as it entered into the African constitutional matrix. By the same token, colonial laws adapted to and incorporated many customary and/or religious laws and practices. In a similar vein, the identity, nature, and purpose of liberal constitutional norms and practices have also been transformed. The quest to solve some of the existential problems posed to the constitutional matrix by the power balance in the social fields at different times and places has made these syncretic changes possible.

Most importantly, these syncretic processes in the constitutional matrix have also brought with it syncretic constitutional designs and practices. Legal syncretism animates the very conception of the African state along with its vertical and horizontal divisions of power, and its notion of constitutional rights. The African state, unlike the Euro-American state, is a syncretic state created through international law *from above* and African indigenous laws *from below*. International law reimagined and reconfigured Africa *from above* into world society as a colony in the late nineteenth century and then recognized it as an equal sovereign into the community of nations in the mid-twentieth century in the form of a European-style territorial state with a defined population, territory, government, and sovereignty. Additionally, it bestowed on the territorial state (both colonial and postcolonial) formal internal autonomy and external protection. Within the contours of these territorial states, African indigenous laws have been reconfigured *from below* in order to provide the state with the necessary infrastructure and resources for its internal operation. At the center of this syncretic configuration lies the written constitutional system, which primarily provides legitimacy and—to the extent possible—the institutional and normative context for the practice of constitutionalism. This syncretic constitutional configuration challenges conventional wisdom regarding the nature of the African state, as well as its relationship with society and the international community, by transcending the artificial binaries of formal vs informal, state vs non-state, legitimate vs illegitimate, weak state vs strong state, etc, in the conception and practice of constitutionalism.

In turn, the syncretic nature of the African state necessitates the reinterpretation and redeployment of the classic theories of vertical state organization. As a result, the classic federal and unitary theories are not only modified and transformed in the African state, but the federal spirit and unitary logic are also blended together therein. As a result, while the unitary states in Africa incorporate federalist principles and practices and have a general federalist ambition, the federal states draw heavily from the unitary theory and have a general unitary impulse.

In a similar vein, even though the horizontal division of power accepts the formal structure of separation of powers from liberal constitutional theory, its internal organization and power allocation are animated by legal syncretism. The legislature in many African states is a dual house of representation based on both the liberal notion of popular sovereignty and the traditional form of sovereignty. While the direct election of members of the legislature through regular elections embodies the notion of popular sovereignty, the incorporation and reconfiguration of traditional authorities in both the legislature as well as the business of legislation—albeit to different degrees and in different forms—show the traditional conception of sovereignty. Through such legislative design, citizens have dual forms of representation. By the same token, while the executive branch takes the form or shape of either a presidential or parliamentary system of government, its substantive powers are inspired by the *modus operandi* of the Colonial Governor. As a result, in contrast with the core of the doctrine of separation of powers, executive power in Africa—more often than not—is personalized and the executives are imperial. Likewise, the judiciary fuses persons and laws from customary and/or religious laws together with statutory laws and this concomitantly channels a syncretic judicial structure and philosophy.

Similarly, the Bill of Rights regime configures rights rooted in both the liberal tradition and African cultures. Such constitutional design has transformed the nature and identity of constitutional rights in Africa; these rights are not only entitlements that limit the power of the state, but are also duties which impose obligations on the part of the individual towards the state, the community, and the family. Moreover, constitutional rights rest in a diverse normative universe that has plural senses of justice, equal treatment, and equal concern.

Precisely because legal syncretism animates and permeates the constitutional designs and practices in Africa, these constitutional designs and practices, in turn, have their own unique features and purposes. A closer inspection of federalism, the executive, and women's constitutional rights—as representatives of the various aspects of constitutional designs and practices—in the selected case studies of Nigeria, Ethiopia, and South Africa, reveals how African constitutionalism is a result of the syncretism of the various constitutive elements of the constitutional matrix. Although federalism in Africa shares the forms, structures, and discursive practices of liberal constitutional theory, its normative articulations and institutional frameworks are animated by syncretic configurations, and these have concomitantly transformed its purpose, fundamental elements, and operation—albeit in different ways. In addition to unitary theory, which is inherent to the federal experiments, federalism is also blended with the military principle of organization in Nigeria, ethnicity and socialism in Ethiopia, and liberalism and Ubuntu in South Africa. As a result, the normative and institutional frameworks of federalism are animated by these syncretic elements.

Furthermore, as the primary purpose of federalism in Africa is the accommodation of ethnonational diversity and the maintenance of territorial integrity, it does not necessarily need the practice of liberal constitutionalism or democracy to survive, nor is it incompatible with unlimited government to operate—provided that the government is committed to the syncretic federal logic. This is the reason why federalism manages to operate and survive in Nigeria and Ethiopia largely in the absence of liberal constitutionalism. In contrast, even though the original logic for federalism in South Africa was the accommodation of ethnic and racial diversity, it was the acceptance of liberal constitutionalism by the key constitutional actors that maintained the classic purposes of federalism in the final Constitution. Hence, the operation of federalism in South Africa does require the practice of liberal constitutionalism.

Similarly, the executive branch is also the syncretic result of the various constitutive elements in the constitutional matrix. While the African executive adopts the forms and structures of either a presidential or parliamentary system from liberal constitutional theory—as the offspring of the doctrine of separation of powers, it draws its substantive executive powers from the *power-enabling* aspects of the different elements in the constitutional matrix. To this end, it uses the African traditional system of government as a discursive practice with which to establish an imperial and strong executive, while, in fact, it seems to constitutionalize the theory of colonial government. The truth of the matter is, that in addition to the absence of a unitary African traditional theory of government, the centralized political systems in precolonial Africa had an inbuilt system of separation of powers and checks and balances. However, the colonial theory of government ushered in one-man governance under the leadership of the Colonial Governor. Hence, there is an implicit acceptance of the colonial theory of government in postcolonial constitutionalism and the constitutions have rarely been used to limit the substantive powers of the executive, but rather to enlarge and/or safeguard it. The result is the transformation of executive power into personalized power, and the President or Prime Minister into an Imperial President or Premier.

In this respect, presidentialism in Nigeria and parliamentarianism in Ethiopia are adopted with the objective of centralizing and consolidating executive power in the person of the Chief Executive in a way that upsets the doctrine of separation of powers, and even the overall federal structure. However, the African executive also establishes its power and structure drawing from the *power-limiting* aspects of the different elements in the constitutional matrix. Consequently, the power of the executive is limited, its power is dispersed, and, ultimately, imperial ambition is constrained. South Africa is a good example of this type of limited executive. The acceptance of the limited theory of government in South Africa has led to a construction of executive power that is personally and institutionally dispersed and diffused, building on the *power-limiting* aspects of both liberal and indigenous notions of power.

By the same token, women's constitutional rights are also the results of the syncretic relations between rights rooted in the liberal tradition and those rooted in customary and religious systems.[1] Thus, while the women's constitutional rights regime in Africa converges with the liberal notion of women's rights as incorporated in international human rights instruments, it also diverges from the same, as it includes the notion of rights as found in customary and religious laws and practices. However, such syncretism comes in different forms and shapes: while there is a general blend and transformation of women's rights rooted in both the liberal and customary systems in Nigeria, Ethiopia, and South Africa, there is also a symbiotic relationship in Nigeria between the women's rights of the liberal tradition and those found in Islamic law. The syncretism between women's rights as found in both the liberal tradition and customary laws comes mainly *from above*, ie, from the apex judicial or quasi-judicial organs, although such syncretism also arises *from below*, ie, from changes in the customary laws of the community based on their own initiative, as we find in South Africa. This syncretic configuration creates spaces and interactions for the enforcement of women's rights in multiple, overlapping, and sometimes competing avenues through creative procedural innovation and normative commitment to syncretism, rather than choosing one over the other. Although the advantage of legal syncretism to women's rights is contingent upon several factors in time and place, it certainly offers better options to women than what the universalists and cultural relativists prescribe in the human rights debate.

[1] Indeed, women have to struggle for their liberal or customary/religious rights for their materialization. See for instance Aili Mari Tripp, 'Conflicting Agendas? Women's Rights and Customary Law in African Constitutional Reform' in Susan H Williams (ed), *Constituting Equality: Gender Equality and Comparative Constitutional Law* (Cambridge University Press 2009) 173–94; Mary Hames, 'Rights and Realities: Limits to Women's Rights and Citizenship after 10 Years of Democracy in South Africa' (2006) 27 Third World Quarterly 7, 1313–27.

From the comprehensive study of African constitutionalism contained in this book, we can draw several observations, three of which are most fundamental. First, that legal syncretism as a theory clearly captures and explains the nature, identity, and structure of African constitutionalism in epistemologically conscious, theoretically defensible, and methodologically sound ways. By taking African constitutionalism across time and space seriously, legal syncretism gives due emphasis to African constitutional designs and practices on their own terms, without falling into the traps of legal centralism and legal pluralism. By doing so, it offers a unique theoretical perspective with which to understand the socio-economic, cultural, and political contexts that give rise to—and influence—the different constitutional designs, and, consequently, transform and shape the constitutional practices. Furthermore, it clearly accounts for the internal workings of the African state through a holistic investigation of its biosphere and by zooming into its vertical and horizontal divisions of power and notion of constitutional rights. By deploying multidisciplinary approaches and materials in order to explain, analyze, and capture the various aspects of constitutional designs and practices, it offers a better account of what African constitutionalism really is, in both its normative articulations and empirical realities. Following from this, legal syncretism helps to identify more clearly the achievements, challenges, and pathologies of African constitutionalism.

Second, that legal syncretism offers key theoretical tools and practical insights for assessing and evaluating the performance of African constitutionalism. As legal syncretism situates the phenomenology of African constitutionalism within broader temporal and spatial perspectives, along with the resultant complex socio-economic and political contexts, it sheds more light on the origin, development, and transformation of constitutional systems in general, and their unique designs and practices in particular. On the one hand, this helps to understand why a constitutional system comes into being in the first place and how it aims to address its raison d'être. On the other hand, this also helps to understand the nature and purpose of the specific constitutional designs put in place—in order to achieve the general aims of the constitutional systems—and their consequent practices. The tools of constitutional assessment that are drawn in such ways can provide better accounts of the performance of African constitutionalism and the state of constitutional government in Africa than the Western liberal tools of constitutional assessment which usually record and register constitutional failure. In this respect, for example, the discussion on federalism in Chapter 4 casts some light on how legal syncretism provides useful tools for evaluating the performance of African constitutionalism. Based on the standards of success and failure in classic federal theory, the viability of federalism in Nigeria and Ethiopia is an anomaly, and its performance is largely a failure. But this assessment ignores the true nature of federalism and its dynamics in these countries. However, if we consider the transformation of its purpose, fundamental elements, and operation in these states, the viability of federalism is not an anomaly and its performance is not largely a failure.

Third, that legal syncretism provides important theoretical and practical insights to constitution-builders in Africa regarding the making, revision, and enforcement of constitutions. Legal syncretism helps constitution-builders to both identify the achievements, recurring challenges, and pathologies of African constitutionalism as well as trace the underlying causes in a comprehensive manner. This enables them to maintain the current achievements and direct their attention and efforts to finding new solutions to the challenges and pathologies of African constitutionalism. As discussed in Chapter 7, constitution-builders now have a general theory for future constitutional designs and practices—from broader issues of sovereignty to restructuring political power, from reforming the legal system to maintaining and improving the practice of constitutional jurisgenesis—drawn from African constitutional experiences, from precolonial times to the present. Hence, legal syncretism offers constitution-builders in Africa new insights for reimagining the purpose, substance, and scope of constitutions and constitutionalism in order to fully realize the right to self-determination of African states and peoples, and to execute their constitutional promises for and by themselves.

In this book I have explored African constitutionalism, which has thus far been understudied and has attracted little attention in the field of comparative constitutional law. While the thesis and analysis of this book are theoretically and comparatively rich, historically and contextually informed, temporally and spatially extensive, it is only intended as the starting point and not the final word on African constitutionalism. Its chief contribution to the study of African constitutionalism is the 'paradigm shift' it introduces. By 'paradigm', following Thomas Kuhn, I mean a constellation of beliefs, values, theories, and techniques shared by members of a given scientific community that supplies the foundation for the further practice and development of its discipline.[2] As this book demonstrates, the legal centralist and the legal pluralist paradigms do not give us a clear account of African constitutional changes, designs, and practices across time and space and, consequently, do not have the necessary theoretical lens and practical tools for the diagnosis, improvement, and consolidation of African constitutionalism. In both of these paradigms, the political, legal, and constitutional theories that underpin constitutions and constitutionalism as categories of analysis and practice conceal the true nature and structure of African constitutionalism. The legal syncretic paradigm, on the other hand, not only offers us a new perspective for understanding both the past and present of African constitutionalism, but also supplies us with the theoretical foundations and practical tools for its future diagnosis, improvement, and consolidation by piercing the veils of the legal centralist and legal pluralist paradigms. This book, therefore, both presents the complex terrain of African constitutionalism to scholars, policy makers, and development practitioners, while also setting a future research agenda with a new paradigm. In this regard, future research can be directed towards examining and understanding the various aspects of constitutional designs and practices through legal syncretism in different African states. Additionally, it would be extremely useful to study how future constitutional designs and practices should build on, and respond to, the different elements of the African constitutional matrix. I hope that this book's theoretical insights and methodological designs go beyond Africa and inspire comparative constitutional studies elsewhere as well, especially in the postcolonial world of the global south.

[2] Thomas S Kuhn, *The Structure of Scientific Revolutions* (3rd edn, University of Chicago Press 1996) 176–79.

Index

For the benefit of digital users, indexed terms that span two pages (e.g., 52–53) may, on occasion, appear on only one of those pages.